COPYRIGHT AND PATENT LAWS FOR THE AGE OF ARTIFICIAL INTELLIGENCE

This book responds to the need to distinguish human creations from those produced by AI.

It does so by tracing human attributes of authorship and inventorship in statutory requirements for protection and ownership in European copyright and patent laws.

Its main contribution lies in exposing shortcomings in how the laws are applied in the UK, Germany and France. It shows that the human origin of creations is traditionally inferred from their expressive form or technical character. Given the advancements in AI, such inferences are no longer legitimate. What is more, these shortcomings may eventually lead to granting copyright or patent protection where none is lawfully permitted or sufficiently justified. To remedy the situation, this book offers doctrinal and conceptual amendments and proposes law reforms to implement them.

This book guides authorities, practitioners and students through the main arguments of the debate concerning copyright and patents for objects entirely or partly generated by AI. It also makes original contributions to advance the ongoing academic and policy debates on AI and intellectual property law.

Copyright and Patent Laws for the Age of Artificial Intelligence

Authorship and Inventorship Revisited

Eva Janečková

•HART•
OXFORD • LONDON • NEW YORK • NEW DELHI • SYDNEY

HART PUBLISHING

Bloomsbury Publishing Plc

Kemp House, Chawley Park, Cumnor Hill, Oxford, OX2 9PH, UK

1385 Broadway, New York, NY 10018, USA

Bloomsbury Publishing Ireland Limited, 29 Earlsfort Terrace, Dublin 2, D02 AY28, Ireland

HART PUBLISHING, the Hart/Stag logo, BLOOMSBURY and the Diana logo are trademarks of Bloomsbury Publishing Plc

First published in Great Britain 2025

A catalogue record for this book is available from the British Library.

A catalogue record for this book is available from the Library of Congress.

Library of Congress Control Number: 2025930945

ISBN: HB: 978-1-50997-623-2
ePDF: 978-1-50997-625-6
ePub: 978-1-50997-624-9

Typeset by Compuscript Ltd, Shannon

For product safety related questions contact productsafety@bloomsbury.com

To find out more about our authors and books visit www.hartpublishing.co.uk. Here you will find extracts, author information, details of forthcoming events and the option to sign up for our newsletters.

To Václav and Killian

PREFACE

This book is based on my DPhil thesis defended in 2023 at Oxford. Despite numerous transformations and reformulations, it cannot be concealed that this book incorporates research done by an early career researcher. As such, this book is probably still naively ambitious, at instances it may come across as unnecessarily defensive and would, unquestionably, benefit from some narrowing down. Though imperfect, I believe that this book as well as early career scholarship in general have their place in Academia. They both, as I hope, tend to be refreshing, offer bolder arguments and are less afraid of experimentation and thinking out of the box (because often there is no box yet).

And, most importantly, this book, as any other early career research work, would not have seen the light of day without the invaluable support received from more experienced scholars. My sincere thanks go to my supervisor, Professor Justine Pila, for the fruitful and vivid discussions we had, for her endless support and admirable patience with me, to examiners of the DPhil thesis, Professors Robert Burrell and Matthias Leistner for their constructive comments and kind treatment and to Professors Dev Gangjee, Lionel Bently and Noam Shemtov who commented on and helped me with this research at its various stages. Needless to say, any errors or omissions in the text are mine.

I also thank the anonymous reviewers for their pertinent comments. Actually, the Bull's head on the cover is a sort of response to one of them. The review questioned whether this book does not consist of two separate essays, one on patents and the other one on copyright, being just stuck together. And yes, it is plausible to see just a handle and a saddle or just a patent law part and a copyright law part. But I hope that this book will also enable you to appreciate an integrated whole, a Bull's head, a human intellectual creation.

I would like to express my thanks to Tania Cheng-Davies and Yin Harn Lee, my kind colleagues that I am lucky to have at Bristol, whose support and flexibility made work on this book more effective.

I thank wholeheartedly Professor Josef Drexl who gave me the opportunity to start this intellectual adventure by offering me a GRUR scholarship to study at the Munich Intellectual Property Law Center, one of the best places to study intellectual property law in Europe, and who has supported me in my academic career. My thanks also go to the Max Planck Institute for Innovation and Competition in Munich for hosting me as a guest researcher and granting me access to their library collections which proved instrumental to writing this book.

And foremost, I thank my family for their love and support.

Eva Janečková
Bristol, 30 September 2024

CONTENTS

Preface ..... *vii*
Table of Cases ..... *xi*
Table of Legislation ..... *xix*
Table of International Treaties ..... *xxi*

1. Introduction 1
Formulation of the Problem 1
Significance of this Research 3
Methods and Scope 4
Structure and Content 7

2. AI: Why does AI Matter to Intellectual Property Law? 8
Introduction 8
What is Artificial Intelligence? 8
Aspects of AI Relevant for Intellectual Property 12
The Ensuing Questions 19
Conclusion 24

3. The Relevant Justifications for Copyright and Patents 25
Introduction 25
Human Intellectual Creations 27
Intrinsic Values of Human Intellectual Creations 36
Social Values of Human Intellectual Creations 42
Value of Expressive Subject Matter and Non-Obvious Technical Subject Matter 45
Conclusion 50

4. Inventorship in European Patent Law 51
Introduction 51
Inventorship in Positive Law 51
Inventorship in the EPC 62
Reflections of Human Inventorship in Patentability Requirements 69
Conclusion 78

5. **Inventorship in the Application Practice in the UK, Germany and France** **79**
Introduction 79
Epistemic Approaches to the Invention Requirement 79
Epistemic Approaches to the Inventive Step Requirement 87
Conclusion 97

6. **EU Authorship** **99**
Introduction 99
EU Copyright Protection in Two Tracks 99
Human Aspects in the Originality Standard 109
Reflection of Personality 119
Application of the EU Copyright Subsistence Criteria to AI Productions 121
Conclusion 122

7. **Authorship in the UK, Germany and France** **125**
Introduction 125
Authorship in Positive Law 125
Computer-generated Works in the UK 142
Conclusion 147

8. **Authorship in the Application Practice in the UK, Germany and France** **148**
Introduction 148
Reflections of Authorship and the Epistemic Approaches in the UK 148
Reflections of Authorship and the Epistemic Approaches in France 155
Reflections of Authorship and the Epistemic Approaches in Germany 162
Conclusion 169

9. **Reforms and Ways Forward** **171**
Final Overview 171
Refining the Conceptions of Human Inventorship and Authorship 174
Amending the Epistemic Approaches 177

10. **Conclusion** **186**

Bibliography *191*
Index *203*

TABLE OF CASES

EU

Case C-203/02 The British Horseracing Board [2004] EU:C:2004:695 102
Case C-5/08 Infopaq International A/S v Danske Dagblades Forening [2009] ECR I-6569, EU:C:2009:465 .... 105–07, 109, 111, 113, 115, 119, 123–24, 127–29, 131, 138, 144, 149–50, 154, 163, 189
Case C-393/09 Bezpečnostní softwarová asociace v Ministerstvo kultury [2010] ECR I-13971, EU:C:2010:816 .... 100, 178
Joined cases C-403/08 and C-429/08 Football Association Premier League Ltd and Others v QC Leisure and Others, and Karen Murphy v Media Protection Services EU:C:2011:631, [2011] ECR I-9083, [2012] 1 CLRM (29) 769 ECJ 110
Case C-277/10 Martin Luksan v Petrus van der Let Luksan [2012] EU:C:2012:65 117
Case C-406/10 SAS Institute Inc v World Programming Ltd [2012] EU:C:2012:259 .... 101, 115, 124
Case C-145/10 Eva-Maria Painer v Standard VerlagsGmbH and Others [2012] ECDR (6) 89, EU:C:2011:798 114
Case C-604/10 Football Dataco Ltd and Others v Yahoo! UK Ltd and Others [2012] EU:C:2012:115 .... 102–03, 111, 113, 151
Case C-128/11 UsedSoft GmbH v Oracle International Corp [2012] EU:C:2012:407 100
Case C-201/13 Johan Deckmyn and Vrijheidsfonds VZW v Helena Vandersteen [2014] EU:C:2014:2132 .... 35, 106, 121
Case C-160/15 GS Media BV v Sanoma Media Netherlands BV and Others [2016] EU:C:2016:644 .... 35, 121
Case C-310/17 Levola Hengelo BV v Smilde Foods BV [2018] EU:C:2018:899 105
Case C-469/17 Funke Medien NRW GmbH v Bundesrepublik Deutschland [2019] EU:C:2019:623 .... 114–15, 124
Case C-476/17 Pelham GmbH and Others v Ralf Hütter and Florian Schneider-Esleben [2019] EU:C:2019:624 .... 5, 105
Case C-683/17 Cofemel – Sociedade de Vestuário SA v G-Star Raw CV [2019] EU:C:2019:721 .... 107, 111–12, 116, 119–20, 122, 148, 163, 176

Case C-161/17 Land Nordrhein-Westfalen v Dirk Renckhoff [2018] EU:C:2018:634 ... 120
Case C-833/18 SI and Brompton Bicycle Ltd v Chedech / Get2Get [2020] EU:C:2020:461 ... 104, 109–10, 116, 122, 176, 178

EPO

Alcan/Aluminium Alloys, T 465/92 of 14 October 1994, EP:BA:1994:T046592.19941014 ... 87
Broccoli/PLANT BIOSCIENCE, G 0002/07 of 9 December 2010, EP:BA:2010:G000207.20101209 ... 36, 70
Classification method/COMPTEL, T 1784/06 of 21 September 2012, EP:BA:2012:T178406.20120921 ... 80
Combustion engine, T 0426/88 of 9 November 1990, EP:BA:1990:T042688.19901109 ... 75
Decision of 27 January 2020 on patent applications EP 18 275 163 and on EP 18 275 174 ... 63
Decision R 0005/13 of 10 February 2014, EP:BA:2014:R000513.20140210 ... 88
Decision T 0914/02 of 12 July 2005, EP:BA:2005:T091402.20050712 ... 80
Decision T 1317/08 of 15 May 2012, EP:BA:2012:T131708.20120515 ... 88
Decision T 2197/09 of 20 November 2014, EP:BA:2014:T219709.20141120 ... 74
Designation of inventor/DABUS J 0008/20 of 21 December 2021, EP:BA:2021:J000820.20211221 ... 63–65, 68–69
Estimating sales activity/DUNS LICENSING ASSOCIATES, T 0154/04 of 15 November 2006, EP:BA:2006:T015404. 20061115 ... 70. 79–80, 87
Factor-9/JOHN HOPKINS, T 1329/04 of 28 June 2005, EP:BA:2005:T132904.20050628 ... 70
Friction reducing additive, G 0002/88 of 11 December 1989, EP:BA:1989:G000288.19891211 ... 73
Genentech/Expression in yeast, T 445/91 of 20 June 1994, EP:BA:1994:T045591.19940620 ... 75, 88
Odour selection/QUEST INTERNATIONAL, T 0619/02 of 22 March 2006, EP:BA:2006:T061902.20060322 ... 80
Serotonin receptor/ELI LILLY, T 0241/95 of 14 June 2000, EP:BA:2000:T024195.20000614 ... 73
Simulation Method, G 0001/19 of 10 March 2021, EP:BA:2021:G000119.20210310 ... 71
Tomatoes/State of Israel, G 0001/08 of 9 December 2010, EP:BA:2010:G000108.20101209 ... 36, 70–72, 80, 174, 183
Two identities/COMVIK, T 0641/00 of 26 September 2002, EP:BA:2002:T064100.20020926 ... 74, 88

UNITED KINGDOM

Actavis Group PTC EHF v ICOS Corporation [2019] UKSC 15, [2019] Bus LR 1318 .... 77, 79, 91, 97
Actavis UK Ltd v Novartis AG [2010] EWCA Civ 82, [2010] FSR 18 .... 89, 91
Actavis UK Ltd v Eli Lilly & Co [2017] UKSC 48, [2017] Bus LR 1731 35
Aerotel Ltd and Telco Holdings Ltd [2006] EWCA Civ 1371, [2007] Bus LR 634 82
AT&T Knowledge v Comptroller General of Patents [2009] EWHC 343, [2009] Bus LR D51 82
BDI Holding GmbH v Argent Energy Ltd [2019] EWHC 765 (IPEC), [2019] FSR 25 54
Biogen Inc v Medeva Plc [1996] UKHL 18, [1997] RPC 1 .... 81, 90
Cala Homes (South) Limited v Alfred McAlpine Homes East Limited (No 1) [1995] FSR 818 (Ch) 127–28, 131, 147, 151, 153, 155, 187
Conor Medsystems Inc v Angiotech Pharmaceuticals Inc [2008] UKHL 49, [2008] 4 All ER 621 90
Creation Records Ltd and Others v News Group Newspapers Ltd [1997] EMLR 444 (Ch) 152–53
Cummins v Bond [1927] 1 Ch 167 .... 19, 129, 131, 152–53
Edgeberry v Stephens (1693, 1738) 90 ER 1162 32
Exxon Corporation and Others v Exxon Insurance Consultants International Ltd [1982] Ch 119, [1982] RPC 69 .... 149, 153
Fisher v Brooker [2009] UKHL 41, [2009] FSR 25 .... 35, 128, 131
Fylde Microsystems Ltd v Key Radio Systems Ltd [1998] FSR 449 (Ch) 128, 131, 151
Gemstar-TV Guide International Inc v Virgin Media Ltd [2009] EWHC 3068 (Ch), [2010] RPC 10 82
Generics (UK) Ltd v H Lundbeck A/S [2007] EWHC 1040 (Pat), [2007] RPC 32 89–91
George Hensher Ltd Appellants v Restawile Upholstery [1976] AC 64 (HL) 153–54
H Lundbeck A/S v Generics (UK) [2008] EWCA Civ 311, [2008] RPC 437 89
Haberman v Jackel Intl Ltd [1999] FSR 683 .... 77, 90, 92
Hadley v Kemp [1999] EMLR 589 (ChD) 128, 131
Henry Brothers (magherafelt) Ltd v The Ministry of Defence and the Northern Ireland Office [1997] RPC 693 55
Hospira (UK) Limited v Genentech, Inc [2015] EWCA Civ 57, [2015] CN 229 91
HTC Europe Co Ltd v Apple Inc [2013] EWCA Civ 451, [2013] RPC 30 82
IDA Ltd v University of Southampton [2006] EWCA Civ 145, [2006] RPC 21 55–56

Johns-Manville Corporation's Patent [1967] FSR 327 89–90
Kogan v Martin [2019] EWCA Civ 1645 [2020] FSR 3 .... 126–27, 129, 131, 148, 153, 155
Ladbroke (Football) Ltd v William Hill (Football) Ltd [1964] 1 WLR 273 (HL) 151
LucasFilm Ltd v Ainsworth [2011] UKSC 39, [2012] 1 AC 208 .... 149, 153
Macmillan & Co Ltd v Cooper (1924) 40 TLR 186 (PC) 152
Martin v Kogan II [2021] EWHC 24 (Ch), [2021] FSR 10 .... 129–30, 147, 177–78
MedImmune Ltd v Novartis Pharmaceuticals UK Ltd [2012] EWCA Civ 1234, [2012] 10 WLUK 325 90
Merchandising Corp v Harpbond [1983] FSR 32 (CA) 152–53
Michael Mitchell v British Broadcasting Corporation [2011] EWPCC 42, [2011] 12 WLUK 734 153
Molnlycke AB and Another v Procter & Gamble Limited and Others (No 5) [1992] FSR 549 92
Newspaper Licensing Agency Ltd and others v Meltwater Holding BV and others [2011] EWCA Civ 890, [2012] Bus LR 53 149
Nichia Corporation v Argos [2007] EWCA Civ 741, [2007] Bus LR 1753 77
Norowzian v Arks Ltd and Others (No 2) [1999] EWCA Civ 3018, [2000] FSR 363 149
Nova Productions Ltd v Mazooma Games Ltd [2006] EWHC 24 (Ch), [2006] RPC 14 .... 23, 143
Novartis AG v Generics (UK) Limited [2012] EWCA Civ 1623 89
Positec Power Tools (Europe) Ltd v Husqvarna AB Chancery Division [2016] EWHC 1061 (Pat), [2016] Bus LR 714 77
Pozzoli SPA v BDMO SA [2007] EWCA Civ 588, [2007] Bus LR D117 89–90
Response Clothing Ltd v The Edinburgh Woollen Mill Ltd [2020] EWHC 148 (IPEC), [2020] FSR 25 .... 100, 148
SAS Institute Inc v World Programming Ltd [2013] EWHC 69 (Ch), [2013] RPC 17 .... 144, 150
Sawkins v Hyperion Records Ltd [2005] EWCA Civ 565, [2005] 1 WLR 3281 .... 128–29, 131, 149–54
Shazam Productions v Only Fools The Dining Experience [2022] EWHC 1379 (IPEC) [2022] FSR 25 100
Sheeran and others v Chokri and others [2022] EWHC 827 (Ch) [2022] FSR 15 179
Stephen Thaler v Comptroller General of Patents Trade Marks and Designs [2021] EWCA Civ 1374, [2021] 9 WLUK 172 .... 20, 48, 53, 188
Stephen Thaler v The Comptroller-General [2020] EWHC 2412 (Pat), [2020] 9 WLUK 227 68

Thaler v Comptroller General of Patents, Designs and Trade Marks [2023] UKSC 49, [2024] Bus LR 47 .... 20, 52, 67
Temple Island Collections Ltd v New English Teas Ltd [2012] EWPCC 1, [2012] FSR 9.......... 144, 150–51
University of London Press Ltd v University Tutorial Press Ltd [1916] 2 Ch 601 (Ch).......... 48, 150
University of Southampton's Applications [2005] RPC 220 54
Walter v Lane [1900] AC 539 (HL).......... 129, 131, 151–53
Yeda Research and Development Co Ltd v Rhone-Poulenc Rorer International Holdings Inc [2007] UKHL 43, [2008] RPC 1 ....32, 52–54, 56

GERMANY

Antiblockiersystem, Decision of 13 May 1980, X ZB 19/78 [1980] GRUR 849..........86
Atemgasdrucksteuerung, Decision of 17 May 2011, X ZR 53/08 [2011] GRUR 903..........60
Buchhaltungsprogramm, Decision of 14 July 1993, I ZR 47/91 [1994] GRUR 39.......... 140, 147, 187
Coverversion, Decision of 11 December 1997, I ZR 170/95 [1998] GRUR 376 142
DABUS, Decision of 11 June 2024, X ZB 5/22 .... 59, 87, 175
Decision of 20 September 1955, I ZR 194/53BGHZ 18, 175/177 [1955] NJW 1753..........165
Decision of 1 December 1977, 20 U 46/77 [1978] GRUR 640..........164
Decision of 26 September 1980, I ZR 17/78 [1981] GRUR 267..........165
Decision of 27 May 1981, I ZR 102/79 [1981] GRUR 820..........167
Decision of 22 June 1995, I ZR 119/93 [1995] GRUR 581..........165
Decision of 30 January 1996, 5 U 7926/95..........166
Decision of 29 April 1999, I ZR 65/96 [1999] ZUM 644..........166
Decision of 6 September 2005, X ZR 15/02 (Nr 53), BeckRS 2005, 12492..........96
Decision of 16 April 2015, I ZR 225/12 [2015] GRUR 1189..........165
Disiloxan, Decision of 27 February 1969, X ZB 11/68 [1969] GRUR 265...... 77, 97
Dynamische Dokumentengenerierung, Decision of 22 April 2010, Xa ZB 20/08 [2010] GRUR 613..........85
Erfindungen mit Bezug zu Geräten und Computerprogrammen, Decision of 24 February 2011, X ZR 121/09 [2011] GRUR 610..........85
Geburtstagszug, Decision of 13 November 2013, I ZR 143/12 [2014] GRUR 175 169
Inkasso-Programm, Decision of 9 May 1985, I ZR 52/83 [1985] GRUR 1041 167–68
Kranhäuser, Decision of 26 February 2009, I ZR 142/06 [2009] GRUR 1046 ....139–40, 142

Logikverifikation, Decision of 13 December 1999, X ZB 11/98 [2000] GRUR 498 85
Maschinenmensch, Decision of 10 July 2002, 5 U 41/01 [2003] GRUR-RR 33 137–38
Miturheberrecht bei "Memoiren", Decision of 14 October 1952, 4 U 82/52 [1953] GRUR 499 139
Pippi-Langstrumpf-Kostüm, Decision of 17 July 2013, I ZR 52/12 [2014] IIC 467 166
Pneumatische Einrichtung, Decision of 6 October 1981, X ZR 57/80 [1982] GRUR 95 .... 59, 69
Rosaroter Elefant, Decision of 19 October 1994, I ZR 156/92 [1995] GRUR 47 138
Rote Taube, Decision of 27 March 1969, X ZB 15/67 [1970] IIC 136 .... 23, 72, 84, 86, 174
Satellitenfoto, Decision of 30 May 1989, 16 O 33/89 [1990] GRUR 270 .... 23, 136, 142
Solange Du da bist, Decision of 24 November 1955, 6 U 916/55 [1956] GRUR 432 138
Spanplatten, Decision of 5 May 1966, I ZR 110/64 [1966] GRUR 558 .... 59–60, 87
Steuerungseinrichtung für Untersuchungsmodalitäten, Decision of 20 January 2009, X ZB 22/07 [2009] GRUR 479 84–85
Steuervorrichtung, Decision of 18 May 2010, X ZR 79/07 [2010] GRUR 817 .... 59, 61, 64, 69
Vorausbezahlte Telefongespräche, Decision of 7 March 2006, X ZR 213/01 [2006] GRUR 663 96
Wildverbißverhinderung, Decision of 10 November 1970, X ZR 54/67 [1971] GRUR 210 60
Wrapped Reichstag – Christo, Decision of 24 January 2002, I ZR 102/99 [2003] IIC 570 .... 166, 169

FRANCE

Cour de cassation, Decision of 13 November 1973, n° 71-14.469 134
Cour de cassation, Assemblée Plénière, Decision of 7 March 1986, n° 83-10.477 158
Cour de cassation, Decision of 3 November 1988 (1989) 142 RIDA 299 133
Cour de cassation, Decision of 2 March 1999, n° 97-10.179 157
Cour de cassation, Decision of 28 November 2000, n° 98-17.891 157
Cour de cassation, Decision of 19 December 2000, PIBD 2001 721 III 277 .... 77, 95

Cour de cassation, Decision of 5 February 2002 (2002) 193 RIDA 373 133
Cour de cassation, Decision of 8 October 2002, PIBD 2002 754 III 564...............94
Cour de cassation, Decision of 25 April 2006, JCP E 2006, 1806 57
Cour de cassation, Decision of 13 November 2008, n° 06-19.021........................157
Cour de cassation, Decision of 22 September 2011, n° 09-71.337........................158
Cour de cassation, Decision of 14 February 2012, PIBD 2012
960 IIIB 263...67
Cour de cassation, Decision of 17 October 2012, n° 11-21.641...........................158
Cour de cassation, Decision of 20 November 2012, PIBD 2012 III 857 94
Cour de cassation, Decision of 22 January 2014, n° 11-24.273............................157
Cour de cassation, Decision of 6 January 2021, n° 19-14.205..............................135
Cour d'Appel de Bordeaux, Decision of 31 January 2005 (2005)
204 RIDA 298 162
Cour d'appel de Paris, Decision of 19 January 1978, PIBD 1978 111 348 94
Cour d'appel de Paris, Decision of 20 April 1989 (1990) 143 RIDA 317 134
Cour d'appel de Paris, Decision of 14 January 1992 (1992) 152 RIDA 198.........134
Cour d'appel de Paris, Decision of 16 January 1992 (1992) 152 RIDA 204.........133
Cour d'appel de Paris, Decision of 21 November 1994 (1995)
164 RIDA 381 159
Cour d'appel de Paris, Decision of 20 November 1996 (1997)
173 RIDA 321 135
Cour d'appel de Paris, Decision of 13 November 2002, PIBD 2003
762 III 201 94
Cour d'appel de Paris, Decision of 28 February 2007 (2007) 212
RIDA 312...159
Cour d'appel de Paris, Decision of 26 June 2018, PIBD 2018
1101 IIIB 573..57
Cour d'appel de Toulouse, Decision of 22 March 1999, PIBD 1999
679 III 273 57
TGI de Paris, Decision of 10 April 1992, PIBD 1992 529 III 483 57
TGI de Paris, Decision of 11 October 2011, n° 08-00.908.....................................57
TGI de Paris, Decision of 27 June 1997, PIBD 1997 III 661 161
TGI de Paris, Decision of 19 January 2005, PIBD 2006 807 III 254.......................94
TGI de Paris, Decision of 6 October 2009 (2010) 226 RIDA 506........................160

AUSTRALIA

IceTV Pty Ltd v Nine Network Australia Pty Ltd [2009] HCA 14,
239 CLR 458..35
Telstra Corp Ltd v Phone Directories Co Pty Ltd (2011) 90 IPR 1........................23
Thaler v Commissioner of Patents [2021] FCA 879 ....20, 49–50

UNITED STATES

Association for Molecular Pathology (AMP) v Myriad Genetics Inc,
133 S Ct 2107 (2013).. 35, 184
Diamond v Chakrabarty, 100 S Ct 2204, 2208, 65 L Ed 2d 144 (1980)........... 23, 35
Feist Publications Inc v Rural Telephone Service Co Inc (1991)
499 US 340 35
Mazer v Stein, 347 US 201, 219 (1954)...43
Thaler v Hirschfeld 1:20-cv-903 (LMB/TCB) (ED Va Sep 2, 2021)......................184

TABLE OF LEGISLATION

EU LAW

Directive 96/9/EC of 11 March 1996 on the legal protection of databases [1996] OJ L 77/20 .... 102–03, 116
Directive 98/44/EC of 6 July 1998 on the legal protection of biotechnological inventions [1998] OJ L 213/13) 74
Directive 2001/29/EC of 22 May 2001 on the harmonisation of certain aspects of copyright and related rights in the information society [2001] OJ L 167/10 .... 5, 99–100, 103–09, 117, 120–21, 124, 145
Directive 2004/48/EC of 29 April 2004 on the enforcement of intellectual property rights [2004] OJ L 195/16 109
Directive 2006/115/EC of 12 December 2006 on rental right and lending right and on certain rights related to copyright in the field of intellectual property (codified version) [2006] OJ L 376/28 .... 103, 117
Directive 2006/116/EC of 12 December 2006 on the term of protection of copyright and certain related rights [2006] OJ L 372/12 108
Directive 2009/24/EC of 23 April 2009 on the legal protection of computer programs [2009] OJ L 111/16 100
Regulation (EU) 1257/2012 of of 17 December 2012 implementing enhanced cooperation in the area of the creation of unitary patent protection [2012] OJ L 361/1 176
Regulation (EU) 1260/2012 of 17 December 2012 implementing enhanced cooperation in the area of the creation of unitary patent protection with regard to the applicable translation arrangements [2012] OJ L 361/89 176
Directive 2019/790 of 17 April 2019 on copyright and related rights in the Digital Single Market and amending Directives 96/9/EC and 2001/29/EC [2019] OJ L 130/92 5
Regulation (EU) 2024/1689 laying down harmonised rules on artificial intelligence (Artificial Intelligence Act) [2024] OJ L144/1 .... 17, 188

FRANCE

Code de la propriété intellectuelle (Loi n° 92-597 du 1er juillet 1992 relative au code de la propriété intellectuelle).............32, 56, 131, 155, 174
Code pénal 181

GERMANY

Gesetz über Arbeitnehmererfindungen of 25 July 1957 (BGBl I S 756) as amended..37
Urheberrechtsgesetz of 9 September 1965 (BGBl I S 1273)....................36, 136–37, 162–63, 167, 169
Patentgesetz of 16 December 1980 (BGBl I S 1) 32, 64, 86, 174
Strafgesetzbuch of 13 November 1998 (BGBl I S 3322)...181

UNITED KINGDOM

Patents Act 1977 ....37, 52–53, 64, 81–82, 89, 184–85
Copyright, Designs and Patents Act 1988............................. 5, 29, 36, 125, 146, 148
Fraud Act 2006..181

UNITED STATES

35 US Code..184

TABLE OF INTERNATIONAL TREATIES

Agreement on a Unified Patent Court 16351/12 [2013] OJ C 175 176
Agreement on Trade-Related Aspects of Intellectual Property Rights 52, 72
Berne Convention for the Protection of Literary and Artistic Works
1886, as amended on 28 September 1979 ....26, 28–29, 31, 36, 38, 47, 102, 106–08, 120, 125, 143–44, 146, 148
Convention on the Grant of European Patents (European Patent Convention) of 5 October 1973 as revised by the Act revising Article 63 EPC of 17 December 1991 and the Act revising the EPC of 29 November 2000 ....6–7, 72, 51
Implementing Regulations to the EPC.. 63, 65, 180
Paris Convention for the Protection of Industrial Property 1883
as revised at Stockholm in 1967 ....26–27, 31, 36, 38, 51–52, 67
Protocol on Jurisdiction and the Recognition of Decisions in respect of the Right to the Grant of a European Patent 64
Vienna Convention on the Law of Treaties 1969 .... 62, 74

1

Introduction

This book is about how advancements in artificial intelligence (AI) challenge European copyright and patent laws and how the laws should be updated to meet these challenges. It is unique as it adopts the perspective of human intellectual creative activity and, through this lens, analyses the positive law concerning authorship and inventorship. This book is also distinctive as it links authorship and inventorship for entitlement purposes with the statutory requirements for protection and by examining how the relevant norms are applied by European authorities. It is based on extensive legal research into copyright and patent laws and the application practices at European level, in the UK, France and Germany. The significance of this book rests in offering subtle doctrinal solutions and reforms to the respective laws.

Formulation of the Problem

This book's starting point is that such AI-driven systems exist that are capable of determining expressive elements of literary, dramatic, musical and artistic works or non-obvious features of technical advances without the relevant human intervention or understanding. If realised, such productions made entirely or partly by an AI-driven system (AI productions) would have no immediate human creator and, at the same time, there may be indistinguishable from human-made inventions and works.

The above is a necessary simplification of what, in reality, may be a colossal production process involving complex interactions between a variety and a number of human and AI-driven systems' inputs being present at its different stages: from machine learning processes to the post-creative fine-tuning of the outputs. Yet, the process of creating or inventing *stricto sensu* need not involve any human being in the authorial or inventorial capacity with respect to the final expressive subject matter or technical advance. This book gives examples of AI productions with respect to which, as it appears, the AI-driven systems had (functionally) replaced some of the human decision-making that is relevant for giving rise to authorship and inventorship.

Given the technological changes in production processes, the emergence of AI productions present a novel problem for copyright and patent laws. For the first time in human history, human beings involved in the processes of production of expressive or technical subject matter may not be the direct and immediate creators and hence are, to some extent, disconnected from the final output.[1] This disconnect challenges our long-held assumptions about authorship and inventorship and the habit of making inferences about human origin of subject matter from their expressive or technical character. Thereby it impacts on copyright subsistence and patentability assessment.

There is a growing body of literature on AI and its implications for intellectual property law. Some scholars advocate for treating outputs generated by AI-driven systems as any other works or inventions because, as they argue, they pose no novel problem for current law,[2] or because there is no explicit requirement for human authorship[3] and inventorship respectively,[4] or under the condition that humans are still, somehow, involved in the process.[5] A contrary view has been supported with reference to the human authorship requirement,[6] and the need to find a human to whom copyright or patent rights can be attached.[7] Against this background, the main original contribution of this book lies in asking and answering the following, more subtle, but no less fundamental, questions. Would the authorities find out that an expressive subject matter that takes the form of a traditional work was not authored by a human being? Would the authorities detect that a technical advance subject to a patent application was not made by a human being if patent applicants were holding this information back?

Ultimately, this book seeks to uncover whether AI productions are likely to end up being protected by copyright and patents even if they lack a human creator. Naturally, it makes sense to ask these questions only if the lack of human creator matters for copyright and patent protection. This is not uncontroversial in the literature. Therefore, this book clarifies the role of human intellectual creative activity and the conceptions of authorship and inventorship and resolves some preliminary issues.

It is a central principle of modern intellectual property law that copyright and patents are reserved for human intellectual creations (ie authorial works and inventions) for the benefit of their human creators and this book argues that this

[1] A similar observation was made by Boyden: 'Computer-generated Works Destabilize Copyright Law's Approach to Authorship by Obscuring the Connection between the Creative Process and the Work.' Bruce Boyden, 'Emergent Works' (2016) 39 *Colum JL & Arts* 377, 380.

[2] James Grimmelmann, 'There's No Such Thing as a Computer-Authored Work – And It's a Good Thing, Too' (2016) 39 *Colum JL & Arts* 403, Daria Kim, '"AI-Generated Inventions": Time to Get the Record Straight?' (2020) 69 *GRUR International* 443.

[3] Annemarie Bridy, 'Coding Creativity: Copyright and the Artificially Intelligent Author' [2012] *Stan Tech L Rev* 5.

[4] Colin Davies, 'An Evolutionary Step in Intellectual Property Rights – Artificial Intelligence and Intellectual Property' (2011) 27 *Computer Law & Security Review* 601.

[5] Ana Ramalho, 'Patentability of AI-generated Inventions: Is a Reform of the Patent System Needed?' Available at: https://papers.ssrn.com/sol3/papers.cfm?abstract_id=3168703, accessed 1 April 2019.

[6] Pamela Samuelson, 'Allocating Ownership Rights in Computer-Generated Works' (1986) 47 *U Pitt L Rev* 1185, 1199 and Ralph Clifford, 'Intellectual Property in the Era of the Creative Computer Program: Will the True Creator Please Stand Up' (1997) 71 *Tul L Rev* 1675, abstract.

[7] Jane Ginsburg and Luke Budiardjo, 'Authors and Machines' (2019) 34 *Berk Tech LJ* 343 Abstract.

should remain so. To maintain the status quo, the encounter of AI productions and copyright and patent laws forces us to engage properly and afresh with what it means to bring a human intellectual creation into existence. This requires us to leave, for a moment, the perspective of a protected subject matter and adopt the perspective of the intellectual creative activity preceding the subject matter, determining its existence as a human intellectual creation and thus making it eligible for protection.

From this perspective, the book first analyses the conceptions of authorship and inventorship and demonstrates the link between human authorship and copyright subsistence requirements and human inventorship and patentability requirements. Building on the logical indispensability of the link, it examines whether, and if so how, the current legal requirements for protection reflect the human aspects of creation. Finally, and most importantly, this book scrutinises the ways in which authorities apply the legal requirements for protection. This is carried out with a view to determining whether they take the human aspects of creation appropriately into consideration. Another aim is to establish whether the authorities are equipped with such epistemic approaches, methods and tools that would enable them to distinguish a human-made invention or work from other subject matter.

Significance of this Research

Both copyright and patents have a statutory basis and since the authorities are bound by the respective statutes, they are obligated to use such epistemic approaches, methods and tools that enable them to apply statutory norms adequately. This book's focus on the authorities' epistemic approaches and their application practices is thus important for preserving the coherence and integrity of the modern copyright and patent law systems. Coherence not only helps to achieve respect for law, but it also helps to generate a greater good – the rule of law.[8]

In more consequentialist terms, without adequate epistemic approaches the authorities are likely unable to distinguish subject matter eligible for protection from other subject matter (albeit expressive or technical). Given the emergence of AI productions there is now an increased risk of granting protection where none is lawfully permitted or justified. If ineligible AI productions end up being protected because of flawed law or application practices, the commons would be deprived of expressive subject matter or non-obvious technical advances without appropriate justification. This would impact adversely on downstream innovation, freedom to

[8] For instance, Ion Fuller cites coherence as one of the principles of what he called 'the inner morality of law'. Jeremy Waldron, 'The Rule of Law' in Edward Zalta (ed), *The Stanford Encyclopedia of Philosophy* (*plato.stanford*, Summer 2020). Available at: https://plato.stanford.edu/archives/sum2020/entries/rule-of-law/, last accessed 31 December 2021.

conduct business and the right to work by unjustifiably appropriating resources and opportunities. Furthermore, getting the epistemic approaches right is of the utmost relevance to the normative questions of whether, and if so how, to protect AI productions (with no human creator). If, in the future, new systems are introduced to protect AI productions (eg by *sui generis* rights or neighbouring rights) and, there are no adequate epistemic approaches in place, this will result in more opportunities to game the systems.

Methods and Scope

Although this research responds to the advancements in AI, neither the capabilities of AI-driven systems nor defining the AI-generated or AI-assisted outputs[9] lie at its heart. Rather, it brings human intellectual creative activity to the fore. This book thus explores the role of inventors in devising an inventive invention and the role of authors in creating an authorial work by means of doctrinal research. It unpacks the conceptions of human authorship and human inventorship and aims to refine them so that they can be useful in the novel context. This book also traces human aspects of creation in the copyright subsistence and patentability requirements. It does so with the aid of descriptive and interpretative analyses of the requirements for a work, originality, an invention and inventive step. The sources of these requirements, the statutory texts, are given purposive interpretation.[10] The international treaties are construed by means of literal, systematic and teleological interpretation and, where illuminating, with reference to their preparatory documents and reports on their drafting.[11]

This book addresses copyright and patent laws side by side. The reason is that, as advocated here, these bodies of law share the same core, ie they protect only human intellectual creations. Although today the notions of human intellectual creations and mental labour are associated with copyright rather than with patents, this has not always been the case. As researched by Professors Sherman and Bently, historically, the language of creativity was used in 'all areas of law which granted property rights in mental labour',[12] including patent law. According to them, the

[9] The need for formulating definitions of AI-assisted or AI-generated was mentioned for instance in World Intellectual Property Organization, 'Revised Issues Paper on Intellectual Property Policy and Artificial Intelligence' (wipo, May 2020). Available at: www.wipo.int/meetings/en/doc_details.jsp?doc_id=499504, last accessed 17 December 2021.

[10] In the sense that Professor Burrows put forward: 'When we talk of "purpose", we are looking for the policy behind the statute or statutory provision.' Andrew Burrows, *Thinking About Statutes: Interpretation, Interaction, Improvement* (CUP 2018) 19.

[11] The interpretation of international treaties is guided by Silke von Lewinski, 'Principles of Interpretation' in Jörg Reinbothe and Silke von Lewinski (eds) *The WIPO Treaties on Copyright* 2nd edn (OUP 2015) [6.0.4]–[6.0.8].

[12] Brad Sherman and Lionel Bently, *The Making of Modern Intellectual Property Law: The British Experience, 1760–1911* (CUP 1999) 44.

creativity underpinnings form a common ground and are shared by copyright and patent laws: 'the model of creativity employed by the law was not limited to literary property nor was it restricted to the late eighteenth century'.[13]

This book is concerned with copyright in authorial works (or author's rights). There are several reasons why this book does not discuss copyright in entrepreneurial works, ie sound recordings, films, broadcasting, typographical arrangements of published editions[14] and press publications.[15] First, while authorial works are understood as products of human intellectual and creative choice and skill, entrepreneurial works are, as put by Professor Bently and others, 'product[s] of technical and organisational skill' effectuated by corporations.[16] Hence, the nature of entrepreneurial works is, in this respect, quite different from the nature of authorial works.

Further, copyright in authorial works is designed to reward and incentivise individual creativity and mental labour, whereas the neighbouring rights came to existence as a response to a contemporary need to protect investment in technology, ie 'investment in recording studios, technicians, mastering, record manufacturing and distribution'.[17] This makes the rationale for the protection of entrepreneurial works fundamentally different from the rationale for copyright in authorial works.

Admittedly, copyright in entrepreneurial works can be utilised to cover AI productions that take the form of literary or artistic works. Copyright will arguably subsist in a sound recording of music composed by an AI-driven system as well as in a (non-original) film consisting of moving images created entirely by an AI-driven system. With that comes a corresponding scope of protection which is limited to the signal and does not extend to the protection of the content. As put by Richard Arnold, '[i]t will be appreciated that copying the signal necessarily involves copying the content, but copying the content does not necessarily involve copying the signal'.[18] Hence, protection of AI productions via 'signal' rights would not be effective.

[13] ibid.

[14] All in the Copyright, Designs and Patents Act 1988 (CDPA), s 1(1)(b), (c).

[15] Directive 2019/790 of 17 April 2019 on copyright and related rights in the Digital Single Market and amending Directives 96/9/EC and 2001/29/EC [2019] OJ L 130/92, Art 15 relevant for the EU Member States.

[16] Lionel Bently and others, *Intellectual Property Law* 6th edn (OUP 2022) 38.

[17] Bernt Hugenholtz, 'Neighbouring Rights are Obsolete' (2019) 50 *IIC* 1006, 1007.

[18] Richard Arnold, 'Content Copyrights and Signal Copyrights: The Case for a Rational Scheme of Protection' (2011) 1 *Queen Mary J Intell Prop* 272, 272. Similarly, Hugenholtz ibid, 1011. Hence, a musical composition created by an AI-driven system may be freely re-created and re-recorded or adapted for other performance or images from the film created by an AI-driven system may be freely re-created provided no part of the sound recording itself or the (non-original) film itself is taken (or taken by means of a photograph in case of the film). CDPA, s 17 interpreted in the light of the Directive 2001/29/EC of 22 May 2001 on the harmonisation of certain aspects of copyright and related rights in the information society [2001] OJ L 167/10, art 2(c) nad (d) and C-476/17 *Pelham GmbH and Others v Ralf Hütter and Florian Schneider-Esleben* [2019] EU:C:2019:624, ruling 1. The making of an adaptation of sounds from a sound recording or moving images from a (non-original) film is allowed because only '[t]he making of an adaptation of the work is an act restricted by the copyright in a literary, dramatic or musical work'. CDPA, s 21(1).

Since this book is focused on human authorship and human aspects of creation reflected in copyright subsistence criteria, neighbouring rights fall outside its scope because these aspects are not required for their protection. Put differently, since human intellectual creative activity is the main methodological discriminator of what is relevant for this book, then, under such a prism and perhaps paradoxically, an authorial work has more in common with an invention than with an entrepreneurial work.

It should also be noted that European copyright regimes may contain exceptions to the general rule that authorial works must be created by natural persons. For instance, since the end of the nineteenth century, journals, encyclopaedias and dictionaries (later referred to as collective works) have received special treatment in France. A juridical person can originally be entitled to enjoy author's rights in these collective works because of its assumed ability to conceive the project of creating a collective work and take an active part in its composition and editing.[19] It is the decision to embark on creating a collective work that is made at the beginning of the process of creation which is regarded as crucial and thus makes the juridical person merit the initial entitlement to the result.[20] However, such exceptions arising ad hoc out of temporary, specific needs of certain markets or industries do not impact on the principled need for human authorship in authorial works.

As its title suggests, this book is devoted to protection of human intellectual creations in European patent and copyright (author's rights) laws. Hence, the doctrinal, conceptual and normative parts of research are conducted in European patent law, EU copyright law and national patent and copyright (author's rights) laws of the United Kingdom, France and Germany. These jurisdictions were selected because they emerge from different legal traditions while adhering to the harmonised EU copyright subsistence requirements and identical patentability requirements enshrined in the European Patent Convention.

The main idea is that the shared standards and norms, besides their 'autonomous' life at the European level, are (supposed to be) transposed into national laws where they, in turn, interact with national traditional conceptions and requirements until they find a final form in the application practices of national authorities. This choice of jurisdictions thus promises an analysis of a wider spectrum of application practices and epistemic approaches which, at the same time, stem from the same legal bases. While this book is not primarily comparative, in exceptional instances it was impossible to resist the temptation to compare.

The choice of the United Kingdom, France and Germany was motivated by pragmatic reasons because these countries aspire to be the AI leaders in Europe. Given their developed economies, skilled human capital and the amount of state funding being poured into research, they seem to be on their way to achieving it. It is anticipated that the research results contained in this book will be tested in real

[19] André Bertrand, *Droit d'auteur* 3rd edn (Dalloz Action 2010) 204–05.
[20] ibid.

life in the not-too-distant future. Hence, AI productions are expected to emerge in higher numbers in these countries and, at least in the first phase, be tried before British, French and German national authorities.

This book reflects the state of the art in AI and law as on 31 July 2024.

Structure and Content

This book is structured as follows: Chapter 2 introduces the developments in AI, the two most promising AI techniques and the capabilities of the state-of-the-art AI-driven systems which have tabled the novel problem and led to this research. Chapter 3 explains the basic notions used in this book such as human intellectual creations, human authorship and human inventorship. It also outlines the historical and theoretical reasons for upholding the status quo and preserving copyright and patents for human intellectual creations. Chapter 4 tackles human inventorship in European patent law and analyses the UK, French and German conceptions of inventorship. It also brings answers as to whether the origin of an invention matters for granting a European patent under the European Patent Convention and how, if at all, the requirements for an invention and inventive step reflect the human aspects of creation. Chapter 5 searches for reflections of human aspects of creation in the national patentability requirements and examines national authorities' treatment of these requirements. It addresses the central problem of this book: do the authorities employ adequate epistemic approaches and methods to distinguish a human-made invention from other subject matter? Chapter 6 offers an original view on construction of EU authorship. Chapter 7 analyses the conceptions of human authorship in UK, French and German copyright laws and identifies what one must do to become an author. Chapter 8 is the copyright law counterpart of Chapter 5 and searches for reflections of human aspects of creation in the national copyright subsistence requirements and examines national authorities' treatment of these requirements. It also answers the central question: do the authorities employ epistemic approaches and methods that enable them to distinguish a human-authored work from other subject matter? Chapter 9 summarises the main findings, proposes to refine the conceptions of authorship and inventorship and recommends and justifies certain legal reforms. Chapter 10 concludes.

2

AI: Why does AI Matter to Intellectual Property Law?

Introduction

This chapter aims to define the AI-driven systems of this book's interest and describe the aspects in which the advancements in AI challenge the European copyright and patent laws. First, it introduces artificial intelligence as a field of human activity, its ambitions and the current state of the art. This introduction builds mainly on the work of computer scientists and other experts who have been working in AI for several decades such as Michael Wooldridge or Stuart Russel. This chapter also appreciates certain thorny terminological issues and common misunderstandings.

In short, this book is interested in AI-driven systems that have two capabilities. The first capability is producing outputs that are prima facie indistinguishable from those made by human beings (eg traditional works or inventions). The second relevant capability is that they can determine expressive elements and non-obvious technical features of their outputs. In relation to the second capability, this chapter highlights how limited the human understanding of and control over the creative processes that involve AI-driven systems may be.

What is Artificial Intelligence?

The field of AI is deemed to have been established in a summer school organised by mathematicians and (early) computer scientists in Darthmouth College in New Hampshire in 1956.[1] It stems from the fields of mathematics, logic and computer science. It also experienced stages at which its advancements were propelled by probability theories, statistics, economics and neuroscience.[2]

Despite having written a few decades of its own history, no universally accepted definition of AI itself has been formulated to date. Neither have its goals been

[1] Michael Wooldridge, *The Road to Conscious Machines. The Story of AI* (Penguin 2020) 50. Michael Wooldridge is a Professor of Computer Science at the University of Oxford who has worked in the field of AI for several decades.

[2] ibid 165.

unanimously settled.[3] Professors Russell and Norvig in their textbook summarise that most definitions of AI are concerned either with thought processes and reasoning or with behaviour. This implies that the goal of AI designers is to design machines that think like humans or machines that perform tasks that normally require intelligence when performed by humans.[4] In more specific terms, as put by Professor Wooldridge, '[w]e build agents and delegate our preferences to them; these agents act rationally on our behalf to carry them out, using rational decision-making as exemplified by von Neumann and Morgenstern's expected utility theory [...]'.[5]

Predictions as to when machines will achieve a human level of intelligence (in terms of thinking or acting) or even outperform it have captured the imaginations of many.[6] In 2014, world-leading physicists and computer scientists Hawking, Tegmark and Russell asserted that

> [t]here are no fundamental limits to what can be achieved: there is no physical law precluding particles from being organized in ways that perform even more advanced computations than the arrangements of particles in human brains. An explosive transition is possible, although it may play out differently than in the movie: as Irving Good realized in 1965, machines with superhuman intelligence could repeatedly improve their design even further, triggering what Vernor Vinge called a 'singularity'.[7]

To put these two pieces of information together, the ambitions surrounding AI are high and apparently have no physical law standing in their way. Tests to measure whether an AI-driven system achieves human-level thinking or acting have already been proposed. The well-known example is the Turing test which looks at predictability of outputs. As stated by Turing and others,

> [t]he extent to which we regard something as behaving in an intelligent manner is determined as much by our own state of mind and training as by the properties of the object under consideration. If we are able to explain and predict its behaviour or if there seems to be little underlying plan, we have little temptation to imagine intelligence.[8]

It follows that a Turing-like test would contain a set of criteria or questions which interrogators ask to uncover rules-based thinking on the other side. If human

[3] ibid 2.

[4] Stuart Russell and Peter Norvig, *Artificial intelligence: A Modern Approach* 3rd global edn (Pearson 2016) 1–2.

[5] Wooldridge (n 1) 162. The same (modern) definition of AI was offered by Stuart Russell 'BBC Reith Lectures 2021 – Living with Artificial Intelligence. Transcript of the Lecture' 5 (BBC 1 December 2021). Available at: www.bbc.co.uk/programmes/m001216j, last accessed 12 December 2021.

[6] Oren Etzioni, 'No, the Experts Don't Think Superintelligent AI is a Threat to Humanity' (*MIT Technology Review*, 20 September 2016). Available at: www.technologyreview.com/s/602410/no-the-experts-dont-think-superintelligent-ai-is-a-threat-to-humanity/?utm_campaign=internal&utm_medium=homepage&utm_source=top-stories_3&set=602438, last accessed 22 December 2021.

[7] Stephen Hawking, Max Tegmark and Stuart Russell, 'Transcending Complacency on Superintelligent Machines' (*Huffpost*, 19 April 2014). Available at: www.huffingtonpost.com/stephen-hawking/artificial-intelligence_b_5174265.html?guccounter=1, last accessed 22 December 2021.

[8] Alan Turing and others, 'Can Automatic Calculating Machines be Said to Think?' (1952) in Jack Copeland (ed), *The Essential Turing* (OUP 2004) 491.

interrogators can discover a purely rules-based, predictable thinking behind the responses given in the course of testing, they are unlikely to believe that they were in a conversation with a fellow human.[9] The downside of this test is that the extent to which the interrogators regard something as behaving in an intelligent manner is determined as much by their own beliefs and experience as by the properties of the interrogated object.

Alternatively, the Lovelace test, proposed by Professor du Sautoy, examines whether the creative process undertaken by a machine is 'repeatable [...] and yet the programmer is unable to explain how the algorithm produced its output'.[10] This would mean that a machine is able to add something more to the input in the process of creation which did not occur accidentally. Though this test eliminates the possibility of human interrogators projecting intelligence onto the machine, the downside is that it relies on honesty of the designers' pledge that they are unable to explain how the output was produced.

Despite (not yet) encountering machines which would fare well in general affairs, there is evidence of state-of-the-art AI-driven systems performing amazingly when carrying out narrowly specified tasks that are executed in a customised, friendly environment.[11] In more concrete terms, there are two components of AI which enabled these recent achievements and deserve a closer look: machine-learning and neural networks.

Machine-Learning

Machine learning is a sub-field of AI that deals with machines which 'compute a desired output from a given input, without being given an explicit recipe for how to do this'.[12] This contrasts with conventional computing where the 'recipe' for computation is given to the machine. Machine-learning algorithms can mine data, discover a function from them and then use it to solve prediction problems in future situations (inductive learning).[13] The training of a machine learning algorithm (MLA) involves statistical analysis, including inductive logic, applications of probability theories which enable decision-making under uncertainty and providing feedback. A human designer's choices of parameters for training an MLA such as a training dataset, probability theory, probability distribution and type of feedback, are interrelated and largely depend on the task that the MLA

[9] Diane Proudfoot and Jack Copeland, *The Oxford Handbook of Philosophy of Cognitive Science* (OUP 2012) 4.

[10] Marcus du Sautoy, *The Creativity Code: How AI is Learning to Write, Paint and Think* (4th Estate 2019) para 6.29.

[11] For examples see Wooldridge (n 1) 220–21.

[12] ibid 169.

[13] Clarence Chio and David Freeman, *Machine Learning and Security: Protecting Systems with Data and Algorithms* (O'Reilly 2018) 9–10. Russell and Norvig (n 4) 693.

should perform. These choices determine the type of learning and naturally have a significant impact on the nature of outputs generated by the MLA.

There are three basic types of machine learning. Under supervised learning, an MLA is fed with training data that has been labelled by a designer or there may be human feedback provided in the process of learning. The MLA is given hypotheses which it tests against the authorised input-output pairs to find the underlying function between the input and the output.[14] In this case, the human designer is in control of choosing a reliable training dataset, the key features (attributes) in data and the starting hypothetical function. The role of the MLA is to perform function approximation and make predictions for novel (never seen) data.[15]

Under unsupervised learning, the MLA is tasked to search for patterns on its own, usually by means of clustering, ie allocating data to clusters.[16] This means that the MLA is left to learn just on output data, without any feedback or training dataset, designated attributes or starting hypothetical function. Therefore, it is not as influenced by the biases in labelled data or by the assumptions made by human designers as it would have been under supervised learning. Nonetheless, for instance in clustering, human designers must supply the MLA with some context to enable it to plot the data, ie estimate the distribution over the number of clusters and estimate which cluster each point belongs to.[17] Additionally, human designers must choose and apply a probabilistic model to make sense of the data plot (the output).

Finally, the third type of machine learning, reinforced learning, is used in behaviour training and the feedback consists of giving reward and punishment signals upon action driven by the MLA.[18] Here, the human interference with the MLA training is reduced to an ex-post evaluation of its performance. Typically, this happens at the end of a training game when the MLA receives the information whether it has lost or won and hence it learns from its previous mistakes – 'it can use this information to learn an evaluation function that gives reasonably accurate estimates of the probability of winning from any given position'.[19]

It follows that the types of learning offer various degrees of human designers' control over the form of outputs in the training phase and afterwards. While the supervised learning is encumbered with bias in the labelled data and assumptions made at its beginning, the interpretation of outputs is rather straightforward. Conversely, the unsupervised learning may be relatively free from bias in the training dataset and other initial assumptions, yet somewhat constrained by choice of probabilistic models to interpret the final outputs. The reinforced learning, in effect, imitates learning of animals or children. When the latter is coupled with neural networks structure it yields impressive results.

[14] Russell and Norvig (n 4) 695.
[15] Kevin Murphy, *Machine Learning: A Probabilistic Perspective* (MIT Press 2012) 3.
[16] Russell and Norvig (n 4) 694.
[17] Murphy (n 15) 10–11.
[18] ibid 10.
[19] Russell and Norvig (n 4) 831.

Neural Networks

One of the most promising machine learning techniques is neural networks. The idea of neural networks originated in the field of psychology. This dates to 1958 when Rosenblatt published his work on the perceptron – a probabilistic model for information storage and organisation in the brain.[20] Nowadays, neural networks are experiencing a revival thanks to some non-methodological developments, such as the accessibility of vast amounts of data, the availability of efficient computing hardware, eg graphics processing units,[21] and one important methodological step. The methodological game changer rests in the implementation of more layers of networks with different structure and different roles in the whole network.[22] Thereby the networks became deep neural networks.

Neural networks are composed of interconnected nodes (artificial neurons) which carry a mathematical model.[23] These nodes receive and process inputs from their neighbouring nodes and generate an output if activated. Their activation depends on (i) a weighted sum of all incoming inputs, (ii) a so-called activation function and (iii) an activation threshold.[24] Advanced neural networks also incorporate a so-called backpropagation function which enables the network to send feedback backwards (to the nodes in the previous level) and compute gradients of error and then optimise the weights accordingly.[25] Initially, the weights and activation thresholds can be set to random values and they adjust continually during the training.[26] In recent years, AI became popular thanks to a wide-spread use of generative AI in tools such as GPT-4, Dall-E, Midjourney, Stable Diffusion and Co-Pilot. Generative AI systems are based on foundation models using the transformer architecture.[27] These models can abstract from the context, recognise and predict any repeating patterns or motifs, including words, pixels, music notes or computer code.

Aspects of AI Relevant for Intellectual Property

The key message from the above is that there is a variety of AI techniques with various properties.[28] These properties, their settings and architectures (for

[20] Frank Rosenblatt, *The Perceptron: A Theory of Statistical Separability in Cognitive Systems (Project Para)* (Cornell Aeronautical Laboratory 1958).

[21] Alice Roberts and Michael Wooldridge, *Artificial Intelligence* (Penguin Books 2018) 40.

[22] Matt Taddy, 'The Technological Elements of Artificial Intelligence' (*NBER* February 2018). Available at: www.nber.org/papers/w24301.pdf, last accessed 22 December 2021.

[23] Russell and Norvig (n 4) 729.

[24] Wei Di, Anurag Bhardwaj, Wei, Jianing, *Deep Learning Essentials: Your Hands-on Guide to the Fundamentals of Deep Learning and Neural Network Modeling* (Packt Publishing 2018) 83.

[25] ibid 87.

[26] Larry Hardesty, 'Explained: Neural Networks' (*MIT News* 14 April 2017). Available at: https://news.mit.edu/2017/explained-neural-networks-deep-learning-0414, last accessed 22 December 2021.

[27] Ashish Vaswani and others, 'Attention is All you Need' 31st Conference on Neural Information Processing Systems (NIPS). Advances in Neural Information Processing Systems. (2017) 30 arXiv:1706.03762.

[28] Many more are described in Russell and Norvig (n 4).

neural networks) represent a trade-off between exploiting the full potential of AI-driven systems and interpretability of their outputs. The less controlled the AI-driven systems the more questionable the responsibility for the outputs and attribution of the outputs to the people behind those systems. This book is interested only in those AI-driven systems that (i) can produce outputs indistinguishable from those made by human beings and (ii) can determine expressive elements and non-obvious technical features of their outputs autonomously (ie without relevant human intervention or understanding).

Prima Facie Indistinguishability of Outputs

To make this more concrete, some real-life examples are used to demonstrate how AI productions look and feel like and how they come to being. To begin with a notorious example of painting imitating Rembrandt's style – an AI-driven system was allowed to collect and process data from Rembrandt's paintings, and was tasked to generate a portrait of a Caucasian man of a certain age, with certain appearance features and facing to the right based on those data.[29] Allegedly, to a layman, even a Rembrandt fan, the painting would look authentic, as if it were Rembrandt's own.[30] Although, as admitted by those behind The Next Rembrandt project, the resulting painting would not confuse experts.[31]

Another group of researchers focused on designing an AI-driven system to generate sonnets. The resulting sonnets, as far as stress and rhyme were concerned, were evaluated as 'indistinguishable from human-written poems'.[32] On the whole, they were evaluated 'as nearly indistinguishable from published poems by humans'[33] whereas experts found them to 'lack readability and emotion'.[34]

Further, audiences at the Camden and Edinburgh Fringe theatrical festivals struggled to detect with certainty whether a particular improvisational scene they watched was performed by a human behind a robot or by an AI-driven robot. This was allegedly due to the immediate and contextual responses produced by the

[29] ING, Video on making the Next Rembrandt (*Next Rembrandt*, undated). Available at: www.nextrembrandt.com/, last accessed 22 December 2021.

[30] Martin Veitich, 'The Story Behind Rembrandt's Last, 3D-printed Masterpiece' (*IDG Connect*, 8 June 2016). Available at: www.idgconnect.com/article/3579984/the-story-behind-rembrandt-s-last-3d-printed-masterpiece.html, last accessed 22 December 2021.

[31] ibid. Another thing is the likelihood of confusion as to the origin of the physical carrier. The Next Rembrandt painting came out of a 3D printer so it could hardly be confused with a centuries-old oil on canvas. Nevertheless, in contrast to a painting, for a work which is originally digital, such as a digital photograph or a piece of software, it could be extremely difficult to tell the origin only based on experience with the carrier.

[32] Jey Han Lau and others, 'Deep-speare: A joint neural model of poetic language, meter and rhyme' Proceedings of the 56th Annual Meeting of the Association for Computational Linguistics (*arXiv*, 10 July 2018). Available at: https://arxiv.org/abs/1807.03491, last accessed 22 December 2021.

[33] ibid 1.

[34] ibid.

AI-driven robot.[35] As the designers of the AI-driven robot claim, 'approximately half the audience members believed that an AI was performing flawlessly alongside human improvisor(s)'.[36]

In the domain of patent law, only a handful of people openly admit that AI-driven systems can produce technical advances indistinguishable from those made by humans. Professor Abbott writes that an AI-driven system modelled after biological evolution processes produced technical advances that were granted patents in the US.[37] The following patent claim lists an invention allegedly invented by an AI-driven system:

> A neural network based prototyping system for prototyping construction of a device from a plurality of known components, wherein a desired relationship between inputs and outputs of the device being prototyped is known, comprising: […].[38]

This claim does not differ to an appreciable extent from the following (comparable) inventive concept which was devised by human inventors: 'A computer implemented process for training neural networks to their optimal training point, the process comprising the steps of: initializing neural network node weight values […]'.[39]

Another patent claim describing another technical advance allegedly produced by an AI-driven system without a human inventor:

> A food or beverage container comprising: a wall defining an internal chamber of the container, the wall having interior and exterior surfaces and being of substantially uniform thickness; wherein the wall has a fractal profile with corresponding convex and concave fractal elements on corresponding ones of the interior and exterior surfaces; and wherein the convex and concave fractal elements form pits and bulges in the profile of the wall.[40]

The patent application containing the claim above cited a piece of prior art – a seamless can – invented by a team of inventors from Japan:

> A shock resistant seamless can comprising a side wall having an inside surface and an outside surface formed from a laminate of a metal substrate and a thermoplastic resin

[35] Kory Mathewson and Piotr Mirowski, 'Improvised Comedy as a Turing Test, 31st Conference on Neural Information Processing Systems', Workshop on Machine Learning for Creativity and Design (*arXiv* 23 November 2017). Available at: https://arxiv.org/abs/1711.08819, last accessed 22 December 2021.

[36] ibid.

[37] Ryan Abbott, 'I Think, Therefore I Invent: Creative Computers and the Future of Patent Law' (2016) 57 *BC L Rev* 1079, 1086.

[38] Neural network based prototyping system and method, US patent 5852815A expired. Available at: https://patents.google.com/patent/US5852815A/en, last accessed 22 December 2021. Claimed by Stephen Thaler as presented in Abbott (n 36) 1085.

[39] Optimum cessation of training in neural networks, US patent 6119112A. Available at: https://patents.google.com/patent/US6119112A/en?q=Neural+network&q=based&assignee=International+Business+Machines+Corporation, last accessed 22 December 2021.

[40] Food container, European patent application EP3564144A1. Available at: https://worldwide.espacenet.com/patent/search/family/063915228/publication/EP3564144A1?q=pn%3DEP3564144, last accessed 13 December 2021.

> layer provided on the inside surface of the can side wall, wherein the inner surface of the side wall resin layer opposite the metal substrate comprises a plurality of dotted projections.[41]

The technical advance with (allegedly) no human inventor seems indistinguishable from the human-made inventions.

There is a wealth of literature listing more examples of AI productions that are regarded as indistinguishable from human-made objects.[42] Hopefully, the above examples are sufficient to give a flavour of the achievements of some AI-driven systems. As the human audiences (whose testimonies were referred to above) evaluated by their own senses, the AI productions they have encountered were so expressive or technical that they found them prima facie indistinguishable from human-made subject matter. Recalling the Turing test, it is plausible to assert that some of the above-listed outputs would pass the test in natural conditions, eg at the Camden and Edinburgh Fringe festivals.

AI-driven Systems that can Determine Expressive or Non-obvious Technical Elements of their Outputs

The second capability that makes some AI-driven systems relevant for copyright and patent laws is that they can autonomously determine expressive or non-obvious technical elements of their outputs. The difficulty with this claim is that it can be either verified by examining the process of creation or accepted bona fide in statements of the people behind the AI-driven systems. Since at the moment there is no obligation to submit to such an examination nor are there any specific methods for such an examination in place, one is left to proceed by relying on the veracity of expert statements.[43]

For instance, such a human-free determination of expressive elements probably happened in the case of the Next Rembrandt project. The designers had openly described the nature of choices and the origin of the expressive elements.[44] To reiterate, they instructed the system to design a portrait of a Caucasian man of age between thirty and forty, with facial hair, in contemporary clothing and facing

[41] Seamless can, US patent US5803301A, Decision of the US PTO of 8 September 1998. Available at: https://worldwide.espacenet.com/patent/search/family/063915228/publication/EP3564144A1?q=pn%3DEP3564144, last accessed 13 December 2021.

[42] Patrick Goold, 'Artificial Authors: Case Studies of Copyright in Works of Machine Learning' (2020) 67 *J Copyright Soc'y USA* 427; Ben Hattenbach and Joshua Glucoft, 'Patents in an Era of Infinite Monkeys and Artificial Intelligence' (2015) 19 *Stan Tech L Rev* 32; Christian Hartmann and others, 'Trends and Developments in Artificial Intelligence Challenges to the Intellectual Property Rights Framework' (*invir*, 2020). Available at: www.ivir.nl/ivir-study-for-european-commission-on-ai-and-ip/, last accessed 13 December 2021.

[43] The risks of bias or dishonesty in the statements are mitigated by checking them against expert sources – professors of computer science with years of experience in the field of AI, namely Professors Wooldridge and Russell.

[44] ING (n 28).

to the right. As follows from the designers' testimonies, this choice was driven by data availability and other effectiveness considerations.[45] The AI-driven system then generated the portrait based on data gathered under the chosen subject's profile. Hence, the expressive elements of the portrait, such as the colours, shapes, light, shade, etc, and their arrangement were determined by the evaluative process within the AI-driven system and the input data. It seems that no human being was directly and immediately involved in the process of making decisions about the visually expressive details of the resulting painting.

Another example may be AI-driven systems that produced technical solutions in the DARPA 2016 Cyber Grand Challenge, 'the world's first all-machine cyber hacking tournament'.[46] The competing AI-driven systems were able to find flaws in their own systems, reason about them, patch them and look for flaws in the competing systems and attack them, all in real time and autonomously, ie without any human input in the course of the contest. Under such circumstances, the resulting technical elements of the solutions towards patching and attacking were directly and immediately determined by the competing systems.

Lastly, drug discovery appears to be the promised land for the application of AI-driven systems to technical problems. In 2020, an AI-driven system identified a highly effective antibiotic – with a given name *halicin*.[47] According to the scientists supervising the process of invention, the system learnt representations of molecules 'automatically, mapp[ed] molecules into continuous vectors [... and designed ...] molecular representations that are highly attuned to the desired property'.[48] They further described the approach of the system as analytical, using abstracted information about molecular representation that are normally inscrutable and unavailable to human beings. This allowed structurally different antibiotics to be identified.[49]

From this example, it follows that the system was given the task of finding a compound with a desired property in relation to *E.coli*, ie a technical problem was presented to the system. The system then crawled chemical libraries and ranked *halicin* as very high with respect to the desired property, ie it found the technical solution. Ranking *halicin* so highly was a result that no human being involved in the process was able to control or had prior knowledge of.

If the processes run on the above-mentioned AI-driven systems can be repeated and, at the same time, it is true that there is no way in which it can be explained how the outputs are produced, those AI-driven systems would pass the Lovelace test. These achievements and processes are difficult to translate into the language of social science and humanities.

[45] ibid 1'44'.

[46] Dustin Fraze, 'Cyber Grand Challenge (CGC) (Archived)' (*US Department of Defense*, undated). Available at: www.darpa.mil/program/cyber-grand-challenge, last accessed 22 December 2021.

[47] Jonathan Stokes and others, 'A Deep Learning Approach to Antibiotic Discovery' [2020] Cell 688, 689.

[48] ibid.

[49] ibid.

Legal scholars often disagree on whether AI-driven systems are a mere tool, or they come up with their outputs autonomously. For instance, law Professor Blok writes that 'artificial intelligence did not take the initiative to invent. It was used by humans as a tool in the inventive process. In that sense, artificial intelligence does not invent autonomously'.[50] Or, Kim writes that 'it is doubtful whether computers can, at all, be autonomous from humans and perform computation "on their own"'.[51] Handling these arguments requires the utmost sensitivity to the context. In some contexts, they are right.

Undoubtedly, there are AI-driven systems with no level of autonomy. These are, however, of no interest to this book. The various applications of MLAs in the cyber security domain may serve as examples. When focusing on illegitimate activities, a supervised pattern recognition may be used for MLA training in detecting spam in incoming email based on the observed predictable attributes of a spam, eg containing words 'lottery', 'cheap', 'offer', etc.[52] Alternatively, an MLA based on Bayesian inferential statistics which can extract patterns from larger amounts of information without being distracted by noise may be used in intrusion detection systems.[53] In these settings, the systems are indeed mere tools.

Another context is the higher-order realm. AI-driven systems are no source of motivation (in the sense of taking the initiative to invent or create) or intentionality (in the sense of setting out the high-order objective, eg find an antibiotic). Hence, the AI-driven systems (of interest in this book) are not required to be autonomous in the sense that they would go about their own business. Nor are there autonomous in the sense that they would generate inventions with no human intervention whatsoever.[54] However, as shown in the examples above, these systems are sufficiently autonomous to find a way to solve complex, narrowly specified technical problems on their own. This is also supported by the Preamble to the EU AI Act: 'AI systems are designed to operate with varying levels of autonomy, meaning that they have some degree of independence of actions from human involvement and of capabilities to operate without human intervention.'[55]

When Professor Wooldridge describes current AI-driven systems, he does not shy away from using the term 'autonomy'. For instance, he comments on the achievements of a Deep Mind's AI-driven system as follows: 'it learned how to

[50] Peter Blok, 'The Inventor's New Tool: Artificial Intelligence – How Does It Fit in the European Patent System?' (2017) 39 *EIPR* 69,70.

[51] Daria Kim, '"AI-Generated Inventions": Time to Get the Record Straight?' (2020) 69 *GRUR International* 443, 446.

[52] Chio and Freeman (n 13) 13.

[53] Bazara Barry and Anthony Chan, 'Intrusion Detection Systems' in Peter Stavroulakis and Mark Stamp (eds), *Handbook of Information and Communication Security* (Springer 2010).

[54] Professor Straus questions the possibility of DABUS inventing autonomously 'with no human intervention' in Joseph Straus, 'Artificial Intelligence and Patenting: Some Lessons from "DABUS" patent applications' (2022) 44 *EIPR* 348.

[55] Regulation (EU) 2024/1689 laying down harmonised rules on artificial intelligence (Artificial Intelligence Act) [2024] OJ L144/1, rec 12.

play [the game of Go] to a super-human level without any human supervision at all: it just played against itself'.[56] In relation to another system which learnt to cheat in a game in order to play more efficiently, he wrote: '[t]his was not anticipated by Deep Mind's engineers: it was autonomously learned by the program'.[57]

Moreover, from the perspective of people working in the field of AI, there is a crucial difference between the 'autonomous' AI techniques and conventional computing. As mentioned above, the AI-driven systems (of this book's interest) operate upon being given an abstract guidance and a definition of an objective (imagine a magic goldfish or a genie from a lamp[58]) and they do not require precise instructions for computation, ie the recipe.[59] As everyone knows from everyday life, there is a qualitative difference between performing under an abstract guidance and performing under precise, step-by-step instructions. It would thus be a stretch to call both – a conventional computer and an AI-driven system – tools of the same rank. Insisting on this nuance between following a guidance and following a recipe, the conventional computer may be called a tool that follows a recipe,[60] whereas an AI-driven system (or a magic goldfish) is rather a means to an end.

The take-home message from the above is that, in the field of AI, some concepts, such as autonomy or intelligence, may not mean the same thing as in the context of social sciences and humanities.[61] In this book, the term autonomy in the context of AI means freedom from human control when making choices rather than autonomy in the Kantian sense of exercising autonomous free will when making decisions.[62] (Put differently, autonomy in this sense is more likely to mean 'freedom from' than 'freedom to' as coined by Erich Fromm).[63] Equally, intelligence

[56] Wooldridge (n 1) 199.

[57] ibid 195.

[58] Metaphors of this kind are used by Wooldridge (n 1) 261 and Russell (n 5) 10 as well. They do not intend to create an allure of fancy or mystery but rather communicate the level of abstraction of the instructions given to a machine and the absence of clear instructions how to achieve the goal.

[59] Wooldridge (n 1) 169.

[60] To indulge in pedantry, even the computer is not a tool in ordinary language. According to Oxford English Dictionary, a tool means '[a]ny instrument of manual operation' (Johnson); a mechanical implement for working upon something, as by cutting, striking, rubbing, or other process, in any manual art or industry.' Oxford English Dictionary Online (*EOD*, December 2020). Available at: www.oed.com/, last accessed 31 December 2021. Hence using a laptop as a tool would mean using only the hardware as a lever or hammer for instance.

[61] Some legal scholars prefer referring to 'automation' instead of 'autonomy' in the context of AI, eg Kim (n 50). Other legal scholars refer to AI-driven systems as not only autonomous but also creative, unpredictable, independent, rational, evolving, eg Shlomit Yanisky Ravid and Xiaoqiong Liu, 'When Artificial Intelligence Systems Produce Inventions: An Alternative Model for Patent Law at the 3A Era' (2018) 39 *Cardozo L Rev* 2215. This confusion of terms causes appreciable misunderstandings among legal scholars commenting on the developments in AI.

[62] Robert Johnson and Adam Cureton, 'Kant's Moral Philosophy' in Edward Zalta (ed), *The Stanford Encyclopedia of Philosophy* (*plato.stanford*, Spring 2021). Available at: https://plato.stanford.edu/archives/spr2021/entries/kant-moral/, last accessed 11 December 2021.

[63] Erich Fromm, *Escape from Freedom* (first published Farrar & Rinehart 1941); Erich Fromm, *Strach ze svobody* (Portál 2014).

is more likely to mean rationality and advanced computation[64] than intelligence based on consciousness.[65]

These meanings of autonomy and intelligence are legitimate also given the fact that although the Turing test and the Lovelace test aim at scrutinising intelligence and autonomy respectively, passing them does not require consciousness or Kantian autonomy. For the purposes of this book, it is also pertinent to mention that, for copyright to subsist or for grant of patent, the current laws do not explicitly require human beings to be in the state of Kantian autonomy or consciousness when making a work or an invention.[66]

Finally, recent advancements in AI brought opaqueness and inscrutability of AI-driven systems' inner workings which is significant in the legal context. There are sensory and intellectual observations of the inner workings of the AI-driven systems or, better say, a lack thereof. As put by Wooldridge, 'the intelligence they embody is opaque. The expertise that a neural network has captured is embodied in the numeric weights associated with the links between neurons, and, as yet, we have no way of getting at or interpreting this knowledge'.[67] According to other accounts, human designers also struggle to track causality in the systems' decision-making processes and retrieve reasons for their concrete decisions.[68]

This carries important implications for assumptions of authorship and inventorship and application of copyright and patent laws. As the examples of the antibiotic discovery or making the Rembrandt-style painting illustrate, human beings who deploy AI-driven systems may neither have control over the concrete form of the final outputs nor the ability to grasp those outputs intellectually before they are completed.

The Ensuing Questions

Admittedly, there is more than one plausible way in which challenges that the advancements in AI create for copyright and patent laws can be phrased. Without making any taxonomic claims regarding how these issues should be formulated, they, nonetheless, must be somehow conceptually captured and separated so

[64] Hawking, Tegmark and Russell (n 7).

[65] Some philosophers argue that it is not correct to describe AI-driven systems as intelligent because they do not have human consciousness. See talks given by Professors John Searle and Luciano Floridi at the conference 'Technology and the Human Future' (YouTube, 25 October 2016). Available at: www.youtube.com/watch?v=b6o_7HeowY8, last accessed 6 September 2018.

[66] Gernot Schulze, 'UrhG § 7 Urheber' in Thomas Dreier and Gernot Schulze (eds), *Urheberrechtsgesetz* 6th edn (CH Beck 2018) [3]. *Cummins v Bond* [1927] 1 Ch (EWHC Ch) 167, 168. André Bertrand, *Droit d'auteur* 3rd edn (Dalloz Action 2010) 140.

[67] Wooldridge (n 1) 188.

[68] Will Knight, 'The Dark Secret at the Heart of AI' (*MIT Technology Review*, 11 April 2017). Available at: www.technologyreview.com/s/604087/the-dark-secret-at-the-heart-of-ai/, last accessed 22 December 2021.

that they can be addressed in a structured manner. Therefore, these issues are condensed into the following, interrelated questions:

(i) Does current law recognise an AI-driven system as inventor or author (and hence is it permissible to designate an AI-driven system as inventor or author)?
(ii) Can an AI-driven system devise inventions or create works?
(iii) Should any changes to law be introduced to accommodate AI productions that have no human creator (ie no author or inventor)?

So far, there are judicial decisions concerning question (i). The authorities around the world have 'almost uniformly rejected the designation of an artificial intelligence as an inventor on the grounds that only a natural person can be designated as an inventor'.[69] Since copyright subsistence does not require any formalities in many countries, the US decision of the District Court of Colombia (currently under appeal) may be referred to. The US Copyright Office refused to register a piece of visual art allegedly created 'autonomously' by an AI-driven system because it 'lacked human authorship and thus no copyright existed in the first instance'.[70] Hence, the question of whether it is permissible to designate an AI-driven system as inventor or author under current patent and copyright laws, appears to have been answered in multiple jurisdictions in the negative.

Questions (ii) and (iii) were subject to numerous public consultations and policy initiatives launched by policy makers and governmental agencies across the world.[71] While these are not the main concerns of this book, several preliminary items related to them should be clarified. The normative issue (iii) is addressed mainly in Chapter 3.

Question (ii) – whether an AI-driven system can devise inventions or create works – is tackled briefly below. Though first it should be acknowledged that since there is no universally accepted definition of AI even in the AI field itself, the questions (as formulated above) are tainted with some terminological uncertainty.

[69] German Federal Supreme Court, Decision of 11 June 2024, X ZB 5/22 [28]. See decisions from other jurisdictions: *Thaler v Comptroller General of Patents, Designs and Trade Marks* [2023] UKSC 49; [2024] Bus LR 47 and *Stephen Thaler v Comptroller General of Patents Trade Marks and Designs* [2021] EWCA Civ 1374; [2021] 9 WLUK 172 for the UK, *Thaler v Vidal* [2022] 2021–2347 (Fed Cir 2022) for the USA, *Thaler v Commissioner of Patents* [2021] FCA 879 for Australia and *Thaler v Commissioner of Patents* [2023] NZHC 554 for New Zealand.

[70] *Thaler v Perlmutter* [2023] 22-1564 (BAH) 6.

[71] United States Patent and Trademark Office, 'Public Views on Artificial Intelligence and Intellectual Property Policy' (*USPTO*, 6 October 2020). Available at: www.uspto.gov/about-us/news-updates/uspto-releases-report-artificial-intelligence-and-intellectual-property, last accessed 17 December 2021, World Intellectual Property Organization, 'Revised Issues Paper on Intellectual Property Policy and Artificial Intelligence' (*wipo*, May 2020). Available at: www.wipo.int/meetings/en/doc_details.jsp?doc_id=499504, last accessed 17 December 2021, UK IPO, 'Impact Assessment' (*gov*, 29 October 2021). Available at: https://assets.publishing.service.gov.uk/government/uploads/system/uploads/attachment_data/file/1029930/impact-assessment.pdf, last accessed 16 December 2021, Japan Intellectual Property Strategy Headquarters, 'Intellectual Property Strategic Program 2016' (*kantei.go* May 2016). Available at: www.kantei.go.jp/jp/singi/titeki2/kettei/chizaikeikaku20160509_e.pdf, last accessed 17 December 2021.

Therefore, this book advocates for framing the AI challenge and, more specifically, the issues of copyright subsistence and patentability of AI productions around the relevant human activity. The underlying logic is that the issues of copyright subsistence and patentability depend on the definition of human activity or human intervention that is required for existence of an invention or an authorial work.[72] Then, whenever a human activity corresponding to the definition has indeed been involved in the process of devising or creating a particular subject matter, the resulting subject matter (or certain parts thereof) will constitute a human-made invention or work.

Coming back to the question (ii), as the following chapters will show, the relevant process and relevant intellectual inputs in inventing and creating have traditionally been conceived of relatively narrowly in the selected European jurisdictions. For instance, no legal basis was found to regard a person who merely states the objective, gives general ideas or initiates the process of inventing or creation as the actual inventor or author. Rather, at the factual level, the activity of inventing corresponds to solving a narrowly specified technical problem and the activity of creating corresponds to choosing expressive elements. Hence, a short sharp answer to question (ii) may be that evidence shows that there are AI-driven systems capable of inventing and creating in such a narrow and factual sense (and no general artificial intelligence is necessary for such tasks).

In contrast with the above answer, this book approaches the activities of devising inventions and creating works (for patenting and copyright purposes) as purely human intellectual creative activities. It follows that AI-driven systems cannot invent or create in this 'human-centred' sense of inventing or creating simply because they are not human beings. Yet, there are AI-driven systems that can determine expressive elements or non-obvious technical features of subject matter without inventing or creating in the legal sense. Bringing this together, this basically means that if human beings determine expressive elements or non-obvious technical features of subject matter (and thereby create or invent in the factual sense), this activity produces legal effects (because, as human beings, they also create and invent in the legal sense). Whereas if the same is done by an AI-driven system, no legal effects ensue. To put this from a subject-matter-centred perspective, not every (convincingly) expressive or non-obvious technical subject matter can automatically be considered a human-made invention or work.

One may also ask a slightly different question which actually makes more sense than the general question of issue (ii), ie whether a particular subject matter was (de facto) made by a human being or by other means. The answer to such a question is that it depends on the facts. Though this sounds rather straightforward, the legal sense and the factual sense of inventing and creating sometimes

[72] This approach is also taken by Jane Ginsburg and Luke Budiardjo, 'Authors and Machines' (2019) 34 *Berk Tech LJ* 343 Abstract.

get muddled. For instance, some argue that because authorship and inventorship require conception then every expressive or non-obvious technical subject matter must have a human author or inventor. One must only look for them diligently.

For instance, Professor Shemtov in his study on inventorship concludes that

> under French law an inventor is a person who is actively involved in the conception of the invention [...], by definition, every invention has a conception phase and that conception is at present, as well as in the foreseeable future, limited to human faculties, notwithstanding the involvement of a sophisticated AI system featuring an unpredictability element. This being so, it follows that every invention may have been conceived by at least one human actor; it is this actor who is likely to be the inventor under French law.[73]

The above reasoning essentially goes as follows: since every invention must *de lege lata* have a conception phase and this phase is limited to human faculties, then every invention 'may have' a *de facto* human inventor.

No doubt that now and in the near future there will be natural persons who will be intellectually involved in the processes of production of expressive subject matter or technical advances. However, that does not necessarily mean that these people will contribute to their conception in the authorial or inventorial capacity.

This book treats these AI-generated challenges as a novel problem. Yet, these challenges are analogous to those which copyright and patent laws have encountered in the past. For instance, some academics treat AI-driven systems as mere tools and thus similar to cameras or general-purpose computers.[74] The use of cameras and computers, however, brought about a new type of subject matter, ie a photograph and a computer program. This prompted questions whether the new subject matter belonged to literary or artistic domain.[75] In contrast, it is not questionable whether AI productions belong to the literary or artistic domain because they take the established forms of expression. Hence, the use of AI-driven systems has different implications for copyright law than the introduction of cameras and computers.

Some compare AI productions with computer-generated works and regard the debate about their potential protection as a mere protraction of a debate about

[73] Noam Shemtov, 'A Study on Inventorship in Inventions Involving AI Activity' (*EPO* February 2019) 18–19. Available at: http://documents.epo.org/projects/babylon/eponet.nsf/0/3918F57B010A3540C125841900280653/$File/Concept_of_Inventorship_in_Inventions_involving_AI_Activity_en.pdf, last accessed 17 December 2021.

[74] Bernt Hugenholtz and João Quintais, 'Copyright and Artificial Creation: Does EU Copyright Law Protect AI-Assisted Output?' (2021) 52 *IIC* 1190.

[75] This builds on research done by Cooper who describes the struggles of early photographers for artistic status and photography for being accepted as one of the artistic domains. Elena Cooper, *Art and Modern Copyright: The Contested Image* (CUP 2018) 15, 26 ff. In the case of computer programs, Professor Samuelson and others write about the struggles to justify the protection of computer programs as literary works. Pamela Samuelson and others, 'A Manifesto Concerning the Legal Protection of Computer Programs' (1994) 94 *Columbia L R* 2308, 2315–20.

protection of computer-generated works from the end of the 1980s.[76] However, the state-of-the-art computers of that period did not possess the capabilities of today's AI-driven systems and would not have passed the Turing and Lovelace tests. More specifically, their achievements were mediocre (a piece of code or a database)[77] and their outputs were mostly pre-determined by hard-coded, precise instructions (the recipe). Hence, the implications for copyright law are different due to the difference in quality and processes of creation of their outputs.

There is also some similarity between AI productions and works that owe their existence to multiple creators such as Wikipedia, open-source software, or folklore due to the diverse origins of the contributions and complexity in the process of creation.[78] With respect to these complex works, there are doubts about the allocation of copyright because of collective authorship,[79] the nature of collaboration and subsequent adaptations within a certain community.[80] Despite sharing some of the concerns regarding entitlement, the AI productions suffer from possibly having no human creator, instead of having too many creators, hence the implications for copyright subsistence are different.

In patent law, patentability of natural subject matter like bacteria, a sequence of human genes or animal-breeding processes seem to have posed a similar challenge as patentability of AI productions. The similarity lies in the potential absence of human inventor and (consequently) absence of an invention. Some understood that the implications for patent law were to establish whether biotechnology belongs to the fields of technology.[81] Others asked whether human ingenuity and sufficiently transformative acts were involved in the making of the natural subject matter.[82]

[76] Provisions on computer-generated works were adopted also in the UK (in more detail in Chapter 7), Ireland, India, New Zealand and Hong Kong.

[77] In Australia, copyright in a database with no human author was assessed in *Telstra Corp Ltd v Phone Directories Co Pty Ltd* (2011) 90 IPR 1. In the UK, copyright in a computer-generated work was warranted in *Nova Productions Ltd v Mazooma Games Ltd* [2006] EWHC 24 (Ch), [2006] RPC 14. In Germany, copyright in photographs made by a machine was rejected in *Satellitenfoto*, Decision of 30 May 1989, 16 O 33/89 [1990] *GRUR* 270.

[78] Ravid and Liu (n 60), too, regard the complexity in the process of creation as a key feature of the problem.

[79] For a description of and research on the problem of collective authorship see Daniela Simone, *Copyright and Collective Authorship* (CUP 2019) 2.

[80] The difficulties with attributing authorship of folklore to a specific person is cited in Agnès Lucas-Schloetter, 'Folklore' in Silke von Lewinski (ed), *Indigenous Heritage and Intellectual Property* (Kluwer Law International 2004) 296. Similarly, Professor Sherman cites (but does not defend) one of the objections against copyright in Aboriginal art. The objection is that its creator is the community rather than an identifiable individual. Brad Sherman 'From the Non-original to the Ab-original: A History' in Brad Sherman and Alain Strowel (eds), *Of Authors and Origins: Essays on Copyright Law* (Clarendon Press 1994) 123.

[81] *Rote Taube*, Decision of 27 March 1969, X ZB 15/67 [1970] IIC 136, 138. See also Joseph Straus, 'Biotechnologische Erfindungen – ihr Schutz und seine Grenzen' [1992] *GRUR* 252, 258.

[82] *Diamond v Chakrabarty*, 100 S Ct 2204, 2208, 65 L Ed 2d 144 (1980) 310. Justine Pila and Paul Torremans, *European Intellectual Property Law* 2nd edn (OUP 2019) 73.

While the arguments made under the latter approach are useful for this book, the problems are different. The AI productions are not taken directly from nature and, in practice, are unlikely to ring the biotech bell and attract the caution that is associated with patenting natural processes or products. The known examples of technical advances that allegedly are AI productions have an allure of technical character which makes them highly indistinguishable from human-made inventions and thus likely to fly below the biotech radar.

Conclusion

This chapter concludes that the following technical facts are relevant for copyright and patent laws: there are AI-driven systems that can determine expressive elements of literary or artistic subject matter or non-obvious technical features of technical advances; they allegedly can do it without human intervention or understanding. In technical terms, such AI-driven systems could be based on deep neural networks that use various types of training, ie involving a combination of various levels of human interference with training and absence of human intervention and understanding in the process of creation (of final outputs; not creation of the neural network architecture or training the MLA).

Copyright and patent laws and policies thus face an unprecedented situation: the AI-driven systems having (functionally) replaced some of the human decision-making in the processes of creation of literature, art and technology. In many cases this led to the existence of expressive subject matter without a human author that are indistinguishable from human-authored works and to non-obvious technical advances without a human inventor that are indistinguishable from human-made inventions.

The documented achievements of some AI-driven systems legitimise the ongoing debates concerning authorship and inventorship in the age of AI. These encompass factual, doctrinal and normative questions of authorship, inventorship and the creation of works and inventions which are often intermingled. These overlaps, together with legal scholars, judges and policy makers holding different opinions on the capabilities of AI-driven systems (or using different vocabulary to describe them) and different policy preferences hinder the development of constructive dialogues. What is needed is to shift the focus away from AI (for a moment) and direct it at what copyright and patent laws are really about: protection of authors and inventors and their intellectual creations.

3

The Relevant Justifications for Copyright and Patents

Introduction

This chapter sets out the conceptual and theoretical background for the chapters that follow. It frames the key terms such as human intellectual creations, author, inventor and human intellectual creative activity with reference to scholarly work and to examples of historical development of those terms.[1] This framing and the corresponding theoretical framework will inform this book's perspective and shape its normative proposals.

Copyright and patents have traditionally and in principle been reserved for human intellectual creations and this chapter argues that this should remain the case in the foreseeable future.[2] First, this is because human intellectual creations carry certain specific intrinsic and social values which other objects, no matter how expressive or technical they may be, do not. Second, even if some compelling arguments for protection of expressivity, technicality and inventiveness as such can be found, these arguments, if standing alone, are not solid and robust enough to justify property in expressive or non-obvious technical subject matter as such (regardless of their origin).

The intrinsic and social values of human intellectual creations are abstracted from deontic and utilitarian justificatory theories. Given the limited space, this chapter prioritises those theories that justify the proprietary aspect[3] of copyright

[1] Though this book's focus is on laws of the UK, France and Germany, this chapter also makes references to US scholarship and doctrine for several reasons. First, their intellectual influence goes beyond the US borders. Second, this chapter understands the key terms in a broader sense and searches for some common ground in which search the US accounts may be helpful. Third, these references should also offer more insights into the 'common law' countries tradition (though copyright and patents have a statutory basis in the US as well as the UK) and thereby balance out the continental law scholarship and doctrine which would otherwise be dominating.

[2] This is not the same as to say that intellectual property rights are justified. Rather, this book adopts Machlup's conclusions concerning justifications for patents (and dares to extend them to copyright) in the respect that once a society has established copyright and patent systems, then the policy recommendation is to 'muddle through' and refrain from abolishing them. Fritz Machlup, *An Economic Review of the Patent System* (Committee Print 1958) 80.

[3] Property in the sense advanced (in the intellectual property context) by Merges, 'The most important core principle of the institution of private property is this: it assigns to individual people control over individual assets.' Robert Merges, *Justifying Intellectual Property* (Harvard University Press 2011) 5.

and patents and those theories that were trending in the economic and political discourse towards the end of the nineteenth century. This is because these theories were arguably part of the Zeitgeist at the time of drafting of the Paris Convention 1883[4] and the Berne Convention 1886[5] in the European cultural milieu and, as such, they likely influenced and co-constructed the concepts and framework used in these treaties.[6]

Naturally, the preparatory and drafting meetings leading to these treaties were taking place against the backdrop of complex socio-economic realities that made the international consensus on protection of author's and inventor's rights possible, such as international piracy,[7] internationalisation of trade[8] or the sense of opportunity to lead by example.[9] Nonetheless, authors, inventors and their interests were in the forefront and at the heart of the drafting activities as the resolutions and proclamations made in the course of the preparatory and drafting works reveal.[10]

For instance, Numa Droz, the president of the 1886 Conference, described the drafting work of the Berne Convention as 'the solemn consecration of a principle of law and justice, and its effect to tighten the bonds that should unite mankind, apart from which it will undoubtedly contribute to the encouragement and multiplication of the noblest products of human ingenuity'.[11]

In a similar vein, the resolutions agreed by the Vienna Patent Congress 1873 on protection of inventions, in the words of Ladas, 'affirmed the natural right of the inventor'.[12] And they did so for the following reasons:

> The sense of right among civilised nations demands the legal protection of intellectual works. (b) This protection affords [...] the only practical and effective means of introducing new technical methods [...] to the general knowledge of the public. (c) The protection of invention renders the labour of the inventor remunerative, and induces

[4] Paris Convention for the Protection of Industrial Property 1883, as revised at Stockholm in 1967 (Paris Convention).

[5] Berne Convention for the Protection of Literary and Artistic Works (Paris Act of 24 July 1971), as amended on 28 September 1979 (Berne Convention).

[6] These theories were also widely debated in times when the benefits of intellectual property were questioned and their future existence was at stake. This concerns mainly the patent abolishment debates in the UK and Prussia, see Louise Duncan, *The Role of Theoretical Debate in the Evolution of National and International Patent Protection: from the French Revolution to the Paris Convention of 1883* (Brill 2021).

[7] ibid 30.

[8] Duncan (n 6) 213.

[9] Michel Pelletier and Edmond Vidal-Naquet, *La Convention D'Union pour la Protection de la Propriété Industrielle* (Librarie Recueil Sirey 1902) 8.

[10] Traces of natural rights theories, reward- and incentive-based justificatory theories can be found in the copyright and patent discourses in the UK, Germany and France, though they did not enjoy an equal influence and popularity.

[11] Sam Ricketson, *The Berne Convention for the Protection of Literary and Artistic Works: 1886–1986* (Kluwer 1987) 891.

[12] Stephen Ladas, *International Protection of Industrial Property* (Harvard University Press 1930) 74. This merely presents a consensus at an international level and does not necessarily mean that all domestic patent systems were based on natural law theories.

thereby competent men to devote time and means to the introduction and practical application of new and useful technical methods and improvements [...].[13]

This book thus regards the values and ideas embodied in justice and labour-based theories of property and reward- and incentive-based justificatory theories as influential in times when nations were brought together to protect the rights of authors and inventors, thus likely underpinning the minimal common ground laid down in these treaties.[14]

Human Intellectual Creations

This book uses the term 'human intellectual creations' as an overarching notion for works and inventions. At this level of abstraction, the term 'human intellectual creations' captures the essence of inventions and works, ie that they are productions of human mind. According to Plaisant, French diplomat and treatise writer, the term 'intellectual rights' (used to denote both author's and inventor's rights) was coined in the nineteenth century to embrace 'all categories of rights applicable to the creations of human brain'.[15]

Authorship and inventorship are understood as relationships between an author/inventor and their work/invention. These relationships are regarded as having been established through human intellectual creative activity[16] (which term should later be defined for normative purposes based on doctrinal research). The constitutive role of human intellectual creative activity for intellectual property has been recognised for some time. More specifically, according to Professors Sherman and Bently, mental labour and the process of creativity were the main concern of intellectual property law in the eighteenth and the first half of the

[13] The resolutions as they are quoted in Sam Ricketson, *The Paris Convention for the Protection of Industrial Property A Commentary* (OUP 2015) 35. Though commentators Pelletier and Vidal-Naquet called these resolutions to be mere platonic wishes which did not turn into anything practical. See Pelletier and Vidal-Naquet (n 9) 9.

[14] Ricketson ibid, 10.

[15] Marcel Plaisant, *Traité de droit conventionnel international concernant la proprieté industrielle* (Librairie du Recueil Sirey 1949) 6. He attributed coinage of the term to Edmond Picard, a Belgian lawyer in his work of 1879.

[16] For instance, this term is used in the Explanatory Memorandum to the Computer Programs Directive, 'As far as the property right is concerned, a computer program, in common with other works protected by intellectual property legislation, is the result of a creative intellectual human activity.' Proposal for a Council Directive on the legal protection of computer programs COM(88) 816 final – SYN 183; 89/C 91/05) [2.2.]. It is also used in scholarship, eg by Laligant, who mapped the developments in the concept of originality in French law from the mid-nineteenth to the end of the twentieth centuries. In his monograph, he writes that 'by using the term "work of the mind" the legislator suggests that the protectable work by author's rights must be a product of human intellectual creative activity'/ *'le législateur suggère déjà, par l'emploi de l'expression "œuvre d'esprit" que l'œuvre protégeable au titre du droit d'auteur doit être le produit d'une activité mentale fabricatrice de l'homme'*. Olivier Laligant, *La véritable condition d'application du droit d'auteur : Originalité ou création?* (Presses Universitaires d'Aix-Marseille 1999) 14.

nineteenth centuries.[17] They claim that human mental labour was 'the most influential organising principle of pre-modern intellectual property law'.[18] They also observe that, in modern law, 'creativity reappeared in the form of the requirements of originality and non-obviousness, in which applicants had to show, in effect, that their respective works were creative'.[19]

This book uses the terms 'author' and 'inventor' as normative concepts. They will be used in the sense outlined below, unless defined with reference to a specific legislative act or case law. In the copyright law part, author is understood as the author-creator, ie a natural person who, as put by Professor Ricketson, 'is an intellectual creator in the literary or artistic sphere'.[20]

The Berne Convention assumes the human nature of authors. According to Ricketson, during the Berne Convention drafting process, 'there was very little debate about the subject, so it seems only logical to interpret "authors" and "authorship", for purposes of the Convention, as pertaining to the persons who created such works'.[21] The human nature of authors is implied by Article 6bis of the Berne Convention which provides for moral rights of authors.[22] Moral rights are associated with human beings only and hence the assumption embodied in that provision was that the author is a human being. Copyright is also largely justified by the author's natural rights on the basis of, as put by Professor Ginsburg, 'personal creativity, and that largely underpins the Berne Convention'.[23]

Professor Dietz also supports the proposition that the notion of author was used in the Berne Convention to denote exclusively a natural person who created the work. In his words, 'an examination of the whole system of the Berne Convention up to the last revisions in Stockholm/Paris also reveals that only natural persons who have created works are considered authors'.[24] He adds that the absence of an explicit definition of author in the Berne Convention and national differences in the conceptions of author and authorship should not be interpreted as if the recognition of the author-creator is optional (in the Berne Convention's legacy).[25]

According to Dietz, in common law countries, there may be a confusion between (i) authorship as original creation (in fact) and (ii) authorship as original attribution for ownership purposes.[26] He defends the conceptual purity of authors

[17] Brad Sherman and Lionel Bently, *The Making of Modern Intellectual Property Law* (CUP 1999) 173.

[18] ibid.

[19] ibid 200.

[20] Ricketson (n 11) 893.

[21] Sam Ricketson, 'The 1992 Horace S. Manges Lecture – People or Machines: The Berne Convention and the Changing Concept of Authorship' (1991) 16 *Colum-VLA JL & Arts* 1, 8.

[22] 'Independently of the author's economic rights, and even after the transfer of the said rights, the author shall have the right to claim authorship of the work and to object to any distortion, mutilation or other modification of, or other derogatory action in relation to, the said work, which would be prejudicial to his honor or reputation.' Berne Convention, art 6bis(1).

[23] Jane Ginsburg, 'People Not Machines: Authorship and What It Means in the Berne Convention' (2018) 49 *IIC* 131, 134.

[24] Adolf Dietz, 'The Concept of Authorship under the Berne Convention' (1993) 155 *RIDA* 26.

[25] ibid 4 and 10.

[26] ibid 38.

as creators against other persons in whom national copyright laws may initially vest the rights and, at that occasion, call them authors. He argues that, for instance, the work-for-hire doctrine is just an implicit assignment by virtue of the copyright statute which is actually compliant with the creator doctrine because 'at least for a logical second at the moment of creation of the work, authors under the [Berne] Convention are the original owners of the copyright'.[27]

Authorship, ie the relationship between the author and their work, is concerned with what one must do to become an author. Despite the differences in national conceptions of author, some basic and common understanding of the underlying activity may be formed. Most prominently, according to a comparative study conducted by Professor Ginsburg and in her words, 'an author is (or should be) a human creator who, notwithstanding the constraints of her task, succeeds in exercising minimal personal autonomy in her fashioning of the work'.[28] She adds that 'most national copyright laws agree that mere execution does not make one an author. An "author" conceives of the work and supervises or otherwise exercises control over its execution'.[29] Hence, this book adopts the minimalistic view that the relevant authorial human intellectual creative activity consists of conceiving and executing the work (or exercising a control over the execution). A work is then viewed as the result of an activity by which a human being conceives a work and gives it a form (or an expression).

The chosen conception of author is, admittedly, individualistic and based on the personal nature of the relationship between the author and their work. For these characteristics, it has been subject to criticism. Legal and other scholars question whether the romanticised view of author is not detached from the reality of how authorial works come to existence.[30] Even in France, the continental bastion of authors, some regard the Romantic conception of an author to belong to the past because nowadays works are created in teams, by consumers, on collaborative platforms and that new processes of creation tend to blur the line between an author and a user-manipulator.[31]

However, a question more pertinent to this book is whether copyright laws are bound to mimic perceptions of authorship trending in literary or art theory. As Professor Bently writes, 'the histories fail to establish conclusively any causative, necessary or determining link between the legal and the literary. All there

[27] ibid 40. The 'logical second' argument does not, however, apply to the UK law for instance. Under the Copyright, Designs and Patents Act 1988, s 11(2) copyright never vests in the employee. Michael Tappin and others, *Laddie, Prescott and Vitoria: The Modern Law of Copyright* 5th edn (Lexis 2018) [11.25].

[28] She compared the laws of the USA, the UK, Canada, Australia, France, Belgium and the Netherlands. Jane Ginsburg, 'The Concept of Authorship in Comparative Copyright Law' (2003) 52 *DePaul L Rev* 1063, 1092.

[29] ibid, 1072.

[30] For references to and comments on the literature see Lionel Bently, 'Copyright and the Death of the Author in Literature and Law' (1994) 57 *MLR* 973.

[31] André Lucas, Agnès Lucas-Schloetter and Carine Bernault, *Traité de la propriété littéraire et artistique* 5th edn (LexisNexis 2017) 174.

is a complimentary and reinforcing connection, a parallel development'.[32] Undoubtedly, social and cultural preconceptions about creativity play a role in making laws and judicial decisions.

It is also true that contemporary creative processes feature 'collective, collaborative, individualistic, professional and user-generated'[33] creativity. For instance, Professor Zemer argues that every work stems from collaboration between the public and authors and that 'the public contributes invaluable skill and expertise by virtue of maintaining and providing social and cultural properties'[34] which is a copyright eligible contribution in the sense of providing 'detailed concepts, data and emotions'.[35] In a sense, it is true that the public maintains language, for instance, and individual words can be seen as 'detailed data'. But property right for contribution in the form of maintaining language and individual words goes against the fundamentals of the established copyright systems. There is little point in having copyright if the public would be a joint author of every work. This would turn an exclusive (and an exclusionary) right into an inclusive enterprise.

Professor Zemer also draws an analogy between how trade marks derive their attractiveness from the joint effort of their authors and consumers and applies this logic to copyright works. He calls both subject matter 'social construct[s]'.[36] But at such an abstract level, many things privately owned are social constructs, including money or leasehold.[37] Therefore, this understanding of authorship is hardly reconcilable with the idea of copyright as private property (or a property-like right).

Regardless of the valid observations that human beings do not create in a vacuum, but rather within various social and cultural contexts and networks, under the influence of many external determinants and using commons such as language or colours, the starting position adopted in this book is that human beings create as individuals nonetheless. They do so because, first, at the physiological level, there are no collective or platform brains, just individual brains. As phrased by Czech neuropathologist Koukolík, '[e]veryone from the eight billion people who live on the Earth is a neurobiological individual. Every brain is biologically,

[32] Lionel Bently, 'Copyright and the Death of the Author in Literature and Law' (1994) 57 *MLR* 973, 978. See also Professor Lavik's scepticism about the potential of humanities to develop 'more effective concepts, definitions and distinctions for the purposes of copyright law'. Erlend Lavik, 'Romantic Authorship in Copyright Law and the Uses of Aesthetics' in Mireille van Eechoud (ed), *The Work of Authorship* (Amsterdam University Press 2014) 79.

[33] Giancarlo Frosio, *Reconciling Copyright with Cumulative Creativity: The Third Paradigm* (Edward Elgar Publishing 2018) 4–5. Frosio investigates creativity from the perspective of interplay between community, law and market.

[34] Lior Zemer, *The Idea of Authorship in Copyright* (Ashgate 2007) 199.

[35] ibid.

[36] ibid.

[37] Assuming some sort of free market-based economy, money or leasehold are also social constructs as their existence and their value are derived from the joint effort of persons transacting them and the public.

psychologically and socially individual, the history and experience of every brain is equally individual'.[38] He also adds that we are individuals with a personal history and, at the same time, we are members of our cultural surroundings and its history and we are also members of human species and its history.[39]

Second, individual and personal creativity can be perceived as a part of dialogue between an individual author and others, and this dialogue may happen in teams or on collaborative platforms. Similarly, Professor Ng argues that '[t]he author's creativity as expressed in any work of literature or art represents the sine qua non of creative engagement with other authors, communities, and the rest of the society'.[40] Or, as put by Professor Drahos,

> authors, composers, musicians and scientists move in traditions and cultures which they react to or against. Equally a story about creativity which sees it as an outcome of tradition or other social forces ignores the capacity of individuals to step outside of social norms. Creative individuals are in one respect rule breakers.[41]

This book echoes the view that cultural and societal determination of author's mind and means of expression do not rule out perceiving literary and artistic works as results of one's intellectual and creative activity.

When addressing patent law, an inventor is understood to be an inventor-creator, ie a natural person who is 'the actual deviser of the invention'.[42] The moral right of inventor to be mentioned as such in the patent was added to the Paris Convention during the London Revision Conference 1934, however leaving it open to the national laws to determine who the inventor is.[43]

The concept of inventor does not have the relatively widely recognised conceptual base compared to the one of author nor has it such a strong natural rights' backing.[44] This may also be due to the fact that while the Berne Convention was built on the legacy of specialised bilateral treaties for protection of author's rights, the objects of protection under the Paris Convention were previously addressed only by a special provision or two in trade agreements.[45]

Nonetheless, normative reflections of the inventor-creator principle are apparent in patent laws. Besides the inventor's moral right, a person who comes up

[38] '*Každý z osmi miliard lidí, kteří jsou dnes na Zemi, je neurobiologický jedinec. Každý mozek je biologicky, psychologicky i sociálně individuální, historie a zkušenosti každého mozku jsou rovněž individuální.*' František Koukolík, *Já. O mozku, vědomí a sebeuvědomování* (Karolinum 2024) 132. In this book Koukolík popularizes international research in his field with a special focus on the self, consciousness and self-consciousness.

[39] ibid.

[40] Alina Ng, *Copyright Law and the Progress of Science and the Useful Arts* (Edward Elgar Publishing 2011) 94.

[41] Peter Drahos, *A Philosophy of Intellectual Property* (ANU Press 1996) 61.

[42] Patents Act 1977, s 7(3).

[43] Ricketson (n 11) 389.

[44] Drahos (n 41) 29. Drahos adds that English law did not see inventions as results of creative activity, ie 'inventors merely uncover what is already there. [...] The idea that inventors create nothing confuses the pre-existence of the laws of nature with their novel application.' ibid.

[45] Pelletier and Vidal-Naquet (n 9) 5, Duncan (n 6) 210.

with an invention has an 'inventor's right'[46] and right to file a patent application before (and logically so) a patent is granted.[47] The mere fact of inventing thus produces legal effects preceding the grant of the patent (which goes against the logic of patent as a mere privilege granted by a state). Inventorship is also protected if the patent is granted to another, independent inventor who was the first to file a patent application. In such a case, the inventor who was overtaken in the race to the patent office has the right to continue the use which began before the priority date of the issued patent.[48]

Historically (and this is covered in a brief and necessarily simplified manner), patents as proprietary rights in intangible objects 'emerged from the very tangible world of artisanship and crafts'.[49] Hence the first inventors were artisans and craftsmen. The first patent statute which was enacted in Venice derived inventor's rights from 'the very fact of his invention'[50] rather than from a privilege granted by state. Individual rebellions against Renaissance guilds underscored the role of individual inventors and their ingenuity. For instance, a patent for the architect Brunelleschi was justified by 'his own ingenuity and invention'.[51]

In Elizabethan England patents also served to attract import of new technology through welcoming their carriers and embodiments, ie foreign craftsmen, and artisans.[52] Following a public resentment against royal prerogatives, the Statute of Monopolies 1623 prohibited them with few exceptions, including patents for 'the true and first inventor'.[53] London barrister Hindmarch commented in 1846 that English courts permitted granting patents to persons who brought 'such [new] arts and manufactures *within the realm* [italicised in the original]'[54] and this was interpreted as including persons who imported new inventions to England. In *Edgeberry v Stephens*, the court interpreted the Statute of Monopolies as having 'intended to encourage new discoveries useful to the kingdom, whether learned and acquired by study or travel [...]'.[55]

[46] '*Erfinderrecht*' in German for instance. Josef Kohler, *Deutsches Patentrecht* (Verlag von F Bensheimer 1878) 77. Lord Walker called the right arising out of the act of invention as 'a sort of inchoate property in the invention' *Yeda Research and Development Co Ltd v Rhone-Poulenc Rorer International Holdings Inc* [2007] UKHL 43, [2008] RPC 1, [53].

[47] EPC, art 60.

[48] Patents Act 1977, s 64; Patentgesetz of 16 December 1980 (BGBl 1981 I S 1) (German Patent Act) § 12, Code de la propriété intellectuelle (Loi n° 92-597 du 1er juillet 1992 relative au code de la propriété intellectuelle, as amended) (French Intellectual Property Code) art L613-7.

[49] Joanna Kostylo, 'Commentary on the Venetian Statute on Industrial Brevets (1474)' in Lionel Bently and Martin Kretschmer (eds), *Primary Sources on Copyright (1450–1900)* (2008). Available at: www.copyrighthistory.org, last accessed 20 April 2021.

[50] ibid.

[51] Pamela Long, 'Invention, Authorship, "Intellectual Property" and the Origin of Patents: Notes Toward a Conceptual History' (1991) 32 *Technology and Culture* 846, 881.

[52] Christine MacLeod, *Inventing the Industrial Revolution* (CUP 2009) 11.

[53] Statute of Monopolies 1623. As quoted in Kostylo (n 50).

[54] William Hindmarch, *A Treatise on the Law relating to Patent Privileges for the Sole Use of Inventions; and Practice of Obtaining Letters of Patents for Inventions* (V&R Stevens & GS Norton, and W Benning & Co 1846) 27.

[55] *Edgeberry v Stephens* (1693, 1738) 90 ER 1162.

Other lawyers of the day commented that apart from importers being treated as the inventors, 'the words "true and first inventor" are narrowly construed, and a patent is invalid if the author of the invention is not the patentee'.[56] Less than a century later, White QC wrote that it is a sound practice to include as inventors 'all those who have made any discernible personal contribution to the final result'.[57] The UK abandoned patents for importation and amended the law in favour of the actual deviser of invention on recommendation of the Banks Committee 1970.[58]

The French patent system was founded on the personal character of patent rights by a decree in 1762.[59] Historically, a patent could be granted to the author of the invention or to another person to whom the right of the inventor was validly transferred.[60] From Blanc's account of the French Patent Statute of 8 July 1844 one learns that the act of granting a patent was merely declaratory, ie merely recognising an already existing right of the inventor to their invention. As put by Blanc, '[e]very new discovery or invention in all the areas of industry vests in its author, under the conditions and for the time determined hereafter, the exclusive right to exploit to his profit the said discovery or invention'.[61]

In the 1843 Parliamentary reports accompanying patent law reforms in France, the proposed abolition of patents for improvements was justified on the grounds that they prompt inventors to share even premature conceptions which are then picked up by 'certain industrial speculators, the true hornets of the inventive genius [...] paralysing in their hands the development'[62] as well as the exploitation of the ideas to the detriment of their inventors.[63] Patents for imported inventions were proposed to be abolished because they were a mere 'prize in the race'[64] and were denounced as a 'theft from the public domain'.[65]

The first patent statute for the German Empire was adopted in 1877 thanks to, inter alia, the influence of the Association of German Engineers and promotion of advantages of (an improved) patent system by its member and inventor

[56] James Johnson and Henry Johnson, *An Epitome of the Law and Practice connected with Patents for Inventions* (Longmans Green, & Co. 1894).

[57] Blanco White, *Patents for Inventions and the Registration of Industrial Designs* 3rd edn (Stevens & Sons 1962) 185.

[58] Maurice Banks, *The British Patent System* (Her Majesty's Stationery Office 1970) Cmnd 4407.

[59] Jean Marc Mousseron, *Le droit du breveté d'invention* (Librairie générale de droit et de jurisprudence 1961) 239.

[60] Etienne Blanc, *L'inventeur breveté, code des inventions et des perfectionnements* 3rd edn (Cosse 1852) 256.

[61] '*Toute nouvelle découverte ou invention dans tous les genres d'industrie, confère à son auteur, sous les conditions et pour les temps ci-après déterminé, le droit exclusif d'exploiter à son profit ladite découverte ou invention*' ibid 254.

[62] '*certains spéculateurs industriels, véritables frelons du génie d'invention, [...] paralysant ainsi entre leurs mains le développement*' Adrien Huard and Michel Pelletier, *Répertoire de législation et de jurisprudence en matière de brevets d'invention* (Librairie générale de jurisprudence 1885) 28.

[63] ibid.

[64] '*que le prix de la course*' ibid 29.

[65] '*un vol fait au domaine public*' ibid.

Werner Siemens.[66] According to Professor Beier, the aspects of inventions which made the invention patentable were evolving from the concept of inventor's objective contribution to the concept of technological progress.[67] Later, from around 1914 in the practice of the Imperial Court, patentable subject matter was required to demonstrate a certain degree of inventiveness which operated together with the requirements of novelty and technological progress.[68] In 1923, the German Imperial Court held that 'a mere objective enrichment of technology does not suffice; the invention must rest on a creative intellectual activity not lying close [being obvious] to an average-skilled man'.[69] The Patents Act of 1936 was said to make, in the words of judge Lindenmaier, 'the creative act of the inventor a condition for patent protection'.[70]

Building on the conception of inventor-creator, this book adopts the understanding of inventing activity as advanced by Robinson, US patent treatise writer of the end of the nineteenth century. In Robinson's view, patent eligible inventions must involve

> (1) An idea conceived by the inventor; (2) An application of that idea to the production of a practical result. Neither of these elements is alone sufficient. An unapplied idea is not an invention. The application of an idea, not original with the person who applies it, is not an invention. Hence, the inventive act in reality consists of two acts; one mental, the conception of an idea; the other manual, the reduction of that idea to practice.[71]

As Professors Pottage and Sherman comment, Robinson would treat also a discovery (even if made by chance) as a patentable invention if 'the inventor had understood it well enough to describe how to reproduce it'.[72]

In this latter respect, the present understanding differs from Robinson's and aligns with the current European patent law understanding of invention. As formulated by Professor Pila, inventions are understood as 'technical teachings, namely, subject matter involving technical character, in the sense of depending for their existence on some human intervention in the material world utilizing the forces of nature to produce a causal, perceivable, and repeatable result'.[73]

[66] Duncan (n 6) 199–201. Duncan also explains other economic and political factors that contributed to passing the Patent Statute of 1877.

[67] Friedrich-Karl Beier, 'Zur historischen Entwicklung des Erfordernisses der Erfindungshöhe' [1985] *GRUR* 606, 615. Beier was a director of the Max Planck Institute for Foreign and International Patent, Author's Rights and Competition Law, Munich.

[68] ibid.

[69] '*Eine nur objektive Bereicherung der Technik reiche nicht aus; die Erfindung müsse auf einer "schöpferischen Geistestätigkeit" beruhen, dem Durchschnittsfachmann nicht nahegelegen haben*.' ibid.

[70] Lindenmaier, 'Die schöpferische Leistung als Voraussetzung der Patenterteilung' (1939) 3 *GRUR* 153.

[71] William Robinson, *Law of Patents for Useful Inventions* (Little, Brown 1890) 77.

[72] Alain Pottage and Brad Sherman, *Figures of Invention: A History of Modern Patent Law* (OUP 2010) 61.

[73] Justine Pila, *The Subject Matter of Intellectual Property* (OUP 2017) 115.

One may object that the focus of this book on human intellectual creations or human intellectual creative activity is simply outdated. However, the conceptions of author, inventor and their personal relationship to works and inventions did not cease to occupy the central place in copyright laws and perhaps, less obviously, in patent laws. Works and inventions currently enjoy a robust, generous and (ever-) expanding protection which is often justified by reference to the underlying human intellectual creative activity being poured into their immediate creation.[74]

The last few decades witnessed a revival of human creativity underpinnings in the reasonings of courts. According to the US Supreme Court, copyright subsists only in works which are 'original and are founded in the creative powers of the mind [and are …] the fruits of intellectual labor'.[75] For the High Court of Australia, creativity is one of the 'aspects of a mental process which produces an object, a literary work, a particular form of expression which copyright protects'.[76] The UK House of Lords held that having a good idea and composing a piece of music are activities that clearly merit copyright.[77] The House of Lords also stressed that property in human intellectual creations

> provide an incentive to innovation and creativity. A person who has a good idea, as [the joint author] did when he composed the well-known organ solo that did so much to make the song in its final form such a success, is entitled to protect the advantage that he has gained from this and to earn his reward.[78]

Copyright subsistence in the cases above hinged on the origin of the subject matter in the human mind or mental processes and its eventual production or realisation through labour.

In patent law, the significance of human intellectual creative activity resurfaced in the context of biotechnological inventions. In *Diamond v Chakrabarty*[79] and *AMP v Myriad Genetics*,[80] the US Supreme Court effectively distinguished between a process of providing access to a non-naturally occurring substance (the isolation of genes from natural DNA) and a process of creating a non-naturally

[74] By way of illustration, the Court of Justice of the European Union repeatedly instructed national courts that the (copy/author's) rights should be given broad interpretation (Case C-160/15 *GS Media BV v Sanoma Media Netherlands BV and Others* [2016] EU:C:2016:644 para 30) and exceptions to rights must be interpreted strictly (Case C-201/13 *Johan Deckmyn and Vrijheidsfonds VZW v Helena Vandersteen* [2014] EU:C:2014:2132 para 22); a favourable treatment of author or their successors in title in the three-step test Christophe Geiger, Jonathan Griffiths and Reto Hilty, 'Towards a Balanced Interpretation of the "Three Step Test" in Copyright Law' (2008) 30 *EIPR* 489; extension of duration of copyright; generous doctrine of equivalents not only in Germany but now in the UK too *Actavis UK Ltd v Eli Lilly & Co* [2017] UKSC 48, [2017] Bus LR 1731.

[75] *Trade-Mark Cases*, 100 US 82, 25 LEd 550 (1879) 94, embraced in *Feist Publications Inc v Rural Telephone Service Co Inc* (1991) 499 US 340 at 344–45, 347.

[76] *IceTV Pty Ltd v Nine Network Australia Pty Ltd* [2009] HCA 14, 239 CLR 458, 47, 49.

[77] *Fisher v Brooker* [2009] UKHL 41, [2009] 1 WLR 1764.

[78] ibid [8].

[79] *Diamond v Chakrabarty*, 100 S Ct 2204, 2208, 65 L Ed 2d 144 (1980) 310.

[80] *Association for Molecular Pathology (AMP) v Myriad Genetics Inc*, 133 S Ct 2107 (2013) 2116.

occurring substance (the synthetic making of cDNA or bacterium). Significantly, only the substances resulting from the latter process are patent eligible because only the devising of those substances involves human intellectual creative activity.

The European Board of Appeal of the European Patent Office in *Tomatoes/State of Israel* made a general statement that the 'essence of invention' is 'human intervention in a process in order to bring about a desired result'.[81] The Enlarged Board of Appeal thus interpreted the concept of invention as requiring 'human intervention'[82] or an intentional abstention therefrom.[83]

From among legal scholars, Professor Merges in his book Justifying Intellectual Property makes a case for the relevance of human intellectual creative activity in the 'Internet era',

> [...] the new technologies of dissemination have not changed one important fact: creative works still require effort, and (in many cases) a projection of the individual will, or personality. Since effort and individuality are the essence of IP, property rights in creative works continue to make sense even in the Internet era.[84]

Now intellectual property faces the challenge posed by new technologies of creation which fact makes the human creativity underpinnings of copyright and patent systems even more pertinent.

Intrinsic Values of Human Intellectual Creations

The intrinsic values of human intellectual creations are given by their human origin. Human intellectual creations embed and mirror their human creator's dignity and personality. The respect for human dignity is the rationale behind moral rights: the paternity right with respect to both, inventions[85] as well as works,[86] the right to divulge the work and the right to integrity of work.[87] Moral rights and the right

[81] *Tomatoes/State of Israel*, G 0001/08 of 9 December 2010, EP:BA:2010:G000108.20101209 [6.4.2.3] and the same [6.4.2.1]. The same also *Broccoli/PLANT BIOSCIENCE*, G 0002/07 of 9 December 2010, EP:BA:2010:G000207.20101209, [6.4.2.1].

[82] ibid [6.4.2.1]. It may be objected that the EBA contrasts 'human' to 'natural/biological intervention' in this decision. In the present view, it rather contrasts the effects of a human intervention and natural 'intervention' of sexual crossing on the resulting subject matter. The EBA distinguishes between technical steps that (i) merely enhance or assist the biological processes and those that (ii) change the result. In principle, inventions in all technical fields secure their technical character through human intervention in the nature. This applies to inventions in computer science (eg utilising electricity), chemistry (eg utilising properties of various materials), mechanics (eg utilising natural laws of motion), etc.

[83] ibid [6.4.2.3]. For a more in-depth analysis of the case, see Chapter 4.

[84] Merges (n 3) 24–25.

[85] Art 4ter Paris Convention also see Georg Bodenhausen, *WIPO Guide to the Application of the Paris Convention* (BIRPI 1968), 64. EPC, art 62.

[86] Berne Convention, art 6bis.

[87] French Intellectual Property Code, art L121-1-121-9, right to object to derogatory treatment of work under the Copyright, Designs and Patents Act 1988, s 80 and Urheberrechtsgesetz of 9 September 1965, BGBl. I S. 1273 (Author's Right Act) § 14.

to fair remuneration for one's creation[88] are those rights in intellectual property that can almost without a dispute be regarded and treated as human rights.[89] More solemn proclamations to this effect may be found in the Universal Declaration on Human Rights 1948[90] or International Covenant on Economic, Social and Cultural Rights.[91] These two fundamental rights thus share with other human rights their sanctity, universality and inalienability.

The degree to which human dignity or personality is recognised as a justificatory reason differs across jurisdictions. It is truly foundational in Germany where (i) a personal right in invention arises upon its creation,[92] and (ii) 'intellectual property […] is simply recognised by legislation'[93] and not created. Also, the personal and economic dimensions of author's rights (moral and economic rights) create a unity under the monistic theory.[94] Dignity and personality-based reasons to justify intellectual property seem to resonate similarly in France. As put by Professor Desbois, author's rights are 'not considered instruments of a policy inspired by opportunistic considerations, [or] by a concern to stimulate intellectual creation; [but rather] they constitute modes of expression of respect owed to works of the mind and their creators'.[95] In jurisdictions where the protection of human dignity and personality is secured via protection of one's creations, replacing 'human' with 'AI' and protecting subject matter with no human creator (author or inventor) would be a nonsense.

In contrast, in the UK, the language of investment, eg investment of labour and effort,[96] rather than the language of dignity or personality has traditionally been used. As for patents, historical petitions for patents in England cited, as put

[88] In France, inventors-employees have a right to supplementary remuneration or fair price under the French Intellectual Property Code, art L.611-7. In the UK, the inventor-employees have a right to additional compensation under Patents Act 1977, ss 40(1) and 41. In Germany, inventor-employees have a right to fair compensation under §9 of the Employees' Inventions Act of 25 July 1957 as amended ('*Gesetz über Arbeitnehmererfindungen*').

[89] French Constitutional Council confirmed the status of intellectual property as a human right. See in Pascal Kamina and others, 'France' in Burton Ong (ed) *International Copyright Law and Practice* annually updated (LexisNexis 2024) §1[4]. See also Paul Torremans, 'Copyright (and Other Intellectual Property Rights) as a Human Right' in Paul Torremans (ed), *Intellectual Property Law and Human Rights* (3rd edn, Wolters Kluwer 2015) 226. Peter Yu, 'Reconceptualizing Intellectual Property Interests in a Human Rights Framework' (2007) 40 *UC Davis L Rev* 1039, 1081.

[90] 'Everyone has the right to the protection of the moral and material interests resulting from any scientific, literary or artistic production of which he is the author', art 27(2).

[91] 'The States Parties to the present Covenant recognize the right of everyone: [… t]o benefit from the protection of the moral and material interests resulting from any scientific, literary or artistic production of which he is the author', art 15(1)(c).

[92] Maximilian Haedicke, '§3 Ownership A. Inventor and Inventor Right' in Maximilian Haedicke and Henrik Timmann (eds), *Patent Law: A Handbook on European and German Patent Law* (CH Beck 2014) 244.

[93] *Tonband v Grundig Reporter*, German Supreme Court, 18 May 1955, BGHZ 17, 266 as cited in Silke von Lewinski, *International Copyright Law and Policy* (OUP 2008) 38–39.

[94] Karl-Nikolaus Peifer, 'UrhG § 11 Allgemeines' in Gerhard Schricker and Ulrich Loewenheim (eds), *Urheberrecht* 6th edn (CH Beck 2020) [3].

[95] Henri Desbois, *Le droit d'auteur en France* 3rd edn (Dalloz 1978) 7.

[96] von Lewinski (n 93) 46.

by Professor MacLeod, '"the great charge, labour, cost and pains" (or similar sacrifices) that the petitioner had expended on his invention'.[97] This may lead to the impression that, in the UK a hypothetical extension of copyright or patents to any expressive or non-obvious technical subject matter respectively would leave human dignity intact and require mere cosmetic changes in law, eg with respect to patent application forms and derivation of title.

In such a case, moral rights in common law jurisdictions could just become obsolete without impacting on the force of economic rights. Yet, even in the traditional common law jurisdiction, there is something to lose by relinquishing the value of human origin. There is a social value in correct attribution because, as Professor Ginsburg argues, attribution assists the public with its orientation on the market, similarly to trade marks.[98] She adds that attribution enhances the communication function of works because it enables the audience to perceive it with its origin in mind and interpret it accordingly.[99]

This social value is not carried by AI productions with no human creator. Since an AI-driven system merely determines expressive elements but does not communicate anything (in the sense of communication as association), there can hardly be any enhancement of communication. Attribution of expressive elements to the AI-driven system could then work as an assurance that there is no communication. With respect to technology, knowing its origin is crucial for trust and its implementation. How much trust would a piece of technology made entirely or partly by an AI-driven system enjoy, especially in defence, cyber security or medicine?

The human origin of human intellectual creations is crucial for justification of property as a natural right. The rhetoric of justice and desert was employed at preparatory and drafting meetings leading to the Paris Convention 1883 and the Berne Convention 1886. The 1878 Congress in Paris (preceding the Berne Convention 1886) focused first on those principles that promised some united approach of the countries. One of the passed resolutions stated that: '[t]he right of author in his work constitutes, not a concession by the law, but one of the forms of property which the legislature must protect'.[100] Delegates to the Vienna Patent Congress 1873 managed to agree only on a few principles because of the profound differences in the then existing patent law systems.[101] Among the few agreed points, the Congress, as put by Ladas, 'affirmed that "the right of the inventor is a right of property that the civil law does not create, but simply regulates"'.[102]

Under the natural law theories of property, states merely recognise or affirm natural rights; these rights are properly justified by and derived from human

[97] MacLeod (n 52) 13.

[98] Jane Ginsburg, 'Moral Rights in a Common Law System' (1990) 1 *Ent L R* 121, 122.

[99] ibid.

[100] Ricketson (n 11) 46. This formulation likely builds on the French theoretical basis for protection of author's rights, for more details see Duncan (n 6) 5 ff.

[101] Stephen Ladas, *Patents, Trademarks and Related Rights. National and International Protection. Vol I* (Harvard University Press 1975) 62.

[102] ibid.

attributes such as labour, personality or dignity. For instance, Pufendorf, an eighteenth-century German scholar, argued that property in things is justified through 'labour and cultivation by men' because it would be 'improper that a man who had contributed no labour should have right to things equal to his by whose industry a thing had been raised or rendered fit for service'.[103] Thereby, the contribution of labour that renders the work fit for use, eg composing a musical work that can be listened to in the process of creation makes property in that work justified.

In the common law tradition, John Locke is often cited when it comes to labour-based justifications of property.[104] In his Second Treatise of Government, he writes that a human being has a property in their person and body and that through the use of their body, they can have property in the direct and immediate fruits of their labour and exclude others from using that property.

> The labour of his body, and the work of his hands, we may say, are properly his. Whatsoever then he removes out of the state that nature hath provided, and left it in, he hath mixed his labour with, and joined to it something that is his own, and thereby makes it his property. It being by him removed from the common state nature hath placed it in, it hath by this labour something annexed to it, that excludes the common right.[105]

Merges interprets Locke's theory as having the end goal surviving and thriving with the aid of appropriation justified by labour.[106] Adopting this interpretation, it becomes clear that only human beings are capable of labouring in this sense.

Justification of appropriation based on the relationship between a human creator and their creation was metaphorically described by German philosopher Hegel. Also, Professor Radin finds Hegel's idea of embodied will useful in justifying property.[107] He recognises the process of 'imposing a form on a thing' as one of few justified ways how to take possession of a thing.[108] He elaborates further on how something can become existent as an object of property:

> It is only through the development of his own body and mind, essentially through his self-consciousness's apprehension of itself as free, that he takes possession of himself and becomes his own property and no one else's. This taking possession of oneself, looked at from the opposite point of view, is the translation into actuality of what one is according to one's concept, i.e. a potentiality, capacity, potency. In that translation one's self-consciousness for the first time becomes established as one's own, as one's object also and distinct from self-consciousness pure and simple, and thereby capable of taking the form of a 'thing'.[109]

[103] Samuel Pufendorf, *De Jure Naturae et Gentium* (Ex officina Knochiana, 1744) as cited in Stephen Buckle, *Natural Law and the Theory of Property: Grotius to Hume* (OUP 2002) 102.

[104] Merges (n 3) 31 ff, Drahos (n 41) 28.

[105] John Locke, *Second Treatise of Government* (Alex Catalogue 1994) s 27.

[106] 'A theory about why individual appropriation helps people to survive and thrive' Merges (n 3) 40.

[107] Margaret J Radin, *Reinterpreting Property* (University of Chicago Press 1994) 47.

[108] Georg Hegel, *Philosophy of Right* as translated in Thomas Knox, *Hegel's Philosophy of Right* (OUP 2015) [54] and [56].

[109] ibid [57].

To put it simply: (i) there is a pure and simple self-consciousness (ii) which becomes one's own through the person taking the possession of oneself and (iii) as the person expresses what she is and she owns, such as her attainments, erudition, talents and this becomes embodied in something external and alienated,[110] the result can be thus regarded as property of that person.

An object can become a property of its creator because it originates in the alienation of (or a part of) creator's own self-consciousness. The object becomes an embodiment of their will;[111] hence the act of making the object creator's own can be regarded as a definitional element of the object itself. Hegel also distinguishes two stages of this alienation – making the self-consciousness one's own which is inward facing (internal) and giving a form to an object which is an activity upon the outer world. It is noteworthy that the above theories employ human intellectual creative activity that is immediately and directly bringing a new thing into being, ie in the intellectual property context determining its expressive or non-obvious technical elements.

Some may object that human personality does not justify copyright and patents to an equal measure. In technical fields, in contrast with literature or arts, creators face more constraints to express their personalities. As Professor Hughes writes, computer programmers may be constrained in embellishing their works, 'but even they can embellish their works to suit at least some of their own predilections. The genetic researcher or the aerospace engineer are even more constrained; their slightest embellishments may be dangerous indeed.'[112] He closes his discussion on the scope for expression of personality by stating that

> [t]he individual must have some internal connection to the claimed property. This connection need not be that the object 'expresses' the owner's personality. It may be simply that the owner identifies himself with the object. With inventions, the object may precede the personality stake, but with time the scientist or engineer comes to identify himself with his scientific or technological advances.[113]

Indeed, when one approaches personality holistically and focuses on the human forces in the process of creation, one can immediately appreciate the relationship between an inventor and their inventions. Inventors have to employ their cognitive and personality traits such as ingenuity, mental endurance and conscientiousness in solving technical problems regardless of how many embellishments they can afford to insert into the final outcome.

Outside the natural law theories but not dissimilarly, prominent English thinkers, namely Adam Smith, Jeremy Bentham and John Stuart Mill, regarded patents as just compensation and reward for a person's mental labour and experimental endeavours.[114] In US patent law, Professor Mossoff puts the labour theory under

[110] ibid [43].
[111] ibid [53].
[112] Justin Hughes, 'The Philosophy of Intellectual Property' (1988) 77 *Georgetown LJ* 287, 330.
[113] ibid.
[114] Matthew Fisher, 'Classical Economics and Philosophy of the Patent System' [2005] *IPQ* 1, 8–10.

the spotlight. He refers to an influential US Supreme Court decision of 1834 in which the labour argument was embraced: 'That every man is entitled to the fruits of his own labour must be admitted.'[115] Further, the US Patent Act 1836 refers to labour and desert policy when justifying the duration of patent rights which should secure 'for inventors the fruits of their inventive labors'.[116]

It may plausibly be argued that to bring about pretty, useful or innovative AI productions requires human intellectual activity in the form of formulating a technical problem, giving a suitable prompt, preparing a training dataset, training an algorithm, tinkering with the results, etc. However, the activity poured into the preparation of a dataset is a human intellectual creative activity in relation to that dataset, not the consequent productions. The activity poured into training an algorithm, adjusting its weights, setting up the parameters is a human intellectual creative activity in relation to that algorithm, not the consequent productions. There are other legal means to protect datasets or algorithms such as trade secrets or unfair competition.[117]

If these preparatory, up-stream activities or high-level inputs such as giving a guidance or supplying principles to an AI-driven system were to be rewarded, the putative authors or inventors would need to justify how these activities differ from the same kind of activities in the processes not involving an AI-driven system to preserve the fairness and labour/desert-based rationale. For instance, why should there be inventorship for persons who prepare datasets to be crunched by AI-driven systems while there is no inventorship for persons (usually called assistants) who prepare datasets for further processing by other persons? Why should there be inventorship for deploying an AI-driven system, if there is no inventorship for using a microscope (to solve a particular problem)?[118] This would also mean rewarding those who have access to AI-driven systems or microscopes and their output out of which any ordinarily skilled expert would make the ensuing technical teachings. This is analogous to procuring a (relatively) exclusive access to certain information, describe its practical use for industry, formulate it as a technical teaching and present it as one's own invention (eg appropriation of indigenous knowledge, biopiracy).

One may also think of post-creative activities such as rearranging elements, editing, mere reduction to practice, etc. and some argue that the person who does this post-creative activity on an AI production should be rewarded by copyright[119] or patents. However, why should the post-creative activity on AI productions not be treated as any other follow-on creativity? If no new authorial work or invention of inventive quality emerges due to the transformative nature of the post-creative

[115] *Wheaton*, 33 US at 658 as quoted in Adam Mossoff, 'Who Cares What Thomas Jefferson Thought about Patents – Reevaluating the Patent Privilege in Historical Context' (2007) 92 *Cornell L Rev* 953, 988.

[116] As expressed by Circuit Justice McLean as quoted in Mossoff, ibid 1006.

[117] Jean-Marc Deltorn and Franck Macrez, 'Authorship in the Age of Machine Learning and Artificial Intelligence' in Sean M O'Connor (ed), *The Oxford Handbook of Music Law and Policy* (OUP 2019).

[118] It may be argued that the inventive bit is done by the person who comes up with an idea how to use an AI-driven system to produce technical solutions in an inventive way. And this is plausible if such an inventive use of AI-driven system passes an adjusted obviousness test, including a question whether a person skilled in the art would use an AI-driven system to solve such a problem and if so in which ways.

[119] Pamela Samuelson, 'AI Authorship?' (2020) 63 *ACM* 20, 22.

activity (which would become an intellectual creative activity in relation to the new subject matter), then there is no reason for reward in the form of copyright in or patents for an incremental improvement, mere new edition or finetuning.

In this connection, the US Patent and Trademark Office (USPTO) issued inventorship guidance where it states that a mere reduction to practice does not earn inventorship.[120] This is distinguished from 'the doctrine of simultaneous conception and reduction to practice'.[121] Pursuant to that doctrine, 'in some instances, an inventor may only be able to establish a conception by pointing to a reduction to practice through a successful experiment'.[122] As the guidance continues, this doctrine is sometimes helpful when 'the inventor does not have a reasonable expectation that they would produce the claimed invention'.[123] However, setting up and deploying an AI-driven system to solve a certain problem does not produce an invention by accident (because AI-systems work deterministically).

On a more general level, if there are no good (meta-)reasons for which the labour/desert-based reasons should assist in extending the meritorious activity to the pre-creative and post-creative activities in relation to human intellectual creations, then for the moment it is difficult to see any good reasons for such an extension in favour of AI productions.

Social Values of Human Intellectual Creations

Human intellectual creations are valuable because they advance the progress of science and learning and the flourishment of culture. In this vein, under the Statute of Anne 1709/10, the role of authors in production of literary works took precedence over the role of book disseminators. In the words of Professor Deazley, the 'Parliament focused upon the social contribution the author could make in the encouragement and advancement of learning'.[124] The Act also explicitly stated that copyright should encourage 'learned Men to compose and write useful Books'[125] and hence indicated the meritorious intellectual creative activity: composing and writing.

The US Constitution vesting the powers to enact legislation in intellectual property matters in the Congress signifies its importance to the New World's settlers. As put by one of the federalists, James Madison, the Congress should have the respective powers

> to promote the progress of science and useful arts, by securing, for a limited time, to authors and inventors, the exclusive right to their respective writings and

[120] USPTO, 'Inventorship Guidance for AI-Assisted Inventions' Docket No PTO–P–2023–0043.
[121] ibid.
[122] ibid.
[123] ibid.
[124] Ronan Deazley, 'Commentary on the *Statute of Anne* 1710' (2008) in Lionel Bently and Martin Kretschmer (eds), *Primary Sources on Copyright (1450–1900)*. Available at: www.copyrighthistory.org, last accessed 20 April 2021.
[125] ibid.

> discoveries. [...] The copyright of authors has been solemnly adjudged, in Great Britain, to be a right of common law. The right to useful inventions seems with equal reason to belong to the inventors.[126]

In the mid-twentieth century, the US Supreme Court concurred and explained the rationale for the powers of the Congress in consequentialist economic terms.

> The economic philosophy behind the clause empowering Congress to grant patents and copyrights is the conviction that encouragement of individual effort by personal gain is the best way to advance public welfare through the talents of authors and inventors in 'Science and useful Arts.'[127]

These accounts reveal a shared underlying logic: patents and copyright (are expected to) incentivise certain activity through rewarding that activity. The instrumentality of talents of authors and inventors is widely acknowledged and mainly relied on in common law countries.

Professor Machlup, who conducted an economic review of the US patent system in the mid-twentieth century, found that 'the profit expectations connected with the hope for a patent monopoly may induce inventive talents to exert their efforts'.[128] He further acknowledges that even after the ways of organising research and innovation in technology have changed over time, the ultimate task – to induce inventive talents to exert their effort – remains unchanged.[129]

Professor Ginsburg's research debunks the stereotype that the concern with public interests is more prevalent in common law countries. She asserts that the first copyright laws in France as well as the USA were based on the furtherance of private as well as public interests which were, as she puts it, 'of equal weight'.[130] She shows that the education policy was at the forefront in France[131] almost as much as in the USA and that reward for 'men of industry or of talents'[132] was as important in the USA as in France. The US and French examples illustrate how the goal of advancing learning and education may go hand-in-hand with the goal of providing incentives to create to individuals.

The progress of science, advancement of learning and flourishment of culture usually evokes producing more technology, more books, more music and more art[133] (which nowadays may not necessarily mean more human intellectual

[126] James Madison, 'Federalist No. 43' (Library of Congress, undated). Available at: https://guides.loc.gov/federalist-papers/text-41-50#s-lg-box-wrapper-25493407, last accessed 21 March 2021.
[127] *Mazer v Stein*, 347 US 201, 219 (1954).
[128] Machlup (n 2) 23–24.
[129] ibid 36.
[130] Jane Ginsburg, 'A Tale of Two Copyrights: Literary Property in Revolutionary France and America' (1991) 147 *RIDA* 125, 143.
[131] ibid 163.
[132] ibid 145 quoting a US historical source.
[133] 'The social value of utilitarian works lies principally if not exclusively in their ability to perform tasks [...] or satisfy desires more effectively or at lower costs.' Peter Menell, 'Intellectual Property: General Theories' in Boudewijn Bouckaert and Gerrit De Geest (eds) *Encyclopedia of Law & Economics. Vol II* (Edward Elgar 2000) 130.

creations, see Chapter 2). However, on a more granular level, one can appreciate a social value unique to producing human intellectual creations as opposed to mere having more of expressive or non-obvious technical artifacts. Applying the work of psychoanalyst Fromm to the situation at hand, by producing human intellectual creations, society becomes richer in writers, artists and inventors and thus more learned and cultured through an active, direct and creative engagement of its members with letters, music, arts and technical puzzles.[134] In contrast, current research reveals that using AI-driven systems damages human creative capabilities by flattening and re-structuralising neuronal pathways (in human brains).[135]

A special social added value can be perceived in the processes of creation and invention in which human beings work together and learn from each other. Practising and nurturing the traditions of authorship or inventorship, ie know-how, in creating works or problem solving, that pass from generations of writers, musicians, artists and engineers to new generations of writers, musicians, artists and engineers has its own social value. Pedagogy would call this practice apprenticeship and spells out the social benefits of 'enculturation, [...] participation in a social group, and [preservation of] competence and social identity in relation to the community of practice'.[136] Putting subject matter without human creators on an equal footing with human intellectual creations may, eventually, mean that the traditions of creating and problem solving, including skills and knowledge that cannot be readily datafied (ie turned into data) will vanish.

In addition, there is a social value in the attribution of a work or an invention (which presupposes transparency as to their origin) because it fuels incentives to create. According to Professor Quaedvlieg, mentioning a name of the author on a copy of work is important to establish their reputation, especially for those authors 'who seriously pursue creative career'.[137] A survey conducted on a sample of approximately 9,000 European inventors in the early 2000s shows that '[t]he inventors consider monetary rewards and other rewards like career advances or benefits less important than personal and social rewards, like personal satisfaction, prestige, reputation, and the contribution to the performance of the organization'.[138] To realise those reputational rewards and incentives the creators must, first, create something and, second, they must be recognized and named as inventors or authors. Needless to add that all the justifications for intellectual

[134] Erich Fromm, *To Have or to Be?* (Bloomsbury 2012).

[135] Research as reported in Christian Mammen and others, 'Creativity, Artificial Intelligence and the Requirement of Human Authors and Inventors in Copyright and Patent Law' (*Ssrn*, 17 July 2024). Available at: https://papers.ssrn.com/sol3/papers.cfm?abstract_id=4892973, accessed 31 July 2024.

[136] Daniel Pratt, 'Good Teaching: One Size Fits All?' (2002) 93 *New Directions for Adult and Continuing Education* 5, 10.

[137] Antoon Quaedvlieg, 'Authorship and Ownership: Authors, Entrepreneurs and Rights' in Tatiana-Helenē Synodinou (ed), *Codification of European Copyright Law: Challenges and Perspectives* (Wolters Kluwer Law & Business 2012) 202.

[138] Alfonso Gambardella and others, 'The Value of European Patents – A Survey of European Inventors – Final Report of The PatVal EU Project' (*europa*, January 2005). Available at: http://ec.europa.eu/invest-in-research/pdf/download_en/patval_mainreportandannexes.pdf, last accessed 31 December 2021.

property that are incentives-based are applicable exclusively to self-conscious creators capable of responding to such incentives.

Value of Expressive Subject Matter and Non-Obvious Technical Subject Matter

Finally, the value that copyrighted works and patented inventions carry due to their expressivity or technicality and inventiveness must be addressed. These qualities correspond to the secondary patentability requirements in European patent law (novelty, inventive step, industrial application) and the requirement of (literary, dramatic, musical or artistic)[139] form in copyright laws of the UK, Germany and France.

Not all commonly cited justifications for intellectual property rest on the human origin of works and inventions. For instance, Hardin, in his seminal article *The Tragedy of the Commons*, argues that scarce resources are more sustainably managed as private property or under exclusive rights than as the commons.[140] He warns against a tragic depletion of resources that are accessible to everyone in an uncontrolled way and in certain case he even calls '[t]he alternative of the commons […] too horrifying to contemplate'.[141]

However, the practice has shown that in the case of private property there can be too much of a good thing. Heller and Eisenberg point to the fact that the privatisation of biomedical research in the USA led to obstacles in the form of overlapping patent rights owned by different private parties which, in effect, impeded the downstream innovation.[142] In a similar vein, Professor Shapiro shows how patent thickets in the telecommunications industry increased transaction costs and harmed innovation.[143]

Another account that justifies property in technical solutions is social contract theory. Under this theory, patent rights are a consideration offered by the public in exchange for knowledge disclosed by the inventor. A direct consequence of introducing this theory was a new patentability criterion – the sufficiency of disclosure of the invention. For instance, Machlup refers to this set of reasons as exchange-for-secrets theory because it is oriented towards disclosing inventions in a sufficient (or enabling) manner rather than keeping them secret.[144] It is noteworthy though that the social

[139] In the UK; for the EU copyright it would be 'providing enough creative freedom' and in France and Germany a perceivable form of expression would suffice, see Chapters 6 and 7.

[140] Garrett Hardin, 'The Tragedy of the Commons' (1968) 162 *Science* 1243, 1244–45.

[141] ibid 1247. Though one may wonder how this 'cold war'-style narrative was transplanted to the intellectual property discourse.

[142] Michael Heller and Rebecca Eisenberg, 'Can Patents Deter Innovation? The Anticommons in Biomedical Research' (1998) 280 *Science* 698, 699.

[143] Carl Shapiro, 'Navigating the Patent Thicket: Cross Licenses, Patent Pools, and Standard Setting' (2000) 1 *Innovation Pol'y & Econ* 119.

[144] Machlup (n 2) 21.

contract theory has never operated self-sufficiently. Historically, it rather stands on the shoulders of reward- and incentive-based theories as it does not consider disclosing a subject matter that has not been previously devised by a human being.

Another social value rendered by patent system (independently of the origin of invention) is formulated by Professor Kitch in his prospect theory. He observes that the patent system promotes an efficient allocation of opportunities (prospects).[145] However, he does not claim, nor can it be inferred from the prospect theory, that one should have a patent system as, otherwise, opportunities would not have been allocated efficiently. Moreover, as Kitch himself acknowledges, his prospect theory is only complementary to rewards theory (which is, as already demonstrated above, founded on the human inventor–creator principle).[146]

From a utilitarian perspective, ie that of maximising the overall good in society, one may legitimately ask two questions. First, do expressivity or technicality and inventiveness as such bring anything valuable? This would make a good subject for a longer debate, but this book takes the stance that expressive or technical and inventive properties as such are neither good nor bad for society. The obvious examples of their ambivalence are genetic engineering, nuclear fission, cyber security detection tools, pornography or Machiavelli's *The Prince*. Their utility depends on their use and the mere fact of their disclosure does not guarantee their use for good ends.

To be more accurate, their disclosure does not even guarantee their use. As argued by economist Schumpeter, '"getting new things done" is not only a distinct process but it is a process which produces consequences that are an essential part of capitalist reality'.[147] The claim that a mere disclosure does not automatically guarantee the overall good (nor any goods actually) was validated during the Covid-19 pandemic. On 3 February 2022, it was announced that South African scientists had managed to create a copy of Moderna's vaccine.[148] Despite this project presumably having been assigned the utmost urgency and one could imagine the laboratories having been run 24/7, it took almost eight months to bring a disclosed technical solution to practice because of raw material shortages and lack of a complete recipe for creation of the vaccine.[149]

Further, utility is needs, preferences and time sensitive. For instance, an invention made by the Max Planck Institute's scientist Karl Ziegler for which he also won a Nobel Prize in 1963, enabled the widespread use of plastics for everyday

[145] Edmund Kitch, 'The Nature and Function of the Patent System' (1977) 20 *J Law Econ* 265.

[146] ibid 266.

[147] Joseph Schumpeter, 'The Creative Response in Economic History' (1947) 7 *Journal of Econ Hist* 149, 152.

[148] Amy Maxmen, 'South African scientists copy Moderna's COVID vaccine' (*nature*, 3 February 2022). Available at: www.nature.com/articles/d41586-022-00293-2, last accessed 4 February 2022.

[149] ibid. The 'almost eight months' was calculated from the date of when the last patent covering Moderna's mRNA-1273 COVID-19 VACCINE was granted, ie on 26 June 2021 to the announcement. Moderna, 'Program Patents' (*moderna*, undated). Available at: www.modernatx.com/patents, last accessed 4 February 2022.

objects like shampoo bottles or plastic bags.[150] This invention, once acclaimed as a progress of science, may nowadays be regarded as a progress towards extinction, especially by those concerned about the state of the environment to which the wide use of plastics contributed.

The economic reasonings for granting a time-limited monopoly revolve around the argument that, but for the monopoly, the expressive or non-obvious technical subject matter would not have been brought to light because their production incurs a high fixed cost while their subsequent use or reproduction by others incurs only a low variable cost.[151] Since the limited space of this chapter does not allow us to delve into the law and economics literature, it must suffice to acknowledge that the reality is more complex than this model of market failure suggests.

Whether one can plausibly rely on the market failure argument in justification of intellectual property depends on parameters with different values from market to market, eg market structure, elasticity of demand, and the effects of intellectual property on market power. As Professors Landes and Posner point out, the adequacy of incentives to invent differ depending on the height of the fixed costs, possibilities to invent around and availability of substitutes on the market.[152] This necessarily creates a discrimination between the fields of technology to which inventions belong. For instance, while patents for pharmaceutical inventions would arguably be justified, patents for software not in an equal measure.

Professor Breyer takes books as example and estimates how the abolition of copyright would impact any incentive to produce them. He arrives at different conclusions for different kinds of book precisely because of different market characteristics.[153] He shows that college textbooks could be viable without copyright, whereas elementary and high school textbooks would experience difficulties. As he reasons, this is because college books are more profitable and their authors would likely write them anyway in the course of their employment.[154] In contrast, elementary and high-school textbooks are less profitable and their authors are usually employed by publishers who would be directly hit by the abolition of copyright.[155] Hence copyright, too, appears to be necessary to incentivise production only under certain circumstances.

Since patents are there for subject matter in all technical fields and copyright for any literary, dramatic, musical or artistic subject matter[156] and since the

[150] Birgit Fenzel, 'Patent solution in a canning jar' (*Max-Planck-Gesellschaft* 11 August 2014). Available at: www.mpg.de/8361429/flashback-ziegler, last accessed 31 December 2021.

[151] Carl Shapiro and Hal Varian, *Information Rules* (Harvard Business School Press 1999) 21.

[152] William Landes, Richard Posner, and Richard Posner, *The Economic Structure of Intellectual Property Law* (Harvard University Press 2003) 300.

[153] Stephen Breyer, 'The Uneasy Case for Copyright: A Study of Copyright in Books, Photocopies, and Computer Programs' (1970) 84 *Harvard L R* 281, 309ff.

[154] ibid 310.

[155] ibid.

[156] As explained in the Introduction, this book concerns copyright in the classic Berne Convention works. Entrepreneurial works such as sound recordings or audiovisual recordings are outside its scope.

market failure argument works only under certain circumstances on the market, patents and copyright do not seem to be fully justified or justified equally under all circumstances.

Therefore, the universal character of protection of inventions and works may only be explained and likely stems from their human origin and justificatory theories that hinge upon it (eg labour theories, rewards- and incentives-based justificatory theories). None of the market failure-based theories can explain or justify the universality and equality with which the law treats works (coming from any literary or artistic sphere) and inventions (coming from any technical field).

The last category of reasons worth addressing are intellectual property fallacies. They are mostly based on the argument that protection is justified because bringing a subject matter into being requires some investment (even if not extraordinarily high or even if not in the form of human intellectual creative activity) and this investment should be protected from free riders.

One of its iterations is reaping without sowing, ie a holder of a subject matter should be able to exclude others from its use so that the others do not reap where they have not sown. It implies that, as Spence put it, 'it is wrong to reap without sowing if someone else, and in particular the sower, has a stronger claim to that which is reaped'.[157] However, as Spence points out, the problem is that the phrase assumes that there is a person who has a better right than anybody else and this assumption cannot be justified by the phrase itself.[158]

Another example is Justice Peterson's rule of thumb '[…] there remains the rough practical test that what is worth copying is prima facie worth protecting'.[159] This test, too, stands and falls with the assumption that there is a person with a better right in the work than the person using the work. And it also includes an assumption that there is a protectable work. A similar argument was made by Justice Birss re the position of Dr Thaler, the owner of an AI-driven system DABUS: '[l]ooking at Dr Thaler's position as it stands, it is not obvious that there is any other person with a better right than Dr Thaler's to be granted patents for these inventions but if there is then they can come forward'.[160]

In this line of thinking, the underlying reason seems to be that protection must be granted if someone claims it. But just because nobody with a better title comes forward, it does not and should not make the claimant or applicant entitled. Hence, these arguments do not justify why the subject matter is or should be protected. If need be, they may serve well for protection of investment by trade secrets, unfair competition or unjust enrichment (provided further conditions are met).[161]

[157] Michael Spence, 'Justifying Copyright' in Daniel McClean and Karsten Schubert (eds), *Dear Images: Art, Copyright and Culture* (Ridighouse 2002) 396.

[158] ibid.

[159] *University of London Press Ltd v University Tutorial Press Ltd* [1916] 2 Ch 601 (Ch) [608].

[160] *Stephen Thaler v Comptroller General of Patents Trade Marks and Designs* [2021] EWCA Civ 1374, [2021] 9 WLUK 172 [85].

[161] The protection of investment is a valid argument for protection by neighbouring rights if those subject matter correspond to entrepreneurial works.

Some also argue that copyright and patents should be granted for AI productions with no inventor in order to spur innovation. For instance, the UK IPO in relation to AI and IP states that any intervention should (first) 'encourage innovation in AI technology or promote the use of AI for the public good; and [second] not undermine IP's wider role in promoting human creativity and innovation'.[162] The innovation argument was also used by Beach J for the Federal Court of Australia. He construed the statutory term of inventor 'in a manner that promotes technological innovation and the publication and dissemination of such innovation by rewarding it, irrespective of whether the innovation is made by a human or not'.[163]

As for the (simplified) stipulation that intellectual property promotes innovation, whether any innovation is in practice delivered depends on other factors that are external to intellectual property law.[164] As put by Shapiro in a nutshell, while the prospect of temporary market power (which may or may not come with intellectual property) spurs innovation (Schumpeter), once a firm is an incumbent it will refrain from disruptive innovation (Arrow) unless it fears being superseded by another, more innovative firm.[165] In addition, as argued by Professor Ghidini and Cavani and endorsed by Professors Drexl and Lowenheim, mere investment does not justify intellectual property: 'IP can perform a dynamic (and pro-competitive) mission only if it protects, within the statutorily set time (and other) limits, not investments as such, but specific intellectual achievements, statutorily qualified as worthy of such protection.'[166]

The weakness of the statements that copyright and patents are the right tools to spur innovation in AI is that they lack grounding in evidence.[167] In fact, the available evidence suggests the contrary. The available evidence shows that AI productions are being produced under legal uncertainty about their intellectual property status. To take the area of drug discovery as an example, in 2020 and 2021 alone, the firms using AI in drug discovery managed to raise sums ranging from $100 million to $500 million per funding call or an IPO.[168]

Hence, it is questionable whether there is any actual need for a regulatory intervention to spur innovation in such a thriving industry. A more pertinent question is whether the absence of copyright and patents decrease incentives to

[162] UK IPO, 'Impact Assessment' (*gov* 29 October 2021). Available at: https://assets.publishing.service.gov.uk/government/uploads/system/uploads/attachment_data/file/1029930/impact-assessment.pdf, last accessed 18 December 2021.

[163] *Thaler v Commissioner of Patents* [2021] FCA 879 [124].

[164] See for instance Edwin Mansfield, *The Economics of Technological Change* (Longmans 1969) 102.

[165] Carl Shapiro, 'Competition and Innovation: Did Arrow Hit the Bull's Eye?' in Josh Lerner and Scott Stern (eds), *The Rate and Direction of Inventive Activity Revisited* (University of Chicago Press 2012) 400.

[166] Gustavo Ghidini and Giovanni Cavani, 'The Relationship Between the Unfair Competition Regime and IP Law' in Niklas Bruun and others (eds.) *Transition and Coherence in Intellectual Property Law* (CUP 2021) 467, 474.

[167] In case of the UK IPO this is forgivable because the UK IPO's call for views aims at gathering the evidence.

[168] Neil Savage, 'Tapping into the drug discovery potential of AI' (*Nature*; 27 May 2021). Available at: www.nature.com/articles/d43747-021-00045-7, last accessed 31 December 2021.

use AI-driven systems in the production of technology, novels, music, computer programs or art. Given the present lack of answers and solid empirical evidence of the need for a positive regulatory action, the compelling reasons for protecting subject matter other than human intellectual creations are still awaited.

Conclusion

This chapter concludes that if copyright and patents are justified then only for those literary or artistic expressive subject matter and non-obvious technical advances that are human intellectual creations. The justificatory reasons based on human dignity, fairness and labour/desert lend the copyright and patent systems their universality and moral high ground. Protection of subject matter that lack human authorship and human inventorship cannot be justified on the same grounds as human intellectual creations. Besides missing the intrinsic values of human intellectual creations, this subject matter should not be put on an equal footing with human intellectual creations because their processes of production do not bring the social added values of the processes involving human authorship and inventorship.

In other words, any potential expansion of copyright and patent protection to protect subject matter other than human intellectual creation is not justified by the current human dignity, fairness, labour/desert-based theories and incentives to create. Incentives to produce and invest, market failure or fair competition reasons are not, if standing alone, compelling, robust nor sufficiently validated by evidence to justify the protection in all literary, artistic and technical fields.

Relatedly, some frame the normative issue as 'Why not?', ie why not protect expressive or non-obvious technical subject matter with no human creator by using copyright or patents respectively.[169] But this framing ignores the fact that, for centuries, human authors and human inventors have been challenged to give good reasons why they merit protection and why the benefits of the protection are likely to outweigh any associated costs. As a result, the current copyright and patent systems are built on positive reasons. Chief among them are those that refer to the intrinsic and social values of human intellectual creations.

[169] For instance, the Federal Court of Australia has surrendered to this tempting question of why not in *Thaler v Commissioner of Patents* (n 160) [121].

4

Inventorship in European Patent Law

Introduction

Adopting the view that the justification of patents for inventions is based on human inventorship, the legal concept of human inventorship must first be defined. Another related issue is whether human inventorship matters for patentability or whether European patents can be granted regardless of the origin of technical solutions subject to patent applications.

This chapter argues that in European patent law the origin of an invention is relevant for patentability. This becomes obvious when the European patent law is read holistically, in light of its theoretical underpinnings and factual assumptions of national patent laws. This chapter also sheds more light on the link between inventorship and patentability and how the former could inform the assessment of the latter with a view to distinguishing human-made inventions from other subject matter.

This chapter begins by exploring conceptions of inventorship for ownership purposes under patent laws in the UK, France and Germany. Then it interrogates the role of the long-established assumptions about human inventorship in the European Patent Convention (EPC)[1] as well as the examination practices of the European Patent Office (EPO). Finally, this chapter identifies reflections of human inventorship in the EPC patentability criteria to support the argument that human inventorship is needed under European patent law.

Inventorship in Positive Law

Inventorship in the Paris Convention

The first international patent law instrument, the Paris Convention, does not explicitly address the nature of inventorship. Nonetheless, it guarantees the moral right of inventors to be named as such in a patent.[2] Because of the personalist

[1] Convention on the Grant of European Patents (European Patent Convention) of 5 October 1973 as revised by the Act revising Article 63 EPC of 17 December 1991 and the Act revising the EPC of 29 November 2000.

[2] Paris Convention, art 4ter: 'The inventor shall have the right to be mentioned as such in the patent' read in conjunction with Georg Bodenhausen, *WIPO Guide to the Application of the Paris Convention*

nature of moral rights, they are associated with human beings only. Hence, an inventor, in the sense of the Paris Convention, may be assumed to be a human being. According to Professor Ricketson, recognising and providing for the moral right of the inventor caused no noteworthy controversies among the parties to the Paris Convention.[3] There are no indications that the Paris Convention countries would have regarded inventors as including any other entities than human beings. Human inventorship was not debated as a potential condition for granting patents. But the reason might have been that the Paris Convention did not aim to harmonise substantive patent law.[4]

Inventorship in the UK

The Banks Committee tasked with drafting recommendations on reforming the UK patent system quoted White QC when stating the object and purpose of patent protection,

> [t]he basic theory of the patent system is simple and reasonable. It is desirable in the public interest that industrial techniques should be improved. In order to encourage improvement, and to encourage also the disclosure of improvements in preference to their use in secret, any person devising an improvement in a manufactured article, or in machinery or methods for making it, may upon disclosure of his improvement at the Patent Office demand to be given monopoly in the use of it for a period of sixteen years. After that period it passes into the public domain; and the temporary monopoly is not objectionable, for if it had not been for the inventor who devised and disclosed the improvement nobody would have been able to use it at that or any other time, since nobody would have known about it.[5]

The Patents Act 1977 defines 'inventor' as the actual deviser of the invention.[6] This provision was interpreted, most prominently, by Lord Hoffmann as meaning 'the natural person who came up with the inventive concept' in *Yeda*.[7] When contemplating possible inventorship by a machine in *Thaler*,[8] the UK Supreme

(BIRPI 1968), 64 wherein it is explained that the right under Article 4ter is 'commonly called a moral right.'

[3] Sam Ricketson, *The Paris Convention for the Protection of Industrial Property A Commentary* (OUP 2015) 389.

[4] ibid 443 ff. The Agreement on Trade-Related Aspects of Intellectual Property Rights sets out substantive patentability requirement for an invention and an inventive step. However, it does not define those notions and they are left to be defined 'in good faith' by the Members. Carlos Correa, *Trade Related Aspects of Intellectual Property Rights: A Commentary on the TRIPS Agreement* 2nd edn (OUP 2020) Ch 9.

[5] Blanco White, *Patents for Inventions and the Registration of Industrial Designs* 3rd edn (Stevens & Sons 1962) 1–2.

[6] Patents Act 1977, s 7(3).

[7] *Yeda Research and Development Co Ltd v Rhone-Poulenc Rorer International Holdings Inc* [2007] UKHL 43, [2008] RPC 1, [20].

[8] *Thaler v Comptroller General of Patents, Designs and Trade Marks* [2023] UKSC 49, [2024] Bus LR 47.

Court followed *Yeda* and reiterated that the inventor within the meaning of the Patents Act 1977 is required to be a natural person.[9]

In the *Thaler* case, Dr Thaler was the appellant and patent applicant who claimed that an AI-driven system known as DABUS autonomously and solely created several inventions subject to his patent applications.[10] Dr Thaler requested to be granted patents for the respective inventions based on his ownership of DABUS which he also named as the inventor on the patent applications. In the patent applications, Dr Thaler also explicitly stated that he was not the inventor.[11]

Against the facts of the case, the UK Supreme Court affirmed the Court of Appeal's findings that 'DABUS is not and was not an inventor of any new product or process described in the patent applications. It is not a person, let alone a natural person and it did not devise any relevant invention'.[12] The Court of Appeal also added that inventors as creators enjoy moral rights under the Patents Act, s 13(1)[13] which further substantiates the conclusion that an inventor must be a natural person.

Coming back to *Yeda*, Lord Hoffmann therein embraced Laddie J's understanding of inventor as 'the natural person who came up with the inventive concept' and summarised the preceding case law that

> [t]he word 'actual' denotes a contrast with a deemed or pretended deviser of the invention; [...] It is not enough that someone contributed to the claims, because they may include non-patentable integers derived from prior art [...] Deciding upon inventorship will therefore involve assessing the evidence adduced by the parties as to the nature of the inventive concept and who contributed to it. In some cases this may be quite complex because the inventive concept is a relationship of discontinuity between the claimed invention and the prior art.[14]

This succinct paragraph contains several important points. First, the designation of the actual deviser as the inventor and the correct attribution of the right in invention is not a mere formality but it matters for entitlement to the patent.[15] Lord Walker called the right arising out of the act of invention 'a sort of inchoate property in the invention' to be fully realised by the grant of a patent.[16]

[9] ibid [56].
[10] ibid [5].
[11] ibid [6].
[12] ibid [73].
[13] *Stephen Thaler v Comptroller General of Patents Trade Marks and Designs* [2021] EWCA Civ 1374, [2021] 9 WLUK 172 [121].
[14] *Yeda* (n 7) [20].
[15] Also Lord Hoffmann in ibid [19]: 'In my opinion, therefore, the first step in any dispute over entitlement must be to decide who was the inventor or inventors of the claimed invention. Only when that question has been decided can one consider whether someone else may be entitled.'
[16] ibid [53].

Second, the relevant activity or contribution is relatively narrowly defined. The inventor is not any person intellectually involved in production of the invention. Only those natural persons who actually 'came up with the inventive concept'[17] are inventors. This does not necessarily mean that every step in the process of inventing must be planned and anticipated, particularly not in the trial-and-error method of inventing. For instance, the *Yeda* case concerned an invention resting on a combined treatment with a monoclonal antibody which was 'surprisingly discovered'.[18] Even though the monoclonal antibodies were supplied by another scientist, Weizmann scientists were the ones who 'had started with an antibody-drug conjugate but during the course of research they "unexpectedly discovered that the unconjugated mixture of drug and antibody in the control produced synergistic and beneficial results"'.[19]

The Weizmann scientists were basically testing two things: a drug and an antibody to find out which one rendered better results. They ended up with a discovery that it was the two of them combined and that was claimed to constitute the inventive concept. They mentioned that their discovery was surprising, but this did not seem to have lessened their claim before the House of Lords.[20] Hence, coming up with an inventive concept need not mean to predict the results of experiments with precision.

Third, it is arguable that the above passage by Lord Hoffmann signals the link between conception of the inventive concept and the requirement for an inventive step. More specifically, Lord Hoffmann equates the inventive concept with 'a relationship of discontinuity between the claimed invention and the prior art'.[21] This discontinuity evokes the proverbial gap between the invention and the territory accessible to a person skilled in the art.[22]

This is further supported by comments made by Hacon HHJ in *BDI Holdings*. He summarises that the 'inventive concept' has been used in the following contexts aside from entitlement: (a) in determining the scope of a patent claim and in this context it was equated with '"the inventive core" of the claim, to be ascertained by focusing on the problem underlying the invention'[23] and (b) in the assessment of obviousness (ie the absence of an inventive step) and in this context it was equated with 'the essence of the claim'.[24] Hacon HHJ commented that these meanings do not seem to differ much if at all from the one given to the inventive concept in *Yeda*.

[17] *University of Southampton's Applications* [2005] RPC 220, 234.
[18] *Yeda* (n 7) [4].
[19] ibid [11].
[20] ibid [4].
[21] ibid [20].
[22] Though the notion of 'inventive concept' is not crystal clear. As noted by practitioners Gibbins and Grant, the notion needs to be 'treated with particular caution. In three respects it is used in mutually inconsistent ways'. David Gibbins and Gregor Grant, '"Inventive Concept" – Is It A Good Idea?' (2005) 5 *EIPR* 170.
[23] *BDI Holdings GmbH v Argent Energy Ltd* [2019] EWHC 765 (IPEC), [2019] FSR 25 [18].
[24] ibid [19].

Another often-cited case discussing inventorship dealt with Professor Howse's idea of a cockroach trap which worked on the principle that the insects' feet alight on electrostatic talcum powder, they slip onto a fly paper and die.[25] After learning of this idea, Mr Metcalfe of IDA suggested to Professor Howse that magnetic powder should bring certain advantages over electrostatic talcum powder.[26] Following this suggestion and thanks to powders supplied by IDA, Professor Howse's students conducted some routine experiments. They found out that the suggestion worked, and the University of Southampton filed for a patent containing the known technical features of the trap and magnetic powder.

The Court of Appeal held that the inventor in the sense of the actual deviser was Metcalfe because the contribution brought by Professor Howse was common general knowledge for those in the art. As put by Jacob LJ, '[t]here was nothing inventive about it and I do not see how Professor Howse could fairly be described as an inventor. The "heart" [of the invention] was Mr Metcalfe's idea and his alone.'[27]

Hence, by suggesting the use of magnetic powder, Metcalfe effectively came up with the inventive concept which made him the inventor. Or put differently, he provided the technical feature that implied the inventive step. Similarly to Lord Hoffmann's account of inventorship, Jacob LJ understands the activity of inventing in *IDA* narrowly (eg, excluding students who conducted routine experimentation) and seems to focus on the technical feature(s) thanks to which the invention passes the inventive step test.

Determining inventorship depends on when the invention is complete in the sense that it is enabling. The Court of Appeal made clear in *IDA* that supplying a non-enabling idea is not sufficient.[28] In the words of Jacob LJ, '[t]hose who contribute enough information by way of necessary enablement to make the idea patentable would count as "actual devisors", having turned what was "airy-fairy" into that which is practical.'[29]

In *Henry Brothers*,[30] the Patents Court emphasised the aspect of making an invention useful for inventorship to arise. The court held that '[o]ne must seek to identify who in substance had been responsible for the inventive concept, namely the combination: whose idea it had been which turned a useless collection of elements into something which would work'.[31] Although the implication of responsibility could justify a broader scope of inventing, the latter part of the sentence narrows it down to creating an idea that makes the invention useful.

[25] *IDA Ltd v University of Southampton* [2006] EWCA Civ 145, [2006] RPC 21 [2].
[26] ibid [3].
[27] ibid [33].
[28] ibid [39].
[29] ibid.
[30] *Henry Brothers (Magherafelt) Ltd v The Ministry of Defence and the Northern Ireland Office* [1997] RPC 693, [1997] 6 WLUK 52.
[31] ibid 706.

All in all, to merit the status of an inventor under UK patent law, a natural person must be the originator of the inventive concept or contribute information necessary to make the idea patentable, eg to make the invention work.[32] Contributions as to providing resources,[33] entrepreneurial or managerial contributions[34] are unlikely to merit inventorship.

Inventorship in France

Historically, under the Patent Statute 1844, the grant of patent was merely declaratory to recognise the right of the inventor to their invention.[35] This is no longer the case and, pursuant to the French Intellectual Property Code, the grant of patent is constitutive of the exclusive rights to exploit the invention.[36] The Minister presenting the bill for the Patent Statute 1844 avoided any solemn proclamations concerning the raison d'être of patent law by saying that patent law '[…] exists and it exists without contestation from 1791. The inventor could not exploit his discovery without the society; the society could not enjoy the discovery without the will of the inventor'.[37] According to Professor Mathély, patents are granted for several reasons,

> [f]irst, the reason is justice. An inventor brings something good to the world of commons. This contribution requires a recognition, a compensation. Second reason is effectivity. It is widely recognised that one of the essential engines of human activity is personal interest. As it is in general interest to stimulate research and in order to achieve it, it is necessary to secure income for inventors. Finally, there is the economic necessity and utility. The research is costly.[38]

Under the Code, in principle, the right to the patent belongs to the inventor; any exceptions therefrom exist only on a statutory basis, namely inventions by employees or hosted researchers.[39] If the inventor at hand does not fall into any

[32] *IDA v The University of Southampton* (n 25) [39].

[33] *Yeda* (n 7) [11].

[34] Lionel Bently and others, *Intellectual Property Law* 6th edn (OUP 2022) 637.

[35] Étienne Blanc, *L'inventeur breveté, code des inventions et des perfectionnements* 3rd edn (Imprimerie et librairie Cosse 1852) 256.

[36] *Code de la propriété intellectuelle* (Loi n° 92-597 du 1er juillet 1992 relative au code de la propriété intellectuelle, as amended) (French Intellectual Property Code or Code) art L 611-1. See also Jean-Michel Bruguière, *Code de la propriété intellectuelle* 25th edn (LexisNexis 2024) 484.

[37] '[…] *ce qui existe, et ce qui existe sans contestation depuis 1791. L'inventeur ne peut exploiter sa découverte sans la société; la société ne peut en jouir sans la volonté de l'inventeur;*' Blanc (n 35) 6.

[38] '*D'abord, une raison de justice. L'inventeur apporte un bienfait au monde de ses semblables. Cet apport requiert une reconnaissance, une récompense. En second lieu, une raison d'efficacité. Il est constant que l'un des moteurs essentiels de l'activité humaine est l'intérêt personnel. Comme il est de l'intérêt général de susciter la recherche, il faut y parvenir, accorder un bénéfice aux inventeurs. Enfin, la nécessité et utilité économique. La recherche est coûteuse*' Paul Mathély, *Le nouveau droit français des brevets d'invention* (Librairie du journal des notaires et des avocats 1991) 18–19.

[39] Code, art L611-7 and art L611-7-1. Bruguière (n 36) 538 ff.

of these statutory exceptions, then they themselves are entitled to 'the property in the invention'.[40]

In order to attribute inventorship and decide on entitlement, it is necessary to identify the date 'on which the invention was conceived',[41] ie the date on which the inventor described the characteristics of the invention. If an employee left their employer at a stage of the process of inventing at which the invention could be realised in a short time, the provisions on employees' inventions apply to such an invention.[42] Conversely, the provisions on employees' inventions do not apply to a person who became an employee after 'the essence of the invention which consisted of an idea'[43] was formulated. If none of the relevant facts are explicitly questioned, it is presumed that the applicant is the entitled person.[44]

The above excerpts from case law already provide some clues as to what a person must do to merit the status of inventor: to originate the essence of invention. The Code does not shed more light on the nature of inventorial activity. Neither the cases concerning co-inventorship nor employees' inventions address inventorship in much more detail. For instance, the Court of Appeal in Paris held that to deregister an already registered co-inventor of an invention subject of an issued patent, the claimant must prove that the registered inventor did not intervene in the conception of the invention.[45]

In cases concerning an equitable remuneration for inventors-employees which is a consideration laid down by the Code in exchange for employer's entitlement to the exploitation right, the courts rely on evidence concerning the process of invention and are led by the contributions brought by concrete employees. For instance, the First Instance Court in Paris found that a putative co-inventor collaborated with two other co-inventors to devise a method of avoiding infection by a virus that was based on genetic manipulation carrying the recombinant of the virus.[46] In a discussion with another expert, the putative co-inventor formulated the problem (ie how to obtain the recombinants of adenovirus) and then proposed to build the genomes of adenovirus in E-coli bacteria by genetic recombination, something which had not been done before.[47] During this conversation the co-inventors also realised that some planned steps in the process were not technically necessary, which significantly shortened the process. For these reasons, the putative co-inventor claimed 'to be the engine of

[40] '*la propriété de son invention*'. Cour de cassation, Decision of 25 April 2006, *JCP* E 2006, 1806.

[41] '*que l'invention a été conçue*' TGI de Paris, Decision of 10 April 1992, *PIBD* 1992 529 III 483.

[42] Bruguière (n 36) 541.

[43] '*l'essentiel de l'invention consistait en une idée*' Cour d'appel de Toulouse, Decision of 22 March 1999, PIBD 1999 679 III 273 as referred to in ibid.

[44] Cour d'appel de Paris, Decision of 24 May 1994 as rephrased and referred to in Bruguière (n 36) 538.

[45] Cour d'appel de Paris, Decision of 26 June 2018, *PIBD* 2018 1101 IIIB 573.

[46] TGI de Paris, Decision of 11 October 2011, n° 08-00908.

[47] ibid.

the conception of that invention from the beginning [...] and evaluate[d] his inventive contribution at 40% proportion of co-inventivity'.[48]

In another case decided by the First Instance Court in Paris, the patented invention consisted of the process of manufacturing a printable sheet of paper for marketing purposes which proved to be a success.[49] The inventive concept rested on how the layers of paper were laid to achieve a printable coated-like paper. It was the claimant who had the idea of layering, which layers to use and came up with the technical solution as to how to put the layers together. However, the claimant did not have the technical skills to realise the invention, or, put differently, to make the idea work. Two engineers, biochemists, were tasked with further development of this idea and conducted experiments with various materials. Eventually these engineers were designated as the inventors on the patent.

The court found that the claimant 'was at the origin of the technical and marketing idea of the invention but [he was] not [at the origin of the] technical feasibility in any way, therefore his part in the [process of] invention should be limited to an invention in the course of employment [...]'.[50] The court recognised the claimant's co-inventorship for 'an idea of paper being first grained before being coated, [even though] he did not participate in the conception or realisation of the process which obtained the desired product'.[51]

Though the French courts tend to see the inventor as someone who took part in the conception of the invention, no consistent definition of inventorship has emerged. It transpires that an invention is required to be conceived by a human being. As the case law on employees' inventions shows, it is important to determine the moment when the essence of invention was conceived to determine whether inventorship can be attributed to a specific person. Inventorship under French patent law arises upon the activity of conceiving the essence of invention, similarly to Lord Hoffmann's view of inventing as coming up with the inventive concept.

Inventorship in Germany

As stated in the commentaries on the German Patent Act, the purpose of patent law is to grant patents for 'novel and industrially applicable inventions that rest on inventive activity'.[52] Patents are there to reward the inventor for their inventive

[48] '*Il estime donc qu'il a eu un rôle moteur dans cette invention en concevant l'invention au départ* [...] *et sa quote-part inventive à 40 % du tot*' ibid.

[49] TGI de Paris, Decision of 16 October 2001 *PIBD* 2002 744 III 265.

[50] '*n'est à l'origine que de l'idée technique et marketing de l'invention mais aucunement de sa faisabilité technique, sa part dans l'invention doit être limitée à une invention de mission* [...]' ibid.

[51] '*il a eu l'idée d'un papier d'abord grainé avant d'être couché, n'a pas participé à la conception et à la mise en place du procédé permettant d'obtenir le produit souhaité*' ibid.

[52] '*Der Zweck des Patentrechts, für neue, auf erfinderischer Tätigkeit beruhende und gewerblich anwendbare Erfindungen Patente zu erteilen* [...].' Klaus-Jürgen Melullis, 'Einleitung' in Georg Benkard (ed) *Patentgesetz* 12th edn (CH Beck 2023) [1].

contribution and they also represent a consideration for enabling others to work on the invention.[53] Patents warrant a property-like right that does not precede the positive law, but rather it is given by the lawmakers.[54]

Since the Patent Act 1936, German patent law has followed a so-called inventor doctrine ('*Erfinderprinzip*') according to which 'no invention is conceivable without inventor'.[55] In Germany the inventor's rights are recognised as a result of making an invention without any need for registration or formalities.[56] These rights are regarded as monistic rights and consist of an economic right to a patent[57] and a personal inventor's right.[58] The personal nature of inventor's right means that it cannot be transferred, alienated or waived.[59] Personal rights exist independently of whether the invention will eventually be found patentable or not and can be invoked against certain uses of the invention by third parties.[60] The inventor is originally entitled to the right to a patent pursuant to §6 of the German Patent Act. The right to a patent arises upon completion of the invention and its disclosure.[61]

As Professor Melullis, a former German Federal Supreme Court judge, writes, 'the invention is necessarily the result of human creative activity'.[62] And, with reference to case law, he adds that 'the inventor is the de facto author of the invention, not the person who commissioned its creation or who employs its creator'.[63] Or, in the words of the German Federal Supreme Court: an invention results from 'a creative act of the inventor'.[64] Making an invention is a real act[65] which implies that whether inventing happened and who did it is a question of fact.

In the decision concerning an AI-driven system, DABUS, the German Federal Supreme Court held that an inventor in the sense of the German Patent Act can only be a natural person.[66] The Court also acknowledged that the concept of

[53] ibid.

[54] Alfred Keukenschrijver, 'Einleitung' in Alfred Keukenschrijver and Rudolf Busse (eds) *Patentgesetz* 8th edn (De Gruyter 2016) [57].

[55] '[...] *Patentgesetz von 1936 das "Erfinderprinzip" eingeführt hat und ersichtlich* [...] *davon ausgeht, daß keine Erfindung ohne Erfinder denkbar ist*'. Helmut Schippel, 'BGH 05.05.1966 Ia ZR 110/64 "Spanplatten"' [1966] *GRUR* 558.

[56] Maximilian Haedicke, '§3 Ownership A. Inventor and Inventor Right' in Maximilian Haedicke and Henrik Timmann (eds), *Patent Law: A Handbook on European and German Patent Law* (CH Beck 2014) 243.

[57] The right to a patent is deemed to flow from the inventor's right in invention. *Pneumatische Einrichtung*, Decision of 6 October 1981, X ZR 57/80 [1982] *GRUR* 95.

[58] Haedicke (n 56) 243.

[59] Klaus-Jürgen Melullis, 'PatG § 6 [Recht des Erfinders]' in Georg Benkard (ed), *Patentgesetz* 12th edn (CH Beck 2023) [22].

[60] *Steuervorrichtung*, Decision of 18 May 2010, X ZR 79/07 [2010] *GRUR* 817.

[61] Melullis (n 59) [1], [6], [7].

[62] '*Die Erfindung ist notwendig das Ergebnis menschlicher schöpferischer Tätigkeit*' ibid [31].

[63] '*Erfinder ist der tatsächliche Urheber der Erfindung, nicht derjenige, der ihre Entwicklung in Auftrag gegeben hat oder ihren Schöpfer beschäftigt*' ibid [34].

[64] '*die schöpferische Tat des Erfinders*' *Steuervorrichtung* (n 60) 820.

[65] Christoph Ann, '§ 19. Erfinderprinzip und Erfinderrecht' in Rudolf Kraßer and Christoph Ann (eds), *Patentrecht* 7th edn (CH Beck 2016) [10].

[66] *DABUS*, Decision of 11 June 2024, X ZB 5/22 [21].

inventor has been long understood to mean a natural person 'whose creative activity gave rise to the invention'.[67] It also added that when an AI-driven system is used in the process of inventing, it does not really matter whether the invention rests on an inventive activity as long as it is not obvious to the PSA from the prior art.[68]

With respect to inventorship, the German Federal Supreme Court stated that the applicant must indicate those who 'were involved in the discovery of the teaching subject to the patent application in the legally relevant way'[69] and therefore those who are originally entitled to the invention.[70] However, it stated that such an attribution of inventorship does not require making a contribution in the form of 'a self-contained inventive content'.[71] What counts as the relevant contribution in relation to technical teachings discovered with the aid of AI-driven systems is 'a human contribution that substantially influenced the overall success'.[72] It remains to be seen whether this decision signifies a development of the general understanding of inventorship or whether it introduced a special inventorship standard for the AI context (without appropriate justification).

Outside and preceding the AI context, to claim inventorship, the invention must be completed. As the German Federal Supreme Court explained in *Spanplatten*, this means that the inventor has a clear idea that an invention can be implemented into the practice without any further experiments or tests.[73] In another case, it found that whether an invention is completed ought to be ascertained based on whether it can be worked by an average person skilled in the art, not according to the opinion of the inventor.[74] From this it may be inferred that the invention must be complete to the extent that it is reproducible.

To establish inventorship, the courts are invited to consider the way in which the invention subject of the patent came into being (without limiting themselves to the text of patent claims).[75] It must also be proven which act brought about the invention.[76] This means that a contribution, an idea or suggestion that solves a technical problem is required and thus the process of inventing seems to be delineated by the underlying technical problem.[77]

More specifically, the German Federal Supreme Court found that making an invention involves 'developing one own's knowledge with which one can solve a concrete technical problem by certain technical means and disclosing this

[67] '*deren schöpferischer Tätigkeit die Erfindung entspringt*' ibid [24].
[68] ibid [33]–[34].
[69] ibid [35].
[70] ibid.
[71] ibid [36].
[72] '*ein menschlicher Beitrag, der den Gesamterfolg wesentlich beeinflusst hat*' ibid [38].
[73] *Spanplatten*, Decision of 5 May 1966, I ZR 110/64 [1966] *GRUR* 558.
[74] *Wildverbißverhinderung*, Decision of 10 November 19770, X ZR 54/67 [1971] *GRUR* 210.
[75] *Atemgasdrucksteuerung*, Decision of 17 May 2011, X ZR 53/08 [2011] *GRUR* 903.
[76] ibid.
[77] The problem must be narrow and specific, for instance how to eliminate shaking produced by a motor chain saw in *Motorkettensäge*, Decision of 20 June 1978, X ZR 49/75, [1978] *GRUR* 583. Ann (n 65) [20].

knowledge [...] as an instruction that can be used for technical implementation'.[78] The importance of coming up with an independent and creative contribution to 'the patented inventive concept' was also highlighted in scholarship.[79] In *Motorkettensäge*, the German Federal Supreme Court held that the thoughts and suggestions of both putative co-inventors may have contributed to the invention had they both been pre-conditions for the invention to exist.[80] However, not every pre-condition counts: bringing a common suggestion or a plain, abstract idea does not make one an inventor.[81]

There seems to be some uncertainty about whether the inventorial contribution must be above an average skilled person's performance. On the one hand, Melullis writes that the inventors are those persons who 'made the knowledge'[82] and there is 'a creative contribution' if what the person contributes surpasses the common knowledge and the skills of an average man in the art.[83] On the other hand, in cases of co-inventorship, the bar seems to be rather low: only such contributions which did not influence the overall success and which were non-essential in relation to resolving the technical problem do not count as co-inventorial.[84]

Only the human intellectual creative activity resulting in a solution of the underlying technical problem is relevant for establishing an inventorial contribution.[85] Contributions that are closely linked to the invention but fall short of having the character of intellectual activity such as providing funding, labour, setting up tools, testing prototypes or fulfilling other assistant tasks do not meet the co-inventorship threshold despite their closeness to the actual process of invention.[86] Similarly, Professor Haedicke writes that the mere provision of 'accessories, laboratory space, providing personnel or financial aid do not equate to an inventive process and therefore do not make one entitled to a partial ownership of the patent'.[87] According to another former German Federal Supreme Court judge, Keukenschrijver, drawing a line between a co-inventor and a mere aid is possible only on a case-by-case basis.[88]

[78] *Steuervorrichtung* (n 60) 820.
[79] Martin Chakroborty '§3 Ownership A. Inventor and Inventor Right' in Maximilian Haedicke and Henrik Timmann (eds), *Patent Law: A Handbook on European and German Patent Law* (CH Beck 2014) 250.
[80] *Motorkettensäge* (n 77).
[81] Melullis (n 59) [44].
[82] '*dieses Wissen geschaffen haben*' ibid [35].
[83] '*ein schöpferischer Beitrag*' ibid [50].
[84] *Motorkettensäge* (n 77).
[85] For instance, Melullis (n 59) [44] and for others see below.
[86] Ann (n 65) [17].
[87] Haedicke (n 56) 244.
[88] Alfred Keukenschrijver, '§ 6 Recht auf das Patent' in Rudolf Busse and Alfred Keukenschrijver (eds), *Patentgesetz* 8th edn (De Gruyter 2016) [37].

Inventorship in the EPC

The EPC is an international treaty which ought to be interpreted according to the rules set out in the Vienna Convention of the Law of Treaties (VCLT).[89] Articles 31–33 of the VCLT state that treaties should first be subject to textual and teleological interpretation and in addition, historical interpretation to confirm the meaning rendered by the primary methods or to determine the meaning if the interpretation by the primary methods 'leaves the meaning ambiguous or obscure; or leads to a result which is manifestly absurd or unreasonable'.[90,91]

Under the textual method, one determines the meaning of a term in accordance with the ordinary meaning it has in the context in which it is used. One may compare the language versions of the treaty, assess whether the context is such that it lends the term the meaning it has in plain, everyday language or whether those terms are 'specific legal expressions [which] have to be understood in the sense of their meaning in the legal context',[92] or look at any subsequent agreement or practice among the EPC Contracting States.[93]

Under the teleological method, one determines the object and purpose of the interpreted provision and the treaty and interprets the term in their light. The object and purpose of the EPC is stated in the Preamble as 'to strengthen co-operation between the States of Europe in respect of the protection of inventions, [and to achieve this by] a single procedure for the grant of patents and by the establishment of certain standard rules governing patents so granted'[94] and to establish the European Patent Organisation to act to the above ends.[95]

However, the EPC does not mention a full harmonisation of substantive patent law as its purpose. Some steps towards the unification of substantive law were undertaken in the Convention on the Unification of Certain Points of Substantive Law on Patents for Invention 1963 (Strasbourg Convention 1963) drafted under the auspices of the Council of Europe and signed by its Member States with the view to 'assist[ing] industry and inventors, to promote technical progress and contribute to the creation of an international patent'.[96]

Given the membership overlap between the Council of Europe, the EU and the European Patent Organisation, it is, to some extent, also pertinent to quote

[89] Vienna Convention on the Law of Treaties 1969. Although the VCLT is not formally binding for all the EPC Contracting States, eg Norway, France or Turkey. However, its provisions on interpretation, foremost Article 31, were confirmed by international courts as being applicable as customary international law.

[90] ibid art 32(a)(b).

[91] Axel Metzger, 'Interpretation of IP Treaties in Accordance with Articles 31–33 VCLT' in Henning Grosse Ruse-Khan and Axel Metzger (eds), *Intellectual Property Ordering Beyond Borders* (CUP 2022) Ch 6, Silke von Lewinski, 'Principles of Interpretation' in Jörg Reinbothe and Silke von Lewinski (eds) *The WIPO Treaties on Copyright* 2nd edn (OUP 2015) Ch 6.

[92] Metzger ibid 160.

[93] ibid 162.

[94] EPC, Preamble.

[95] ibid.

[96] Convention on the Unification of Certain Points of Substantive Law on Patents for Invention of 27.11.1963, European Treaty Series 47, Preamble.

the Court of Justice of the European Union on the purpose of patents in the context of the EU free movement of goods.

> In relation to patents, the specific subject matter of the industrial property is the guarantee that the patentee, to reward the creative effort of the inventor, has the exclusive right to use an invention with a view to manufacturing industrial products and putting them into circulation for the first time, either directly or by the grant of licences to third parties, as well as the right to oppose infringements.[97]

This formulation clearly recognises rewarding the creative effort of the inventor as one of patent law primary goals. With the appropriate methods of interpretation and the object and purpose of the EPC in mind, this chapter proceeds to the search for human inventorship in the text of the EPC.

Right to be Named as the Inventor

Under Article 62 of the EPC, the inventor has the right, vis-à-vis the applicant for or proprietor of a European patent, to be mentioned as the inventor before the EPO.[98] This provision gives effect to the moral rights of the inventor.[99] Corresponding to Article 62, Article 81 of the EPC requires the applicant to designate the inventor and 'if the applicant is not the inventor or is not the sole inventor, the designation shall contain a statement indicating the origin of the right to the European patent',[100] namely the way the title was transferred to the applicant.[101] To meet the above requirements of the EPC, it seems crucial to know who the inventor is under these provisions.

A European patent application, which designated the AI-driven system DABUS as the inventor, was rejected by the Receiving Section of the EPO on 27 January 2020. This decision was upheld by the EPO's Board of Appeal in 2021.[102] The application was rejected on the ground of not complying with the requirement to designate the inventor on the patent application under Article 81 of the EPC because 'the inventor within the meaning of the EPC had to be a natural person'.[103]

[97] Case C-15/74 *Centrafarm BV and Adriaan de Peijper v Sterling Drug Inc* [1974] EU:C:1974:114, para 9.

[98] EPC, art 62.

[99] Peter Hess, 'EPC 2000, Art 62' in Richard Hacon and Jochen Pagenberg (eds), *Concise European Patent Law* 2nd edn (Kluwer Law International 2008) 67.

[100] EPC, art 81 and Implementing Regulations to the EPC, rule 19(1).

[101] Travaux préparatoires to the EPC 1973, Minutes of the Munich Diplomatic Conference for the Setting up of a European System for the Grant of Patents, M/PR/I, para 265. Available at: www.epo.org/law-practice/legal-texts/epc/archive/epc-1973/traveaux.html, last accessed 29 March 2021.

[102] *Designation of inventor/DABUS* J 0008/20 of 21 December 2021, EP:BA:2021:J000820.20211221.

[103] The wording of 'natural person' used by the Receiving Section of the EPO is preferred to the wording used by the Board of Appeal 'person with legal capacity' which term encompasses also juridical persons. Decision of the Receiving Section of the EPO posted on 27 January 2020 refusing European patent application No. 18275163.6 as quoted in ibid 3.

The Board of Appeal expressed two important, but also contestable, legal opinions. First, it took the view that it must interpret the concept of inventor uniformly and autonomously[104] and determined its meaning with the aid of the *Oxford English Dictionary*.[105] Second, it found that '[w]hile the concept of inventor does not require any support from domestic legislation, the concept of successor in title implies an interaction with national law'.[106]

This fails to give a due account to the context in which the term inventor is used and the purpose of the EPC. First, the term 'inventor' is used in the context of the inventor's moral right (Articles 62 and 81 giving effect to Article 62) and right to a patent (Article 60 to be discussed below) just for the purposes of applying for and obtaining a European patent. This follows from the title of the chapter 'Persons entitled to apply for and obtain a European patent – Mention of the inventor'.

Given the contexts of application and grant are clearly subservient to the long-term enjoyment of patent rights (after the grant), it would be impractical to give the term 'inventor' any other meaning than it has in national laws which govern entitlement to patents in general. Given also the competence division, ie that the patent rights after the grant and any entitlement disputes are governed by national laws and are in the competence of national authorities,[107] the EPO's competence to uniformly and autonomously interpret the concept of 'inventor' used in the EPC appears unsubstantiated (and historically unused).

Therefore, when applying the EPC provisions referring to 'inventor', the EPO should understand the term as a specific legal expression and in its legal context because the EPC Contracting States define inventors in their national patent laws. To reiterate, the national patent laws in the UK, Germany and France understand an inventor as a natural person who actually devised,[108] made,[109] or originated[110] an invention. This is the meaning (together with the meanings the term has in other EPC Contracting States) that the term 'inventor' under the EPC should assume.

Second, in relation to inventorship, the Board of Appeal held that the EPO is 'entitled to verify that the designation identifies an inventor within the meaning

[104] *DABUS* (n 102) [4.2.2].

[105] ibid [4.3.1].

[106] ibid.

[107] EPC, art 61 and the Protocol on Jurisdiction and the Recognition of Decisions in respect of the Right to the Grant of a European Patent (Protocol on Recognition), art 1. See further the Patents Act 1977, s 7(2), *Patentgesetz* of 16 December 1980 (BGBl 1981 I S 1) ('German Patent Act') §6, French Intellectual Property Code, art L611-6.

[108] Patents Act 1977, s 7(3).

[109] A person gains the status of an inventor when he 'makes an invention, so he himself acquires knowledge how to solve a particular technical problem with certain technical means [...] and he discloses his knowledge [...] as an instruction that can be used for technical implementation'. *Steuervorrichtung* (n 60) [28].

[110] 'The law attributes, [...] the ownership to the invention to a person who is at its origin.' '*La loi attribue* [...] *la propriété de l'invention à la personne qui en est à l'origine*.' Pierre Sirinelli, *Code de la propriété intellectuelle* 24th edn (Dalloz 2024) 669.

of the EPC'.[111] Perhaps the devil is in the detail and one needs to distinguish between having the competence to verify that the designation identifies an inventor and the competence to verify whether the designation identifies the inventor (of the specific invention subject to the patent application it deals with). Clearly, the Implementing Regulations exclude the competence to 'verify the accuracy of the designation of the inventor'.[112] It is tenable though that the EPO has the competence to check whether the designation identifies an inventor in the sense of the EPC, ie in the sense of patent laws of the EPC Contracting States.

In practice, the EPO merely assumes the correctness of the designation[113] and notifies the designated inventor where the applicant is a different person.[114] The EPO also checks whether the patent application complies with the formal requirements,[115] including whether it designates the inventor in a request for granting a European patent if the applicant is the sole inventor,[116] or whether it designates the inventor in a separate document if the applicant is not the inventor or the sole inventor.[117] In case these formal requirements are not met, the patent application shall be refused under Article 90(5) of the EPC.

In *Designation of Inventor/DABUS*, the Board of Appeal also makes clear that the failure to designate a human being as the inventor raises a formal obstacle to the substantive examination of the patent application and thus the grant of a European patent.[118] In practice, however, the formal obstacle to the grant of a European patent can be (pragmatically rather than legally) overcome merely by naming a natural person as the inventor in the European patent application since the identity of the inventor is not verified by the EPO. The possibility of this manoeuvre exposes a shortcoming in the examination system as set out by the EPC and its Implementing Regulations. Consequently, subject matter that have a human inventor on paper only (and do not, in fact, have one) could proceed to substantive examination as if they were inventions devised by human beings.

Right to a Patent

Even if the problem of missing human inventor may seem of little practical consequence in the patent grant proceedings before the EPO (provided applicants

[111] *DABUS* (n 102) [4.3.8].
[112] Implementing Regulations to the EPC, rule 19(2).
[113] 'The EPO must only examine whether the statement filed under Article 81, second sentence, EPC, assuming that it is correct, refers to a situation encompassed by Article 60(1) EPC.' *DABUS* (n 102) [4.2.3].
[114] Implementing Regulations to the EPC, rule 19(3): 'If the applicant is not the inventor or is not the sole inventor, the European Patent Office shall communicate to the designated inventor the information in the document designating him […].'
[115] EPC, arts 78 and 90.
[116] Implementing Regulations to the EPC, rule 41.
[117] ibid rule 19.
[118] *DABUS* (n 102) [4.2.3].

put the name of a natural person forward as a matter of formality), it becomes more intriguing when it comes to entitlement to a European patent. Pursuant to Article 60(1) of the EPC, the right to a European patent shall belong to the inventor or his successor in title.

As put by Melullis, this right comprises the 'inventor's personal right that has as its object the relationship of the inventor to their creation and the personal position and acknowledgment resulting therefrom'[119] and the claim to be granted a patent.[120] The right to a European patent is an expression of a 'fundamental principle of almost all European patent systems'[121] and arises upon completion of the invention.[122] Thus, the right to a patent exists by virtue of the act of invention and precedes the grant of the patent, ie the act of state administration.

Before the EPO, the person deemed entitled to exercise the right to a European patent is the applicant.[123] For this provision, as well as for the EPO's lack of competence to examine the accuracy of designation of inventor and thus the title to patent, a European patent may, in effect, be granted to a person who is not entitled to it, ie in breach of Article 60(1) of the EPC. However, national patents stemming from the European patent can be revoked by national courts of the EPC Contracting States (with the effect *ex tunc* and for the territory of the respective Contracting States) in the post-grant phase, on the ground that its proprietor is not entitled to it (further referred to as lack of entitlement).

To summarise, a European patent is legitimately granted only if it is granted to the human inventor of the underlying invention, the subject of the patent application or their successor in title. Should a European patent be granted despite its proprietor's lack of entitlement, it is open to a revocation attack. If revoked, it is then treated as if it had never been granted in the first place. As the revocation on the ground of lack of entitlement is governed by national laws, the revocation proceedings in the EPC Contracting States differ to some extent. For instance, in the UK, they can only be initiated by a person who was found by the court or the comptroller to be entitled to be granted that patent.[124] In Germany, application for the revocation can be brought only by an interested party and, in case of usurpation only by the injured party.[125] In France

[119] '*Zum einen enthält es das Erfinderpersönlichkeitsrecht, das als weitgehend immateriales Recht vor allem die Beziehung des Erfinders zu seiner Schöpfung und die daraus resultierende persönliche Stellung und Wertschätzung zum Gegenstand hat*' Klaus-Jürgen Melullis, 'Patentfähige Erfindungen' in Georg Benkard (ed), *Europäisches Patentübereinkommen* (CH Beck 2002) [17].

[120] ibid.

[121] Travaux préparatoires to the EPC 1973, Texts Drawn Up by the Drafting Committee of Main Committee I at the Meeting on 12 September 1973, M/74/I/R 1. Available at: www.epo.org/law-practice/legal-texts/epc/archive/epc-1973/traveaux.html, last accessed 29 March 2021.

[122] Haedicke (n 56) 244.

[123] EPC, art 60(3).

[124] Patents Act 1977, s 72(1)(b) in conjunction with s 72(2).

[125] German Patent Act, Nullity Proceedings and Compulsory Licence Proceedings ('*Nichtigkeits- und Zwangslizenzverfahren*') §81(3).

only the inventor or their successor in title can file the application for the revocation on the ground of lack of entitlement.[126]

This excursion to national patent laws, albeit brief, shows that the initiation of national revocation proceedings on the ground of lack of entitlement under Article 138(1)(e) of the EPC lies largely in the hands of the inventor or their successor in title. This is reinforced by the fact that neither the EPO nor the national patent authorities (at least in the UK, France and Germany)[127] check the entitlement *ex officio*. As confirmed by the UK Supreme Court, patent applicants are required 'to indicate rather than establish'[128] legally recognised inventorship and entitlement. The UK Supreme Court also confirmed that the Intellectual Property Office correctly never investigated the identity of the real inventor.[129] Consequently, in practice, in the de facto absence of a human inventor, there seems to be no legal basis for the revocation of a European patent due to lack of entitlement.

To conclude, the EPC system presupposes the existence of an individualised human inventor (this fact stems from the national patent laws) and reflects this normatively, both in the inventor's designation and the entitlement rules under Articles 60(1), 62 and 81 of the EPC. Reading these provisions in line with national definitions of inventor, a natural person who devised an invention is a precondition for the existence of an invention as well as for the legitimate grant of a European patent. Hence, the human origin of invention is of legal significance under the EPC system. However, as the existence of human inventors is taken for granted, the EPC system does not contain any reliable mechanisms to verify inventors' status and accuracy of applicants' entitlement declarations.

Patentability

Leaving the realm of individual inventor's rights and their relative claims, this chapter argues that (general) human inventorship is a necessary condition for patentability. As shown above, the existence of an individualised human inventor and their inventorship are required by the national patent laws, the EPC and the Paris Convention.

The presumption that each invention has an individualised human inventor subsumes a more general belief that an invention originates from a human being. More specifically, under UK, German and French laws, the inventor is defined as

[126] Cour de cassation, Decision of 14 February 2012, *PIBD* 2012 960 IIIB 263.

[127] Intellectual Property Office, *Manual of Patent Practice* (UK IPO 2016) [13.12]. The accuracy of inventor's designation is not verified by the German Patent and Trade Mark Office, German Patent Act, §37. Pursuant to the French Intellectual Property Code, art. 611-15, the INPI does not verify the designation of the inventor.

[128] *Thaler* (n 8) [37].

[129] ibid [51].

a natural person who actually devised, made, or originated respectively an invention. Rephrasing this in a subject matter-centred fashion, an invention is to be understood as something actually having been devised or made by an inventor,[130] ie something which owes its existence to a certain kind of human activity or intervention.

The proposition that the existence of an invention is predicated on human activity or intervention has been made on a number of occasions. For instance, Professor Pila recognises 'origination in an act of human creation (requiring a certain talent or capacity)' as one of the common definitional elements of intellectual property subject matter.[131] Elsewhere, Professor Sherman conceptualises invention as 'a product of a process in which a human agent (or inventor) exercises their inventive skills to build on, modify, or adapt preexisting natural materials'.[132]

Accounts along these lines can also be found in commentaries from civil law jurisdictions. Melullis describes the importance of human activity for the concept of invention as follows: '[a]s a result of an intellectual activity by individualised natural persons the invention is necessarily connected with the inventor; an invention without inventor is not conceivable'.[133] Professor Haedicke writes that 'the prerequisite for every invention [...] is an intellectual process of invention'.[134] It follows that, in principle, if a non-obvious technical subject matter does not have any human inventor and thus lacks human inventorship, not only there is no one entitled to patent, but also, and more fundamentally, there is no invention eligible for patent protection.

It is noteworthy that the connection between human inventorship (or human origin) and patentability of a subject matter has not attracted much attention in modern scholarship. As put by Professors Pottage and Sherman, 'modern patent lawyers so rarely ask the question: what is the invention? [...] Although the requirements for patentability do not include a discrete requirement that applicants be able to show that they have created an invention, it is clear that the invention occupies a pivotal place in patent law'.[135]

Notably, in *Designation of inventor/DABUS*, the EPO's Board of Appeal agreed with the patent applicant that Article 52(1) of the EPC 'is not limited to

[130] An argument along these lines was made by Marcus Smith J in *Stephen Thaler v The Comptroller-General* [2020] EWHC 2412 (Pat), [2020] 9 WLUK 227 [45].

[131] Justine Pila, *The Subject Matter of Intellectual Property* (Oxford 2017) 9. The monograph is focused on European and UK law.

[132] Brad Sherman, 'What Does it Mean to Invent Nature?' (2015) 5 *UC Irvine LR* 1193, 1203. The article analyses US and Australian doctrine.

[133] '*Als Ergebnis einer schöpferischen Tätigkeit individualisierbarer Personen ist die Erfindung notwendig mit einem Erfinder verbunden; eine Erfindung ohne Erfinder ist nicht denkbar*.' Melullis (n 59) 310.

[134] Maximilian Haedicke, '§3 Ownership A. Inventor and Inventor Right' in Maximilian Haedicke and Henrik Timmann (eds), *Patent Law: A Handbook on European and German Patent Law* (CH Beck 2014) 244.

[135] Alain Pottage and Brad Sherman, *Figures of Invention: A History of Modern Patent Law* (OUP 2010) 3.

human-made inventions'.[136] The Board even made an obiter proposition that lack of human inventorship is no hurdle to patentability, ie 'there would be inventions patentable under Article 52(1) EPC, for which no right to a patent is provided under Article 60(1) EPC'.[137] Under the holistic and relational view of patentability and entitlement, this is impossible. To reiterate, the right to a patent is derived from the inventor's right in invention.[138] This right is legally recognised as being the result of 'a creative act of an inventor'.[139] Hence, working through this backwards: without the creative act of an inventor, there is no invention (and hence no patentable invention), further there is no right in invention and, finally, there is no right to a patent. Patent laws in the UK, France, Germany or the USA[140] do not give answers as to how a patentable invention could occur but for the creative act of an inventor. Nor does the EPO.

At any rate, this chapter argues that human inventorship and potential lack thereof have practical implications. Scrutinising the origin of non-obvious technical advances became important with the advancements in AI. It is important for preserving the coherence and integrity of the modern patent system. Granting patents for human-made inventions as well as subject matter with no human inventor would eventually render the patent system incoherent and its outcomes inconsistent because it would mean treating fundamentally dissimilar objects equally. Therefore, it is pertinent to ask whether, and if so how, human inventorship is reflected in statutory patentability requirements.

Reflections of Human Inventorship in Patentability Requirements

Pursuant to Article 52(1) of the EPC, 'European patents shall be granted for any inventions, in all fields of technology, provided they are new, involve an inventive step and are susceptible of industrial application'. Out of these statutory patentability criteria, the following analysis focuses on the requirements for an invention and inventive step. At first glance, the requirement for an invention seems to be the closest reflection of human inventorship in positive law as the invention represents the inventor's contribution to the state of the art.[141] Equally, the requirement for

[136] *DABUS* (n 102) [4.6.2].
[137] ibid.
[138] *Pneumatische Einrichtung* (n 57).
[139] *Steuervorrichtung* (n 60) 820.
[140] USPTO, 'Inventorship Guidance for AI-Assisted Inventions' Docket No PTO-P-2023-0043.
[141] For instance, in German law (until the reform in 1968) the requirement for an invention and the requirement for an inventive activity were not separate. Rather, the achievement or the contribution to the art was understood as the main patentability criterion. See Ralph Nack, 'Inventions and their

an inventive step aims to identify the inventor's intellectual contribution as it is suggested by its anthropomorphic phrasing.[142]

Requirement for an Invention

The requirement for an 'invention' is a self-standing patentability requirement under the EPC[143] and any subject matter must first constitute an invention. The rare instance where the nature of an invention has been more comprehensively considered by the most authoritative interpreter, the Enlarged Board of Appeal of the European Patent Office (EBA),[144] is *Tomatoes/State of Israel.*[145] In response to, inter alia, the referred question of whether a method of crossing and selecting plants escapes the exclusion of Article 53(b) of the EPC of 'essentially biological processes', by virtue of containing an additional feature of a technical nature,[146] the EBA made a general statement that the 'essence of invention' is 'human intervention in a process in order to bring about a desired result'.[147] The EBA thus interpreted the concept of invention as requiring 'human intervention'[148] or an intentional abstention therefrom.[149]

Amenability to Patent Protection' in Maximilian Haedicke and Henrik Timmann (eds), *Patent Law: A Handbook on European and German Patent Law* (CH Beck 2014) [24]. Or, '[t]he definition of an invention as being a contribution to the art [...]'. See *Factor-9/JOHN HOPKINS*, T 1329/04 of 28 June 2005, EP:BA:2005:T132904.20050628, [12].

[142] An invention is required to involve an 'inventive step', or 'inventive activity' pursuant to the EPC, art 56. Similarly, Professor Aplin chooses novelty and inventiveness when giving an account of creativity in patent law. Tanya Aplin, 'Creativity and the Law' in Lee Martin and Nick Wilson (eds), *The Palgrave Handbook of Creativity at Work* (Palgrave 2018). Put in other words, 'creativity reappeared in the form of the requirements of originality and non-obviousness, in which applicants had to show, in effect, that their respective works were creative'. Brad Sherman and Lionel Bently, *The Making of Modern Intellectual Property Law: The British Experience, 1760–1911* (CUP 1999) 200.

[143] *Estimating sales activity/Duns Licensing Associates*, T 0154/04 of 15 November 2006, EP:BA:2006:T015404.20061115, [5].

[144] The EBA is a quasi-judicial body of the EPO. It is tasked with ensuring a uniform application of the EPC, deciding points of law of fundamental importance and with a limited judicial review of decisions of the Boards of Appeal. EPC, arts 112 and 112a.

[145] *Tomatoes/State of Israel*, G 0001/08 of 9 December 2010, EP:BA:2010:G000108.20101209.

[146] Even though the referral concerned interpretation of the EPC, art 53(b) primarily, this question hints at the category of 'as such' non-inventions under the EPC, art 52(2) and their saving through a step of technical nature. Thus, the EBA started answering the question by defining what technicity and an invention under the EPC, art 52(1) mean.

[147] *Tomatoes/State of Israel* (n 145) [6.4.2.3] and the same [6.4.2.1]. The same also *Broccoli/PLANT BIOSCIENCE*, G 0002/07 of 9 December 2010, EP:BA:2010:G000207.20101209, [6.4.2.1].

[148] ibid [6.4.2.1]. It may be objected that the EBA contrasts 'human' with 'natural/biological intervention' in this decision. In the present view, it rather contrasts the effects of a human intervention and natural 'intervention' of sexual crossing on the resulting subject matter. The EBA distinguishes between technical steps that (i) merely enhance or assist the biological processes and those that (ii) change the result. In principle, inventions in all technical fields secure their technical character through human intervention in the nature. This applies to inventions in computer science (eg utilising electricity), chemistry (eg utilising properties of various materials), mechanics (eg utilising natural laws of motion), etc.

[149] ibid [6.4.2.3].

Most recently, in the *Simulation Method* case the EBA dealt with the question of whether parts of a process defined by mathematical concepts such as 'a frustration function' were technical or not (ie this was outside the biotechnology context).[150] In this decision, the EBA distinguished that there are two components of the requirement for an invention – an invention and technicity: 'from Article 52 EPC, it can be concluded that only "technical" inventions are patentable.'[151] However, the EBA refrained from defining what 'technical' means and added that the technicality of the invention 'implies that an object is created, or a process is run with some purpose based on human creativity'.[152] To distinguish an invention from a non-invention, it referred to weather which is clearly not an invention; whereas 'a physical system that can be modelled in the sense of showing how it [weather] works'[153] could be.

From the EBA's case law, mainly *Tomatoes/State of Israel*, it follows that, first, the required human intervention must pursue the goal of achieving a desired result. Second, such an intervention must cause a durable and permanent change in the resulting subject matter (such as a genetic change in a living product[154]) and must be repeatable.[155] Thereby, a causal connection between a human being who intervenes in the world with a view to achieving a desired result and non-natural properties of the materialised result is needed.

To explain this a bit further, this chapter advocates (in line with the above EBA's rulings) the view of inventions as creations, ie reproducible results of a process involving human intervention (which determined its technical elements). In this understanding, a human intervention is an event preceding the invention which intervention is a necessary condition for the invention to exist. Given the required repeatability of the process,[156] this must be true every time the invention was worked. If this is true for every time the invention was worked, then this is also true for its first occurrence (in the sense of human creation).

Some scholarship refers to 'accidental inventions', ie 'accidental discoveries, [which] at least at the moment of the serendipitous event, lack conception'.[157] However, neither the accidental event of discovering a substance nor the discovered substance amount to an invention in the sense of *Tomatoes/State of Israel*. However, a 'serendipper' can turn a discovery into an invention by acquiring knowledge about how to re-create it, how to incorporate it into a process with industrial application, etc.

[150] *Simulation Method* G 0001/19 of 10 March 2021, EP:BA:2021:G000119.20210310 [77].
[151] ibid [75].
[152] ibid [47] and [75].
[153] ibid.
[154] *Tomatoes/State of Israel* (n 145) [6.4.2.3].
[155] ibid [6.4.2.1].
[156] ibid.
[157] Sean Seymore, 'Serendipity' (2009) 88 *NC L Rev* 185, 191.

For practical purposes, the creations in the above sense are transformed into technical teachings which can then be disclosed to allow others in the field to make them. If a subject matter is claimed as a product, then it corresponds to the 'desired result'.[158] If a subject matter is claimed as a process (a method), its qualification for an invention depends on incorporating a human intervention within its steps which intervention is causally determinative of the relevant elements of the desired result.[159] Such causally determinative human intervention is called human 'creative' intervention further on.

The interpretation of inventions as creations in the above sense may be supported by reference to legislative history. The policy documents which accompanied amendments to the EPC in 2000 further corroborate that inventions and creations are synonymous under the EPC framework. Prominently, they state that '[t]he new wording of Article 52(1) EPC plainly expresses that patent protection is reserved for creations in the technical field'.[160] The Comparative Study of Substantive Law further emphasises the role of human origin: 'one can infer from what has been said the rule that the author of a patentable invention must have been presented with a problem and have indicated a solution to it'.[161]

In a landmark decision *Rote Taube* (pre-dating the EPC 1973), the German Federal Supreme Court affirmed that subject matter should not be treated as non-inventions when they involve a methodical utilisation of controllable natural forces and phenomena (not only in the fields of physics, chemistry but also biology) to achieve a causal, perceivable result.[162] The requirement of repeatability of the method and reproducibility of the result were adopted by the EBA in *Tomatoes/State of Israel* to form part of the EBA's interpretation of the notion of 'invention'.

As creations from all technical fields must be treated equally,[163] an identical definition of an invention should apply to subject matter coming from any field

[158] *Tomatoes/State of Israel* (n 145) [6.4.2.3].

[159] ibid [6.4.2.3]. This comes from the part of the decision where the EBA interprets the 'essentially biological process' exception to patentability. In sum, (i) if there is a technical step in a process then the process is an invention; (ii) if the technical step in a process which is based on the sexual crossing of plants and on subsequent selection only serves to perform the process steps of the breeding process then such a process is excluded; and (iii) if, however, the technical step within such a process determines the result to some extent then the process is outside the exception and bounces back to constitute an invention.

[160] Special edition 4/2007 Revision of the European Patent Convention (EPC 2000) Synoptic presentation EPC 1973/2000 – Part I: The Articles Part II Chapter I Article 52 EPC.

[161] Roger Gajac, 'Comparative Study of Substantive Law in Force in the Countries Represented on the Committee of Experts on Patents' EXP/Brev (53) 18 as reproduced in Justine Pila, *The Requirement for an Invention in Patent Law* (OUP 2010) 139. This was prepared in 1953 under the auspices of the Council of Europe and influenced drafting of the EPC 1973 and accompanying Community Patent Convention.

[162] *Rote Taube*, Decision of 27 March 1969, X ZB 15/67 [1970] IIC 136, 138. Also see Joseph Straus, 'Biotechnologische Erfindungen – ihr Schutz und seine Grenzen' [1992] *GRUR* 252, 258.

[163] The Agreement on Trade-Related Aspects of Intellectual Property Rights, art 27(1) prohibits discrimination on the grounds of the field of technology.

of technology. Therefore, the authorities should apply the same standard and have the same task of ascertaining whether a certain subject matter is an invention, including the aspect of its origin. This means asking whether the subject matter constitutes an invention in the sense of (i) the result of the human creative intervention or (ii) the process that incorporates the human intervention within its steps which intervention is causally determinative of the desired result.

Further, the understanding of inventions as creations may be enhanced thanks to its juxtaposition to an unpatentable discovery and systematic reading of the EPC. As put in the Comparative Study of Substantive Law, 'as a general rule, a patent can only protect an invention (a creation) and not a discovery, i.e. the simple taking note of a pre-existant [*sic*] reality'.[164] Inventions are patentable under conditions outlined in Article 52(1). Pursuant to Article 52(2)(a), discoveries shall not be regarded as inventions in the sense of Article 52(1).[165]

In general, a discovery involves finding and disclosing information about the natural world, including the description of properties of a pre-existing matter.[166] A transformation of a discovery into an invention requires 'an act of invention or human ingenuity'.[167] Or, as put by Moufang, a member of the Boards of Appeal, in a more down-to-earth manner, 'a discoverer becomes an inventor when he provides, on the basis of his knowledge, a purposeful instruction to a certain pursuit'.[168] If the discovery concerns a function, its patentability depends on whether or not this discovery enriched the whole teaching with technical elements.[169]

According to Melullis, a discovery that is implemented in a reproducible process may constitute an invention, whereas a mere reformulation of a discovery in the form of a technical teaching does not render it patentable.[170] In *Serotonin receptor/ELI LILLY*, the EPO emphasised that a mere discovery of a property of a receptor, even if it has a pharmacological effect, is not sufficient to claim a therapeutic invention.[171]

> The discovery on which the invention is based, even if representing an important piece of scientific knowledge, still needs to find a practical application in the form of a defined,

[164] Gajac (n 161) 138.

[165] EPC, art 52(2)(a).

[166] Simon Thorley and others, *Terrell on the Law of Patents* 15th edn (Sweet & Maxwell Ltd 2000) [2]–[69] (not included in the 19th edn); Sigrid Sterckx and Julian Cockbain, *Exclusions from Patentability: How Far Has the European Patent Office Eroded Boundaries* (CUP 2012) 115.

[167] Sterckx and Cockbain ibid 133.

[168] Rainer Moufang, 'Art 52(2) u (3) EPÜ Ausgeschlossene Nicht-Erfindungen/excluded non-inventions' in Rainer Schulte (ed), *Patentgesetz mit Europäischem Übereinkommen* 10th edn (Carl Heymanns Verlag 2017) [75].

[169] To put it in the words of the EBA: 'A claim to the use of a known compound for a particular purpose, which is based on a technical effect which is described in the patent, should be interpreted as including that technical effect as a functional technical feature.' *Friction reducing additive*, G 0002/88 of 11 December 1989, EP:BA:1989:G000288.19891211.

[170] Melullis (n 119) 346.

[171] *Serotonin receptor/ELI LILLY*, T 0241/95 of 14 June 2000, EP:BA:2000:T024195.20000614, [3.1.2].

real treatment of any pathological condition in order to make a technical contribution to the art and be considered an invention eligible for patent protection.[172]

Generally, it is difficult to formulate the required human intervention that would turn a discovery into an invention more specifically than to say that the discovery must be made a part of a solution to a problem. There is an exception: pursuant to the EU Biotech Directive, a (discovered) naturally occurring biological material may be the subject of an invention if it is isolated from its natural environment or produced by means of a technical process.[173]

Requirement for an Inventive Step

To be patentable, an invention must be inventive in the sense of involving an inventive step or activity[174] as well as achieving some progress or advancement of the state of the art.[175] In relation to human inventorship, the requirement for an inventive activity may seem to play a second fiddle to the requirement for an invention. Nonetheless, this chapter argues that the requirement for an inventive activity reflects human inventorship in requiring a genuine intellectual activity involved in solving the underlying technical problem.

Pursuant to Article 31 of the VCLT, international treaties should be interpreted 'in good faith in accordance with the ordinary meaning to be given to the terms of the treaty in their context and in the light of its object and purpose'.[176] First, the terms of 'inventive step' or 'inventive activity' should be given their ordinary meaning of inventive (intellectual) step or activity. Hence, the activity that is required to be involved in devising an invention under Articles 52(1) and 56 of the EPC means (i) a genuine intellectual activity that is (ii) of a certain quality.

This is supported by the relevance of features of the invention for the assessment of an inventive step. Where an invention consists of both technical and non-technical features, the inventive step is assessed only in respect of those features that contribute to the solution of the technical problem by providing a technical effect[177] (or a further technical effect in case of computer implemented

[172] ibid.

[173] Directive 98/44/EC of 6 July 1998 on the legal protection of biotechnological inventions [1998] *OJ L 213/13)* art 3(2).

[174] English version: Inventive step, German version: *Erfinderische Tätigkeit* (inventive activity) and French version: *Activité inventive* (inventive activity).

[175] A mere disadvantageous modification of the closest prior art does not constitute an inventive step. T 2197/09 of 20 November 2014, EP:BA:2014:T219709.20141120 [5.4].

[176] Vienna Convention on the Law of Treaties 1969, art 31.

[177] *Two identities/COMVIK*, T 0641/00 of 26 September 2002, EP:BA:2002:T064100.20020926 [6]. *Estimating sales* (n 147) [5 e)]. This was embraced by the EBA in *Simulation Method* (n 155) [125] re computer-implemented mathematical models or algorithms.

methods). Hence, the necessary intellectual activity[178] should be involved directly in solving a technical problem and thus be reflected in those features which contribute to the solution.[179]

Further, the required intellectual activity is intended to be of human origin because it is benchmarked against hypothetical decision-making and acts of a notional natural person, the person skilled in the art (PSA). The PSA is a notional expert (or a team of experts) in the technical field of the invention[180] who has common general knowledge, has read all publicly available documents, knows publicly available uses of the technology, understands all languages,[181] and possesses the necessary equipment and technical tools which vary according to the technical field. This person is conservative[182] and unimaginative, therefore they would miss every step that goes beyond ordinary good practice and routine.

In this respect, the PSA standard[183] works similarly to other legal standards of notional persons, such as 'reasonable person' or 'average consumer'. If negligence is to be determined with the aid of a reasonable person standard, it may safely be inferred that it is human negligence that is being considered. Therefore, it seems plausible to conclude that if something is to be determined by reference to a PSA standard, that something is a human activity of a similar nature and under similar circumstances as the standard (otherwise the standard could not justifiably be called a standard). The standard applies in the same manner as other standards, just asking a negative question, ie what a PSA would not have done. Lastly, since the required activity is referred to as 'intellectual' in the EPC drafting documents it is to be understood as being of human origin.

The purpose of the requirement for an inventive activity is to assess whether the invention carries such a technical advancement that is far enough from PSA's playground. No doubt, the inventive activity is to be measured objectively as it follows from Article 56 of the EPC and national patent laws. The interpretation in light of this purpose refuses any regard to subjectivity in the assessment. The purpose of this requirement, ie the objective nature of measurement of the quality, however, does not negate the embedded presumption of a genuine human intellectual activity.

[178] As acknowledged elsewhere, 'while the exercise of (mental) labour and effort is a necessary condition for an invention to be non-obvious, it is not a sufficient condition', Bently and others (n 34) 591.

[179] Naturally, there are many ways in which one comes up with a solution to a technical problem. Some may start from a pre-defined technical problem and devise a solution to it. This will be typical for solutions suggested by AI-driven systems. Others may start with finding an object and then devising its purpose or implementation to solve technical problems. See European Patent Office, *Guidelines* (2021), Part G, Chapter VII [9].

[180] Philip Johnson, 'EPC 2000, Art 56' in Richard J Hacon and Jochen Pagenberg (eds), *Concise European Patent Law* 2nd edn (Kluwer Law International 2008) 52.

[181] *Combustion engine*, T 0426/88 of 9 November 1990, EP:BA:1990:T042688.19901109, [6.4].

[182] *Genentech/Expression in yeast*, T 445/91 of 20 June 1994, EP:BA:1994:T044591.19940620, [5.1.3.3].

[183] Jürgen Kroher, 'Art 56' in Dieter Stauder and Stefan Luginbühl (eds) *Europäisches Patentübereinkommen* 9th edn (Carl Heymanns Verlag 2023) 362.

This can be confirmed with reference to the legislative history. Under the heading 'creative effort', the Comparative Study of Substantive Law references a requirement that 'the invention should represent a manifestation of intelligence which appreciably exceeds the normal train of thought of which any specialist in art would be capable'.[184] Kühnemann's report to which the EPC travaux préparatoires refer as well, formulates 'the requirement of creative effort in an indirect manner so that a realisation of a subject matter that was within the reach of an average expert was excluded from patentability'.[185]

Additionally, a German delegate to the Patents Working Party expressed the view that 'under German law, the concept of *Erfindungshöhe* [inventive level] did not necessarily involve creative effort (flash of genius) on the part of the inventor. It was enough if he broke new ground and applied some intellectual activity'.[186] Further, Kurt Haertel, referred to as 'father of the European patent law'[187] in his study of 1960, writes that while the delegates drafting the EPC were not able to agree on whether patentability should depend on the conception of progress in the art or inventive level, they agreed on 'an explicit formulation of how to evaluate the inventive performance'.[188]

The above accounts testify to hesitations about how to positively define the underlying intellectual activity. On the one hand, the involvement of an inventor's genuine intellectual activity in the process of devising an invention is both presupposed and required. Requiring a genuine intellectual activity is also aligned with the purpose of patent systems as laid out by the CJEU in *Centrafarm*[189] in 1974 and in the labour, reward and incentives-based justificatory theories. On the other hand, when it came to pinning down the intellectual activity, there was evident uncertainty about how to define it.

Finally, this was resolved by adopting a legal presumption of inventive activity: '[a]n invention shall be considered as involving an inventive step if, having regard to the state of the art, it is not obvious to a person skilled in the art.'[190] Hence, inventiveness is measured according to an objective standard of an average expert and a hypothetical of what would have been within their reach. In effect, to make

[184] Gajac (n 161) 16, copy on file with author.

[185] Herbert Kühnemann, 'Report on Technological Progress and Creative Effort as Patentability Criteria' EXP/BRev (60) 5. Available at: https://rm.coe.int/090000168072965b, last accessed 29 March 2021.

[186] Proceedings of the 1st meeting of the Patents Working Party held at Brussels from 17 to 28 April 1961, Document IV/2767/61-E p 18. Available at: www.epo.org/law-practice/legal-texts/epc/archive/epc-1973/traveaux.html, last accessed 29 March 2021.

[187] The website of the City of Munich, 'Kurt-Haertel-Passage' (*Muenchen*, 2003). Available at: www.muenchen.de/rathaus/Stadtverwaltung/Kommunalreferat/geodatenservice/strassennamen/Strassenneubenennung-2003/kurthaertelpassage.html, last accessed 2 December 2021.

[188] Kurt Haertl, *Study on the Fundamental Problems of the Creation of a European Patent Which Stands Next to the National Patents* (Bonn 1960) 27.

[189] *Centrafarm* (n 97).

[190] EPC, art 56.

an inventive invention, an inventor is required to do what an average expert would not have done.

With respect to the inventive activity, the EPO Guidelines for Examination clarify that

> in order to assess whether an inventive step is present it is important for the examiner to bear in mind that an invention may, for example, be based on the following: the devising of a solution to a known problem [... or] the arrival at an insight into the cause of an observed phenomenon (the practical use of this phenomenon then being obvious).[191]

Similarly, despite the proclaimed disregard for the way in which the inventor made their invention or inventor's subjective assessment of their efforts,[192] the UK courts consider so-called secondary evidence relating to the contemporaneous events, industrial response to the invention, the realities surrounding making the particular invention and actual ways of approaching the particular technical problem undertaken at the time of the invention.[193] Telling the actual story of an inventor devising the invention can be favourable to the patentee.[194]

Moreover, the German and French application practices yield a typology of inventive activities. The activities of overcoming technical obstacles, answering a series of objectively difficult questions,[195] reversing a bias, misleading belief or technical stereotype,[196] surprising a PSA,[197] making a selection from among a great number of possible solutions or combining at least three documents of prior art[198] are all indicative of inventive activity.

During the EPC drafting negotiations, in reaction to a Swiss proposal to allow applicants' evidence that they have made progress in the art, Kurt Haertel, President of the German Patent Office and the Chair of the Main Committee I at the Munich Diplomatic Conference commented that 'it had not proved possible to find a better definition than that given in Article 54 of the theoretically objective concept of inventive step, in respect of which, however, subjective elements also played a part in practice'.[199] This account, as well as the practice of courts, recognise that when the inventiveness is disputed, the evidence on subjective elements of the inventive activity is acceptable.

[191] EPO Guidelines (n 179) [9].

[192] *Nichia Corporation v Argos* [2007] EWCA Civ 741 [2007] Bus LR 1753 [13].

[193] A list of secondary factors was provided by Justice Laddie in *Haberman v Jackel Intl Ltd* [1999] FSR 683, 699–701.

[194] *Actavis Group PTC EHF v ICOS Corporation* [2019] UKSC 15, [2019] Bus LR 1318 [71]. *Positec Power Tools (Europe) Ltd v Husqvarna AB Chancery Division* [2016] EWHC 1061 (Pat), [2016] Bus LR 714 [8].

[195] Alfred Keukenschrijver, '§ 4 Erfinderische Tätigkeit' in Rudolf Busse and Alfred Keukenschrijver (eds), *Patentgesetz* 8th edn (De Gruyter 2016) [116].

[196] ibid [48]–[49]. Cour de cassation, Decision of 19 December 2000, *PIBD* 2001 721 III 277.

[197] *Disiloxan*, Decision of 27 February 1969, X ZB 11/68 [1969] *GRUR* 265, 266.

[198] All in Institut national de la propriété industrielle, *La délivrance des brevets et des certificats d'utilité* (INPI 2016) 95.

[199] Travaux préparatoires to the EPC 1973, Vol 42 E, EPO, Munich 1999, M/PR/K/I [82].

Conclusion

The above analysis of patent entitlement disputes in the UK, France and Germany reveals that the inventor is not just any individual who is intellectually involved in the production of inventions. The inventor is only the natural person who has actually devised (the UK), made (Germany) or originated (France) the inventive concept or the essence of the invention.

This chapter argued that human inventorship is reflected and is implicitly present in the requirements for an invention and an inventive step, though no crystal-clear image of human inventorship under the EPC emerges. Nonetheless, if the requirements for an invention and inventive activity are read in the light of their purpose and the underlying factual assumptions (of the EPC Contracting States) it follows that a subject matter must constitute a creation involving an inventive activity. To meet the requirement for an invention, a subject matter must be a result of a human intervention which intervention directly and causally determines its technical elements. To meet the requirement for an inventive activity, a subject matter must constitute a result of a genuine intellectual activity expended on solving a technical problem of such a quality that it makes the invention inaccessible to a PSA. In other words, inventorship may, in principle, be claimed only by the natural person who originated those technical elements of the invention that imply an inventive activity.

Furthermore, with reference to human inventorship stemming from national case law on entitlement, this book argues that the necessary human creative intervention and human intellectual activity of inventive quality must occur in the process of devising the invention (the UK), making the invention (Germany) or conceiving of the invention (France). The process of inventing is understood relatively narrowly in the UK and France and relatively broadly in Germany. The boundaries of the process of inventing are demarcated by the process of coming up with the inventive concept (UK), solving a specific, concrete technical problem completely, including the disclosure of the teaching (Germany) and formulating the idea which forms the essence of the invention without necessarily completing the invention (France).

Consequently, a subject matter that is not the result of required human creative intervention and human intellectual activity of inventive quality cannot be readily accommodated by the EPC system without compromising the system's theoretical basis, foundational factual assumptions and rules on entitlement and designation of the inventor.

5

Inventorship in the Application Practice in the UK, Germany and France

Introduction

The aim of this chapter is to evaluate whether authorities in the UK, France and Germany are able to distinguish inventions made by human inventors from other non-obvious technical advances. First, it identifies and analyses the methods, tools and epistemic approaches used by authorities to apply the legal requirements for an invention and an inventive activity. Since the national patentability criteria are modelled on the EPC and national patent offices and courts should follow the interpretation of those criteria given by the EPO,[1] the differences across the selected jurisdictions may be marginal.

If it is accepted that patentability is conditioned upon the necessary human creative intervention and human intellectual activity of inventive quality being poured into the activity of devising the inventive concept (the UK), making the invention (Germany) or conceiving of the essence of invention (France), then the authorities should ideally examine the process of inventing and how the subject matter came into being.

Epistemic Approaches to the Invention Requirement

European Patent Office

Under the EPC, any subject matter must first qualify for an invention to be granted a patent.[2] Chapter 4 introduced the understanding of an invention as a creation of human origin. To reiterate, 'as a result of an inventive activity of individualised

[1] The settled jurisprudence of the EPO on the interpretation of the EPC should normally be followed. *Actavis Group PTC EHF v ICOS Corporation* [2019] UKSC 15, [2019] *Bus LR* 1318 [56].

[2] *Estimating sales activity/DUNS LICENSING ASSOCIATES*, T 0154/04 of 15 November 2006, EP:BA:2006:T015404.20061115 [5].

persons, the invention is necessarily tied in with an inventor; an invention without inventor is not conceivable'.[3] Against this background, this chapter introduces the more common understanding of invention as a technical subject matter and demonstrates its detachment from the understanding of an invention as a creation.

In practice, a 'requirement of technicality'[4] (or technicity) often takes the mantle of the requirement for an invention. The question of whether this requirement is met arises in the context of categories of subject matter that are excluded from patentability under Article 52(2) as non-inventions.[5] In this respect, the Board of Appeal views the list as a 'negative definition of the notion of invention'.[6] What the listed categories have in common is that they comprise objects which are deprived of any technical character. However, where the claimed technical advance is not limited to an excluded subject matter as such, but it is only directed to an excluded subject matter, it can still qualify for an invention provided its technical character is demonstrated.[7]

In practice, the EPO examiners would just ask whether a subject matter has a technical character. Over time, the Boards have developed the following guidance on technical character. Technical character is to be proven by demonstrating that the subject matter (i) involves technical means, (ii) produces a technical result or (iii) involves a technical field of human activity.[8] Alternatively, it must be demonstrated that the resulting subject matter 'provides a tangible technical effect, such as the provision of a physical entity as the resulting product or a non-abstract activity, such as through the use of technical means'.[9]

In summary, the requirement of technicality is not an adequate substitute for an invention because it is not suitable to detect a lack of human creative intervention involved in devising of the technical solution. The inquiry after technical character does not go as far as to ask whether the required technicity owes its existence to a human creative intervention (*Tomatoes/State of Israel*[10]).

[3] '*Als Ergebnis einer schöpferischen Tätigkeit individualisierbarer Personen ist die Erfindung notwendig mit einem Erfinder verbunden; eine Erfindung ohne Erfinder ist nicht denkbar.*' Klaus-Jürgen Melullis, 'Patentfähige Erfindungen' in Georg Benkard (ed), *Europäisches Patentübereinkommen* (CH Beck 2002) 310.

[4] ibid [5 b].

[5] These include a discovery, scientific theory or mathematical method, aesthetic creations, a scheme, rule or method for performing a mental act, playing a game or doing business, or a program for a computer or the presentation of information.

[6] *Estimating sales* (n 2) [8].

[7] *Odour selection/QUEST INTERNATIONAL*, T 0619/02 of 22 March 2006, EP:BA:2006:T061902.20060322 [2.2].

[8] ibid. Similarly, 'where an intrinsically non-technical solution (mathematical algorithm) seeks to derive a technical character from the problem solved, the problem must be technical'. *Classification method/COMPTEL*, T 1784/06 of 21 September 2012, EP:BA:2012:T178406.20120921 [2.3].

[9] T 0914/02 of 12 July 2005, EP:BA:2005:T091402.20050712 [2.3.6].

[10] *Tomatoes/State of Israel*, G 0001/08 of 9 December 2010, EP:BA:2010:G000108.20101209. For a more detailed analysis see Chapter 4.

United Kingdom

Terrel on the Law of Patents of 1965, ie before the EPC 1973 entered into force and the Patents Act 1977 implemented the EPC patentability criteria, had defined an invention as 'any manner of new manufacture [...] and any new method or process of testing applicable to the improvement or control of manufacture'.[11] In this connection, this edition of *Terrel on the Law of Patents* cites *Reynolds v Herbert Smith & Co Ltd*:

> Discovery adds to the amount of human knowledge, but it does so only ... by disclosing something ... Invention also adds to human knowledge, but not merely by disclosing something. Invention necessarily involves also the suggestion of an act to be done, and it must be an act which results in a new product, or a new result, or a new process, or a new combination for producing an old product or an old result.[12]

According to that commentary, one can turn a discovery into an invention if one 'can describe a method of utilising that principle so as to make it applicable to the production of a new manufacture'.[13]

The Banks Committee, established to report on the state of the patent system and patent law, which also made proposals for the (then) coming Patents Act 1977 expressed reluctance to define the new concept of invention in the new Patents Act or replace the term 'new manner of manufacture'.[14] The Patents Act 1977, as enacted, does not define invention in any way. Nor is any positive definition of invention recognised by the courts.[15]

Most prominently, in the view of Lord Hoffmann, the novelty, inventive step and industrial applicability criteria, when taken in conjunction, probably amount to an invention, unless the grant of a patent for it is excluded.[16] He also adds that: 'I say probably, because in the absence of a definition one cannot say with certainty that one might not come across something which satisfied all the conditions but could not be described as an invention.'[17] At the end of his assessment, he states that '[j]udges would therefore be well advised to put on one side their intuitive sense of what constitutes an invention until they have considered the questions of novelty, inventiveness and so forth'.[18]

Accordingly, in practice, the UK courts address, besides the secondary patentability criteria, only the 'negative definition' of invention. They ask whether the

[11] Guy Aldous, Douglas Falconer and William Aldous, *Terrell on the Law of Patents* 11th edn (Sweet & Maxwell 1965) [9].

[12] *Reynolds v Herbert Smith & Co, Ltd*, 20 RPC 123, 126 as cited in ibid [48].

[13] ibid [49].

[14] Maurice Banks, *The British Patent System* (Her Majesty's Stationery Office 1970) Cmnd 4407, 64.

[15] Douglas Campbell and others, *Terrell on the Law of Patents* 20th edn (Sweet & Maxwell 2024) 2-10–2-15.

[16] *Biogen Inc v Medeva Plc* [1996] UKHL 18, [1997] RPC 1, 41–42.

[17] ibid.

[18] ibid.

alleged invention in question falls within any of the excluded subject matter categories under section 1(2) of the Patents Act 1977.[19] A subject matter is considered not to be excluded from patentability if the contribution contained therein is 'actually technical in nature'.[20] This question was repeatedly discussed in relation to computer-implemented inventions. In those cases, the required technicity was established on the basis of whether the invention produces a relevant technical effect and that depends on the facts of each case.[21]

For instance, in *HTC Europe v Apple*, it was found that 'a method of dividing up the screen of such a device into views and configuring each view as a multi-touch view or a single-touch view using flags with a specific functionality' makes a technical contribution. Its embodiment in software notwithstanding, it 'presents a new and improved interface to application programmers, [...] and makes it easier for them to write application software for the multi-touch device'.[22]

To summarise, in contrast to the EPO's practice, the patentability quest in the UK does not begin with the requirement for an invention, but rather it is closed by it, if at all. Nor is there any specific inquiry into the relationship between an inventor and an invention which is envisaged by virtue of section 7(3) of the Patents Act 1977.[23] In circumstances where a subject matter is directed to an excluded subject matter, the inquiry is focused on whether it makes a technical contribution to the state of the art. At the end of the day, this invention test is reduced to a set of technical questions of fact such as what type of improvement of what type of software (eg a contribution at the level of operating system) counts as an improvement of the hardware (ie the device).[24]

France

An historical commentary to the French Patent Statute of 8 July 1844 lists only two requirements for patentability: novelty and invention. In the context of that statute, Blanc understood an invention as 'a creation of intelligence [... and that is ...] a process or product containing an industrial idea'.[25] Another understanding, offered by Professor Roubier, rested on productive human activity: '[i]n the invention itself, the activity of a human is productive, in the discovery, [the activity] is,

[19] These categories are the same as the ones under EPC, art 52(2).

[20] *Aerotel Ltd and Telco Holdings Ltd* [2006] EWCA Civ 1371, [2007] Bus LR 634 [40].

[21] *Gemstar-TV Guide International Inc v Virgin Media Ltd* [2009] EWHC 3068 (Ch), [2010] RPC 10 [41]–[43], *AT&T Knowledge v Comptroller General of Patents* [2009] EWHC 343, [2009] Bus LR D51 [39]–[41], *HTC Europe Co Ltd v Apple Inc* [2013] EWCA Civ 451, [2013] RPC 30 [154].

[22] *HTC Europe* (n 21) [57]–[59].

[23] '[...] "inventor" in relation to an invention means the actual deviser of the invention [...]'.

[24] See *HTC Europe* (n 21) [154] ff.

[25] '*création de l'intelligence, lorsque, en un mot, le procédé ou le produit contient une idée industrielle*.' Etienne Blanc, *L'inventeur breveté, code des inventions et des perfectionnements* 3rd edn (Cosse 1852) 254.

so to say, receiving [...] what must be rewarded are the arrangements of human activity and not what the nature produced on its own'.[26]

More modern French scholarship, too, juxtaposes an invention and a discovery. Professors Azéma and Galloux comment that 'invention is first a creation which means it needs a separation from an individual who has conceived it and an action on the real world; it fundamentally distinguishes itself from the discovery which is only an apprehension of the real world or an intellectual construct'.[27] For Professor Mathély, an invention is 'every action or endeavour of a human to shape and utilise the nature and the matter'[28] and thus is predicated upon a human creative intervention.

According to Professor Passa, nowadays it is more or less widely recognised that the requirement for an invention is a true, positive and autonomous requirement which is separate from the secondary patentability requirements and excluded subject matter categories.[29] However, as reported by Professor Pollaud-Dulian, French courts do not take it into consideration, or at least they do not do so explicitly.[30]

Interpretation of the requirement for an invention underwent a similar development as at the EPO level and it became framed as a requirement for a technical character. Consequently, French courts adopted invention tests mirroring those applied by the Boards: if a subject matter does not utilise technical means or solve any technical problem, it does not amount to an invention.[31]

It is noteworthy that interpreting an invention as a subject matter with technical character may result in a semantic overlap of the invention requirement and the requirement for industrial applicability. Professors Azéma and Galloux note that the historical condition of industrial character may cover not only the modern requirement for industrial applicability but also the one for invention [as in the past] industrial meant to produce technical goods or results.[32] As this legacy interacts with the current interpretation of an invention, the invention test, if reduced to looking solely for the technical character, may be conflated with the test for industrial applicability. Consequently, according to Professor Passa,

[26] '*Dans l'invention seule, l'activité de l'homme est productive ; dans la découverte, elle est seulement, dit-on, réceptrice.* [...] *ce qu'elle doit récompenser, ce sont les combinaisons de l'activité humaine, et non pas ce que la nature à elle seule produit*' Paul Roubier, *Le droit de la propriété industrielle*, vol 2 (Recueil Sirey 1954) 90.

[27] '*Mais l'invention est d'abord une création c'est-à-dire qu'elle nécessite une séparation d'avec l'individu qui l'a conçue et donc une action sur l'réel ; elle se distingue en cela de la découverte qui n'est qu'appréhension du réel ou construction intellectuelle*' Jaques Azéma and Jean-Christophe Galloux, *Droit de la propriété industrielle* 8th edn (Dalloz 2017) 147–48.

[28] '*Toute action ou entreprise de l'homme pour façonner et utiliser la nature et la matière*' Jérôme Passa, *Droit de la propriété industrielle. Tome 2* 2nd edn (LDGJ 2013) 74 quoting Paul Mathély, 'Le nouveau régime des brevets d'invention' (1969) *Ann prop ind* p 1.

[29] ibid 68.

[30] Fréderic Pollaud-Dulian, *La propriété industrielle* 2nd edn (ECONOMICA 2011) [159].

[31] Passa (n 28) 70.

[32] Jacques Azéma and Jean-Christophe Galloux, *Droit de la propriété industrielle* 8th edn (Dalloz 2017) 158 ff.

this may lead authorities to a conclusion that a certain subject matter is short of industrial applicability, whereas it would have been more appropriate to find a lack of an invention.[33]

In summary, even though, historically, the French saw some human creative activity behind the requirement for invention, in more modern times the technical character has become a convenient proxy for the requirement. Hence, under the current invention test, which follows the EPO's approach, the French courts search for a technical character or technicity rather than human creativity which is actually necessary to produce it. Moreover, given the specifics of the French context, the invention test may happen to check for the same issues as the test for industrial applicability, ie for technical applicability, which renders one of the tests redundant.

Germany

The definition of an invention as a 'teaching of technical content wherein technology depends upon the doctrines of physics and chemistry'[34] originates in the landmark decision *Rote Taube* of 1969. Therein, the German Federal Supreme Court reiterated that objects should not be seen as non-inventions, provided they involve a methodical utilisation of controllable natural forces to achieve a causal, perceivable result, including biological natural forces and phenomena.[35] In another decision, the German Federal Supreme Court held that 'a complete invention entails – in general – instructions on how to use forces, materials or energies of – organic or inorganic – nature to bring about immediately a causal and perceivable result, and [thus] entails solving a task (problem)'.[36]

As further development of German law shows, *Rote Taube* has been superseded in some respects. Firstly, the concept of invention has been overshadowed by the requirement for 'technicity' which is understood as providing 'a solution serving to solve a concrete technical problem with technical means'.[37] As a result, a subject matter is found to constitute an invention if it provides such

[33] Passa (n 28) 68–69.

[34] *Rote Taube*, Decision of 27 March 1969, X ZB 15/67 [1970] *IIC* 136, 138. English translation by the IIC.

[35] ibid.

[36] *Die fertige Erfindung besteht – ganz allgemein – in der Anweisung, Kräfte, Stoffe oder Energien der – belebten und unbelebten – Natur zur unmittelbaren Herbeiführung eines kausal übersehbaren Erfolges zu benutzen, und besteht in der Lösung einer Aufgabe (Problem). Acrylfasern* as quoted in Klaus Bacher, 'PatG § 1 [Voraussetzungen der Erteilung]' in Georg Benkard (ed), *Patentgesetz* 12th edn (CH Beck 2023) [40].

[37] '*die Lösung eines konkreten technischen Problems mit technischen Mitteln* [...]' *Steuerungseinrichtung für Untersuchungsmodalitäten*, Decision of 20 January 2009, X ZB 22/07 [2009] *GRUR* 479 [11].

a solution, or, if it is 'characterised by a piece of knowledge that is based on technical considerations'.[38] What makes some considerations technical or what types of problem can be characterised as technical remains unclear.

Case law as well as legal scholarship submit that this is so by design. Since the concept of the technicity is dynamic[39] and open to assessment[40] it can accommodate subject matter falling into any future branches of the traditional technical fields.[41] As put by Bacher, the current presiding judge of the German Federal Supreme Court, '[t]he definition of the term technicity, and thereby an invention in its patent law sense, must leave room for inclusion of the future developments.'[42] Recently, this potential was realised when the German Federal Supreme Court extended the scope of patentable objects beyond the traditional technical fields of physics, chemistry and biotechnology[43] to cover the technical field of data processing, storing and transmission.[44]

This means that German courts, similarly to the Boards, look for a technical character. In some cases (in particular those involving computer-implemented methods), in order to establish a technical character, it suffices to identify a single technical feature in the invention.[45] For instance, in *Logikverifikation*, a process for hierarchical logic-verification of high integrated switches was found to be an invention because not only (i) the development and design of the particular computer program made the necessary technical considerations available to experts in the field, but also (ii) the technical concept lied in the technical field of chips production and, as a result, (iii) made those chips lighter which was found to be the technical effect.[46]

[38] '[D]*urch eine Erkenntnis geprägt ist, die auf technischen Überlegungen beruht*'. *Logikverifikation*, Decision of 13 December 1999, X ZB 11/98 [2000] *GRUR* 498, 500.

[39] ibid.

[40] '[… p]*atentrechtliche Technikbegriff als abwägungsoffenes Merkmal zu verstehen sei* […]' Herbert Zech, 'Technizität im Patentrecht – Eine intra- und interdisziplinäre Analyse des Technikbegriffs' (*ssrn*, 6 November 2017) 11. Available at: https://papers.ssrn.com/sol3/papers.cfm?abstract_id=3063183, last accessed 7 May 2020.

[41] Ralph Nack, 'Inventions and their Amenability to Patent Protection' in Maximilian Haedicke and Henrik Timmann (eds), *Patent Law: A Handbook on European and German Patent Law* (CH Beck 2014) [13].

[42] Bacher (n 36) [46].

[43] Joseph Straus, 'Biotechnologische Erfindungen – ihr Schutz und seine Grenzen' [1992] *GRUR* 252, 258.

[44] In one case the required technicity was acknowledged because the claimed process run on computer involved 'typical steps of processing, storing and transmission of data via technical devices'. *Erfindungen mit Bezug zu Geräten und Computerprogrammen*, Decision of 24 February 2011, X ZR 121/09 [2011] *GRUR* 610, 612. Also, in an earlier case, the underlying computer program was found to be inherently patentable as it fulfilled the technicity criterion by virtue of processing, storing and transmission of data via a technical device. *Steuerungseinrichtung* (n 37) 480.

[45] *Dynamische Dokumentengenerierung*, Decision of 22 April 2010, Xa ZB 20/08 [2010] *GRUR* 613, 616.

[46] *Logikverifikation* (n 38) 501. The importance of the required technical considerations involved in the working of the invention is also mentioned by Rainer Moufang, 'Patentfähige Erfindungen/patentable inventions Art 52 EPÜ, § 1' in Rainer Schulte (ed), *Patentgesetz mit Europäischem Patentübereinkommen* (Carl Heymanns Verlag 2017) [22].

Among the aspects of technical character, the scholarship lists causality. The use of natural forces must be causally linked with the desired result (*Rote Taube*). What is more, the technical teaching must lead to the result immediately, which means without any intermediary activity of persons.[47] According to Bacher, the difference between technical and non-technical teaching depends on whether 'the desired result is an immediate result of the human (intellectual) activity or whether it was accomplished only by one of those controlled and tamed natural forces'.[48]

In German patent law, as in French law and at the EPC level, the invention can also be understood in contrast with a discovery. According to Nack, the distinction hinges on the relevant activity:

> '[i]nvention' and 'discovery' each describe the product of a particular human activity, that of discovering and that of inventing. These two forms [discovery and invention], therefore, simply mean 'what is discovered' and 'what is invented' and primarily indicate the nature of activity that leads to this acquisition of knowledge.[49]

Melullis adds that if an AI-driven system comes up with a solution to a problem, the production is an invention of that machine.[50] He continues that since the machine is no natural person, this cannot lead to the grant of a patent.[51] As he concludes, 'this does not seem, at the end, to be unjustified because the assessment of patentability of such technical advances, especially with regard to the inventive activity, can hardly be made against the same standards as applicable to natural persons as inventors'.[52]

To summarise, even though in German patent law human beings are traditionally regarded as being the first and primary cause of setting forces of nature into movement and thus creating an invention,[53] neither human creativity nor the process of devising an invention are examined. The invention test is limited to a search for a technical character or technicity. Eventually, this means that the requirement for an 'invention in all technical fields'[54] in effect merges the two definitional elements of (i) invention and (ii) belonging to any of the technical fields into a single concept of 'technicity'. Hence, it seems that any subject matter that relates to a technical field is deemed an invention. This approach ignores the

[47] *Antiblockiersystem*, Decision of 13 May 1980, X ZB 19/78 [1980] *GRUR* 849, 850.

[48] '*das erzielte Ergebnis unmittelbar Ergebnis der menschlichen (Geistes-)Tätigkeit ist oder nur durch eine von dieser beherrschte und gesteuerte Naturkraft bewirkt wurde*' Bacher (n 36) [50a].

[49] However, later in the text Nack does not connect this activity-based distinction with the patentability of a subject matter. Nack (n 41) [149].

[50] Klaus-Jürgen Melullis, 'PatG § 6 [Recht des Erfinders]' in Georg Benkard (ed), *Patentgesetz* 12th edn (CH Beck 2023) [32a].

[51] ibid.

[52] '*Das erscheint im Ergebnis auch deshalb nicht unberechtigt, weil die Bewertung der Patentwürdigkeit solcher Entwicklungen, insbesondere im Hinblick auf die erfinderische Tätigkeit schwerlich mit den gleichen Maßstäben getroffen werden kann, wie sie fur natürliche Person als Entwickler gelten.*' ibid.

[53] Nack (n 41) [15].

[54] *Patentgesetz* of 16 December 1980 (BGBl. 1981 I S. 1) (German Patent Act) §1(1).

possibility that a technical advance may exist which falls within a technical field and which, at the same time, is not an invention.

In this connection, also the German inventor principle seems to be turned upside down. To reiterate, and as also referred to by the German Federal Supreme Court in the German DABUS case,[55] since 'an invention without inventor is not conceivable'[56] then if something looks like an invention (because it has a technical character), some would conclude that it necessarily must have a human inventor. This is a logically plausible inference. However, whether this inference is or is not supported by facts, that is a different question. In reality, there need not to be any human inventor, ie any natural person who would have significantly contributed to the conception of the invention.

Epistemic Approaches to the Inventive Step Requirement

European Patent Office

Pursuant to Article 56 of the EPC, an invention 'shall be considered as involving an inventive step if, having regard to the state of the art, it is not obvious to a person skilled in the art'. In practice, in order to determine whether the technical advance meets the requirement for an inventive step, the Boards use a so-called 'problem-and-solution' test. It comprises the following steps: 'determining the "closest prior art", defining the "objective technical problem" to be solved, and assessing whether or not the claimed invention, starting from the closest prior art and the objective technical problem, would have been obvious to the skilled person'.[57] The outcomes of this test depend heavily on how the concepts of (i) the closest prior art,[58] (ii) a person skilled in the art, and (iii) obviousness are construed. To some extent, these terms have been clarified, yet they remain a matter of judgment.[59]

To reiterate, the inventive step is assessed only in relation to the technical features of the claimed technical advance, ie features contributing to the technical character of the invention.[60] In the words of one of the Boards of Appeal, 'where

[55] *DABUS*, Decision of 11 June 2024, X ZB 5/22 [41].

[56] '[…] *Patentgesetz von 1936 das "Erfinderprinzip" eingeführt hat und ersichtlich* […] *davon ausgeht, daß keine Erfindung ohne Erfinder denkbar ist*' Helmut Schippel, 'BGH 05.05.1966 Ia ZR 110/64 "Spanplatten"' [1966] *GRUR* 558.

[57] European Patent Office, *Guidelines for Examination* (EPO 2021), Part G, Chapter VII [5].

[58] The closest prior art relates to the state of the art which is to be understood as information that are relevant to a certain field of technology. As this element does not have any direct link to human creativity being involved in devising an invention, it is not discussed here in any detail.

[59] *Alcan/Aluminium Alloys*, T 465/92 of 14 October 1994, EP:BA:1994:T046592.19941014 [9.6].

[60] *Estimating sales* (n 2) [5] e).

a feature cannot be considered as contributing to the solution of any technical problem by providing a technical effect it has no significance for the purpose of assessing inventive step'.[61]

The closest prior art amounts to a certain body of knowledge. Information forms part of the prior art if it is made available to the public in such detail that a person skilled in the art can, at the relevant date, work the technical teaching.[62] The closest prior art is information that is 'directed to a similar purpose or effect as the invention or at least belong to the same or a closely related technical field as the claimed invention'.[63] The PSA was introduced in the previous chapter as a notional expert in the technical field of the invention who has common general knowledge, possesses the necessary equipment and technical tools and are conservative[64] and unimaginative in their thinking.

An inventive step is found where the state of the art does not suggest the PSA to take the necessary steps from the prior art towards the claimed invention.[65] Or, put differently, the invention seems obvious to the PSA whenever they see a continuity of mental steps leading from the prior art to the claimed invention that are linked through pointers or hints inherent to their knowledge of the prior art. The inventive step test is thus constructed as hypothetical, objective and focused on what is obvious.

The actual process of devising an invention, or the concrete inventor's steps taken, are merely incidental. Hence, the inventive step test, as currently designed, does not reflect the human aspects of inventing, or what was framed in the previous chapter as a genuine intellectual activity expended on solving a technical problem. In the EPO's decision-making practice, the question of inventive step is considered to be a matter of substantive law.[66]

In summary, when taken from the perspective of the EPO examiners, the inventive step test is designed so that when they construe the invention, the PSA, and determine the closest prior art, they must decide whether there is a chain of obvious steps leading the PSA from the prior art to the invention. Thereby, the emphasis is put on whether the prior art contains enough sufficient pointers that hint at the invention. If the intellectual journey from the prior art to the invention is not interlaced with pointers, nudges, routine procedures or expected results, the invention is likely to pass the inventive step test.

United Kingdom

Historically, under the Patents Act 1949, a patent could be invalidated for being obvious vis-à-vis the state of the art in technology known in the UK before the

[61] *Two identities/COMVIK*, T 0641/00 of 26 September 2002, EP:BA:2002:T064100.20020926 [6].
[62] European Patent Office (n 57) Part G, Chapter IV [2].
[63] ibid Part G, Chapter VII [5.1].
[64] *Genentech/Expression in yeast*, T 445/91 of 20 June 1994, EP:BA:1994:T044591.19940620 [5.1.3.3].
[65] T 1317/08 of 15 May 2012, EP:BA:2012:T131708.20120515 [2.11].
[66] R 0005/13 of 10 February 2014, EP:BA:2014:R000513.20140210 [13].

priority date of the claimed invention. In case law cited in *Terrel on the Law of Patents* of 1982, courts in several cases refer to inventive ingenuity or inventive faculties and make their link to an invention clear:

> If the new use involves no ingenuity, but is in manner and purpose analogous to the old use, although not quite the same, there is no invention [... On the other hand,] a patent for a new use of a known contrivance is good, and can be supported if the new use involves practical difficulties which the patentee has been the first to see and overcome by some ingenuity of his own. An improved thing produced by a new and ingenious application of a known contrivance to an old thing, is a manner of new manufacture within the meaning of the statute.[67]

Section 3 of the Patents Act 1977, currently in force, states that '[a]n invention shall be taken to involve an inventive step if it is not obvious to a person skilled in the art'. Thereby, it establishes a legal presumption that the requirement for an inventive step is fulfilled if the invention is not obvious over certain matters and to a certain notional person. It follows that courts' conclusions concerning an inventive step are conditioned upon their framing of the prior art and the PSA and their understanding of obviousness.

The UK courts have shown a steady reluctance to define the concepts of non-obviousness or obviousness respectively.[68] In this respect, Justice Diplock is often referred to:

> I have endeavoured to refrain from coining a definition of 'obviousness' [...] The correctness of a decision upon an issue of obviousness does not depend upon whether or not the decider has paraphrased the words of the Act in some particular verbal formula. I doubt whether there is any verbal formula which is appropriate to all classes of claims.[69]

The UK courts approach obviousness as a multi-factorial,[70] a kind of jury question, whereby finding obviousness depends on concrete circumstances of the case.[71] The courts developed a test called the 'Windsurfing/Pozzoli test'[72] which culminates by asking whether the identified differences existing between the

[67] *Gadd and Mason* v. *Mayor etc. of Manchester* 9 RPC 516. This case was chosen because 'it has frequently been applied'. William Aldous, David Young, Antony Watson and Simon Thorley, *Terrell on the Law of Patents* 13th edn (Sweet & Maxwell 1982) 138–39.

[68] This approach was summarised in *Novartis AG v Generics (UK) Limited* [2012] EWCA Civ 1623 [57]–[58].

[69] *Johns-Manville Corporation's Patent* [1967] FSR 327, 332.

[70] *Actavis UK Ltd v Novartis AG* [2010] EWCA Civ 82, [2019] Bus LR 1318 [41].

[71] *Generics (UK) Ltd v H Lundbeck A/S* [2007] EWHC 1040 (Pat), [2007] RPC 32 [72], in this part confirmed by the Court of Appeal in *H Lundbeck A/S v Generics (UK)* [2008] EWCA Civ 311, [2008] RPC 437, [24].

[72] The steps of the test are the following: the court (i) first identifies a person skilled in the art and relevant common general knowledge of that person, then (ii) draws an inventive concept from the claim and (iii) determines the differences existing between the matter cited as forming part of the state of the art and the inventive concept of the claim. Lastly, (iv) decides whether, viewed without hindsight, the differences constitute steps which would have been obvious to a person skilled in the art or whether they require any degree of invention. *Pozzoli SPA v BDMO SA* [2007] EWCA Civ 588, [2007] Bus LR D117 [23].

matter cited as forming part of the state of the art and the inventive concept would have been obvious to a person skilled in the art.

One can observe interesting dynamics when it comes to delineating the boundary between the legal term of obviousness and the test used for ascertaining whether the inventive concept would, in fact, have been obvious. As put by Justice Kitchin (as he then was), 'the question of obviousness must be considered on the facts of each case. The court must consider the weight to be attached to any particular factor in the light of all the relevant circumstances'.[73] The relevant circumstances and facts are determined by courts of the first instance. The appellate courts should, in principle, abstain from interfering with the first instance judge's evaluation in questions which are a matter of degree such as obviousness or negligence.[74]

The technical facts enable courts to 'assume the mantle of the normally skilled but unimaginative addressee in the art at the priority date and to impute to him what was, at that date, common general knowledge in the art in question'[75] and to 'understand the thought processes which can lead towards or away from the patented solution'.[76]

Where the activity of devising inventions demands trial and error and plenty of experiments to be undertaken under various levels of uncertainty as to their results, looking for inferential, analogical, and deduction-lead thinking seems inappropriate to answer the obviousness question. Rather, courts ask whether it would have been obvious for a PSA to pursue a particular research pathway with a fair expectation of success.[77]

If, however, the 'expectation of success' aspect somehow disconnects itself from technical considerations, the obviousness question may become more ambiguous and the relevant factors non-technical. As put by Lord Justice Kitchin,

> [w]hether a route has a reasonable or fair prospect of success will depend upon all the circumstances including an ability rationally to predict a successful outcome, how long the project may take, the extent to which the field is unexplored, the complexity or otherwise of any necessary experiments, whether such experiments can be performed by routine means and whether the skilled person will have to make a series of correct decisions along the way.[78]

[73] *Generics v Lundbeck* (n 71) [72].

[74] Lord Hoffmann in *Biogen Inc v Medeva* (n 16) [45]. Where the application of a legal standard such as negligence or obviousness involves no question of principle but is simply a matter of degree, an appellate court should be very cautious in differing from the judge's evaluation.

[75] *Pozzoli SPA v BDMO SA* (n 72) [14].

[76] *Haberman and Another v Jackel Intl Ltd* [1999] FSR 683, 698.

[77] *Conor Medsystems Inc v Angiotech Pharmaceuticals Inc* [2008] UKHL 49, [2008] 4 All ER 621 [42]. In other words, the courts investigate whether a notional PSA 'would assess the likelihood of success sufficient to warrant a trial' *Johns-Manville Corporation's Patent* (n 69) 328.

[78] *MedImmune Ltd v Novartis Pharmaceuticals UK Ltd* [2012] EWCA Civ 1234, [2012] 10 WLUK 325 [91].

In another case, commercial considerations were considered relevant. It did not suffice to show that a PSA could have arrived at the invention, but it needed to be proven that they would have done so.[79] 'Whether he would actually press ahead and implement the idea depends on a host of other, commercial considerations.'[80] Additionally, expectation of success may be influenced by confidence: '[t]he question which the judge had to assess [...] was whether that confidence would have ebbed away so much at the [invention] that the skilled team would no longer have confidence to try it.'[81]

Thereby, non-technical considerations such as commercial considerations, confidence, motives to come up with the solution, the number of possible ways to arrive to the solution, the effort and obstacles on the way and the chances of arriving to the solution[82] have been regarded as relevant. On the one hand, this makes the PSA standard rather flexible and almost alive as it absorbs all the human aspects of inventing and attempts to emulate the process of solving a particular technical problem. On the other hand, such inclusions of non-technical considerations may distort the inventive step test. Following the lead of commercial considerations and confidence may become limitless, as pointed out by Sir Hugh Laddie:

> If the reward for finding a solution to a problem and securing a monopoly for that solution is very high, then it may well be worthwhile for large players to examine all potential avenues [...] What makes something worth trying is the outcome of a simple risk to reward calculation. Yet, if the reward is very large, the avenues worth trying will be expanded accordingly.[83]

Against the background of the Windsurfing/Pozzoli test, a recent case *Actavis v ICOS*[84] is welcomed because of its back-to-basics approach. The UK Supreme Court stressed that the problem-and-solution tests should not be applied mechanistically.[85] This case cautions against the reduction of the assessment of an inventive step to a mere test for non-obviousness as manifested in the invention.

The UK Supreme Court held that an invention can (wrongly) be found inventive only because in its concrete form (eg a 5mg dose in *Actavis v ICOS*) it would have been non-obvious and surprising to the PSA at the beginning of the process of its devising. However, it would be a mistake to infer the involvement of an inventive activity from the non-obviousness of the invention. The non-obvious air of the invention does not make the routine, non-inventive steps (which would have led to its devising) inventive. As reiterated by the UK Supreme Court, the

[79] *Actavis v Novartis* (n 70) [46].
[80] ibid.
[81] *Hospira (UK) Limited v Genentech, Inc* [2015] EWCA Civ 57, [2015] CN 229, CA [46].
[82] *Generics v Lundbeck* (n 71) [72].
[83] Hugh Laddie, 'Patents – What's Invention Got to Do With It?' in David Vaver and Lionel Bently (eds), *Intellectual Property in the New Millennium* (CUP 2010) 93.
[84] *Actavis Group PTC EHF v ICOS Corporation* [2019] UKSC 15, [2019] Bus LR 1318.
[85] ibid [62], [67]–[72].

steps or the activities which would have been undertaken by a PSA in the process of devising the invention are decisive.

In most cases, the primary evidence, ie testimonies of expert witnesses called to court, are conclusive.[86] They serve to identify and give an account of the intellectual world of a notional PSA as well as the common general knowledge and uninventive though informed steps in the field leading from the matter towards the invention. Secondary evidence focuses on historical reality. It provides a reality check where the reconstruction of the obvious way from the prior art to the invention could be unduly tainted by hindsight. As stated by Justice Laddie (as he then was):

> Many patented inventions operate in accordance with simple principles of physics, chemistry or other sciences. [...] So, working from those principles, the solution must be obvious. In such cases it is also easy to take the relevant expert witnesses under cross-examination through a series of logical steps which lead to the solution. The simpler the solution, the easier it is to explain. The easier it is to explain, the more obvious it can appear. This is not always fair to inventors.[87]

Among the secondary evidence one counts sources documenting the contemporaneous events, reactions to the invention, the realities surrounding making the concrete invention and actual ways of approaching the concrete technical problem undertaken at the time of the invention.[88]

In summary, UK courts engage with the process of devising the alleged invention as it would have been hypothetically conducted by the PSA, rather than trying to construe as it had actually happened. In essence, the UK courts search for a strictly non-creative process in order to activate the statutory presumption of an invention being deemed to involve an inventive step if it is not obvious to the PSA.[89]

France

Pursuant to Article L611-14 of the French Intellectual Property Code, 'an invention is deemed to involve an inventive activity, if, for a person skilled in the art, it does not flow from the prior art in an obvious way'.[90] Before this requirement was

[86] *Molnlycke AB and Another v Procter & Gamble Limited and Others (No 5)* [1992] FSR 549, 213.

[87] *Haberman v Jackel* (n 76) 697–98.

[88] A list of secondary factors was provided by Justice Laddie in *Haberman v Jackel* ibid 699–701. To determine whether a development was obvious or not the following matters were relevant: (a) What was the problem which the patented development addressed? (b) How long had that problem existed? (c) How significant was the problem seen to be? (d) How widely known was the problem and how many were likely to have been seeking a solution? (e) What prior art would have been likely to be known to those expected to have been involved in finding a solution? (f) What other solutions were put forward in the period leading up to the publication of the patentee's development? (g) To what extent were there factors which would have held back the exploitation of the solution even if it was technically obvious? (h) How well had the patentee's development been received? (i) To what extent could it be shown that the commercial success was due to the technical merits of the development?

[89] Patents Act 1977, s 3.

[90] '*Une invention est considérée comme impliquant une activité inventive si, pour un homme du métier, elle ne découle pas d'une manière évidente de l'état de la technique.*'

enacted in 1968, the content corresponding to the current conception of the inventive activity used to be identified under the umbrella of the novelty requirement.[91] Back then, the notions of inventive activity and invention were regarded as intertwined:

> No doubt, inventive activity presents itself in the domain of facts in multiple forms; in effect the inventive originality can reside either in the principle of the invention and the idea on which it is founded, or in the means of realisation of the invention and the difficulties that its author had to overcome, or quite simply in the results of the invention and the unexpected advantages which it brings to the industry.[92]

Professor Roubier argued in 1954 that 'it is clear that this kind of inventive activity has an intuitive character'.[93] The inventive activity is 'very ancient in our case law where the inventive idea is often presented as "mother-idea and fundamental" which means that it is the basis of the creation that explains its goal, the problem to which its author applies it in order to solve it'.[94]

Roubier's treatise is often referred to even by recent scholars. His interpretation of novelty as encompassing also non-obviousness was applied in 1956 by a court in Seine[95] and his doctrine of inventive idea was adopted by a court in Paris[96] soon afterwards. But the Court of Appeal in Paris restated in 1961 that there is only one patentability criterion: an objective novelty.[97]

After the enactment of the requirement for an inventive activity in 1968 and in its first years in force, the courts examined also the inventor's process of creation.[98] Nowadays, the modern French approach to interpretation and application of the requirement for an inventive activity closely follows the one of the EPO. French courts conduct a case-by-case analysis of whether an invention would have been obvious to a PSA when compared with the prior art at the priority date. They scrutinise the invention under the objective, problem-and-solution test.[99]

French courts define a PSA as a professional in the technical field where the problem arises which the invention, a subject matter of the patent, proposes to

[91] Passa (n 28) [178].

[92] '*L'activité inventive se présente certainement, dans le domaine des faits avec un aspect multiforme ; il se peut en effet que l'originalité inventive réside, soit dans le principe de l'invention et l'idée qui est à sa base, soit dans les moyen de réalisation de l'invention et des difficultés que son auteur a eu à vaincre, soit tout simplement dans les résultats de l'invention et les avantage inattendus qu'elle a apportés à l'industrie*' Roubier (n 26) 58.

[93] '*il est clair que cette forme d'activité inventive a un caractère intuitif*'; ibid 59.

[94] '*La reconnaissance de cet aspect de l'activité inventive est très ancienne dans notre jurisprudence, où l'idée inventive est souvent présentée comme «l'idée-mère fondamentale», c'est-à-dire celle qui est à la base de la création, qui explique son but, le problème que son auteur s'est appliqué à résoudre*.' ibid 59–60.

[95] Thierry Mollet-Viéville, 'L'instauration du critère d'activité inventive en France' in IRPI (ed), *L'Activité inventive* (Acte de colloque 2019) 15.

[96] Jean-Christophe Galloux, 'La progression du critère de l'activité inventive en droit français' in IRPI (ed), *L'Activité inventive* (Acte de colloque 2019) 21.

[97] ibid 21.

[98] ibid 25–26.

[99] Passa (n 28) [190].

resolve[100] and who possesses average qualities and normal knowledge.[101] One of the aspects of the PSA that may be significant in the AI context is that the PSA is assumed to have at their disposal state-of-the-art tools and machines. For instance, in one case, the PSA was defined as a specialist in security and resilience who has at his disposal specific machines enabling thermal fusion which were available on the market for more than ten years before the date of filing of the patent in question.[102]

In another case, it was held that as the PSA is an engineer in optics of liquid crystals, they are not considered to possess means of computational simulation that an institution like the French National Atomic Energy Commission would do.[103] The attribution of tools and machines to the notional PSA realistically reflects the position of experts in many technical fields whose routine work and its quality depends on them. However, the evaluation of what resources are average or normal and thus justified to form a part of the PSA concept introduces an element of arbitrariness to the assessment.

After a French court puts itself in the shoes of a notional PSA, construed specifically for each individual case, it proceeds to ask whether the PSA would have resolved the problem in the same way as the inventor did by conducting 'every day and normal executive operations'.[104] As found by the French Supreme Court, it is sufficient to establish that 'the state of the art did not suggest the invention without proving an inventive activity'.[105]

Even though French doctrine acknowledges the necessity of the intellectual process resulting in an invention, the inventiveness is to be assessed objectively and externally to that process. For instance, the First Instance Court in Paris held that

> determination of an inventive activity must result, in essence, from an assessment of an intellectual process which led to a realization of the invention taking into account the state of the art at the time of conception of the invention, whereby, in accordance with law, this assessment must be done on the basis of evidence. [... M]ore concretely, the judge must ask himself whether, at the moment when the invention was conceived, for a practitioner in the industry, who is perfectly aware of the prior art, [...] the novel element or novel elements which form the subject matter of the invention were obvious from the prior art.[106]

[100] Cour de cassation, Decision of 20 November 2012, *PIBD* 2012 III 857.

[101] Cour d'appel de Paris, Decision of 19 January 1978, *PIBD* 1978 111 348.

[102] Cour d'appel de Paris, Decision of 13 November 2002, *PIBD* 2003 762 III 201.

[103] TGI de Paris, Decision of 19 January 2005, *PIBD* 2006 807 III 254.

[104] '*des opération d'exécution courante sou normales*' Pollaud-Dulian (n 30) [315].

[105] '*que l'état de la technique et ses connaissances ne suggéraient pas de façon évidente à l'homme de métier de modifier, sans faire preuve d'activité inventive*' Cour de cassation, Decision of 8 October 2002, *PIBD* 2002 754 III 564.

[106] '*la détermination de l'activité inventive doit résulter essentiellement d'une appréciation du processus intellectuel, qui a conduit à la réalisation de l'invention, en fonction de l' état de la technique à l'époque*

French case law, too, developed some indications of inventiveness which have presumptive effects.[107] For instance, the following indicates inventiveness: circumventing an established prejudice,[108] formulation of a novel technical problem, bringing a synergistic effect, unexpected or surprising results, selection from among a great number of possible solutions, combining at least three documents of prior art,[109] etc. One can observe that these indications relate either to the invention, its effects, or other external factors, but neither of them reflects the intellectual process resulting in the invention.

In summary, the French inventive activity test is largely based on the test applied by the EPO. Thereby, it is focused on the invention itself, its effects, and an objective assessment of its standing against the prior art. Statistics show that the current inventive step test is far from perfect. In the years 2008–2016, 45 per cent of litigated French patents were invalidated before French courts with the main reason for invalidation being the lack of inventive activity.[110]

Germany

Pursuant to § 4 of the German Patent Act, 'an invention is deemed to involve an inventive activity if, for a PSA, it does not yield itself from the state of the art in an obvious way'.[111] Traditionally, the inventive activity represents 'a qualitative patentability criterion […] concerned with creativity of the technical advances'.[112] German authorities adopt the same approach as the EPO with a few particularities.

In German tradition, inventive activity seems to have been conceptualised spatially. It is perceived as a border that separates a patent-free area which should be reserved for further uninventive expansion of the prior art and a domain of

de la conception de l'invention, que, d'après la loi, cette appréciation doit se faire d'après le critère de l'évidence ; plus précisément, le juge doit se demander si, au moment où l'invention a été conçue, il était évident, pour un praticien de l'industrie, parfaitement au courant de la technique antérieure, que fussent dégagés clairement et sans effort, de cette technique antérieure, l'élément nouveau ou les éléments nouveaux qui ont fait l'objet de l'invention' Cosmao c. Metériel Moderne Marchand, TGI de Paris, Decision of 17 December 1973, as quoted in Jean-Luc Piotraut and Pierre-Jean Dechristé, *Jugements et arrêts fondamentaux de la propriété intellectuelle* (Technique & Doc 2002) [111].

[107] Institut national de la propriété industrielle, *La délivrance des brevets et des certificats d'utilité* (INPI 2016) 95.

[108] Cour de cassation, Decision of 19 December 2000, *PIBD* 2001 721 III 277.

[109] Institut national de la propriété industrielle, *La délivrance des brevets et des certificats d'utilité* (INPI 2016) 96.

[110] Sabine Agé, 'Introduction de la session' in IRPI (ed), *L'Activité inventive* (Acte de colloque 2019) 67–68.

[111] '*Eine Erfindung gilt als auf einer erfinderischen Tätigkeit beruhend, wenn sie sich für den Fachmann nicht in naheliegender Weise aus dem Stand der Technik ergibt.*'

[112] '*ein qualitatives Kriterium der Patentfähigkeit, […] das auf die Kreativität der technischen Leistung ausgerichtet ist.*' Claus Asendorf, Christof Schmidt and Peter Tochtermann, 'Erfindung auf Grund erfinderischer Tätigkeit' in Georg Benkard (ed), *Patentgesetz* 12th edn (CH Beck 2023) [17].

creative technical achievements.[113] Keukenschrijver writes that a greater distance or a substantial difference from the known, both understood in their qualitative rather than quantitative sense, signal an inventive activity.[114]

According to the German Federal Supreme Court, obviousness is a question of law to be answered through assessment of facts.[115] Put differently, the term of inventive activity is a vague legal term[116] whose content requires a decision evaluating an act on the one hand, and thereby it is formed by the view of the parties, and on the other hand, it is based on factual grounds.[117] The inquiry begins with establishing the key facts relating to the invention and the relevant technical knowledge which are to be ascertained through the eyes of the PSA.[118]

Next, a more detailed set of questions relating to PSA's actions need to be addressed: (a) Which steps would the PSA have had to undertake so that they achieved the solution of the patent in question? (b) Would they have had any instigation or consideration prompting them to set the direction towards the invention? (c) What are the reasons for or against the fact that the PSA would have arrived on the basis of such considerations to the solution proposed in the patent in question?[119]

Though well-elaborated, detailed and well-suited for bureaucratic purposes of patent offices, the German version of the inventive step test does not render flawless results. Statistics show that in the years 2010–2013, 40 per cent of litigated German patents were invalidated and a further 38 per cent were partially invalidated, with 45 per cent of cases citing the lack of inventive activity as the ground for invalidation.[120]

In the German framework, the focus is on the hypothetical process of thinking and acting which would have been performed by a PSA. Whenever an application of known general principles to an individual case required overcoming technical obstacles, solid theoretical considerations or answering a series of objectively difficult questions, an inventive activity was found.[121] Equally, reversing a bias, misleading belief or technical stereotype[122] (without merely diverging from the commonly established practice)[123] testifies to inventive activity. Another

[113] ibid [2].
[114] Alfred Keukenschrijver, '§ 4 Erfinderische Tätigkeit' in Rudolf Busse and Alfred Keukenschrijver (eds), *Patentgesetz* (de Gruyter 2016) [108].
[115] *Vorausbezahlte Telefongespräche*, Decision of 7 March 2006, X ZR 213/01 [2006] *GRUR* 663 [28].
[116] Keukenschrijver (n 114) [8].
[117] Asendorf, Schmidt and Tochtermann (n 112) [5].
[118] Keukenschrijver (n 114) [25]. See also Nack (n 41) [566].
[119] Asendorf, Schmidt and Tochtermann (n 112) [21].
[120] Peter Hess, Tilman Muller-Stoy and Martin Wintermeier, 'Are patents merely "Paper Tigers"?' (*Bardehle Pagenberg* November 2014) 6–7. Available at: www.bardehle.com/en/ip-news-knowledge/publication/detail/are-patents-merely-paper-tigers, last accessed 3 December 2021.
[121] Keukenschrijver (n 114) [116].
[122] ibid [48]–[49].
[123] Decision of 6 September 2005, X ZR 15/02 (Nr 53), *BeckRS* 2005, 12492 [35].

indication of inventive activity is when the PSA would have been surprised by the invention.[124] How the actual inventor arrived at the invention, their career, intensity of their effort or any other such subjective elements are irrelevant.[125] The inventive activity is judged solely according to its results against the prior art.[126] Consequently, the mere existence of an invention coupled with establishing an absence of a non-inventive activity which would have led to it, triggers the statutory presumption of an invention involving an inventive activity.

Conclusion

This chapter concludes that despite the reflections of human inventorship in European patent law, the current epistemic approaches are not sensitive enough to detect the human aspects of inventing. In relation to the requirement for an invention, the concept of 'invention' has been reduced to designate merely a technical feature (the EPO, France), belonging to a technical field (Germany) and a technical contribution (the UK). In practice, upon finding a technical character, authorities tend to conclude that they encountered an invention without asking whether the technical character is due the relevant human creative intervention. This approach ignores the possibility of a subject matter falling within a technical field or having a technical feature that need not constitute an invention because of lack of human origin.

In relation to an inventive step, this chapter found that the notion of 'obviousness' overshadowed the human intellectual aspects of inventing. The obviousness-based approaches can lead to finding non-obviousness in inventions that do not involve the relevant human intellectual activity (as in *Actavis v ICOS*). As concluded in chapter 4, the requirement for an inventive activity should be interpreted as having two components: (i) an involvement of a step (or an activity) (ii) that is of inventive quality. Under the current epistemic approaches, the activity resulting in the invention seems to be taken for granted without being examined. Consequently, only the second component, whether the assumed activity is inventive, is addressed by authorities.

Recently, the UK Supreme Court in *Actavis v ICOS* put the inventive step test back in its place by benchmarking the allegedly inventive intellectual activity against the hypothetical technical intellectual activity of a PSA. The examination of steps of the PSA is limited to solving the technical problem. If in the future

[124] *Disiloxan*, Decision of 27 February 1969, X ZB 11/68 [1969] *GRUR* 265, 266.

[125] Rainer Moufang, 'Erfinderische Tätigkeit/inventive activity Art 56 EPÜ, § 4' in Rainer Schulte (ed), *Patentgesetz mit Europäischem Patentübereinkommen* (Carl Heymanns Verlag 2017) [7].

[126] Christoph Ann, 'Erfinderische Leistung' in Rudolf Kraßer and Christoph Ann (eds), *Patentrecht* 8th edn, (CH Beck 2016) [11]. See also Asendorf, Schmidt and Tochtermann (n 112) [23].

authorities focus strictly on the hypothetical technical PSA's steps instead of a mere impression of non-obviousness that the final subject matter made, the inventive step test will have better chances to detect subject matter whose devising lacked the required human intellectual activity. To achieve this, such a test would also need to be supplemented by a broader disclosure duty of the technical problem and solution imposed on patent applicants (more on this in chapter 9).

6

EU Authorship

Introduction

In contrast to European patent law, in European copyright (author's rights) law it is widely accepted that human origin and the history of creation matter for copyright protection of authorial works. Conceiving of authorship as a relationship between an author and their work, it can be approached from either of its ends – from the perspective of author or from the perspective of work. This chapter looks at the relationship from the perspective of authorial work and its properties to learn more about the underlying activity that makes a person the author and a subject matter their work.

This is a methodological necessity because EU law contains no general definition of 'author'. The explanatory memorandum to the InfoSoc Directive does not explain why. It only mentions that '[i]t is the environment in which works and other subject matter are being created and exploited which has changed – not the basic copyright concepts'.[1] This suggests some stability of the basic concepts (likely including the author and the work), vis-à-vis the ever-evolving creative and exploitative practices. Admittedly, the EU copyright legislation contains no general definition of 'work' either. However, the Court of Justice of the European Union (CJEU) has undertaken a significant effort to define it.[2] For this reason, this chapter focuses on human aspects in the copyright subsistence criteria and the concept of work in the EU legislative acts and the CJEU's case law.

EU Copyright Protection in Two Tracks

EU copyright law is the primary source of definitions and copyright subsistence criteria for certain types of work, namely computer programs and databases.

[1] Proposal for a European Parliament and Council Directive on the harmonization of certain aspects of copyright and related rights in the Information Society of 10 December 1997, COM(97) 628 final 97/0359 (COD).

[2] It is often legitimately questioned whether the CJEU should have done so in the first place. As pointed out by Vousden, the doctrine of autonomous concept comes from the domain of exclusive competence, whereas copyright is considered to fall within the domain of shared competence. Stephen Vousden, 'Infopaq and the Europeanisation of copyright law' (2010) 2 *WIPO J* 197.

Directives that govern copyright in computer program and databases are *leges speciales*[3] in relation to the general InfoSoc Directive. Under the EU copyright scheme, the first step is thus to determine whether a subject matter constitutes a computer program, database or any other subject matter. In relation to other protected subject matter (and subsidiarily for computer programs and databases as well), the InfoSoc Directive provides for a number of exclusive rights for authors in relation to their works.[4] For instance, in *BSA*, the CJEU held that although a graphic user interface cannot be protected by copyright in computer programs, it can still fall under the copyright regime of the InfoSoc Directive, provided it 'is original in the sense that it is its author's own intellectual creation'.[5]

EU copyright law is applicable in the UK subject to the rules under the Retained EU Law (Revocation and Reform) Act 2023 (REULA). REULA gives the UK courts more freedom to depart from EU law which remains an external interpretative aid.[6] At the time of writing (end of July 2024), there had been no changes in the area of copyright. Moreover, between 31 December 2020 (the end of the Brexit transition period when the EU law ceased to apply in the UK) and 1 January 2024 (when REULA entered into force) the UK courts continued to follow the CJEU's case law on copyright subsistence, including interpretation of the concept of work.[7] Therefore, this book treats the UK law as still adhering to the EU copyright subsistence criteria with the caveat that this may change in the future.

Lex specialis – Computer Programs Directive

The first Directive harmonising copyright in relation to a specific subject matter was Directive 91/250/EEC of 14 May 1991 on the legal protection of computer programs.[8] Perhaps surprisingly, the notion of computer program is not defined in the Computer Programs Directive. However, Recital 7 specifies that

> the term 'computer program' shall include programs in any form, including those which are incorporated into hardware. This term also includes preparatory design work leading to the development of a computer program provided that the nature of the preparatory work is such that a computer program can result from it at a later stage.[9]

[3] Case C-128/11 *UsedSoft GmbH v Oracle International Corp* [2012] EU:C:2012:407, para 51.

[4] Directive 2001/29/EC of 22 May 2001 on the harmonisation of certain aspects of copyright and related rights in the information society [2001] OJ L 167/10 (InfoSoc Directive), arts 2–4.

[5] Case C-393/09 *Bezpečnostní softwarová asociace v Ministerstvo kultury* [2010] ECR I-13971, EU:C:2010:816, para 37, reiterated in para 45.

[6] Yin Harn Lee, 'United Kingdom Copyright Decisions and Legislative Developments 2023' (2024) *IIC* 422, 438–39.

[7] See, for instance, *Response Clothing Ltd v The Edinburgh Woollen Mill Ltd* [2020] EWHC 148 (IPEC) [2020] FSR 25 or *Shazam Productions v Only Fools the Dining Experience* [2022] EWHC 1379 (IPEC) [2022] FSR 25.

[8] Directive 2009/24/EC of 23 April 2009 on the legal protection of computer programs [2009] OJ L 111/16 (Computer Programs Directive).

[9] ibid, recital 7.

This inclusive conception of computer program can be interpreted to encompass results of all stages of the process of devising a computer program. Additionally, the Explanatory Memorandum to the Computer Programs Directive defines a computer program as 'a set of instructions the purpose of which is to cause an information processing device, a computer, to perform its functions'.[10] This may be called a purpose-based definition.

The object of protection under the Computer Programs Directive is not, however, a computer program as such but rather 'the expression in any form of a computer program which permits reproduction in different computer languages, such as the source code and the object code'.[11] In *BSA*, the CJEU found that a graphic user interface is not an expression of a computer program because it only 'enables communication between the computer program and the user'[12] and it 'does not enable the reproduction of that computer program'.[13] In *SAS Institute*, the CJEU held that 'functionality of a computer program, the programming language and the format of data files [all of which are] used in a computer program in order to exploit certain of its functions'[14] do not constitute a form of expression of that program. In other words, functionality, programming language or data format are not deemed expressive elements of a computer program.

It follows that the purpose and function of the subject matter are decisive for its qualification as a computer program (and thus for the applicability of the Computer Programs Directive). They are equally important for determining the object of protection under that directive: only those elements of a computer program that are executable (ie able to be run on a computer to enable its reproduction) are deemed expressive of ideas embedded in that computer program (*BSA* and *SAS Institute*).

When it comes to copyright subsistence, the only criterion for protection is the originality of the computer program. This means that a computer program must constitute 'the author's own intellectual creation [and n]o other criteria shall be applied to determine its eligibility for protection'.[15] Authorship is thus central for eligibility for protection.[16]

Again, the Explanatory Memorandum to the Computer Programs Directive can shed some light on the meaning of the term 'computer program' and its originality as perceived by the drafters.

> As far as the property right is concerned, a computer program, in common with other works protected by intellectual property legislation, is the result of a creative intellectual

[10] Proposal for a Council Directive on the legal protection of computer programs COM(88) 816 final – SYN 183; 89/C 91/05) [1.1.].

[11] Computer Programs Directive, art 1(2) and *BSA* (n 5), para 35.

[12] *BSA* ibid para 40.

[13] ibid para 41.

[14] Case C-406/10 *SAS Institute Inc v World Programming Ltd* [2012] EU:C:2012:259, para 39.

[15] Computer Programs Directive, art 1(3).

[16] Lionel Bently and Yin Harn Lee, 'Computer Programs Directive, Art 2' in Bernt Hugenholtz and Thomas Dreier (eds), *Concise European Copyright Law* 2nd edn (Kluwer Law 2016) 248.

> human activity. [… T]he degree of creativity, skill and inventiveness required to devise a program make it no less deserving of protection than other works protected by copyright. The fact that computer programs have a utilitarian function does not change this.[17]

Hence, from the directive, the preparatory materials and CJEU's case law follows that copyright in computer programs is available only for executable elements (the expressive elements) of those computer programs that consist of instructions to run functions (the building blocks) that were selected and combined so that they reflect personality of the individual who did the selection and combination of the instructions.

Lex specialis – Database Directive

A subject matter is eligible for copyright in database under Directive 96/9/EC of 11 March 1996 on the legal protection of databases if it meets the definition of a database under Article 1(2). According to Article 1(2) database means 'a collection of independent works, data or other materials arranged in a systematic or methodical way and individually accessible by electronic or other means'.[18]

Professor von Lewinski comments on Article 1(2) of the Database Directive that the terms systematic and methodological 'mean "according to a plan". Accordingly, the arrangement must be made according to fixed criteria'.[19] She also adds that these criteria should be given a broad interpretation to comply with the Berne Convention.[20]

When the CJEU was interpreting the Database Directive in *Football Dataco*, it held that the selection and arrangement of the dates, times and names of teams in the form of a football fixture list qualified for a database in the sense of the directive.[21] In the same judgment, it also found that '[a]s is apparent from recitals 9, 10 and 12 of that [Database] directive, its purpose is to stimulate the creation of data storage and processing systems in order to contribute to the development of an information market'.[22] The above CJEU's interpretation and academic commentary may be summarised so that the purpose and function of enabling a systematic or methodical organisation of and access to information are definitional of a database.

[17] Proposal (n 10) [2.2.].

[18] Directive 96/9/EC of 11 March 1996 on the legal protection of databases [1996] OJ L 77/20 (Database Directive) art 1(2).

[19] Silke von Lewinski, 'Database Directive' in Michel Walter and Silke von Lewinski (eds), *European Copyright Law. A Commentary* (OUP 2010) 695.

[20] ibid 696.

[21] Case C-604/10 *Football Dataco Ltd and Others v Yahoo! UK Ltd and Others* [2012] EU:C:2012:115, para 26.

[22] ibid para 34. Case C-203/02 *The British Horseracing Board* [2004] EU:C:2004:695, para 30.

Databases in the above sense are protected by copyright if they 'by reason of the selection or arrangement of their contents, constitute the author's own intellectual creation [and n]o other criteria shall be applied to determine their eligibility'.[23] Recital 15 of the Database Directive states that copyright in databases should subsist in 'the selection or the arrangement of the contents of the database [that] is the author's own intellectual creation; whereas such protection should cover the structure of the database'.[24]

The CJEU later confirmed in *Football Dataco* that only the selection and arrangement of data by which the author of the database creates the structure of the database are relevant for copyright.[25] The requirement of originality is met if the author of a database 'expresses his creative ability in an original manner by making free and creative choices'[26] in the selection and arrangement of the contents (ie in the creation of the structure of the database). In negative terms, the CJEU found that a database is not original if 'setting up of the database is dictated by technical considerations, rules and constraints which leave no room for creative freedom'.[27]

It follows that a database must, on the one hand, be arranged in a systematic or methodological way which implies some observable regularity to be imposed by some kind of organising rule to qualify for a database under the Database Directive. On the other hand, the creation of such a database must not be completely constrained by rules. Going beyond the CJEU's rulings, these conditions may be read together as follows: copyright subsists only in those elements of the structure of a database that were determined by rules imposed on it by its author and that were not necessary to achieve a technical result. Similarly to computer programs, authorship is key to establish eligibility. It then follows that copyright in a database is available only for structural elements of those databases that are results of author's own arrangement and selection of the contents of the database.

Besides computers and databases, films have their own definition in the Directive 92/100/EEC of 19 November 1992 on rental and lending rights and on certain rights related to copyright in the field of intellectual property.[28] Herein, film is defined (only for the purposes of that directive) as 'a cinematographic or audiovisual work or moving images, whether or not accompanied by sound'.[29] This may be called a content-based definition. Though films have their 'special' definition, copyright in film falls under the general regime of the InfoSoc Directive.

[23] Database Directive, art 3(1).
[24] ibid recital 15.
[25] *Football Dataco* (n 21) para 32.
[26] ibid para 38.
[27] ibid para 39.
[28] Now Directive 2006/115/EC of 12 December 2006 on rental right and lending right and on certain rights related to copyright in the field of intellectual property (codified version) [2006] OJ L 376/28 (Rental and Lending Directive).
[29] ibid art 2(1)(c).

Lex generalis – InfoSoc Directive

A subject matter may be protected by copyright plainly as a work under the InfoSoc Directive.[30] Some human aspects of creation can be traced already in the objectives and purpose of the InfoSoc Directive. A systematic reading of its Preamble reveals that the primary goal of copyright law harmonisation is to 'foster substantial investment in creativity and innovation, including network infrastructure, and lead in turn to growth and increased competitiveness of European industry […]. This will safeguard employment and encourage new job creation'.[31]

Secondarily, the emphasis is put on achieving smoother functioning of the internal market thanks to increased legal certainty and united approach to the level of protection.[32] Harmonisation of copyright and related rights should also warrant 'a high level of protection, since such rights are crucial to intellectual creation. Their protection helps to ensure the maintenance and development of creativity in the interests of authors, performers, producers, consumers, culture, industry and the public at large'.[33] In this connection, receiving an appropriate reward for their work and investment is postulated as the condition for further creative activity of authors, performers and further investment of producers respectively.[34]

Even though the legislative history reveals that the main agenda of the day was to harmonise the reproduction, communication to the public and distribution rights, together with exceptions and limitations,[35] incentives and reward for creativity flash out prominently in Recitals 9 and 10. Overall, the InfoSoc Directive refers to creativity or intellectual creation eight times.[36]

The authorial creativity as the goal of protection tends to be more accentuated in the context of design and copyright interface. In this context and in the opinion of Members of the European Copyright Society,

> [i]t is well established in EU jurisprudence that the goal of design law is the protection of the investment incurred in creating a design against imitation by competitors, whereas copyright aims to encourage creativity, inter alia by reserving the economic exploitation of works to creators and their assignees.[37]

[30] InfoSoc Directive, arts 2, 3 and 4.
[31] ibid recital 4.
[32] ibid recitals 6 and 7.
[33] ibid recital 9.
[34] ibid recital 10.
[35] Silke von Lewinski, 'Information Society Directive' in Michel Walter and Silke von Lewinski (eds) *European Copyright Law. A Commentary* (OUP 2010) 945.
[36] InfoSoc Directive (n 4).
[37] Estelle Derclaye, 'Opinion of the European Copyright Society in relation to the pending reference before the CJEU in Brompton Bicycle v Chedech/Get2Get (C-833/18)' (2020) 42 *EIPR* 207.

Since the InfoSoc Directive's entry into force in 2001, the CJEU 'has unearthed' the following legal conditions for a subject matter to qualify as a work.[38] First, in *Levola*, the CJEU found that the subject matter must be capable of being identified with sufficient precision and objectivity.[39] This was reiterated in *Pelham* where the CJEU found that a copyright subject matter may be 'very short'.[40] Yet, it must be long and distinct enough to be perceivable and recognisable by human senses.[41]

Second, while individual constitutive elements of a work can be perceived, they cannot be protected by copyright.[42] As found in *Infopaq*, the reason is that the size of a subject matter must be such that allows to 'convey [...] to the reader the originality of a publication such as a newspaper article, by communicating to that reader an element which is, in itself, the expression of the intellectual creation of the author of that article'.[43] According to the CJEU, it was a common ground that the concrete newspaper articles (of which the 11-word extracts in dispute formed parts) were their author's own intellectual creations and this was evidenced from 'the form, the manner in which the subject is presented and the linguistic expression'.[44]

However, the case of 11-word extracts was not as straightforward. The CJEU ruled that such short extracts are eligible if they are 'the expression of the intellectual creation of their author'.[45] And it added that '[i]t is only through the choice, sequence and combination of those words that the author may express his creativity in an original manner and achieve a result which is an intellectual creation'.[46]

Professor Pila criticises the CJEU's approach in *Infopaq* because it 'conceives original works in purely formalistic terms, as compilations of words, sounds, images and human movements'.[47] In contrast, here *Infopaq* is understood as instructing national courts to look for originality in 'the choice, sequence and combination' of words without suggesting that any such compilations are, as they stand, (original) works.[48]

[38] A comprehensive account can be found in Justine Pila, 'The Authorial Works Protectable by Copyright' in Eleonora Rosati (ed), *The Routledge Handbook of EU Copyright Law* (Routledge 2021).

[39] Case C-310/17 *Levola Hengelo BV v Smilde Foods BV* [2018] EU:C:2018:899, para 40.

[40] Case C-476/17 *Pelham GmbH and Others v Ralf Hütter and Florian Schneider-Esleben* [2019] EU:C:2019:624, para 39.

[41] ibid.

[42] Case C-5/08 *Infopaq International A/S v Danske Dagblades Forening* [2009] ECR I-6569, EU:C:2009:465, para 46.

[43] ibid para 47.

[44] ibid para 44.

[45] ibid para 51.

[46] ibid para 45.

[47] Pila (n 38) 72.

[48] In this connection, Professor Torremans ponders whether the criterion of author's own intellectual creation became 'the sole criterion to define the autonomous concept of "a work"', see Paul Torremans, 'The Role of the CJEU's Autonomous Concepts as a Harmonising Element of Copyright Law in the

In efforts to justify the criterion of author's own intellectual creation, the CJEU relies on the Berne Convention.[49] In *Infopaq*, the CJEU states that '[i]t is, moreover, apparent from the general scheme of the Berne Convention, in particular Article 2(5)[50] and (8),[51] that the protection of certain subject-matters as artistic or literary works presupposes that they are intellectual creations'[52] (footnotes added).

There are two plausible ways in which the word 'presupposes' used in *Infopaq* can be understood. 'Presuppose' may mean to presume,[53] or require as a necessary condition.[54] If the CJEU used 'presupposes' in the former sense, it could mean that it is taken for granted that any literary, musical or artistic work in its ordinary meaning (eg a novel, a drama play, a musical composition)[55] is, as a matter of fact, an intellectual creation. This would mean that upon encountering a novel, a painting or a musical composition, one automatically presumes that they have encountered an intellectual creation.

The interpretation of 'presupposes' as 'presumes' also aligns with the conception of work proposed by Professor Pila. She argues that since the notion of 'work' is a common language term and not defined in EU copyright legislation, its meaning and scope should follow its usual meaning in everyday language.[56] Hence, if an expressive subject matter such as a painting or a poem can be subsumed under the meaning that 'work' has in ordinary language, the law should follow suit.

United Kingdom' (2019) 4 *IPQ* 265, 272. Professor Derclaye makes a similar comment on *FAPL* and *BSA*, but argues that this has not been intended by the CJEU in Estelle Derclaye, 'The Court of Justice Copyright Case Law: quo vadis?' (2014) 36 *EIPR* 717 and fn 10.

[49] Plausible criticism of the CJEU's approach to the Berne Convention was raised. According to Professor Derclaye, the CJEU does not use the Berne Convention appropriately because the Berne Convention's minimum standards are not binding in relation to state's own nationals, eg for the EU in relation to EU citizens. Derclaye, ibid 721. In a less critical view adopted by Professor Vousden, 'the relationship between the Berne Convention and EU law is not one of a slavish adherence'. Vousden (n 2).

[50] Berne Convention, art 2(5): 'Collections of literary or artistic works such as encyclopaedias and anthologies which, by reason of the selection and arrangement of their contents, constitute intellectual creations shall be protected as such, without prejudice to the copyright in each of the works forming part of such collections.'

[51] ibid art 2(8): 'The protection of this Convention shall not apply to news of the day or to miscellaneous facts having the character of mere items of press information.'

[52] See *Infopaq* (n 42) para 34.

[53] The term 'presuppose' means to assume, suppose, or postulate beforehand; to take for granted; to presume; to think or believe (something) in advance of actual knowledge or experience. *Oxford English Dictionary* Online (*EOD*, December 2020). Available at: www.oed.com/, last accessed 31 December 2021.

[54] The term 'presuppose' means to require as a necessary preceding condition; to imply or require as something previously or already present or in existence according to the *Oxford English Dictionary* ibid.

[55] Berne Convention, art 2(1) provides examples of literary and artistic works.

[56] Pila (n 38) 30 with reference to Case C-201/13 *Johan Deckmyn and Vrijheidsfonds VZW v Helena Vandersteen* [2014] EU:C:2014:2132 para 19.

The interpretation of 'presuppose' as 'presume' also evokes the pre-modern understanding of protected subject matter in common law. As researched by Professors Sherman and Benly, pre-modern copyright was fragmented, subject-specific and the protected subject matter was perceived as still tied with the tangible object.[57] As they further argue, this was the case until the subject matter became conceived through its belonging to more abstract categories in modern copyright.[58]

Alternatively, if the CJEU intended to give 'presupposes' the conditional meaning, then a subject matter would be required to be an intellectual creation as a pre-condition for being a literary or artistic work in the sense of the Berne Convention.[59] This chapter argues that the CJEU itself leans to the latter, ie the conditional, meaning. This follows from the immediate context in which the word 'presupposes' was used. As held by the CJEU:

> [i]t is, moreover, apparent from the general scheme of the Berne Convention, [...] that the protection of certain subject-matters as artistic or literary works presupposes that they are intellectual creations. Similarly, [...] works such as computer programs, databases or photographs are protected by copyright only if they are original in the sense that they are their author's own intellectual creation. [...] In those circumstances, copyright [...] is liable to apply only in relation to a subject-matter which is original in the sense that it is its author's own intellectual creation.[60]

Under the Berne Convention, the Berne union countries protect 'the rights of authors in their literary and artistic works'.[61] Under Article 2(1) of the Berne Convention, literary and artistic works are understood as 'every production in the literary, scientific and artistic domain, whatever may be the mode or form of its expression'.[62] With reference to Article 2(5) of the Berne Convention, Professors Ricketson and Ginsburg comment that there is 'a clear indication that "intellectual creation" is implicit in the conception of literary and artistic work'.[63] They also add, with reference to the travaux préparatoires for the Brussels Revision Conference, that 'the expression "literary and artistic works" itself meant "personal creation or … intellectual creation within the sphere of letters and the arts"'.[64]

[57] Brad Sherman and Lionel Bently, *The Making of Modern Intellectual Property Law: The British Experience, 1760–1911* (CUP 1999) 17–18.

[58] ibid.

[59] See *Infopaq* (n 42) para 34 and Case C-683/17 *Cofemel – Sociedade de Vestuário SA v G-Star Raw CV* [2019] EU:C:2019:721, para 24.

[60] *Infopaq* (n 42) paras 34–37. In the preparation of this chapter, English, French, German, Czech and Slovak language versions of *Infopaq* were checked. They all permit presumptive as well as conditional meaning.

[61] Berne Convention, art 1.

[62] ibid art 2.

[63] Sam Ricketson and Jane C Ginsburg, *International Copyright and Neighbouring Rights: The Berne Convention and Beyond*, vol I, 2nd edn (OUP 2006) 402.

[64] ibid 403.

Professor Dreier, too, comments that the Berne Convention 'is concerned with creations in the field of literature and the arts'.[65] In addition, Professor von Lewinski writes that '"production" is understood as something originating from the mind of a person, it is also understood as implying originality or creativity, as reflected in the national laws of Berne union countries, even if not explicitly required by the Berne Convention'.[66] Intellectual creation is thus a necessary and implicit condition for protection under the Berne Convention (and that is through the conception of 'literary or artistic work'). Therefore, if the CJEU wished to be in line with the Berne Convention, it seems more likely that it intended to use 'presupposes' in the conditional meaning.

Interpreting 'presupposes' as 'requires as a necessary condition' has further significant implications. This interpretation permits to argue that a subject matter must primarily be an intellectual creation and, only by virtue of being an intellectual creation, it amounts to 'literary and artistic works' in the sense of the Berne Convention. This means that only those novels, paintings, musical compositions, etc. (or parts thereof) that constitute intellectual creations fall within the scope of 'literary and artistic works' in the sense of the Berne Convention. Another implication is that not all novels, paintings, musical compositions, etc. may automatically be regarded as 'literary and artistic works' in the sense of the Berne Convention.

Synthesis

The system and structure of the EU copyright subsistence rules distinguishes two tracks of copyright protection. One track is reserved for computer programs and databases while the other one is for the rest of the works. The problem is that works in the latter track are not defined above and beyond being the author's own intellectual creations. While in the former track, it is possible to conceive of non-original computer programs (or databases) and original computer programs (or databases), the latter track recognises works and non-works only.[67]

Another difference between the subject matter in the two tracks is that computer programs and databases are defined through their purpose and function, whereas the purpose and function of other (types of) protected subject matter cannot be readily drawn from the EU copyright legislation. Neither did the CJEU interpret

[65] Thomas Dreier, 'Berne Convention, Art 2' in Bernt Hugenholtz and Thomas Dreier (eds), *Concise European Copyright Law* 2nd edn (Kluwer Law 2016) 15.

[66] Silke von Lewinski, *International Copyright Law and Policy* (OUP 2008) 122–23.

[67] Photographs seem to be a hybrid. On the one hand, they do not enjoy a special copyright regime like computer programs and databases and straightforwardly fall within the general regime of the InfoSoc Directive. On the other hand, recital 16 of Directive 2006/116/EC of 12 December 2006 on the term of protection of copyright and certain related rights [2006] OJ L 372/12 (Term Directive) speaks of copyright protection of original photographs and other means of protection for other photographs, probably meaning protection for non-original photographs.

the concept of work as requiring any distinct purpose or function (except in negative terms as excluding elements determined by a technical function or rules).[68] Yet, further definitional elements of protected subject matter (such as those given through categorisation of works for instance) would be practical to determine their expressive elements, ie those parts of work that must be proven to be author's own should authorship be claimed successfully.[69]

In conclusion, it is difficult to synthesise more than the following: rights under the InfoSoc Directive protect only expressive elements of subject matter that are author's own intellectual creation.[70] The idea of protection of elements was introduced by the CJEU in *Infopaq*. As Professor Sherman observes, '[b]y suggesting that an element of a work may be protected if it contributes to the originality of the whole, the decision [*Infopaq*] potentially shifts the focus away from a taxonomic inquiry into when a part of a work might be treated as a separate work in its own right'.[71]

In general, copyright in a work subsists from the moment of its creation and no formal registration is required.[72] Reading this together with *Infopaq*, a work is created or comes into existence when its author chooses, sequences and combines the constitutive elements in an original manner. This relatively vague conclusion on general copyright eligibility can be further refined by clarifying what 'author's own intellectual creation' and 'original manner' entail.

Human Aspects in the Originality Standard

Scholarship regularly associates the EU criterion of author's own intellectual creation with originality.[73] Scholarly literature also tends to refer to the free and

[68] Case C-833/18 *SI and Brompton Bicycle Ltd v Chedech / Get2Get* [2020] EU:C:2020:461, para 24. See more detail below.

[69] Building on Justine Pila, 'An Intentional View of the Copyright Work' (2008) 4 *MLR* 535.

[70] For instance, Witten Group proposed the following definition of a work: 'any expression within the field of literature, art or science insofar as it constitutes its author's own intellectual creation'. The Wittem Group, 'European Copyright Code' (2011) 2 *EIPR* 76. Though these definitions are semantically close, this chapter did not adopt the definition of the Wittem Group because it will make use of the notion of 'expressive elements' (and thus adopt a more granular approach) rather than 'an expression' in the analysis that follows. Additionally, the Wittem Group explains in footnote 7 that '"expression" indicates the traditional requirement that works be the result of the author's personal expression'. This suggests that expression can be used interchangeably with creation, whereas this chapter advances the view that an expression or expressive elements are distinct from creation. Similarly, the CJEU makes a distinction between a creation and an expression in *Infopaq* (n 42) para 51: 'if the elements thus reproduced are the expression of the intellectual creation of their author'.

[71] Brad Sherman, 'What is a Copyright Work?' (2011) 12 *Theoretical Inq L* 99, 118. In the quoted part Professor Sherman analysed the EU approach to the concept of work.

[72] Directive 2004/48/EC of 29 April 2004 on the enforcement of intellectual property rights [2004] OJ L 195/16, rec 19.

[73] '[T]he Court of Justice concluded that there was a generalized standard of originality – namely, the "author's own intellectual creation"'. Lionel Bently and others, *Intellectual Property Law* 6th edn

creative choices together[74] and the personal nature of the choices is not traditionally perceived as possibly self-standing. This chapter adopts a novel approach and splits the idiom of free and creative choices into free choices, creative choices and personal choices (which may or may not be cumulated in any given subject matter). The following analysis thus proceeds along the axes of: (i) free choices, (ii) creative choices and (iii) author's own (personal) choice. This should assist in tracing the human aspects of creation.

Free Choices

First, in the CJEU's jurisprudence, the making of free choices is conditioned upon such circumstances that provide the author with, as put by Professor Hugenholtz, sufficient 'freedom of creative choice'[75] to create their work. In *BSA*, the CJEU held that copyright protection is excluded if there is no scope for making choices as to the expressive elements of a subject matter: 'where the expression of those components is dictated by their technical function, the criterion of originality is not met, since the different methods of implementing an idea are so limited that the idea and the expression become indissociable'.[76] In *Brompton Bicycle*, the CJEU confirmed that the possibility of making free, creative choices is limited to the extent to which the subject matter is determined by technical considerations or rules.[77] In *FAPL*, the CJEU found that sporting events do not constitute intellectual creations that are works and this should apply 'in particular to football matches, which are subject to rules of the game, leaving no room for creative freedom for the purposes of copyright'.[78]

From *FAPL, BSA* and *Brompton Bicycle*, it can be inferred that there are circumstances, external to every putative author, such as rules of a game, or constraints

(OUP 2022) 106. 'These works will be protected where they are original in the sense that they are the "author's own intellectual creation". This new EU standard of originality [...]' Tanya Aplin and Jennifer Davis, *Intellectual Property Law: Text, Cases, and Materials* 3rd edn (OUP 2017) 120. Eleonora Rosati, *Originality in EU Copyright: Full Harmonization Through Case Law* (Edward Elgar 2013) 109.

[74] '[I]t is clear that decisions that are limited by functional constraints or "rules" are not to be regarded as "creative choices"'. Bently and others, ibid 109. Aplin and Davis, ibid 126. Annette Kur, 'Unité de l'art is here to stay – Cofemel and its Consequences' (2020) 4 *JIPIL* 290. Professors Loewenheim and Leistner refer to free and creative choices as *'frei kreativer Entscheidungen'* (without a comma between free and creative; two times) as well as *'Gestaltungsspielraum für freie, kreative Entscheidungen'* (with comma; two times) in Ulrich Loewenheim and Matthias Leistner, '§ 6 Schutzvoraussetzungen', in Ulrich Loewenheim and Matthias Leistner (eds), *Handbuch des Urheberrechts* 3rd edn (CH Beck 2021) [5]–[10].

[75] Bernt Hugenholtz, 'Works of Literature, Science and Art' in Bernt Hugenholtz and others (eds), *A Century of Dutch Copyright Law* (deLex 2012) 54.

[76] *BSA* (n 5) para 49.

[77] *Brompton Bicycle* (n 68) para 24.

[78] Joined cases C-403/08 and C-429/08 *Football Association Premier League Ltd and Others v QC Leisure and Others*, and *Karen Murphy v Media Protection Services* EU:C:2011:631, [2011] ECR I-9083, [2012] 1 CLRM (29) 769 ECJ, para 98.

of a technical nature, that prevent the making of free choices. Though it is curious that the creative freedom of an author of a literary work does not seem to be constrained by the rules of grammar, spelling and syntax in the same way.[79]

The case law yields only a negative definition of creative freedom: free choices are possible where the subject matter is not entirely dictated by certain rules, utility or technical function. As authors can only respond to the possibilities offered to them by freedom of choice, they do not determine which choices are free to be exploited for copyright purposes. For instance, if a football game does not provide sufficient freedom for creative and personal choices, it would not do so regardless of whether it was played by robots or by human beings.

Since creative freedom does not contain any human aspects of creation, it is of limited interest to this book. Therefore, the case law on availability of free choices, including the idea/expression dichotomy,[80] is accepted as it is and this book does not delve into the CJEU's reasonings of whether, in principle, an 11-word extract (*Infopaq*)[81] or a football game (*FAPL*)[82] provide enough creative freedom to constitute works.

Creative Choices

Creative choices tend to be understood in several ways. Goold, for instance, understands creative choices as 'creative in the sense that they were aesthetic judgments unconstrained by utilitarian or functional concerns'.[83] But this understanding does not sit neatly with the CJEU expressly excluding aesthetic considerations from the assessment of copyright subsistence in *Cofemel*.[84]

Professor Hugenholtz and Quintais regard creative choices as referring to the level of creativity which is required for copyright to subsist.[85] However, as they observe, the CJEU mentions creative choices and creativity without measuring them in degrees.[86] Indeed, if the CJEU had intended to conceptualise creativity as a standard (as was the case in some EU Members States) it would have to set a threshold. In the absence of any such qualitative threshold in the CJEU's case law, it can be inferred that the CJEU itself probably does not understand creative choices as choices of a certain creative quality.

[79] A similar critical observation can be found with respect to *FAPL* in Justine Pila and Paul Torremans, *European Intellectual Property Law* 2nd edn (OUP 2019) 263.

[80] This is a high-level principle and, as such, it has a limited informational value for this book which digs deeper into what constitutes free, creative and personal choices.

[81] *Infopaq* (n 42).

[82] *Football Dataco* (n 21).

[83] Patrick Goold, 'Artificial Authors: Case Studies of Copyright in Works of Machine Learning' (2020) 67 *J Copyright Soc'y USA* 427, 430.

[84] *Cofemel* (n 59).

[85] Bernt Hugenholtz and João Quintais, 'Copyright and Artificial Creation: Does EU Copyright Law Protect AI-Assisted Output?' (2021) 8 *IIC* 1190, 2021.

[86] ibid.

Similarly, Professors van Gompel and Lavik argue that the wording 'the author's own intellectual creation' suggests a requirement of minimal creativity which they find to be a qualitative element.[87] They also argue that it may be unavoidable for courts to engage in some kind of quality assessment where a distinction must be made between 'just enough creativity' and a commonplace subject matter.[88]

In contrast to the above conceptions of creativity and creative choices, this book argues that CJEU's creative choices should rather be understood in causal terms, ie those that lead to the creation of a work.[89] Somewhat similarly, albeit drawing on US copyright law, Professor Balganesh proposes to examine a 'human act as the cause of relevance from a host of background conditions'[90] and recognises an 'independent copyrightable causation requirement'.[91] For this purpose, he also emphasises the telling potency of the process of creation.[92] When formulating his causation requirement, Balganesh uses analogy with tort law and the theories of causation established therein.[93]

However, neither Balganesh's causation requirement nor tort law theories of causation (such as the NESS test)[94] are followed here because these do not match the needs of EU copyright law.[95] Even if some processes of creation of an authorial work may be complex, they are neither as complex nor as varied as those

[87] Stef van Gompel and Erlend Lavik, 'Quality, Merit, Aesthetics and Purpose: An Inquiry into EU Copyright Law's Eschewal of Other Criteria than Originality' (2013) 236 *RIDA* 101, 107.

[88] ibid.

[89] This is plausible to argue also in the light of other language versions of 'creative' choices. For instance, the German version uses the synonyms '*kreativ*' and '*schöpferisch*' interchangeably while the French one uses '*créatif*' in all cases.

Compare the language versions of *Cofemel* (n 59) para 30: '[...] it follows from the Court's settled case-law that, if a subject matter is to be capable of being regarded as original, it is both necessary and sufficient that the subject matter reflects the personality of its author, as an expression of his free and creative choices [...]'. / '[...] *nach ständiger Rechtsprechung des Gerichtshofs ein Gegenstand erst bzw. bereits dann als Original angesehen werden, wenn er die Persönlichkeit seines Urhebers widerspiegelt, indem er dessen freie kreative Entscheidungen zum Ausdruck bringt* [...]'. / '[...] *il découle de la jurisprudence constante de la Cour que, pour qu'un objet puisse être regardé comme original, il est à la fois nécessaire et suffisant que celui-ci reflète la personnalité de son auteur, en manifestant les choix libres et créatifs de ce dernier* [...]'.

Compare also *Cofemel* (n 59) para 54: 'Second, it is admittedly the case that aesthetic considerations play a part in creative activity.' / '*Zum anderen trifft es zwar zu, dass ästhetische Erwägungen Teil der schöpferischen Tätigkeit sind.*' / '*D'autre part, il est certes vrai que des considérations d'ordre esthétique participent de l'activité créative.*'

[90] Shyamkrishna Balganesh, 'Causing Copyright' (2017) 117 *Colum L Rev* 1, 50.

[91] ibid 9.

[92] ibid 48.

[93] ibid 47.

[94] Sandy Steel, *Proof of Causation in Tort Law* (CUP 2015) 16–17 and 26.

[95] Balganesh himself recognises the limitations of natural causation tests and supplements them with 'legal creation' to sustain the claim: 'Legal creation asks whether the identified human agency ought to lead to an authorship claim as a matter of copyright's goals and principles, even after the court has epistemically identified that agency as the cause of the work.' But this creates its own issues in need of mitigation, see Balganesh (n 90) 61ff.

chains of events that lead to harm which may take an almost infinite number of forms. Second, there are social preconceptions and expectations about creating works that already operate within copyright law.[96] Third, granting copyright under uncertainty is not as acute nor as justified as attribution of liability for harm under uncertainty in tort law. The function of tort law is allocation and redistribution of loss[97] which is different from the objectives of copyright to reward and incentivise creativity.

Should the idea of authorship as causal relationship be entertained further, a revised NESS test proposed by Professor Steel would be a better fit for copyright causation. '[C] counts as a cause of e if it is necessary for the sufficiency of a concretely specified set sufficient for e, where sufficiency may be determined both by physical laws of nature and by the requirement of a rule or set of rules.'[98] This test is based on natural causation and mitigated by legal causation.

An even more suitable option seems to be a purely legal causation test as formulated by Professor Koziol: 'the legally effective cause, a link which certainly has its point of departure in natural causation, but which is determined by legal weightings and can be much narrower than natural causation.'[99] However, if these legally effective causes are translated into the existing copyright law doctrine, one immediately realises that those legally effective causes of authorial works are, in effect, the authorial contributions. Therefore, to keep things simple, this chapter approaches EU creative choices as choices that lead to the creation of a work. In other words, they should be understood as the building or constitutive choices. Further below, the CJEU's case law is analysed through this prism.

To reiterate, the CJEU held in *Infopaq* that what matters for determining the author's own intellectual creation is realising 'the choice, sequence and combination of those words'[100] (ie the constitutive elements or the building blocks of a literary work) through which 'the author may express his creativity in an original manner and achieve a result which is an intellectual creation'.[101] If creative choices are understood as the building or constitutive choices then the creativity mentioned in *Infopaq* should be read as the author's ability to make a subject matter come into being – or 'creative ability' as the CJEU put it in *Football Dataco*.[102]

[96] For example, the only shop in a village has in stock green, black, and yellow paint. Any artist dependent on this stock will necessarily paint with green, black, yellow, brown and/or blue colours (blue and brown and any shades thereof). Thereby, the shop owner's choice as to which colours to stock in his shop is a necessarily sufficient condition for a painting created using these colours. However, the shop owner's stocking choice is legally irrelevant for authorship of the painting, despite its being a contribution that satisfies the NESS test.

[97] James Goudkamp and Donal Nolan (eds), *Winfield & Jolowicz on Tort* 20th edn (Sweet & Maxwell 2020) 1–002.

[98] Steel (n 94) 33.

[99] Helmut Koziol, 'Natural and Legal Causation' in Luboš Tichý (ed), *Causation in Law* (Eva Rozkotová – IFEC 2008) 60.

[100] *Infopaq* (n 42) para 45.

[101] ibid.

[102] *Football Dataco* (n 21) para 38.

In *Funke Medien*, the CJEU found in relation to military reports that

> [...] it is for the national court to ascertain whether, in drawing up those reports, the author was able to make free and creative choices capable of conveying to the reader the originality of the subject matter at issue, the originality of which arises from the choice, sequence and combination of the words by which the author expressed his or her creativity in an original manner and achieved a result which is an intellectual creation [...], whereas the mere intellectual effort and skill of creating those reports are not relevant in that.[103]

In this judgment, the CJEU clearly distinguished the activity of choosing, sequencing and combining the words in the process of drawing up the reports as the only activity relevant for copyright. It contrasted this with the intellectual activity invested in creating the contents of the reports. Therefore, the building choices relevant for copyright were only those concerning the formulation, expression and presentation of the facts (in words) contained in the reports.

In *Painer*, the CJEU stated that, in principle, a portrait photograph can be an eligible subject matter because it allows a photographer to make 'free and creative choices in several ways and at various points in its production'.[104] A non-exhaustive list of choices available to a photographer was suggested by the CJEU.

> In the preparation phase, the photographer can choose the background, the subject's pose and the lighting. When taking a portrait photograph, he can choose the framing, the angle of view and the atmosphere created. Finally, when selecting the snapshot, the photographer may choose from a variety of developing techniques the one he wishes to adopt or, where appropriate, use computer software.[105]

In effect, the CJEU indicated what it regarded as the constitutive elements of a photographic work. However, this is the level of detail into which it rarely goes.[106]

In *Painer* the CJEU suggests that not only choices related to the building blocks of a photograph such as the colour of background, angle of view, etc, but also choices as to the techniques and software count as free and creative choices. While the choices as to the constitutive elements are immediately reflected in the final expression, the choices as to the software, possibly one running machine-learning algorithms, are rather higher-level choices which are not in such an immediate proximity to the final expression.

[103] Case C-469/17 *Funke Medien NRW GmbH v Bundesrepublik Deutschland* [2019] EU:C:2019:623, para 23.

[104] Case C-145/10 *Eva-Maria Painer v Standard VerlagsGmbH and Others* [2012] EU:C:2011:798, para 90.

[105] ibid para 91.

[106] Hugenholtz and Quintais refer to *Painer* in relation to AI-assisted outputs as well. They use it to model the creative process around three stages: conception, execution, redaction. According to them, choices in all these stages should be sufficient to find originality in AI-assisted outputs. So, in contrast to my suggestion, they do not seem to discriminate between choices as to the expressive elements and as to the means, including the use of an AI-driven system. Hugenholtz and Quintais (n 85).

Another example of high-level choices is to decide to take pictures only on sunny days. This undoubtedly will have an impact on the final expression. However, the choices as to the angle of the shot and lighting under which a photographer presses the shutter button rather than the decision to take pictures only on sunny days are immediately reflected in the expression. For this reason, only the former choices should be regarded as the relevant building choices.

In *Funke Medien* the CJEU seems to be clearer on this matter. In that decision, the CJEU did not find the choices as to the creation of the content of the military reports relevant for assessing their copyright eligibility,[107] even though the content of the military reports necessarily had an impact on the final expression (assuming the expression communicated the content). Nonetheless, the choices as to the report content were arguably not as close to the final expression as the choice, sequence and combination of the words.

Similarly to *Funke Medien*, in *SAS Institute*, the CJEU found that the high-level choices of which programming language to use, what the computer program should do (ie its functionality) or data formats do not count as constitutive of the expression of the computer program (though they necessarily have an impact on the expression).[108] By analogy to the *SAS Institute*, the choice of language in which a novel is written has an impact on its expression; however, such a choice does not amount to a creative choice relevant for copyright subsistence.

Hence, only creative choices in the sense of choices that directly and immediately determine the expressive elements and that are made in the process of work's creation are relevant for the assessment of EU originality. This is supported by the CJEU's reasoning in *Infopaq*, *Funke Medien* and *SAS Institute*, with *Painer* being ambiguous. Moreover, *Infopaq* as well as *Painer* imply that whether the choices are creative or not depends not only on the proximity of the choices to the expression but also on the type of subject matter. Therefore, in practice, identifying the right creative choices will be easier in relation to traditional and well-established works such as novels or musical compositions and less so in relation to non-conventional subject matter such as TV programme formats or sports moves.[109]

Author's Own Choices

Author's own choices are implicitly present in the CJEU's copyright assessment. However, they have not yet been addressed separately from the free and creative choices. The author's own (or personal) choices should be understood as referring to the author and their relationship to the work. As the CJEU held in *Painer*, the

[107] *Funke Medien* (n 103) 24.
[108] *SAS Institute* (n 14) paras 39–41.
[109] For further examples see Enrico Bonadio and Nicola Lucchi, *Non-conventional Copyright: Do New and Atypical Works Deserve Protection?* (Edward Elgar Publishing 2018).

choices made by the author must be their own in the sense that, by making those choices, the author stamps 'the work created with his "personal touch"'.[110] The CJEU put the same in other words in *Cofemel*: the work must reflect 'the freedom of choice and personality of its author'.[111]

While Professor Rosati in her comprehensive commentary on EU copyright writes that neither *Cofemel* nor *Brompton Bicycle* 'add [...] anything that was not known already',[112] this book regards *Cofemel* as a significant, albeit consistent, development. This is because it foregrounds personal choice[113] by stating that 'if a subject matter is to be capable of being regarded as original, it is both necessary and sufficient that the subject matter reflects the personality of its author, as an expression of his free and creative choices'.[114] In other words, according to the CJEU, the reflection of author's personality in the final expression is the necessary and sufficient condition for originality.

The problem with conditioning EU copyright on the 'author's own intellectual creation' reflecting the author's personality is that EU copyright legislation does not define the general notion of 'author'. As stated by Professor Quaedvlieg, 'European harmonization on the issue of authorship and ownership is minimal'.[115] Since there is no (general) definition of author in either international or EU instruments, its meaning is left to be determined by the Member States.[116] Recital 16 of the Term Directive states that '[t]he question of authorship of the whole or a part of a work is a question of fact which the national courts may have to decide'.[117]

The exceptions are computer programs and databases which have their authors defined at the EU level, but the real-life effects of these definitions may be questioned. The Computer Programs Directive states that the author of a computer program is the natural person who created the program or the juridical person designated as the right holder if the national law so provides.[118] Similarly, according to the Database Directive, the author of a database is the natural person

[110] *Painer* (n 104) paras 89, 92.

[111] *Cofemel* (n 59) para 54.

[112] Eleonora Rosati, *Copyright and the Court of Justice of the European Union* (OUP 2024) 145.

[113] Scholarship commenting on *Cofemel* focused mostly on the copyright and design law interface, whereas its impact on copyright subsistence attracted little attention. Marianne Levin, 'The *Cofemel* Revolution – Originality, Equality and Neutrality' in Rosati (n 38) 82, Annette Kur, 'Unité de l'art is here to stay – *Cofemel* and its Consequences' (2020) 4 *JIPIL* 290. Matthias Leistner, 'Einheitlicher europäischer Werkbegriff auch im Bereich der angewandten Kunst' [2009] *GRUR* 1114, Eleonora Rosati, 'CJEU Rules that Copyright Protection for Designs Only Requires Sufficient Originality' (2019) 12 *JIPIL* 931. For the problem of overlap see Estelle Derclaye (ed) *The Copyright-Designs Interface* (CUP 2018).

[114] *Cofemel* (n 59) para 30.

[115] Antoon Quaedvlieg, 'Authorship and Ownership: Authors, Entrepreneurs and Rights' in Tatiana-Helenē Synodinou (ed), *Codification of European Copyright Law: Challenges and Perspectives* (Wolters Kluwer Law & Business 2012) 230.

[116] Jeremy Phillips, 'Authorship, Ownership, Wikiship: Copyright in the 21st Century' in Estelle Derclaye, *Research Handbook on the Future of EU Copyright* (Edward Elgar 2009) 204.

[117] Term Directive, recital 16.

[118] Computer Programs Directive, art 2(1).

who created it or the juridical person designated as the right holder by national legislation.[119]

Despite the uncertainty around the concept of author at the EU level, Quaedvlieg reads into EU copyright law a preference for the continental creator doctrine. As he argues: '[w]hilst the software and database directives pretend to refrain from harmonising the allocation of authorship, they circumspectly transpire that a preference is felt for the creator.'[120] He adds that, in the EU, in contrast with the traditional conception of author-creator, the creator doctrine seems to be founded on 'economic considerations of fostering innovation'.[121] It should be added that EU copyright law aims to achieve also non-economic objectives, ie to safeguard 'the independence and dignity of artistic creators and performers'.[122] This clearly indicates that copyright in the EU serves human creators, human performers and their personality attributes.

EU copyright law is slightly more specific about film authorship. In relation to a cinematographic or audiovisual work, its 'principal director shall be considered its author or one of its authors'.[123] The principal director also enjoys special treatment in their capacity as author under EU copyright. In *Luksan*, the CJEU confirmed that a director of a film cannot be deprived of their authorship by the national legislation vesting authorship in other persons (so that the legislation excludes them).[124] The CJEU also held that the author under EU copyright law, here the film director, cannot be deprived of the fair compensation provided for in Article 5(2)(b) of the InfoSoc Directive.[125]

Thus, the CJEU stepped in to protect not only the principal director's authorship as a social status, but also the fundamental economic right flowing from authorship. It did so by making clear that rules vesting those rights in authors are *ius cogens*. Driven by a similar logic, the recitals of the Rental and Lending Directive emphasise that, even if the economic rights are exploited by other persons, the authors and performers should have an inalienable right to equitable remuneration for the rental of their work and fixations of their performance.[126] *Luksan*, as well as the above-mentioned legislation, signal that authorship is taken seriously at EU level.

Nonetheless, neither the Term Directive nor the Rental and Lending Directive explain why the principal director is the one who merits the status of author. The Explanatory Memorandum to the Rental and Lending Directive states that 'at least the principal director of a cinematographic work shall be its author.

[119] Database Directive, art 4.
[120] Quaedvlieg (n 115) 215.
[121] ibid 231.
[122] InfoSoc Directive (n 4) recital 11.
[123] Term Directive, art 2(1). And, 'Member States shall be free to designate other co-authors.' ibid. The same in the Rental and Lending Directive, art 2(2).
[124] Case C-277/10 *Martin Luksan v Petrus van der Let Luksan* [2012] EU:C:2012:65, Ruling 1.
[125] ibid Ruling 3.
[126] Rental and Lending Directive, recital 12.

[… I]t seems useful to take up the proposal of the European Parliament and to safeguard the legal protection for this important group of creative persons in all Member States'.[127] Choosing the director from among all the persons making contributions to creation of films suggests that the EU legislators regard the activity of directing as so important to the creation of a film that it earns the director their status. Or, as put by Quaedvlieg, the principal director's activity is 'central to the creation of the "ensemble" of the film'.[128]

Reading the authorship provision of the Term Directive in conjunction with the case law on originality, it follows that a film is its author's own intellectual creation if the free and creative choices in directing the creation of the film are made personally by its director so that the film reflects their personality. Even if the film (qua work) is not defined, if at least the activity leading to its creation is articulated, individual personal creative choices can be identified.

Synthesis

As shown above, the free, creative and personal choices are, at least conceptually, separable. One can conceive of free choices that are not creative, eg the choice of words when creating a sculpture. There can also be creative choices that are not personal, eg the choice of words made by an AI-driven system when writing a poem. Equally, personal choices in the sense of one's own choices that are neither creative nor free for copyright purposes are conceivable, eg the ensemble of choices of moves when (seriously) playing football. However, can there be personal choices which make the author's personality reflected in the final expression that are not free and creative?

The above search for human aspects of creation reveals that the creative freedom emerges from the CJEU's case law as a vague and unreliable category. The CJEU decides which subject matter does not provide room for creative freedom on an ad hoc basis without clearly formulating any common underlying principle. Nonetheless, it is clear that the creative freedom is rather external to the author and the author is only responsive to what is permitted. If one plays football, no matter how much they aspire to 'create' or 'own' the game, copyright will not subsist in the game. Therefore, for the purposes of detecting human aspects in the EU copyright subsistence criteria, creative freedom can be excluded.

At first glance, the case law gives the impression that free, creative and personal choices are of equal standing. Despite this impression, this chapter argued that the CJEU has elevated the reflection of author's personality to the status of not only the

[127] Proposal for a Council Directive on Rental Right and Lending Right and on Certain Rights Related to Copyright in the Field of Intellectual Property of 30 April 1992, COM(92) 159 final – SYN 319, 2. Available at: https://eur-lex.europa.eu/legal-content/EN/TXT/PDF/?uri=CELEX:51992PC0159&from=EN, last accessed 31 December 2021.

[128] Quaedvlieg (n 115) 228.

necessary but also the sufficient condition for constituting an original work.[129] In this respect, *Cofemel* is as ground-breaking as *Infopaq*. Similarly to *Infopaq* which meant a shift of focus from encapsulation of the subject matter in the traditional categories, *Cofemel* means a shift of focus from free and creative choices to the sole substantive criterion of reflection of personality.

Reflection of Personality

If the CJEU continues to put emphasis on the reflection of personality through making free and creative choices, the CJEU itself and national courts will need to grapple with the concept of personality and how it must be reflected in the work. Primarily, the notion of personality should be given the meaning it has in common, everyday language.[130] Out of the meanings offered by the *Oxford English Dictionary*, and given the context in which the CJEU uses it, the following is the most fitting: personality is '[t]he quality or collection of qualities which makes a person a distinctive individual; the distinctive personal or individual character of a person, esp. of a marked or unusual kind'.[131] Alternatively, the American Psychological Association defines personality as

> the enduring configuration of characteristics and behavior that comprises an individual's unique adjustment to life, including major traits, interests, drives, values, self-concept, abilities, and emotional patterns. Personality is generally viewed as a complex, dynamic integration or totality shaped by many forces, including hereditary and constitutional tendencies; physical maturation; early training; identification with significant individuals and groups; culturally conditioned values and roles; and critical experiences and relationships.[132]

Also, the personality-based theories of property may enrich the understanding of personality for copyright purposes. Both Hegel and Kant give accounts of certain personality attributes on which their justificatory reasons depend. As Hegel writes about the process of self-actualisation through giving a form to things, he refers to dynamic aspects of the self: '[…] the translation into actuality of what one is according to one's concept, i.e. a potentiality, capacity, potency'.[133] Kant relies on

[129] '[I]f a subject matter is to be capable of being regarded as original, it is both necessary and sufficient that the subject matter reflects the personality of its author, as an expression of his free and creative choices'. *Cofemel* (n 59) para 30, discussed more above.

[130] Dissimilarly from 'work', 'personality' clearly is not a special legal term.

[131] Oxford English Dictionary, 'personality (*n.*), sense I.5.b' (*EOD*, June 2024). Available at: www.oed.com/, last accessed 31 July 2024.

[132] APA Dictionary of Psychology, 'Personality' (*dictionary APA*, 19 April 2018). Available at: https://dictionary.apa.org/personality, last accessed 31 July 2024.

[133] Georg Hegel, *Philosophy of Right* as translated in Thomas Knox, *Hegel's Philosophy of Right* (OUP 2015) p 57.

individual free will and human consciousness in the process of appropriation that ultimately serves the expansion of one's freedom and autonomy.[134]

Secondly, any understanding of personality should be formed attentively to the contexts in which the notion is used in EU copyright law. The 'reflection of personality' seems to have appeared first in recital 17 of the (now repealed) Directive 93/98. It stated that '[a] photographic work within the meaning of the Berne Convention is to be considered original if it is the author's own intellectual creation reflecting his personality, no other criteria such as merit or purpose being taken into account'.[135] The CJEU referred to recital 17 in *Painer* when distinguishing between a photographic work and (non-original) photographs: '[a]s stated in recital 17 in the preamble to Directive 93/98, an intellectual creation is an author's own if it reflects the author's personality'.[136] Professor Walter, addressing the legislative history of the Directive 93/98, comments that originality required for computer programs under the Computer Directive served as a model for photographs.[137] However, the Computer Directive does not use the term 'personality'.

Besides the context of photographs, another prominent context was that of *Cofemel*. Against the factual background of this case, the CJEU effectively attempted to draw a line between a work of applied art and (non-original) utilitarian object with reference to 'reflection of personality'.[138] Both these contexts suggest that the 'reflection of personality' was intended to function as a limiting definitional element of the notion of author's own intellectual creation. This means that copyright subsists not in the expression of any intellectual creation, but only in the expression of such an intellectual creation that reflects its author's personality. To give its limiting function full effect, 'personality' should then be construed narrowly.

Lastly, in the light of the purpose and objectives of the InfoSoc Directive, and the objective of a high level of protection in particular, 'personality' should be understood realistically. The more true-to-life the understanding, the more legitimate and sustainable the high level of protection. Additionally, this book argues that a narrow and realistic understanding of the 'reflection of personality' condition would serve authors' interests equally well as the public interests. It would do so by accentuating the human aspects of creation and the intrinsic and social values of human intellectual creations on the one hand and making the expressive subject matter that do not reflect any personality free for the public to use

[134] Robert Merges, *Justifying Intellectual Property* (Harvard University Press 2011) 72.

[135] Directive 93/98/EEC of 29 October 1993 harmonizing the term of protection of copyright and certain related rights [1993] *OJ L 290/9*, rec 17.

[136] Painer (n 104) para 88. See also Case C-161/17 *Land Nordrhein-Westfalen v Dirk Renckhoff* [2018] EU:C:2018:634, para 14.

[137] Michel Walter, 'Term Directive' in Michel Walter and Silke von Lewinski (eds) *European Copyright Law. A Commentary* (OUP 2010) 587.

[138] *Cofemel* (n 59), paras 30 and 54.

on the other. A narrow and realistic understanding of the 'personality' condition would also counterbalance the CJEU's legitimately criticised trend of providing for a robust, generous and (ever-) expanding copyright protection at EU level.[139]

Considering the above, personality for EU copyright purposes may be defined, for instance, as a collection of qualities which makes a person a distinctive individual (in the present), while those qualities are enduring, inherited or acquired throughout the person's life (legacy of the past), and help the person to actualise their potentiality, capacity and potency when the person is wilfully and consciously projecting herself into the world (for the future) in the process of creating an object in the literary or artistic domain. This, of course, is no authoritative definition, but rather one of more possible understandings of personality that could be used in the assessment of copyright subsistence.

Application of the EU Copyright Subsistence Criteria to AI Productions

Given the advancements in AI in particular, a question arises as to whether there could be expressive subject matter that would fall within the literary, scientific and artistic domain and, at the same time, would not express any intellectual creation in the sense of product of human mind. As a matter of fact, such novels, paintings or musical compositions can be generated. While there are AI-driven systems that make free and creative choices in the sense of the CJEU's jurisprudence, these systems can hardly make choices reflecting personality in the sense suggested above. Therefore, those expressive elements that are determined by an AI-driven system do not actually express any intellectual creations nor reflect anyone's personality.[140] Hence, such elements would not amount to work in the sense of the InfoSoc Directive.

To filter out such expressive elements, the EU copyright subsistence criteria should be interpreted so that more emphasis is put on the human aspects of creation, ie the reflection of personality. In this connection, besides the conceptual

[139] For instance, the CJEU repeatedly ruled that the author's rights should be given broad interpretation (Case C-160/15 *GS Media BV v Sanoma Media Netherlands BV and Others* [2016] EU:C:2016:644 para 30) and exceptions to rights must be interpreted strictly (Case C-201/13 *Johan Deckmyn and Vrijheidsfonds VZW v Helena Vandersteen* [2014] EU:C:2014:2132 para 22). Also see the imbalance in the three-step test: Christophe Geiger, Jonathan Griffiths and Reto Hilty, 'Towards a Balanced Interpretation of the "Three Step Test" in Copyright Law' (2008) 30 *EIPR* 489.

[140] It is pertinent to ask whether these objects can reflect the personality of an author of underlying works used in the AI-driven system's training. However, this seems unlikely. As Professor Floridi writes about the relationship between such objects and their intellectual sources, he calls such objects (eg a painting from the Next Rembrandt project) an ectype: 'ectypes can be authentic but unoriginal artefacts' because there is some link to the source, but the subject matter does not originate from that source. Luciano Floridi, 'Artificial Intelligence, Deepfakes and a Future of Ectypes' (2018) 31 *Philos & Technol* 317, 319.

difficulties concerning the notion of personality, an epistemic difficulty presents itself: How do we find and identify the author's personality in the work?

In *Cofemel* the CJEU seems to invite the national court to look for a reflection or manifestation of the author's personality in the subject matter, ie in the final design.[141] In *Brompton Bicycle*, however, the CJEU points to the process of creation as it gives instructions to the national courts to 'account of all the relevant aspects of the present case, as they existed when that subject matter was designed, irrespective of the factors external to and subsequent to the creation of the product'.[142] This should include factors that help 'to reveal what was taken into consideration in [the process of] choosing the shape of the product concerned'.[143]

Given the specific facts of this case, the CJEU seems to have suggested that if certain features of the subject matter, such as its particular shape, were, at some point in time, claimed as technical, possibly even inventive, for the purposes of patent protection, then they can hardly be re-qualified ex post the creation and claimed as choices reflecting author's personality for the purposes of copyright protection.

It makes sense to put the process of creation into the spotlight and *Brompton Bicycle* is the first step in this direction.[144] The fact that the process of creation can reveal more information about the origin of work than the work itself is illustrated by the following example. According to Desbois, a doyen of French copyright law, even if two painters paint the same scenery, each of the two paintings is original because both painters 'have, in effect, expended creative activity, one as the other, when engaging with the same subject independently from each other'.[145] Obviously, one might be unable to tell whether the two paintings were authorial works (or possibly one a copy of another) merely from looking at them, without having any knowledge about their processes of creation. Conversely, the underlying processes of creation reveal that each of the paintings owes its existence to an independent creative activity of each respective author and their own choices, no matter the resemblance of the final results.

Conclusion

Copyright subsistence, as well as the scope of protection, is relatively clear in the case of computer programs and databases since their protected expressive elements are specified in the respective directives. These also provide that authors shall primarily be those natural persons who created the computer programs and databases.

[141] ibid para 54.
[142] *Brompton Bicycle* (n 68) para 37.
[143] ibid para 36.
[144] Though the CJEU did not acknowledge explicitly that such a shift in interpretation was intended.
[145] Henri Desbois, *Le droit d'auteur en France* 3rd edn (Dalloz 1978) 5.

In relation to databases, it can therefore be concluded that copyright subsists only in structural elements (the expressive elements) of those databases whose contents (the building blocks) were arranged and selected so that they reflect personality of the individual who arranged and selected the contents.

Copyright in computer programs is available only for executable elements (the expressive elements) of those computer programs that consist of instructions to run functions (the building blocks) that were selected and combined so that they reflect the personality of the individual who selected and combined the instructions. To reiterate, the materials explaining reasons for harmonising copyright in computer programs proclaim that a computer program is 'the result of a creative intellectual human activity'[146] as any other work.

A similarly structured definition may be offered for films because their authors are defined in the Term Directive. This definition of the author (being the principal director) allows us to conclude that a person can claim authorship of a film if they can prove that the free and creative choices they made when directing the film were personal to them and that the film reflects their personality.

In relation to other subject matter, the general concept of work should be interpreted so that it contains an implicit condition of being an intellectual creation. It can be further inferred from the CJEU's case law that copyright subsists in expressive elements of those works whose building blocks were chosen, sequenced and combined (*Infopaq*) so that they reflect the personality of the individual who made the decisions as to the choice, sequence and combination.

However, a complete picture of copyright subsistence cannot be drawn as further specification of the expressive elements of work (in the general sense) is missing. Neither does EU copyright law lay out any principles for defining expressive elements of work. This could be done through categories of work (as in UK copyright law) or through a positive definition of creative freedom for copyright purposes (what is a literary or artistic domain?) or through the relevant creative activity (as exceptionally done in relation to film).

The problems with identifying expressive elements spill over to identification of the relevant creative choices. If it is unclear which elements are deemed as expressive, then it is difficult to form a clearer idea of the underlying intellectual creation. This complicates the identification of choices that normally lead to its creation, ie creative choices.

In the future, the CJEU may try to fill in these gaps and give more guidance in several ways. It may decide to clear the doubts by positively defining expressive elements of a work and its building blocks. Even if such definitions were achievable, they would likely be too abstract to be practical. Or, the CJEU may put more emphasis on the human aspects of creation. Regardless of whether it does the

[146] Proposal (n 10) [2.2.].

former, it should do the latter. The CJEU should maintain that the reflection of author's personality in the expression is the ultimate indication of (original) work. The CJEU may further shape the interpretation of the concept of work by clarifying its understanding of 'reflection of personality' for copyright purposes. Such a clarification could be supported and informed by the purpose and objectives of the InfoSoc Directive. If the CJEU goes down this path, the evidence and adversarial process on the question of authorship before national courts could do the rest.

At the national level, courts may adopt some principles for assessment of the human aspects of creation that stem from the CJEU's case law. (As the following chapter shows, many equivalent principles already exist at the national level.) Most pertinently in the context of AI productions, the principle of proximity of the result and the relevant creative choices (*Infopaq*) should be observed as the guiding principle when determining creative choices. The closer the choices to the result, the higher the likelihood of them being creative in the sense of the CJEU's jurisprudence and the easier to prove that the author translated their personality into their work through making them. There should be no authorship based on making high-order choices (which flows from *Infopaq*, *Funke Medien* and *SAS Institute* but goes against *Painer*).

In all contexts, the proximity or distance of choices from the result can be discerned more reliably from the process of creation than from the subject matter itself. Then any putative author would need to ascertain how the subject matter in question or some of its elements reflect their personality. Once it is ascertained that the author's personality is reflected in a precisely and objectively identifiable expression, it should follow that the creative choices must have been made and that the subject matter must have offered a sufficient creative freedom to enable the author to stamp their work with their personal touch. This would effectively delegate much of the burden of grappling with authorship to national courts as part of their assessment and evaluation of facts.

7

Authorship in the UK, Germany and France

Introduction

This chapter examines authorship from the standpoint of the author and focuses on what one must do, according to positive law, to become an author. It does so by analysing authorship and authorial contributions for ownership purposes under copyright laws in the UK, France and Germany. More specifically, it looks at the respective constructions of authorship, the significance of the act of creation and activities that constitute the act of creation with a view to conceptualising the relevant human intellectual creative activity.

This task is complicated by the relatively small number of authorship cases. This is likely because authorship is, in principle, presumed (eg if a name purporting to be the author's name appears on copies of the work) until it is disputed.[1] There is also an assumption entrenched that only human beings are capable of creating works in the literary and artistic sphere. Courts thus find themselves seldomly in a position to entertain the nature of authorship.

Despite these difficulties, this chapter selects and analyses the most prominent cases from the UK, France and Germany that touch on authorship. This chapter also highlights the connection between authorship for entitlement purposes and requirements for copyright protection. Building on this connection, it then exposes the flaws in the UK statutory regime for computer-generated works.

Authorship in Positive Law

The United Kingdom

In the UK, copyright in authorial works has a statutory basis and is governed by the Copyright, Designs and Patents Act 1988 (CDPA). The CDPA itself does not state its purpose nor objectives. However, some general sense of copyright law's

[1] Berne Convention, art 15.

purpose and objectives can be drawn from practitioners' and academic commentaries. As put in a leading commentary on the CDPA:

> The original and primary purpose of the copyright laws was and is to encourage and reward authors, composers and artists who create original works […]. A subsidiary purpose was and is to enable authors to prevent premature publication of works; or re-publication of works now repented of. These objects are achieved by giving to the author (or in some cases his employer) and his successors certain exclusive rights to exploit the subject-matter […].[2]

To reiterate, this books deals with copyright in authorial works solely, not with copyright in so-called entrepreneurial works (as explained in the Introduction).

In relation to authorial works, the CDPA defines the author as the actual creator of the work.[3] The *Copinger and Skone James on Copyright* commentary defines the word 'author' as 'the person who originates the protectable elements of that work, whether it be the language used, dramatic incident, musical content or design, as the case may be'.[4] The case law further clarifies the nature of authorship and here it is analysed with the specific focus on the required human intellectual creative activity.

In a recent landmark case on joint authorship, *Kogan v Martin*, the Court of Appeal listed the following aspects of joint authorship, '(a) collaboration, (b) authorship, (c) contribution and (d) non-distinctness of contribution'.[5] Out of these aspects, this book considers just the content discussed under authorship, contribution and to some extent collaboration as relevant.

For the purposes of conceptualising authorship and identifying authorial contributions (and while bearing in mind that joint authorship is a unitary concept[6]), the aspect of collaboration does not need to be analysed at length. This is because collaboration is mainly about, as put by the Court of Appeal, 'the true nature of the interaction between parties in relation to the work',[7] hence it is less about the relationship of each person to the work (ie the 'individualistic' view of authorship).

What is also pertinent in the AI context, collaboration can happen only between 'people who created'[8] the work. Hence, it can be inferred that no collaboration in the sense required by the CDPA is conceivable between a person and an AI-driven system. Similarly, the aspect of non-distinctness of contributions is too specific to joint authorship. The fact of having more authorial contributions that

[2] Michael Tappin and others, *Laddie, Prescott and Vitoria: The Modern Law of Copyright* 5th edn (Lexis 2018) [1.20].

[3] CDPA 1988, s 9(1).

[4] Nicholas Caddick, Gwilym Harbottle and Uma Suthersanen, *Copinger and Skone James on Copyright*, vol I, 18th edn (Sweet & Maxwell 2020) [4–22].

[5] *Kogan v Martin* [2019] EWCA Civ 1645, [2020] FSR 3 [31].

[6] ibid.

[7] ibid [33]. This is not to conceal the fact that in the *Kogan v Martin* case collaboration between the parties was the crucial point on which the case turned. See a commentary on the criterion 'collaboration' in Daniela Simone, '*Kogan v Martin*: A New Framework for Joint Authorship in Copyright Law' (2020) 83 *MLR* 877, 883–885.

[8] ibid [53].

cannot be separated constitutes the rationale behind creating joint authorship as a self-standing legislative category.[9]

Therefore, the following principles formulated by the Court of Appeal in *Kogan v Martin* are relevant for individual authorship:

(i) creating a work comprising the activity of coming up with a 'design as to its general outline'[10] and expanding 'labour of working it out';[11]
(ii) exercising 'skill and effort involved in creating, selecting or gathering together the detailed concepts or emotions which the words have fixed in writing which is protected in the case of a literary or dramatic work, whether the work is one of sole or joint authorship';[12]
(iii) making the right kind of contribution relative to the work in question ('[w]hat counts as an authorial contribution is acutely sensitive to the nature of the copyright work in question'[13]) eg devising a plot is relevant for creation of a dramatic or literary work;[14] and
(iv) contributing elements which expressed person's own intellectual creation in the sense of *Infopaq* (which includes the idea/expression dichotomy considerations).[15]

In the restatement of joint authorship, the Court of Appeal drew on EU copyright law and *Infopaq* (see Chapter 6) and on domestic cases, most prominently *Cala Homes.*[16] In *Cala Homes*, the High Court attributed joint authorship in architectural drawings for a contribution in the form of information concerning design features conveyed verbally or by means of sketches next to a contribution which consisted of skill and expertise in drawing.[17] Putting this (retrospectively) into the framework given in *Kogan v Martin*, the designing of elevations and floor-plans counted as an authorial intellectual input because they were relevant given the nature of the work at stake – a project drawing – and carried detailed concepts and emotions.

The assessment of facts in *Cala Homes* may be less relevant now because it was decided using the pre-*Infopaq* originality standard. If *Cala Homes* were to be decided today, questions might arise as to whether contributing technical information would satisfy the *Infopaq* test. In terms of the process of creation, in *Cala Homes*, the High Court held that the authorial contribution 'must be in the nature of originating and creating something that finds its way into the finished work'[18] on which logic *Martin v Kogan* proceeded.

[9] ibid [47].
[10] ibid [53].
[11] ibid.
[12] ibid [41].
[13] ibid.
[14] ibid [35] and [42].
[15] ibid.
[16] *Cala Homes (South) Limited v Alfred McAlpine Homes East Limited (No 1)* [1995] FSR 818 (Ch), [1995] 7 WLUK 62.
[17] ibid 835.
[18] ibid 834.

In another joint authorship case, *Fisher v Brooker*, the House of Lords affirmed that composing a memorable organ solo at the beginning of the work, and an organ melody which is a counterpoint throughout most of the whole length of the work was a contribution significant enough to amount to an authorial contribution.[19] Also, in relation to a musical work, in *Hadley v Kemp* the High Court held that 'develop[ing] and fix[ing] in [author's] musical consciousness the melody, the chords, the rhythm and the general structure of the song from beginning to end as well as the lyrics'[20] counts as authorial contribution whereas mere singing and playing instruments by other members of a band in their own creative ways did not. The key distinction was drawn between the 'composition or creation of a musical work on the one hand and performance or interpretation of it on the other'[21] with the performance being arguably outside the creative process itself.

That the line between creating and interpreting is difficult to draw follows from *Sawkins v Hyperion.*[22] Mr Sawkins added or modified a figured bass line in two compositions and re-created missing viola parts in respect of a half of another's musical composition with the intention to preserve the identity of another's work.[23] The Court of Appeal considered this enough to amount to an authorial contribution because it produced 'sufficient aural and musical significance to attract copyright'.[24] In the present view, the labour of interpretating and restoring a preexisting musical composition should not have been assessed as creative.

Similarly to *Cala Homes*, *Sawkins v Hyperion* was decided before *Infopaq* and is thus based on the pre-*Infopaq* originality standard. Applying the *Infopaq* standard and, more specifically, if the court were asked whether the re-created work reflected its original author's personality or that of its interpreter, the conclusions might well have been different. This is obvious especially against the factual findings that '[i]t was the aim of Dr Sawkins, so far as was possible, to reproduce faithfully Lalande's music in the form of an accurate edition close to the composer's original intentions'.[25]

The distinction between post-creative and creative activity was made appropriately by Justice Laddie (as he then was) in *Fylde Microsystems.* Justice Laddie found that the skill, time and effort invested into ensuring that a piece of software performed the way it was supposed to, ie a beta-testing activity, did not substantiate claims of authorship.[26] No doubt, the activity of testing software contributes to improvements of the software, enhances its usability (similarly to the musical

[19] *Fisher v Brooker* [2009] UKHL 41, [2009] FSR 25 (2009).
[20] *Hadley v Kemp* [1999] EMLR 589 (ChD), [1999] 4 WLUK 377, 591.
[21] ibid 646.
[22] *Sawkins v Hyperion Records Ltd* [2005] EWCA Civ 565, [2005] 1 WLR 3281.
[23] ibid [21]–[26].
[24] ibid [56].
[25] ibid. [22].
[26] *Fylde Microsystems Ltd v Key Radio Systems Ltd* [1998] FSR 449, [1998] 2 WLUK 20.

score edited by Mr Sawkins) and requires an intellectual activity, but Justice Laddie was correct not to consider it a software-creating activity.[27]

Historically, demonstrating a mechanical executive activity was sufficient for claiming authorship. In *Walter v Lane*, the House of Lords found 'considerable intellectual skill and brain labour beyond the mere mechanical operation of writing'[28] in the activity of taking notes 'in shorthand, word for word, transcrib[ing] them verbatim in longhand, carefully correct[ing] and revis[ing] and punctuat[ing] them'[29] as meritorious of copyright.

Somewhat similarly to *Walter v Lane*, in *Cummins v Bond*, despite the plaintiff not claiming authorship of ideas nor expressions of ideas in the manuscript, she was awarded copyright for her own, very speedy and tiresome automatic writing – 'over 2000 words in an hour and a half without any pause'.[30] In this connection, even contemporary commentators are confident that 'the general principle that an original literary work (other than a database) requires no act of the imagination and no intellectual skill beyond that of knowing how to read and write remains true'.[31]

Walter v Lane was embraced in *Sawkins v Hyperion* as still being good law. The bridge between them was the effort, skill and time the journalist spent in correcting and editing another's speech and the effort, skill and time Mr Sawkins spent in restoring another's compositions. Contrary to the Court of Appeal in *Sawkins v Hyperion*, Richard Arnold still finds *Walter v Lane* to be good law, but only with respect to the need to identify the work and all of its constituent elements that affect its perception (but not in respect of authorship).[32] This chapter agrees with him because, in terms of authorship, *Walter v Lane* is incompatible with the *Infopaq* standard which continues to be followed by the UK courts.

Whilst this remains largely uncommented, the other shared element of *Walter v Lane*, *Cummins v Bond* and *Sawkins v Hyperion* is that in these cases the plaintiffs were standing against defendants with no creative connection to the works whatsoever. Persons with creative inputs and possibly stronger authorship claims than the plaintiffs themselves either did not (Lord Rosebery in *Walter v Lane*) or could not (an external psychic agent in *Cummins v Bond* and the Baroque composer Lalande in *Sawkins v Hyperion*) claim authorship. These cases hence (albeit for practical reasons) skewed authorship towards editing or mechanical activities and thus lowered the pre-*Infopaq* authorship standard.

Coming back to the *Kogan v Martin* litigation, this chapter approaches the decision handed down on retrial, *Martin v Kogan II*,[33] as a model for assessment

[27] ibid.
[28] *Walter v Lane* [1900] AC 539 (HL) 556.
[29] ibid.
[30] *Cummins v Bond* [1927] 1 Ch 167, 168.
[31] Tappin and others (n 2) [3.55].
[32] Richard Arnold, 'Walter v Lane Revisited (Again)' (2021) 2 *IPQ* 67.
[33] *Martin v Kogan II* [2021] EWHC 24 (Ch) [2021] FSR 10.

of authorial character of contributions allegedly made by the putative author, Ms Kogan. More specifically, *Martin v Kogan II* is helpful in adopting a bottom-up approach which is driven by facts, information and evidence concerning putative authors, their personalities and their authorial contributions.

The litigation dealt with authorship of a screenplay for a film about life of Florence Foster Jenkins (FFJ), an American socialite, who aspired to become an acclaimed opera singer. The final screenplay was the result of an iterative process of creation and the final product was preceded by drafts to which Ms Kogan contributed in a different measure. The Court of Appeal held that Ms Kogan could rely on all her contributions towards the final screenplay (but at the same time conceded that her contributions after the third draft were limited).[34]

In *Martin v Kogan II*, ie on retrial, Justice Meade went through the process of creation chronologically and examined interactions of the two putative joint authors, Ms Kogan and Mr Martin. Thereby he was able to determine the point in time when the core of the screenplay (or its identity so to say) was formed. In the words of the judge, the beginning of 2012 was found to be 'a critical time in the creation of FFJ when the characters and key plot events were being shaped'.[35] In principle, an authorial contribution must make it from the conception to the materialisation of what is perceived as the core of the final work.

What is noteworthy, as the work in question was a film screenplay about an amateur opera singer and her musical escapades, substantial part of its identity rested on musicality. As put by Justice Mead, 'the sense is very much that Ms Kogan had and used an ability to exploit musicality as part of the plot and the characterization'.[36] The main contributions made by Ms Kogan were found to lie in 'characterisation, musicality, choice of historical incident and musical terminology'.[37] It transpires that the judge was led by the musicality. The contributions resting on musicality were likely to be attributed to Ms Kogan (in joint authorship), including the idea to use FFJ's life as a motive for the film.[38]

The above 'musicality argument' could be further supported by factual findings that Ms Kogan had a musical personality (or identity) whereas Mr Martin (the other joint author) did not. Mr Martin's own account reinforces the argument: 'Ms Kogan commented that she had been writing since she was three, and he replied that he'd been singing since he was three, so perhaps he should join her on stage.'[39] As Mr Martin did not regard Ms Kogan as a writer with a writing personality, so did he not regard himself as a musician with a musical personality. Hence, the musicality contained in the screenplay could not have been attributed to Mr Martin's personality but rather to Ms Kogan's.

[34] ibid [164].
[35] ibid [150].
[36] ibid [241].
[37] ibid [272].
[38] ibid [107].
[39] ibid [154].

To summarise the above case law, but chiefly *Kogan v Martin, Cala Homes* and *Fisher v Brooker* read in the light of *Infopaq*, to make an authorial contribution a person is required to take part in the intellectual conception of the work and in expressing the work and thereby determining the work's identity. The assessment of authorial contribution begins with identifying the expressive elements of the work and the relevant activity which determines these expressive elements and which is thus relevant relative to the nature of the copyright work (*Kogan v Martin*). This includes activities closer to ideas than the form, eg having an idea to use a particular motive for a film (together with) conceiving of and designing a plot, developing characters and inserting musicality in a screenplay for a musical film or composing a memorable organ solo. According to more recent cases, this likely excludes post-creative activities such as interpreting, restoring, fixation, editing or suggesting improvements (which is supported by *Kogan v Martin, Fylde Microsystems* and *Hadley v Kemp*, but goes against *Walter v Lane, Cummins v Bond* and *Sawkins v Hyperion*).

France

In France, an author's right(s), ie copyright in authorial works, is codified in the *Code de la propriété intellectuelle* (French Intellectual Property Code or Code).[40] The French Intellectual Property Code does not state either its purpose or objectives. In general, these began to develop during the Enlightenment.[41] Since then, they have been subject to debate among French legal scholars. There are political proclamations and court judgments that affirm the natural rights origin of an author's right. Equally, accounts that dispute or vehemently reject this position can be found.[42]

Professors Vivant and Brugière refer to the dualist nature of author's right in France and postulate that this implies that there are two objectives of copyright law. Those are to protect the moral interests of authors and to satisfy their proprietary interests.[43] Similarly, to describe the objective of copyright law in France, Bertrand refers to the CJEU's formulation that 'the essential function of author's right is to secure moral rights in the work and reward the creative effort of the author'.[44]

Professor Gautier defines an author's right as 'the right to exploit a thing created by the mind under such material and moral circumstances as chosen by

[40] Consolidated by the statute n° 92-597 of 1 July 1992 in relation to the intellectual property code, as amended at 26 November 2021.

[41] André Bertrand, *Droit d'auteur* 3rd edn (Dalloz 2010) 8.

[42] For an overview see ibid 42, 48 ff.

[43] Michel Vivant and Jean-Michel Brugière, *Droit d'auteur et droits voisins* 4th edn (Dalloz 2019) 57.

[44] '*La function essentielle du droit d'auteur est d'assurer la protection morale de l'œvre et la remuneration de l'apport créateur de l'auteur.*' Bertrand (n 41) 52 referring to Case T-69/89 *RTE v Commission* [1991] EU:T:1991:39.

the person who was at its origin'.[45] He emphasises two main aspects of author's right: authors retain authority over the work (in particular the right to decide when it will be disclosed to the public); and authors must be compensated for their work.[46] Professor Desbois, whose first treatise was published in 1950, put the human author and humanism at the heart of authors' rights.[47] Under his intellectual influence, humanism became central to the new bill which was later passed into law in 1957 (ie the first modern copyright statute which was codified into the Code in 1992).[48]

Under French Law, the author's right subsists in a work from the moment of its creation.[49] As for the human nature of authorship, French legal scholarship cites the principle that only the natural person who created the work is its author and *ab initio* entitled to author's right.[50] One of the first sentences in the Dalloz commentary states that author's right is the creator's right.[51] Professor Caron describes the human nature of the author as one of the fundamental dogmas of French copyright law.[52]

There is a noteworthy statutory exception to this creator doctrine though.[53] Since the end of the nineteenth century, French law recognises the author's right in journals, encyclopaedias and dictionaries (together referred to as collective works) that initially belong to a juridical person.[54] This does not mean that juridical persons enjoy authorial status. This exception merely creates a legal fiction under which juridical persons are deemed to create in the sense that they initiate a project for a collective work, organise the work of authors of its parts and publish the collective (indivisible) work under their name.[55]

Further, pursuant to article L 111-2 of the Code, '[a] work is deemed created, regardless of whether it is published, due to the fact of bringing into being, even if an incomplete, conception of the author'.[56] The Code does not specify the act of creation in general, just exceptionally, such as in relation to an audio-visual work which is authored by 'a person or persons who bring into being the intellectual

[45] '[…] *le droit d'exploiter une chose créée par l'esprit, dans les conditions matérielles et morales posées par celui qui est à son origine*.' Pierre-Yves Gautier, *Propriété littéraire et artistique* 11th edn (PUF 2019) 25.

[46] ibid.

[47] Christophe Caron, *Droit d'auteur et droits voisins* 6th edn (LexisNexis 2020) 33.

[48] ibid.

[49] French Intellectual Property Code, art L111-1.

[50] Caron (n 47) 179. Bertrand (n 41) 181, Michel Vivant and Jean-Michel Brugière, *Droit d'auteur et droits voisins* 4th edn (Dalloz 2016) 353.

[51] Pierre Sirinelli and others, *Code de la propriété intellectuelle : annoté & commenté* 24th edn (Dalloz 2024) 12.

[52] Caron (n 47) 179.

[53] French Intellectual Property Code, art L113-2.

[54] Bertrand (n 41) 204–5.

[55] Author's rights may belong initially (from the point of creation) to juridical persons also in case of computer programs created by employees or salaried officials. ibid 181. Vivant and Brugière (n 43) 358.

[56] '*L'œuvre est réputée créée, indépendamment de toute divulgation publique, du seul fait de la réalisation, même inachevée, de la conception de l'auteur*.' Code, art L 111-2.

creation of that work'.[57] Caron understands the act of creation that gives rise to author's right as 'an intervention of a human being that is necessarily conscious and modifies the reality'.[58] He adds that 'a robot cannot create in the sense of copyright law'[59] because he does not have human conscience.[60] On the other hand, Vivant and Brugière agree with the Dutch High court which had held that an original creation does not require 'conscious choices'.[61]

Betrand summarises the text of the Code as he writes that the act of creation should be regarded as having two phases, '(i) an intellectual "conception" and (ii) its "realisation" in a material form'.[62] Portron elaborates on account of the 'conception' that it 'is a purely intelligible quality of the "work of the mind"'.[63] Demonstration of its presence in the subject matter enables judges to make conclusions as to the 'imprint of the personality of its author'.[64] Interestingly, the bill which was passed into the first modern French copyright statute of 1957 used words (realisation of) 'the thought of the author'[65] instead of realisation of the 'conception of the author'.

French courts can shed some more light on what a person must do to become a creator in terms of quality and relevance of their activity, its occurrence in the process of creation and the way the activity must determine expressive elements of subject matter. It is noteworthy that French judgments (in particular those coming from the French Supreme Court) do not tend to be as elaborate as those coming from the UK courts, hence they offer relatively limited insights.

When addressing the relevance and quality of contribution in one case, the French Supreme Court reasoned that a chef who was filmed while he was preparing dishes did not manage to prove his creative contribution to the intellectual activities of conceiving, shooting and editing the audio-visual work (that documented his culinary skills).[66] Similarly, the Court of Appeal in Paris found that an artist who supplied information about his life and directly contributed to dialogues for a film about lives of young people in Paris was not the film's author.[67] The reason was that these contributions were not specific and concrete enough

[57] '*Ont la qualité d'auteur d'une œuvre audiovisuelle la ou les personnes physiques qui réalisent la création intellectuelle de cette œuvre*.' Code, art L113-7.

[58] '[U]*ne intervention humaine, qui est nécessairement consciente et qui modifie la réalité*.' Caron (n 47) 60.

[59] '[…] *un robot ne peut pas créer au sense du droit d'auteur* […]' ibid 62.

[60] ibid 64.

[61] Vivant and Brugière (n 43) 163 citing Hoge Raad of 30 May 2008 as taken from Bernt Hugenholtz, 'Chronique des Pays-Bas' (2010) 226 *RIDA* 305.

[62] Bertrand (n 41) 182.

[63] Alexandre Portron, *Le fait de la création en droit d'auteur français* (LDGJ 2021) 57.

[64] ibid.

[65] Jean Escarra, 'Le projet de la loi français sur la propriété littéraire et artistique' (1954) V *RIDA* 3, 9.

[66] Cour de cassation, Decision of 5 February 2002 (2002) 193 RIDA 373. In a similar vein, the fact that a painter and his creative process of painting was the subject of a film did not earn him the status of joint author in relation to that film. Cour de cassation, Decision of 3 November 1988 (1989) 142 *RIDA* 299.

[67] Cour d'appel de Paris, Decision of 16 January 1992 (1992) 152 *RIDA* 204.

in comparison with a contribution in a determined form such as a screenplay in writing, or a direct intervention into shooting of the film with a personal power to make decisions.[68]

According to the Court of Appeal in Paris, a linguist who collected, faithfully transcribed and arranged Cajun words and folklore songs (and had those published in a dictionary and an anthology respectively) did not merit an author's right over the content, ie the individual words or songs.[69] This was despite the effort he had to exert to overcome all the difficulties in the process of their collection and transcription and his argument that the faithfulness of reproduction (of the words and songs) reflected his personality.[70] However, he could claim an author's right in relation to 'the selection and the arrangement'.[71]

A study of oligoelements deficiencies in ruminants was found to be marked by the personality of persons who made the synthesis of scientific knowledge in the field. Whereas a person who made a personal synthesis of the collected information and assumed editing of the synthesis was recognised as the author of the study, a person who collected the sources and gave consultation in the editing phase was not recognised as such. This was because in making his (non-authorial) contribution, he did not interfere with the creative freedom of the author.[72]

That the author-creator's personality must flow from the conception to the realisation of the work and be perceivable in the final subject matter was affirmed by the French Supreme Court in *Guino v Renoir*.[73] A sculptor, Guino, made several sculptures with his own hands based on the original paintings of his teacher, Renoir. The teacher also initiated and directed the creation of the sculptures and assumed their divulgation under his name. However, the teacher could not and did not intervene in the execution of those sculptures. The French Supreme Court reasoned that the underlying sculptures reveal that 'certain postures, certain expressions were accepted and were not dictated [by the teacher] and [they] mark an imprint of the personal creative talent [of the sculptor] and lastly the sculptures would have been different had they been [created] solely by [the teacher]'.[74]

At the same time, the mere act of execution of a work that does not entail any intellectual contribution would not give rise to authorship.[75] There is a recent judgment of the French Supreme Court affirming that authorship may be attributed to a person who did not participate in the execution of a sculpture provided that the underlying 'work had been executed according to his [the author's] instructions

[68] ibid.

[69] Cour d'appel de Paris, Decision of 14 January 1992 (1992) 152 RIDA 198, 201.

[70] ibid.

[71] ibid.

[72] Cour d'appel de Paris, Decision of 20 April 1989 (1990) 143 *RIDA* 317.

[73] Cour de cassation, Decision of 13 November 1973, n° 71-14.469.

[74] '[…] *certaines attitudes, certaines expressions avaient été acceptées et non dictées par b … et marquaient "l'empreinte du talent créateur personnel de guino" et enfin que les sculptures "auraient été autres si elles avaient été l'y … du seul b …"*', ibid.

[75] Portron (n 63) 235.

and under his control'.[76] Portron comments that this was a case of mechanical realisation whereby the person does not express their personality but merely contributes to the expression of another's personality.[77]

As for post-creative activities, Caron, who summarises the case law on restoration and renovation of works, concludes that where the process of restoration of a work requires the most strict fidelity to the image and the spirit of the original work and the restorer did not try to modify the design, arrangement and composition of the preceding work, the restorer does not merit the status of author.[78]

As for pre-creative activities, apparently making a contribution just towards conception but not to later stages of the process of creation is, in general, insufficient. The Court of Appeal in Paris found that the putative joint author intervened during the phase of conception in the renovation of a building. Nonetheless, as he was unable to give evidence of his personal contribution towards the creation of plans or sketches or that he had given precise instructions as to their execution, he was not recognised as joint author (next to the official architect of the renovation project).[79] However, there seems to be an exception to this general rule: as Bertrand writes if one person contributes mere ideas such as their stories or experiences and has them 'rewritten' by another person who gives them the form they are considered joint authors working in collaboration.[80]

To summarise, from the above case law it follows that the French rules on authorship for ownership purposes explicitly require an author's intellectual input in a certain proximity from the result. Contributions that are not immediately determinative of the expressive elements of the outcome do not count as authorial. Those may be contributions made just in the conception phase or those which do not limit the creative freedom of the sole author. This is subject to the established practices in the industry, eg ghost writing.

Though not immediately close to the result, instructions as to the execution of a work can count as authorial if they are precise, concrete and observed so that they determine the expressive elements (*Guino v Renoir*). The precision and specificity of instructions warranting authorship can be a useful discriminator because AI-driven systems tend to be given only high-level, imprecise instructions as to the expressive elements of the final subject matter. The authorial activity must, too, involve making personal decisions and be relevant in relation to the work, ie unlike cooking in relation to making a film or collecting data and editing in relation to writing an article.

[76] '[…] *dès lors que l'œuvre avait été exécutée selon ses instructions et sous son contrôle*'. Cour de cassation, civile, Decision of 6 January 2021, n° 19-14.205.

[77] Portron (n 63) 236.

[78] Caron (n 47) 92.

[79] Cour d'appel de Paris, Decision of 20 November 1996 (1997) 173 *RIDA* 321.

[80] Bertrand (n 41) 184.

Germany

In Germany, an author's right, ie copyright in authorial works, is mainly governed by *Urheberrechtsgesetz* (German Author's Right Act or Act).[81] The purpose and objectives are expressly laid down in §11 stating that '[t]he author's right protects the author with respect to their intellectual and personal relationships to the work and with respect to the use of the work. It equally serves to secure an equitable remuneration for the use of the work.'[82]

The purpose of author's right is further elaborated on in the academic and practitioner's commentaries. Given that German courts, including the German Federal Supreme Court, often quote these commentaries, this chapter also treats them as a valuable source of doctrine. For instance, according to Professor Loewenheim, the Act primarily aims to protect the author.[83] He also quotes the governmental report accompanying the bill which was passed into the Act in 1965 and which grounds author's right in the author: '[i]t is not the work to which the protection relates, but rather the person of the author who stands in the foreground.'[84] According to Professor Bullinger, §1 serves as a Preamble to the Act and helps to clarify its purpose by stating that '[t]he authors of the literature, science and art enjoy protection for their works as provided by this statute.'[85] Professor Schulze, too, emphasises that, according to the text of the Act, the protection is to be enjoyed by authors, not works.[86]

Unsurprisingly then, pursuant to §§12–15 of the Act, the initial beneficiaries of author's right are the authors. Attribution of authorship to a juridical person is inconceivable. This principle is also followed by German courts. For instance, the State Court in Berlin ruled that even if a juridical person maintains satellites that made photographs it does not have the right to be named as the author on the photographs.[87]

In this connection, it is of some consequence that German copyright law adheres to a monist theory under which author's right is characterised by an indivisible unity of economic and moral rights.[88] This means (among other things)

[81] *Urheberrechtsgesetz* of 9 September 1965 (BGBl. I S. 1273) as amended.

[82] '*Das Urheberrecht schützt den Urheber in seinen geistigen und persönlichen Beziehungen zum Werk und in der Nutzung des Werkes. Es dient zugleich der Sicherung einer angemessenen Vergütung für die Nutzung des Werkes*' German Author's Right Act, § 11.

[83] Ulrich Loewenheim, 'UrhG § 1 Allgemeines' in Gerhard Schricker and Ulrich Loewenheim (eds), *Urheberrecht* 6th edn (CH Beck 2020) [1].

[84] '*Nicht das Werk, auf das sich der Schutz bezieht, sondern die Person des Urhebers steht im Vordergrund.*' ibid, citing AmtlBegr. BT-Drs. IV/270, 37.

[85] '*Die Urheber von Werken der Literatur, Wissenschaft und Kunst genießen für ihre Werke Schutz nach Maßgabe dieses Gesetzes.*' Winfried Bullinger, '§2 Urheberrecht' in Artur-Axel Wandtke and Winfried Bullinger, *Praxiskommentar Urheberrecht* 6th edn (CH Beck 2022) [1].

[86] Gernot Schulze, '§1 Allgemeines' in Thomas Dreier and Gernot Schulze (eds), *Urheberrechtsgesetz* 7th edn (CH Beck 2022) [1].

[87] *Satellitenfoto*, Decision of 30 May 1989, 16 O 33/89 [1990] *GRUR* 270.

[88] Schulze (n 86) [1].

that author's right is, in principle, not assignable.[89] The monistic approach together with the creator doctrine have as their implication that a juridical person may use works only by virtue of a licence or a statutory provision (which is in case of works made in the course of employment, computer programs and films).[90]

Pursuant to § 7 of the German Author's Right Act, the author is the creator of the work. The creator is understood to be 'the natural person who in fact made the work on their own by their personal intellectual performance […]'.[91] According to Leowenheim and Peifer, the creation requires an individual intellect that only human beings possess.[92] No specific intention, will or legal capacity are required for creation of a work and thus (in the absence of any formalities) for author's right to subsist.[93]

According to a different commentary, a work is created even if it is not completed. To create a work, it suffices to make the first authorial contributions.[94] The ideas and instructions can count as authorial contributions as soon as they are so concretised that they constitute a personal intellectual creation.[95]

Whether an individual creative contribution was made in the course of creating the work is a question of fact.[96] What counts as authorial contribution depends on the work in question. For example, in an infringement case involving the publication of pictures of a sculpture made for the purposes of a film, the defendants were trying to argue that since the director and the author of the film's screenplay were famously obsessed with detail, they must have given such intricate instructions as to the appearance of the sculpture that it allegedly precluded the sculptor's authorship.[97] The Higher Court in Hamburg reproached the defendants for not submitting any evidence of such instructions. The court concluded, on the basis of 'common life experience',[98] that works of art are created by the people who make them. Given the fact that in this case the author had 'achieved a certain level of recognition as a sculptor',[99] the court held that the creation and especially the arrangement of shapes originated from the sculptor.[100]

[89] Ulrich Loewenheim, '§10 Der Urheber A. Der Werkschöpfer' in Ulrich Loewenheim (ed), *Handbuch des Urheberrechts* 3rd edn (CH Beck 2021) [3]. Michael Grünberger and Adolf Dietz 'Germany' in Lionel Bently and Burton Ong (eds) *International Copyright Law and Practice*, vol 2 annually updated (LexisNexis 2024) §4[1][b].

[90] Ulrich Loewenheim and Karl-Nicholaus Peifer, '§11 II. Einheitliches Urheberrecht' in Gerhard Schricker and Ulrich Loewenheim (eds), *Urheberrecht* 6th edn (CH Beck 2020) [3]. Dorothee Thum, 'UrhG § 7 Urheber' in Artur-Axel Wandtke and Winfried Bullinger, *Praxiskommentar Urheberrecht* 6th edn, (CH Beck 2022) [5] fn 12.

[91] '*diejenige natürliche Person, die das Werk durch eine persönliche geistige Leistung* […] *selbst geschaffen hat*' Thum (n 90) [1]. Similarly Schulze (n 86) [2].

[92] Loewenheim and Peifer (n 90) [2].

[93] ibid.

[94] Thum (n 90) [9].

[95] ibid [29].

[96] ibid [46].

[97] *Maschinenmensch*, Decision of 10 July 2002, 5 U 41/01 [2003] *GRUR-RR* 33.

[98] '*angesichts der allgemeinen Lebenserfahrung*' ibid 34.

[99] '*er als Bildhauer eine gewisse Anerkennung erlangt hatte*' ibid 34.

[100] ibid 34.

The court then continued (obiter) that even if precise instructions as to the execution of a sculpture had been given, these must have been communicated in a (visual) form which was liable to capture the shape of the sculpture, eg by producing studies and sketches.[101] The court added (obiter) that 'especially in the field of sculpture to establish (joint-) authorship it would be necessary that the specifications are so precise that the sculptor is deprived of the possibility to exercise his own creative activity when giving form to the sculpture.'[102]

Somewhat similarly, the German Federal Supreme Court held that if a defendant sought to claim that drawings of a pink elephant were made according to their precise instructions they have to bring concrete evidence forward.[103] Otherwise and in principle, having a mere idea of a pink elephant character and making suggestions as to its creation for an advertisement campaign does not constitute a personal intellectual creation.[104]

In another case, a putative joint author claimed they merit authorship for suggesting a title for a film (which was not adopted), a film-within-a-film concept, an opening scene and a general idea of depicting the cruelty of film industry. The latter three elements made it to the screenplay and eventually to the film. It was not disputed that these contributions were made during a single meeting of the putative joint author and the presumed author of the screenplay.[105] However, the Higher State Court in Munich embraced the lower court's finding that these contributions were fragmentary and, as such, short of authorial nature.[106]

More specifically, the Higher State Court in Munich acknowledged that the idea of an opening scene depicting a fire accidentally breaking out during a film shooting originated with the claimant and was inspired by his real life experience, however it considered the claimant's story to amount to mere reporting, not a protectable story; a mere provision of facts and data that do not constitute a literary work.[107] In the words of the court, 'in order to be protectable, the story must be produced through a creative activity and it thus rests on the imagination of the person who claims it as his own and it must be invented by him'.[108] The condition to invent a story would seem too demanding in the light of further developments, in particular *Infopaq*.

In contrast, the Higher State Court in Cologne decided that a journalist writing up a memoir based on interviews merits authorship because his contributions

[101] *Maschinenmensch* (n 97) 34.

[102] '*Gerade im Bereich der Bildhauerei wäre es für eine (Mit-)Urheberschaft Dritter erforderlich, dass die Vorgaben bereits so präzise sind, dass dem Bildhauer die Möglichkeit eigener schöpferischer Tätigkeit bei der Ausformung einer Figur genommen ist*.' ibid 34.

[103] *Rosaroter Elefant*, Decision of 19 October 1994, I ZR 156/92 [1995] *GRUR* 47.

[104] ibid.

[105] *Solange Du da bist*, Decision of 24 November 1955, 6 U 916/55 [1956] *GRUR* 432, 432.

[106] ibid 434.

[107] ibid.

[108] '*die Fabel auch durch schöpferische Tätigkeit hervorgebracht sein. daß sie also auf der Phantasie dessen, der sie für sich beansprucht, beruhen, daß sie von ihm erfunden sein muß, wenn sie schutzfähig sein soll*'. ibid 434.

were not limited to mere transcription or mere editorial corrections.[109] Rather, the journalist was found to have 'independently created a manuscript that was based on information given orally by the interviewee in two interviews, and that the manuscript demonstrated an unmistakenly individual journalistic character in the way the material was structured and presented'.[110] The journalist's contributions towards the manuscript were regarded equally authorial as those made by the interviewee. The interviewee contributed her own recount of her life experiences.[111] There is an obvious discrepancy in the reasonings of the Higher State Court in Munich and the Higher State Court in Cologne in how they evaluated authorship for telling one's own life experiences. However, in both cases, those persons who structured and arranged the material and produced the final version of the work were recognised as authors or joint authors respectively.

Further, commentaries provide a summary of the case law in relation to non-authorial contributions. The non-authorial contributions are typically based on activities that demand some intellectual activity; however, they are not regarded as creative in relation to the final output. Such activities include auxiliary activities done under precise instructions of authors such as gathering, filtering and arrangement of the material for creation, systematic preparation of the material or making editorial corrections,[112] or behaving in compliance with artist's visions and merely executing his instructions.[113]

Interestingly enough (and similar to the German approach to inventorial contributions), there are different authorship standards applicable to those named as the author on the copies of work and thus those who enjoy the presumption of authorship and others. In 2009 in *Kranhäuser*, the German Federal Supreme Court ruled to the effect that a contribution made by a joint author who was named as such when the work was published does not have to be of strictly authorial quality.[114] Under such circumstances, even a minor creative contribution to a work produced in collaboration, if the contribution is not divisible from the whole, merits joint authorship.[115] This approach changes the dynamic before the court: if someone wishes to challenge joint authorship of another who enjoys presumption of authorship, they should prove that the presumed joint author made only 'entirely irrelevant creative contributions'.[116] In *Kranhäuser*, the presumed author maintained their authorial status because they contributed 'linear structures

[109] *Miturheberrecht bei "Memoiren"*, Decision of 14 October 1952, 4 U 82/52 [1953] *GRUR* 499.

[110] '*sondern auf Grund mündlich erteilter Informationen, die ihm bei zweimaligem Besuch der Kronprinzessin in Beantwortung von Fragen erteilt wurden, selbständig ein Manuskript erstellt, das sowohl in der Gliederung des Stoffes wie in der ganzen Art der Darstellung eine unverkennbar individuelle journalistische Prägung aufweist*'. ibid.

[111] ibid.

[112] Thum (n 90) [36], [38].

[113] Gernot Schulze, 'UrhG § 7 Urheber' in Thomas Dreier and Gernot Schulze (eds), *Urheberrechtsgesetz* 7th edn (CH Beck 2022) [9].

[114] *Kranhäuser*, Decision of 26 February 2009, I ZR 142/06 [2009] *GRUR* 1046.

[115] ibid.

[116] ibid 1047.

spanning over the Rhein basin'[117] to the common architectural design and these contributions were found to fall within the art of city development planning.

Importantly, only contributions made within a certain circumscribed process of creation were taken into consideration, namely those made in a certain workshop during which the work was deemed to have been produced.[118] A similar emphasis was placed on the process of creation in *Buchhaltungsprogramm*, where the German Federal Supreme Court held that a contribution made in the preparatory stage can be considered authorial if it is 'a creative contribution to the integrated creative process of completing the work'.[119]

Buchhaltungsprogramm concerned a computer program for foreign currency book keeping 'in the form of a direct display on the screen (without the need to go into sub-menus) [that] was regarded as original and creative; the manner of the incorporation was good and surprising and in its chosen form of realisation it presents an above-average performance'.[120] When formulating the specification for that computer program, a client (a company dealing with data organisation and processing) gave instructions for development of the program to a software company, including particular steps to be taken to broaden the scope of data processing, conduct some checks and evaluations at certain points. The software company translated these specifications and requirements into a computer language. The client also contributed by structuring the data and preparing a special balance sheet structure so that it could be directly incorporated into the computer program. In this case, the sum of (contributions made on behalf of the client) towards creation of data processing methods which were implemented in the computer program merited joint authorship in the computer program.[121] It may be questioned whether such contributions were not rather towards general ideas and the functionality of the program. In contrast, the Higher State Court in Cologne found that a mere assignment to create software and giving specifications to that end without conducting any actual coding does not make one a joint author of the resulting computer program.[122]

Statutory Presumptions of Authorship

The above cases mostly concern disputes over joint authorship. Such disputes arise if there are at least two persons claiming authorship which enables the parties

[117] ibid.
[118] ibid.
[119] '*einen schöpferischen Beitrag zum einheitlichen Schöpfungsprozeß der Werkvollendung leistet*' *Buchhaltungsprogramm*, Decision of 14 July 1993, I ZR 47/91 [1994] *GRUR* 39.
[120] ibid.
[121] ibid.
[122] *Entwurfsmaterial*, Decision of 8 April 2005 [2005] ZUM-RD 333, 335 as summarised in Gernot Schulze, 'UrhG § 8 Miturheber' in Thomas Dreier and Gernot Schulze (eds), *Urheberrechtsgesetz* 7th edn (CH Beck 2022) [8].

to assert, prove or challenge authorship in the testimonies and other evidence. However, in the *de facto* absence of a (human) author-creator, there seems to be no person entitled to challenge usurpation of copyright by a non-author. Moreover, there are statutory presumptions of authorship which may cover up the absence of the author-creator.

Under the CDPA, for instance, if 'a name purporting to be that of the author appeared on copies of the work as published or on the work when it was made, the person whose name appeared shall be presumed, until the contrary is proved, to be the author of the work'.[123] This means, in effect, that if persons who appear to be the authors remain unchallenged, the actual authorship will hardly ever be scrutinised by the courts or the public.[124] It is unclear whether the 'person whose name' in the presumption of authorship is intended to mean a natural person only or whether this includes a juridical person.[125]

The French copyright law contains a presumption to the same effect, ie '[t]he status of author belongs, unless the contrary is proven, to the person or persons under whose name the work was divulged'.[126] Paying lip service to the creator doctrine, French courts have actually allowed juridical persons to enjoy not only economic rights but also moral rights *ab initio*, including the right to publish the work under their name.[127] The French Supreme Court found that in the absence of objections by any natural person or persons claiming authorship, the work (in this case photographs) may be treated as a collective work and may be published under the name of the juridical person.[128] This was a noteworthy development because such ruling was made for the first time in relation to third parties, the alleged infringers.[129] It was justified by better exploitation reasons and the statutory presumption of authorship.[130]

Hence, if a juridical person publishes a work under their name, they gain (retrospectively) moral rights, including the right to publish the work under their name. This resembles a money laundering scheme in the sense of having an object of a wrong origin and running it through a certain scheme at the end of which an object with a tolerable origin emerges. Under such a framework, the absence of authorship is undiscoverable.

[123] CDPA 1988, s 104(2).

[124] Ryan Abbott, 'Artificial Intelligence, Big Data and Intellectual Property: Protecting Computer Generated Works in the United Kingdom' in Tanya Aplin (ed), *Research Handbook on Intellectual Property and Digital Technologies* (Edward Elgar 2020) 325.

[125] More likely it means only a natural person's name. This can be inferred indirectly from the way in which this presumption is addressed in Tappin and others (n 2) [5.153].

[126] '*La qualité d'auteur appartient, sauf preuve contraire, à celui ou à ceux sous le nom de qui l'œuvre est divulguée.*' French Intellectual Property Code, art L113-1.

[127] Cour de cassation, Decision of 24 March 1993 as found in Vivant and Brugière (n 43) 356.

[128] ibid.

[129] Agnès Robin, 'Question de procedure: une présomption prétorienne' in Michel Vivant (ed), *Les grands arrêts de la propriété intellectuelle* 3rd edn (Dalloz 2020) 291.

[130] Vivant and Brugière (n 43) 356.

In Germany, the presumption of authorship is effective only with respect to the person of author but does not warrant copyright protection.[131] In contrast with the French arrangements, a juridical person does not have the right to be named as the author.[132] However, as follows from the German Federal Supreme Court's decision in *Kranhäuser*, presumed authors enjoy a comparative advantage because they only need to adhere to a lower authorship standard to defend their presumed authorship.

To summarise, in the absence of author-creator and thanks to the presumptions of authorship there seems to be no one who would be legally entitled to challenge whether an expressive subject matter owes its existence to an act of creation that would give rise to authorship. While the presumptions of authorship might have fulfilled their purpose in the nineteenth and twentieth centuries, in the light of the advancements in AI, they are no longer substantiated. If they remain in force, there is a risk that they will unjustifiably strengthen the position of those in possession of expressive subject matter that lack human authorship.

Computer-generated Works in the UK

In copyright law, it is widely acknowledged that concepts of authorship and originality are synonymous[133] or twin concepts.[134] The concept of originality in positive law gives expression to the personal relationship between the author-creator and their work.[135] Originality is usually approached as one of the characteristics of a copyright work. For instance, Professor Pila conceives of an authorial (original) work as 'an expressive production of an author' and thus 'having a certain history of production'.[136] She identifies two definitional elements of a subject matter eligible for EU copyright: intangibility and 'origination in an act of human creation'.[137] According to Professor Hugenholtz, '[w]ithout a "work" there is no author and there are no exclusive rights'.[138] It follows that if a subject matter does not have any human author, not only there is no one entitled to copyright, but also (and more fundamentally in the context of AI-driven systems) there is no authorial (original) work.[139]

[131] *Coverversion*, Decision of 11 December 1997, I ZR 170/95 [1998] *GRUR* 376.

[132] *Satellitenfoto*, Decision of 30 May 1989, 16 O 33/89 [1990] *GRUR* 270.

[133] Jane Ginsburg, 'The Concept of Authorship in Comparative Copyright Law' (2003) 52 *DePaul L Rev* 1063, 1078.

[134] Mireille van Eechoud, 'Voices Near and Far. Introduction' in Mireille van Eechoud (ed), *The Work of Authorship* (Amsterdam University Press 2014) 7.

[135] Bertrand (n 41) 54.

[136] Justine Pila, *The Subject Matter of Intellectual Property* (OUP 2017) 148.

[137] ibid 9.

[138] Bernt Hugenholtz, 'Works of Literature, Science and Art' in Bernt Hugenholtz and others (eds), *A Century of Dutch Copyright Law* (deLex 2012) 34.

[139] Similarly, in Tanya Aplin and Giulia Pasqualetto, 'Artificial Intelligence and Copyright Protection' in Rosa Maria Ballardini, Petri Kuoppamäki and Olli Pitkänen (eds), *Regulating Industrial Internet*

The connection between author-creator and the requirements for copyright protection does not seem to be reflected equally well in the UK statutory framework for so-called computer-generated works (CGW). The CDPA defines computer-generated as 'generated by a computer in circumstances such that there is no human author of the work'.[140] Section 9(3) of the CDPA provides that if such a CGW is a literary, dramatic, musical or artistic work, 'the author shall be taken to be the person by whom the arrangements necessary for the creation of the work are undertaken'.[141]

To date, the only CGW positively identified in case law were composite frames created for the purposes of (and in the course of) playing a video game in *Nova Productions v Mazooma*.[142] Authorship under section 9(3) of the CDPA was attributed to Mr Jones who 'devised the appearance of the various elements of the game and the rules and logic by which each frame is generated and he wrote the relevant computer program'.[143] Kitchin J (as he then was) rejected the player of the game as the potential author of composite frames under section 9(3) of the CDPA because he has not 'undertaken any of the arrangements necessary for the creation of the frame images. All he has done is to play the game'.[144]

The conclusion that player's input was not a necessary arrangement in the sense of section 9(3) of the CDPA can be disputed.[145] Arguably, but for the activity of playing the game, the frames would not have been created. What is more, but for the way the game was played by a particular player, the frames would not have been created in a manner they were. Therefore, the player arguably determined the final expression of the frames.[146]

Stepping away from *Nova Productions v Mazooma*, this chapter argues that in principle it is difficult to apply the CGW provisions convincingly. The CGW are ambiguous because they invite at least two distinct lines of argument. Both involve hurdles on the way to copyright protection. The first line of argument assumes CGW constituting works in the sense of the Berne Convention and thus requiring some originality. In contrast, the second line of argument assumes CGW not falling within the concept of 'work' in the sense of the Berne Convention.

Through IPR, Data Protection and Competition Law (Wolters Kluwer 2019): '[i]f no intellectual creativity has been exerted, then no work warranting copyright protection has been created.'

[140] CDPA 1988, s 178.

[141] ibid, s 9(3).

[142] *Nova Productions Ltd v Mazooma Games Ltd* [2006] EWHC 24 (Ch), [2006] RPC 14.

[143] ibid [105].

[144] ibid [106].

[145] This comment concerns the causation element of the 'necessary arrangements' only. For a more detailed discussion, see Jani McCutcheon, 'Curing the Authorless Void: Protecting Computer-Generated Works Following IceTV and Phone Directories' (2013) 37 *Melb U L Rev* 46.

[146] In addition, the judgment is confusing as it finds in paragraph 104 that the composite frames are artistic works and 'were created by Mr Jones or by the computer program which he wrote'. In the context of the judgment, 'or' meant an inclusive disjunction. But then it is unclear how these two can possibly occur at the same time, ie how a subject matter can be deemed to have been created by Mr Jones in authorial capacity and, at the same time, to have been created by a computer program and hence not to have any human author.

First, if section 9(3) of the CDPA when referring to 'literary, dramatic, musical or artistic work' (LDMA work) means 'the rights of authors in their literary or artistic works'[147] in the sense of the Berne Convention, copyright subsistence in a computer-generated LDMA work is pre-conditioned on them being an intellectual creation (or on originality) in the first place. In the UK, an LDMA work is original if it involves author's skill, labour and judgment (at the level required in *Infopaq*) poured into the activity of creating the given type of authorial work.[148]

To reiterate the connection between the author-creator and originality, in cases where there is no author-creator, there is no authorial (original) work and hence copyright cannot subsist, regardless of whether there is a person in whom it could be vested according to the statute. As put succinctly by Bently and others, 'it is difficult to see how the existing criterion of originality, which focuses on the relationship between the author and the work, can be applied to computer-generated works'.[149]

Some argue that CGW 'if otherwise original, should not be denied copyright protection solely because they are computer-generated'[150] or that a computer-generated work should be defined as 'generated by a computer in circumstances such that the computer, if a natural person, would be an author'.[151] Or, 'if the creation of the same work would have required the exercise of a substantial amount of skill, labour, etc. had it been done by a human author, the requirement of originality is satisfied though the work be generated by a computer'.[152] These accounts basically suggest that a computer should just swap their place with a human author. The computer's activity would replace the activity required for originality provided it were of the same kind.

Since some AI-driven systems can produce authorial-like inputs in terms of kind and quantity, the only aspect in which the human authors are special is that they are human beings, have personality and hence can make personal decisions reflecting their personality. Therefore, to make the above arguments work, one would need to imagine originality in a piece of literature or art that, in fact, does not have any because it was not authored by a human being.

Or, perhaps, such originality must be of a different kind. As put in the *Copinger and Skone James* commentary, '[i]t is suggested that the relevant skill and labour is that of the person by whom the arrangements necessary for the creation of the work were undertaken'.[153] The literature offers a range of candidates for a person whose arrangements are necessary: AI-driven systems' designers, datasets providers,

[147] Berne Convention, art 1.

[148] This follows from *Temple Island Collections Ltd v New English Teas Ltd* [2012] EWPCC 1 [2012] FSR 9 [53], *SAS Institute Inc v World Programming Ltd* [2013] EWHC 69 (Ch) [2013] RPC 17 [52].

[149] Lionel Bently and others, *Intellectual Property Law* 5th edn (OUP 2018) 117–18.

[150] McCutcheon (n 145) 46.

[151] Abbott (n 124) 323.

[152] Tappin and others (n 2) [22.44].

[153] Caddick, Harbottle and Suthersanen (n 4) (vi) Computer-generated works.

investors, operators.[154] In the absence of any further legal guidance, there is no legal limitation as to the range of the relevant activities.[155] Some tackle this by proposing to select the relevant originality and the fictious author of a CGW on a case-by-case basis.[156]

However, such an ad hoc approach does not provide legal certainty as to the rewards and incentives to create which is necessary for copyright to serve its purpose and realise its objectives.[157] Even if these proposals were tenable, there is no good reason or justification for treating unequally persons who conduct the same activity. A person who has an idea of a subject of a painting and prompts an AI-driven system to paint it would be vested in copyright in the CGW. However, a person who has an idea for a painting and tells a friend to paint it has no copyright in the ensuing work. Is there anything inherently better about prompting a machine what to produce in contrast with instructing a human being what to paint? Moreover, vesting copyright in a person who merely undertakes arrangements necessary for the creation of an LDMA work is not justified by the property theories as already demonstrated in Chapter 3.

The legislative history does not provide satisfactory answers as to the social needs or regulatory problems that the CGW provisions were meant to address. The Whitford Committee saw no issues. Understandably, in 1977, the present issues brought by the advancements in AI could hardly be anticipated. The Committee recommended to rely on the concept of author and praised 'the simplicity of this approach as giving further support to our decisions against making any other person or persons the author of the output'.[158]

A White Paper that followed a decade later stated that '[i]t appears that no practical problems arise from the absence of specific authorship provisions in this area. The Government has therefore concluded that no specific provisions should be made to determine this question'.[159] It was added that '[i]f no human skill

[154] In fact, all these activities such as assembling the computer, plugging in the computer, switching the computer on, etc are necessary arrangements. Had it not been for a person who has built the computer or who has hired the person who had built the computer, the CGW would not have existed and so on and so forth. See more in Ana Ramalho, 'Will Robots Rule The (Artistic) World? A Proposed Model for the Legal Status of Creations by Artificial Intelligence Systems' (2017) 21 *J Internet L* 1 arguing for possibly all of them depending on various factors. McCutcheon (n 146) 53, Jean-Marc Deltorn and Franck Macrez 'Authorship in the Age of Machine Learning and Artificial Intelligence' in Sean M O'Connor (ed), *The Oxford Handbook of Music Law and Policy* (OUP 2019), Bruce Boyden, 'Emergent Works' (2016) 39 *Colum JL & Arts* 377, 385.

[155] McCutcheon provides a list of five activities derived from the case law on joint ownership in films. To what extent activities necessary for making a film are translatable into LDMA categories can be questioned. McCutcheon (n 145) 64.

[156] McCutcheon (n 145) 55. Jean-Marc Deltorn, 'Deep Creations: Intellectual Property and the Automata' (2017) 4 *Frontiers in Digital Humanities*. Available at: https://doi.org/10.3389/fdigh.2017.00003, last accessed 19 April 2021.

[157] In the EU, copyright is meant to safeguard 'the independence and dignity of artistic creators and performers'. InfoSoc Directive, recital 11.

[158] House of Commons, *Copyright and Designs Law* (Whitford Report, Cmnd 6732, 1977) [516].

[159] Department of Trade and Industry, *Intellectual property and innovation* (White Paper, Cmnd 9712, 1986) [9.7].

and effort has been expended then no work warranting copyright protection has been created'.[160]

The good reasons for protecting CGW may be purely instrumentalist. However, these may not be sufficient to justify the breadth and strength of the rights currently enjoyed by authors. Moreover, there are no good reasons for discriminating between authorial LDMA works and computer-generated LDMA works in terms of an originality standard.

The second line of argument assumes that the 'literary, dramatic, musical or artistic work' referred to in section 9(3) of the CDPA 1988 is a special category of subject matter that lies outside the Berne Convention regime. As such, it possibly does not require any originality at all. This makes sense given the particularities of the CGW regime, namely the attribution of copyright to a person who makes the necessary arrangements, including taking care of production costs; the duration of copyright[161] and exemptions from moral rights.[162]

In the same vein, Goold calls the provision on CGW unnecessary, and he sees its only purpose if 'we agree that it is not subject to the originality requirement'.[163] He continues that, however, in such a case 'the effect of the provision is to expand protection to non-original computer-generated works. Yet there is no compelling natural rights or utilitarian reason for doing so'.[164] This book agrees. Moreover, it argues that the proposition that the provisions on CGW expand protection to non-original LDMA works is incompatible with a systematic reading of the CDPA. Given that section 1(1) of the CDPA provides an exhaustive enumeration of works eligible for copyright protection, ie '(a) original literary, dramatic, musical or artistic works, […]'[165] and given it explicitly refers to 'original' LDMA works, the proposition that the provisions on CGW expand protection to non-original LDMA works contradicts literal and contextual interpretation of section 1(1) of the CDPA.

To summarise, the CGW provisions are unhelpful in making a distinction between authorless and original (authorial) works. As Bently and others pointed out, these provisions are ambiguous as to the kind of originality which is required in relation to computer-generated works.[166] On top of that, as shown above, these provisions do not solve the problem of copyright subsistence in an LDMA subject matter that lacks human authorship. This is because within the CDPA they are not operational: neither with authorial originality, originality of a special kind nor absence of originality. Hence, the main take away from the above is that it is crucial to have an adequate method for distinguishing authorial works (original LDMA

[160] ibid [9.8].
[161] CDPA 1988, s 12(7).
[162] ibid s 79(2) and 81(2).
[163] Patrick Goold, 'The Curious Case of Computer-generated Works under the Copyright, Designs and Patents Act 1988' (2021) 2 *IPQ* 120, 129.
[164] ibid.
[165] CDPA 1988, s 1(1).
[166] Bently and others (n 149) 117–18.

works) from other expressive subject matter before one embarks on regulating rights in the latter.

Conclusion

Besides the requirement of authorial contributions being of the right kind and sufficient amount, the decisions and intellectual inputs of the author-creator must immediately determine the expressive elements of the subject matter. (These choices correspond to 'creative choices' in EU copyright law.) Hence, the author must exercise creative activity in the sense that they directly and immediately determine the expressive elements of the final subject matter. Other contributions, albeit intellectual and perhaps even of the right kind, but made outside the process of creation itself, such as handling data, the pre-selection of raw material, mere execution or the provision of abstract ideas are traditionally regarded as non-authorial.

Cases in which authorship was questioned reveal that only the person whose identity is channelled in an undisrupted fashion from the work's conception, via its composition to its materialisation can claim authorship. The importance of legacy of author's identity is visible in *Cala Homes*, *Guino v Renoir* and *Buchhaltungsprogramm*. In these cases, the joint authors gave form to their works and guided their execution by contributing their own conceptions, emotions or giving precise instructions as to the expressive elements and the joint authors-executors adopted some of the elements without necessarily foregoing their own creative freedom. Proof of such a legacy can be drawn from the process of creation. Taking *Martin v Kogan II* as an example, the chronological approach to the events and sensitivity to the context of creation permits to track authorial contributions and their flow from conception through composition into materialisation of the work. Thereby, the authors can prove their personality and identity have been channelled into the work.

8

Authorship in the Application Practice in the UK, Germany and France

Introduction

This chapter looks at whether national copyright subsistence criteria in the UK, France and Germany reflect human aspects of creation. The focus is on national conceptions of (original) work and the interplay between categories of work (or the form of work) and originality as two key copyright subsistence criteria. This chapter also identifies and analyses epistemic approaches that national authorities employ when they apply the copyright subsistence criteria. Are the established epistemic approaches suitable to distinguish an authored work from authorless expressive subject matter? Finally, this chapter considers how the identified human aspects of creation could possibly be applied to AI productions.

Reflections of Authorship and the Epistemic Approaches in the UK

Categories of Work

In the UK, a subject matter must fall under one of the statutory categories of authorial work, ie a literary, dramatic, musical, or artistic work (LDMA) category.[1] These categories continue to be regarded as the starting point for claiming copyright in the UK[2] even though the finite nature of the categories is, arguably, contradictory to the CJEU's rulings in *BSA*, *Cofemel* and the Berne Convention. Yet, the significance of a correct categorisation was stressed recently by the Court of Appeal as it re-categorised a screenplay from a literary work to a dramatic work.[3]

A literary work is defined as any work 'other than a dramatic or musical work, which is written, spoken or sung, and accordingly includes a table or compilation,

[1] Copyright, Designs and Patents Act 1988 (CDPA), s 1(1)(a).

[2] The UK retains a fluid, closed-list subject matter. *Response Clothing Ltd v The Edinburgh Woollen Mill Ltd* [2020] EWHC 148 (IPEC), [2020] FSR 25 [64].

[3] The Court of Appeal in *Kogan v Martin* [2019] EWCA Civ 1645, [2020] FSR 3 [66] rejected the conclusion of the first instance judge that a screenplay is a literary work.

a computer program, preparatory design material for a computer program and a database'.[4] In *Exxon*, Stephenson LJ defined literary work as 'something which was intended to afford either information and instruction, or pleasure in the form of literary enjoyment, whatever those last six words may add to the word "pleasure"'.[5]

However, in *NLA v Meltwater*,[6] the Court of Appeal found that headlines and article extracts of 256 characters can, in principle, and will in many instances (eg in the circumstances of the case at hand) contain 'elements which are the expression of the intellectual creation of the author of the article as a whole'.[7] Despite *Exxon* and *NLA v Meltwater* being similar in dealing with a short arrangement of characters, the court in the latter case did not delve into discussing whether the extracts were literary works in the sense of affording information or pleasure but rather relied on the *Infopaq* standard.

Dramatic works are defined as including 'a work of dance or mime'.[8] Additionally, the Court of Appeal held in *Norowzian*, that dramatic work 'should be given its ordinary and natural meaning, which was a work of action, with or without words or music, which was capable of being performed before an audience'.[9] For instance, if a film can be performed, including being played on a screen, before an audience, it falls within the definition of dramatic work.[10]

Musical works are defined as works 'consisting of music, exclusive of any words or action intended to be sung, spoken or performed with the music'.[11] The Court of Appeal found in *Sawkins v Hyperion* that the meaning of a musical work is to be taken from ordinary language: 'as indicated in the dictionaries, the essence of music is combining sounds for listening to. Music is not the same as mere noise. The sound of music is intended to produce effects of some kind on the listener's emotions and intellect'.[12]

Artistic works are enumerated in the CDPA and encompass a graphic work, photograph, sculpture or collage, irrespective of artistic quality, a work of architecture being a building or a model for a building, or a work of artistic craftsmanship.[13] These sub-categories are then defined separately. For instance, a sculpture 'includes a cast or model made for purposes of sculpture'.[14] In *Lucasfilm*, an Imperial Stormtrooper helmet was found not to be a sculpture because it did not correspond to the ordinary meaning of the word.[15] Nor was it found to constitute

[4] CDPA 1988, s 3(1).

[5] *Exxon Corporation and Others v Exxon Insurance Consultants International Ltd* [1982] Ch 119, [1982] RPC 69 [88].

[6] *Newspaper Licensing Agency Ltd and others v Meltwater Holding BV and others* [2011] EWCA Civ 890, [2012] Bus LR 53.

[7] ibid [85].

[8] CDPA 1988, s 3(1).

[9] *Norowzian v Arks Ltd and Others (No 2)* [1999] EWCA Civ 3018, [2000] FSR 363, 363–64.

[10] ibid.

[11] CDPA 1988, s 3(1).

[12] *Sawkins v Hyperion Records Ltd* [2005] EWCA Civ 565, [2005] 1 WLR 3281.

[13] CDPA 1988, s 4(1).

[14] ibid s 4(2)(b).

[15] *Lucasfilm Ltd v Ainsworth* [2011] UKSC 39, [2012] 1 AC 208 [44].

a work of art because it 'was utilitarian in the sense that it was an element in the process of production of the film'.[16]

Skill, Labour and Judgment

In more recent UK copyright cases, eg *Temple Island* or *SAS Institute v WPL*, the courts referred to the EU author's own intellectual creation alongside the traditional judge-made skill, labour and judgment test[17] and have accommodated the EU language of 'intellectual creation'[18] and 'form of expression'.[19] Moreover, the UK originality assessment entails considerations corresponding to those mentioned at EU level, namely the considerations of the nature of the activity expended, ie the skill, labour and judgment, and whether these were expended in the creation of the work.

The UK conception of originality can be traced back to Peterson J who, in *University of London Press*, held that '[t]he originality which is required relates to the expression of the thought. But the Act does not require that the expression must be in an original or novel form, but that the work must not be copied from another work – that it should originate from the author'.[20] Against the facts of the case, setting mathematical papers required 'the exercise of brainwork, memory, and trained judgment, and even the selection of passages from other authors' works involved careful consideration, discretion, and choice'.[21]

More recent cases refer to the need to identify the required and relevant input of the author – 'author's own substantial and independent effort, skill and time'[22] or, 'the expression of the skill and labour [...] in *Infopaq* terms, [...] intellectual creation'.[23] Put in pre-*Infopaq* words, to meet the originality requirement, '[b]oth individual creative input and sweat of brow may be involved and will be factors in the overall evaluation'.[24]

Moreover, the skill, labour and judgement must be invested in the right activity with regard to the work in question.[25] There is a general agreement that slavish copying, no matter how laborious, could not give rise to an original work.[26]

[16] ibid.

[17] 'These elements above derive from and are the expression of the skill and labour exercised by Mr Fielder, or in *Infopaq* terms, they are his intellectual creation.' *Temple Island Collections Ltd v New English Teas Ltd* [2012] EWPCC 1, [2012] FSR 9 [53].

[18] ibid [53].

[19] *SAS Institute Inc v World Programming Ltd* [2013] EWHC 69 (Ch), [2013] RPC 17 [52].

[20] *University of London Press Ltd v University Tutorial Press Ltd* [1916] 2 Ch 601, 608–09.

[21] ibid 604.

[22] *Sawkins v Hyperion* (n 12) [16].

[23] *Temple Island* (n 17) [53].

[24] *Sawkins v Hyperion* (n 12) [83].

[25] Hugh Laddie, Peter Prescott and Mary Vitoria, *The Modern Law of Copyright and Designs*, vol I 4th edn, (LexisNexis 2011) 94.

[26] *Sawkins v Hyperion* (n 12) [31] and [77].

While slavish copying is understood as performing 'an easy mechanical function',[27] a verbatim transcription of a speech given in public was deemed to be more than mere copying.[28]

In now superseded[29] case law on data compilations, ie in *Ladbroke v Hill*,[30] the House of Lords did not distinguish between the skill, labour and judgement that had gone into the creation of a business idea and the skill, labour and judgement involved in the creation of the expression. More concretely, Lord Hodson appreciated that the production of betting coupons involved 'the selection of headings showing the choice of bets offered by the plaintiffs is itself shown to have been the result of skill and labour expended on them'.[31] He further added that he 'cannot accept that preparatory work must be excluded in this case so as to draw a line between the effort involved in developing ideas and that minimal effort required in setting those ideas down on paper'.[32] This demonstrates that if the process of creation is framed too widely then the relevant activity can encompass creating raw data, ideas and concepts, rather than expressing the data, ideas and concepts in literary or artistic form.

Besides the exclusion of mechanical copying and creation of ideas or data from copyright relevant activities, the relevance of activity is relative to the type of work. In relation to a photograph, in *Temple Island*, the relevant skill, labour and judgement is that poured into choosing the motif, angle of shot, light and shade, illumination, and exposure.[33]

In *Cala Homes*, the relevant intellectual input was 'the skill of making marks on paper or some other medium'[34] and 'the words or lines and the skill and effort involved in creating, selecting or gathering together the detailed concepts, data or emotions'.[35] In relation to software, it was found that only the skill, labour and judgement invested in the actual programming is relevant for the originality assessment and not the 'skill, time and effort [expended] on testing the software'.[36]

In addition, the author's skill, labour, and judgement, taken as a whole, must be of a sufficient (qualitative and quantitative) degree[37] and hence of sufficient transformative character. As stated by the Privy Council in 1924, '[t]he labour, skill

[27] ibid [82].
[28] *Walter v Lane* [1900] AC 539 (HL) recognised as good law per Mummery LJ in *Sawkins v Hyperion* (n 12) [33].
[29] In the light of Case C-604/10 *Football Dataco Ltd and Others v Yahoo! UK Ltd and Others* [2012] EU:C:2012:115.
[30] *Ladbroke (Football) Ltd v William Hill (Football) Ltd* [1964] 1 WLR 273 (HL).
[31] ibid 286.
[32] ibid 287.
[33] *Temple Island* (n 17) [51].
[34] *Cala Homes (South) Limited v Alfred McAlpine Homes East Limited (No 1)* [1995] FSR 818 (Ch) 835.
[35] ibid.
[36] *Fylde Microsystems Ltd v Key Radio Systems Ltd* [1998] FSR 449 (Ch) 457.
[37] *Sawkins* (n 12) [77]. '[O]riginality is a matter of degree depending on the amount of skill, judgment or labour that has been involved' *Ladbroke* (n 30) 277–78. '[…] sufficient aural and musical significance to attract copyright protection'. *Sawkins* (n 12) [56].

and capital should be expended sufficiently to impart to the product some quality or character which the raw material did not possess, and which differentiates the product from the raw material'.[38] In *Sawkins v Hyperion*, the Court of Appeal found in 2005 that though a relatively modest one, the contribution may still count as sufficient, ie 'performing indications, tempo and performance practice indicators'[39] in case of musical work, if the contribution has 'sufficient aural and musical significance'.[40]

The cases of *Walter v Lane*[41] and *Cummins v Bond*[42] suggest that, except for the slavish copying, the requirement may be reduced to an execution of the relevant skill and any creative choices are automatically assumed to having been communicated in the execution. This outdated and pragmatic version of originality notwithstanding, the UK law on originality, on the whole, reflects human authorship in natural person's own intellectual input that is of sufficient transformative character and poured into the activity typical for creation of the given category of work.

Courts' Epistemic Approach to the Criteria

Since a subject matter must first fall within a statutory category of authorial work, this makes it possible to perceive the subject matter as a work within that category. Professor Pila formulates this as a necessity: 'in order to perceive a work *qua* work one must perceive it in relation to a category of work'.[43] This perception through the lens of a category is advantageous also in enabling determination of the expressive elements of the subject matter (something with which EU copyright law struggles). The categories also function as a filter. In *Merchandising Corp v Harpbond* a facial make up was denied copyright on the basis that it was found not to be a painting and thus an artistic work.[44] Similarly, in *Creation Records v News Group*, an arrangement of objects around members of a band containing a Rolls Royce in a swimming pool, a hotel, a scooter and other objects 'seemingly unrelated to each other'[45] was found not to fit into any of the categories. Examining the process of creation, Lloyd J found that

> I do not see how the process of assembling these disparate objects together with the members of the group can be regarded as having anything in common with sculpture or with artistic craftsmanship. No element in the composition has been carved, modelled or made in any of the other ways in which sculpture is made.[46]

[38] *Macmillan & Co Ltd v Cooper* (1924) 40 TLR 186 (PC) 188.
[39] *Sawkins* (n 12) [56].
[40] ibid.
[41] *Walter v Lane* (n 28).
[42] *Cummins v Bond* [1927] 1 Ch 167, 168.
[43] Justine Pila, 'Copyright and Its Categories of Original Works' (2010) 30 *OJLS* 229, Abstract.
[44] *Merchandising Corp v Harpbond* [1983] FSR 32 (CA).
[45] *Creation Records Ltd and Others v News Group Newspapers Ltd* [1997] EMLR 444 (Ch) 447.
[46] ibid 449.

Hence, the criterion of belonging to a category operates as the first, and for the less traditional works also the last, discriminator.

In principle, and as recently confirmed in *Kogan v Martin*,[47] placing a subject matter into the right category is the first hurdle to overcome on the way to copyright subsistence. When conducting this categorisation, UK courts are guided by the ordinary meanings of the statutory categories.

Once a subject matter is put into an LDMA category, UK courts look at the human intellectual creative input (consideration, discretion and choice) poured into activity relevant for creation of that particular category of work coupled with the human transformative act (writing, drawing, correcting, punctuating, etc) causing the final creation – a work – to exist. Hence, in theory, the application of the requirement of originality should contain examination of the authorial contribution in the process of creation of the work. The UK courts have experience with examining the process of creation, just in different contexts. They do so, for instance, in infringement proceedings if the defendant asserts independent creation, eg as in *Mitchell v BBC*.[48]

Unless and until the courts are prompted to examine the process, they primarily focus on the subject matter, ie the form of expression, rather than on the intellectual endeavours preceding the result (*Merchandising Corp v Harpbond, Lucasfilm, Exxon, Hensher Ltd Appellants v Restawile*). There are cases, though, in which courts focused on the process of creation and human inputs (*Ladbrook v Hill, Creation Records v News Group*).

In contrast, in joint authorship cases or other cases where authorship was disputed (*Walter v Lane, Cummins v Bond, Sawkins v Hyperion, Cala Homes*), the evidence concerning the creative process is regarded as the most relevant. On the whole, in the absence of a challenge to authorship and thus an inquiry into the process of creation, the courts are less likely to investigate the process on their own motion.

Application of the UK Copyright Subsistence Criteria to AI Productions

The LDMA categories do not seem to render any reflections of human aspects of creation. They rather stem from traditional understanding of the respective categories in ordinary language. Professor Pila emphasises the importance of intentionality to all the LDMA works. According to her, '[a]n LDMA is, and ought to be, an intentional expression of an LDMA idea; meaning an intentional expression of a particular idea associated with a tradition of LDMA authorship'.[49]

[47] *Kogan v Martin* (n 3).
[48] *Michael Mitchell v British Broadcasting Corporation* [2011] EWPCC 42, [2011] 12 WLUK 734.
[49] Justine Pila, 'An Intentional View of the Copyright Work' (2008) 71 *MLR* 535, 557.

Adopting this view, the LDMA categories could reflect human authorship in their intentionality aspect.

Some of the definitions of LDMA works indeed contain references to intentionality (ie literary work and musical work). The House of Lords in *Hensher v Restawile* relied on intentionality when defining works of artistic craftsmanship.[50] According to Lord Simon of Glaisdale and Lord Kilbrandon, the artistic character (of a work of artistic craftsmanship) must be assessed in an objective way while taking 'the intent of the creator and its result' as decisive and 'the conscious intention of the craftsman [as] the primary test' respectively.[51]

Otherwise, the UK copyright subsistence criteria do not seem suitable to detect lack of human authorship. What also seems problematic in the UK copyright law is the scope of protection. This can be demonstrated on *Sawkins v Hyperion*.[52] To reiterate, Mr Sawkins' contributions consisted of adding or modifying a figured bass line in two compositions and re-creation of missing viola parts in respect of a half of musical compositions from the public domain.[53] The defendants objected that Mr Sawkins was not engaged 'in creation of a musical work at all'.[54] But Jacob LJ (as he then was) held that 'the sort of work done by Dr Sawkins should be encouraged. It saves others the time and trouble of re-creation of near-lost works, but in no sense creates monopoly in them. If someone wants to use Dr Sawkins' short cut, they need his permission'.[55] This sounds sensible and fair, but the effects were such that the musical compositions were taken out of the public domain and placed under the wings of Mr Sawkins' copyright and the scope of protection covered the whole musical work (not just the additions and modifications).[56] Analogically, there may be a similar risk of copyright covering the whole work whereby its expressive elements were determined to a large extent by an AI-driven system and a human being contributed only in a negligible manner. This could be mitigated by following *Infopaq*'s granular approach (ie 'if the elements thus reproduced are the expression of the intellectual creation of their author').[57]

Another issue, gaining importance given the advancements in AI, is the proximity of choices to the final subject matter. If a process of creation involves human designers and an AI-driven system whereas the latter is the last link in

[50] *George Hensher Ltd Appellants v Restawile Upholstery* [1976] AC 64 (HL).
[51] ibid 95 and 97.
[52] *Sawkins* (n 12).
[53] ibid [21]–[26].
[54] ibid [42].
[55] ibid [86].
[56] A different view on *Sawkins v Hyperion* and other 'original recreative works' can be found in Burton Ong, 'Originality from Copying: Fitting Recreative Works into the Copyright Universe' (2010) 2 *IPQ* 165. However, his conclusions on the telling potency of the process of creation concur with the present view: '[I]t is submitted that the originality analysis should centre on *how* the copying process was carried out – the degree of intellectual skill, effort and labour exercised in the process of recreating the antecedent work.' ibid 178.
[57] *Infopaq International A/S v Danske Dagblades Forening* ECLI:EU:C:2009:465.

the chain of creation that 'has the final say about what goes in and what stays out',[58] then given the obscurity of an AI-driven system's workings, practically no human designer's choices entering the AI-driven system's decision-making process would exit the system as those made by human designers (unless these choices were hard-coded).

Under the current courts' construction of joint authorship, if one of human collaborators has the final say, this does not mean that 'there can be no joint authorship'.[59] As put by Justice Laddie in *Cala Homes*, the contribution 'must be in the nature of originating and creating something that finds its way into the finished work'.[60] However, the rules on joint authorship (as a whole set of rules) are not applicable (not even by analogy) to the AI context since joint authorship is a unitary concept[61] and since there is no collaboration of the people[62] between a machine and a human being. However, there is no reason why the way in which the courts approach creative processes and attribution at the occasion of interpreting joint authorship could not be applied in the AI context by analogy. For instance, the guidance that a human input that finds its way into the final work counts towards authorship makes sense also in respect of AI productions. If this is accepted, then the scope of protection should follow closely only those human choices that are reflected in the final work which should be supported by evidence.

Reflections of Authorship and the Epistemic Approaches in France

Work of the Mind

In French law, the author of a work (a work of the mind)[63] enjoys exclusionary author's right(s) which subsist in the work on the basis of its creation.[64] To reiterate, the work is conceptualised as author's creation that takes an original form.[65] It may come as surprise that the French Intellectual Property Code does not mention originality as a general copyright subsistence criterion and that originality is

[58] *Kogan v Martin* (n 3) [50].
[59] ibid [51].
[60] *Cala Homes* (n 34) 834.
[61] *Kogan v Martin* (n 3) [31].
[62] ibid [33].
[63] '*l'oeuvre de l'esprit*'.
[64] Code de la propriété intellectuelle (Loi n° 92-597 du 1er juillet 1992 relative au code de la propriété intellectuelle, as amended as of 26 novembre 2021) (French Intellectual Property Code) art L111-1.
[65] André Lucas and Pierre Sirinelli, 'L'originalité en droit d'auteur' (1993) 23 *JCP* 253, 254. Pierre-Yves Gautier, *Propriété littéraire et artistique* 11th edn (Presses Universitaires de France 2019) 51.

regarded as a judge-made condition.[66] Historically, according to Professors Lucas and Sirinelli, the formulations related to originality rather translated the courts' will 'to make a recognition of the objective existence of a contribution, a personal work (without discussing the banality or the originality as a discriminating criterion) or aimed at admitting the paternity of the person to that contribution'.[67]

Laligant, the author of a monograph on originality, writes that the requirement of originality can be inferred from the Code, ie in his words, '[…] by using the expression "work of the mind" [the legislator suggests] that the work protected by author's right must be a product of intellectual creative activity of a human being'.[68] At any rate, nowadays the criterion of originality is commonly and widely considered as 'implict and undisputable'.[69]

A comprehensive analysis of French copyright cases from the eighteenth century to the end of the twentieth century produced by Laligant, distinguishes two model conceptions of originality. Under the first conception, a work is required to carry an imprint of its author's personality, including courts' expressions such as 'result of a personal work',[70] or 'a mark of personal talent' (subjective originality).[71] The second conception requires a work to be new in the sense that it 'does not reproduce any previous creation'[72] (it is not copied), including the work being distinct from other works of the same genre (objective originality).[73] According to Laligant, in some judgments these two conceptions were used interchangeably[74] or in conjunction with one another.[75]

As for the epistemic approaches, which are the main concern of this chapter, Laligant identified the following approaches in the courts' assessment of copyright subsistence. The courts tended to ask

> whether the work in question is, or is not an object of privilege (1st period[76]); then they asked in a more confusing way whether the work in question is, or is not, novel, original [, sufficiently individual] (2nd period[77]); and lastly […] the notion of "sufficient

[66] ibid 254.

[67] '[…] *la volonté de faire reconnaître l'existence objective d'un apport, d'un travail personnel (sans en discuté la banalité ou l'originalité comme critère discriminatoire) ou visaient à faire admettre la paternité d'une personne sur cet apport*.' ibid.

[68] '[…] *le législateur suggère déjà, par emploi de l'expression " œvre de l'esprit " que l' œvre protégeable au titre du droit d'auteur doit être le produit d'une activité mentale fabricatrice de l'homme*.' Olivier Laligant, *La véritable condition d'application du droit d'auteur: Originalité ou création?* (Presses Universitaires d'Aix-Marseille 1999) 14.

[69] '[…] *implicite et indiscutable*.' Frédéric Pollaud-Dulian, *Le droit d'auteur* 2nd edn (ECONOMICA 2014) [167].

[70] '*résultat d'un travail personnel*' Laligant (n 68) 68.

[71] '*marque d'un talent personnel*' ibid 66 ff.

[72] '*ne reproduit pas une création antérieure*' ibid, 113 and 66.

[73] ibid 113.

[74] ibid 98.

[75] ibid 89.

[76] Footnote added: dated from 1793 to ca 1900, ibid 123.

[77] Footnote added: dated from 1900 to 1988–1990, ibid 123–25.

individuality" has been replaced, under the effect of the supremacy of the subjective conception, by the [notion of] intellectual effort (3rd period[78]).[79]

Although it is now established that originality is understood as the imprint of the author's personality,[80] the ways in which courts address it still vary. In some cases, the courts searched for originality in the activity of creating the work. For instance, the French Supreme Court dismissed an appeal by a putative author against appellate court's reasoning that 'the activities [leading to the work] did not translate any individual imagination nor any effort to [bring about a] personal creation'[81] and affirmed it as sufficient.

In contrast, in a case involving a piece of conceptual art, the French Supreme Court specified the activity that translated author's personality to the work. More specifically, it found that placing a word in a certain fashion, in golden letters and with a particular graphic design, in a particular setting featuring shabby door, a handle in the shape of a cross and a wrecked wall, when perceived as a whole, the combination 'implies aesthetic choices translating the personality of the author'.[82] The fact that the assemblage did not fall into any of the traditional categories of work did not pose a barrier to its protection.

In other cases, the French Supreme Court omitted any reference to the activity and only mentioned the relevant aspects of the work in question. In one of the recent cases, it reproached the appellate court for finding copyright work based on the absence of anteriority of all the elements of the work and on the new character of the choices, but it 'did not specify in what [aspects] those choices, no matter how arbitrary they may be, bear the imprint of the personality of their author'.[83] In another case, the French Supreme Court dismissed an appeal against a decision in which the appellate court found no copyright in a kitchen utensil because its 'realisation was solely dictated by the function assigned to the object without [the process of] creation bearing an imprint of the personality of the author'.[84]

While in principle originality implies making arbitrary choices and a reflection (or a translation) of author's personality in the work,[85] in relation to computer programs, the courts lean towards different criteria. In a landmark decision *Pachot*,

[78] Footnote added: dated from 1988–1990 to 1999, ibid 125.

[79] '*ils se demandent si l'œuvre en cause est ou non objet de privilège (1e période); celle ensuite où ils se demandent plus confusément si l'œuvre en cause est, ou non, nouvelle, originale (2e période); celle enfin où l'expression "individualité suffisante" est supplantée, sous effet du primat de la conception subjective, par celle "d'effort intellectuel" (3e période)*'. ibid 122.

[80] Lucas and Sirinelli (n 65) 255.

[81] '*ces travaux ne traduisaient aucune fantaisie particulière ni un effort de création personnelle*' Cour de cassation, Decision of 2 March 1999, n° 97-10.179.

[82] '*cette combinaison implique des choix esthétiques traduisant la personnalité de l'auteur*' Cour de cassation, Decision of 13 November 2008, n° 06-19.021.

[83] '*n'a pas caractérisé en quoi ces choix, pour arbitraires qu'ils fussent, portaient l'empreinte de la personnalité de leur auteur*' Cour de cassation, Decision of 22 January 2014, n° 11-24.273.

[84] '*réalisation étant commandée par la fonction assignée à l'objet, sans création portant l'empreinte de la personnalité de l'auteur*' Cour de cassation, Decision of 28 November 2000, n° 98-17.891.

[85] Lucas and Sirinelli (n 65) 256.

the French Supreme Court (in a Plenary Assembly) did not allow an appeal against the approach of the first instance judge who required the putative author to submit evidence of 'a personalised effort going beyond a simple implementation of automatic and binding logic and that the effort is materialised in an individualised structure'[86] of the computer program. In another paragraph of the same decision, the requirement was framed as bringing about a work 'bear[ing] the mark of [author's] intellectual contribution'.[87]

Pachot is treated as a good authority on copyright in computer programs even after the Computer Directive came into force and the developments in CJEU's case law notwithstanding.[88] From *Pachot*, it follows that the personalised effort must be translated in an individualised structure of the computer program. While *Pachot* made it clear that copyright depends on leaving a trace of author's intellectual contribution, uncertainty remains as to how to identify such a contribution.[89] In line with the *Pachot* reasoning, in 2011, the French Supreme Court approved an appellate court's decision which was based on a factual finding that there was an intellectual contribution that consisted of writing a computer program according to 'methods distinct from those used for existing computer programs'.[90]

Recent judgments lean towards the imprint of personality criterion also in cases involving computer programs. In 2012, the French Supreme Court found insufficient evidence to show the distinctiveness of a solution proposed by the computer program in comparison with other solutions already available.[91] Therein, the French Supreme Court held the appellate court did not provide a sufficient legal basis for its decision as it failed to specify 'in what [aspects] the choices evidence the appropriate intellectual contribution and the personalised effort of the person who created the computer program as these solely confer the character of a protected original work [...]'.[92]

Despite courts' and scholars' fixation on the concept of originality as the 'cornerstone'[93] of the author's right, Professors Lucas and Sirinelli point out that, first, it should be determined whether the expressive subject matter falls within the domain of literary and artistic property.[94] This means asking whether the subject matter takes a concrete form that is perceivable by human senses, identifiable with objectivity

[86] '*d'un effort personnalisé allant au-delà de la simple mise en œuvre d'une logique automatique et contraignante et que la matérialisation de cet effort résidait dans une structure individualisée*' Cour de cassation, Assemblée Plénière, Decision of 7 March 1986, n° 83-10.477 (Rapp M Jonquères).

[87] ibid.

[88] Pierre Sirinelli and Alexandra Bensamoun, 'Case Law Section' (2018) 255 *RIDA* 125, 182.

[89] Lucas and Sirinelli (n 65) 257.

[90] '*selon des méthodes distinctes de celles utilisées pour les logiciels précédents*' Cour de cassation, Decision of 22 September 2011, n° 09-71.337.

[91] Cour de cassation, Decision of 17 October 2012, n° 11-21.641.

[92] '*en quoi les choix opérés témoignaient d'un apport intellectuel propre et d'un effort personnalisé de celui qui avait élaboré le logiciel litigieux, seuls de nature à lui conférer le caractère d'une œuvre originale protégée*' Cour de cassation, Decision of 17 October 2012, n° 11-21.641.

[93] Lucas and Sirinelli (n 65) 253.

[94] ibid 259.

and precision and provable.[95] According to Professor Gautier, the concretisation of an idea is 'an act of arriving at a sufficient precision as to the future work [...] it is the determination of contours that are not of a vague theme, [nor have their] subject still blurry'.[96] Among the subject matter not of the right form, one finds beauty contests, a method of commercialisation of a work, an idea of a TV programme or an edition of works which merely share a certain number of common characteristics.[97]

What role is there for typology and categorisation of works in French copyright law? Comparatively to the UK, not a prominent one. Article L112-2 of the French Intellectual Property Code lists objects that are, by way of example, works of the mind. Scholars offer their definitions of types of work, eg Gautier defines a literary work as an object communicating thoughts fixed in writing and perceived with sight as well as those expressed vocally[98] or Desbois defines musical work as a composition of melody, harmony and rhythm.[99] Desbois distinguished literary works, musical works and works of art based on their distinct processes of creation.[100] For instance, he identified the stages of creation of a literary work as 'ideas, composition, expression'.[101]

However, the categorisation of works is something on which academics dwell more than the courts. According to the Court of Appeal in Paris, the protection does not depend on whether the subject matter is of a specific genre but only on its original character.[102] Similarly, the fact that a textbook is not specifically mentioned among the statutory categories does not carry any drawbacks for its copyright eligibility.[103] In other cases French courts have recognised the author's right in hairstyles, webpages, sound and light performance, etc.[104]

Courts' Epistemic Approach to the Criteria

The next question is whether and, if so, where and how courts actually check fulfilment of the criteria. Originality is treated as a question of law by French courts. As such, it requires a legal assessment and cannot be delegated to an expert. Yet, experts may assist with identifying any facts and pointers towards its recognition.[105] Making a conclusion on whether a work is original is the domain of judges of the first instance

[95] Christophe Caron, *Droit d'auteur et droits voisins* 6th edn (LexisNexis 2020) 67–82.
[96] '*c'est le fait de parvenir à une précision suffisante quant à l'œuvre future [...] c'est la détermination des contours de ce qui n'est pas un vague thème, un sujet encore flou*' Gautier (n 66) 58.
[97] André Lucas, *Propriété littéraire et artistique* 5th edn (Dalloz 2017) 83–84.
[98] Gautier (n 65) 61–72.
[99] Henri Desbois, *Le droit d'auteur en France* 3rd edn (Dalloz 1978) 134.
[100] ibid 11.
[101] '*idées, composition, expression*' ibid.
[102] Cour d'appel de Paris, Decision of 28 February 2007 (2007) 212 *RIDA* 312.
[103] Cour d'appel de Paris, Decision of 21 November 1994 (1995) 164 *RIDA* 381.
[104] André Lucas, Agnès Lucas-Schloetter and Carine Bernault, *Traité de la propriété littéraire et artistique* 5th edn (LexisNexis 2017) 97–98.
[105] Michel Vivant and Jean-Michel Brugière, *Droit d'auteur et droits voisins* 4th edn (Dalloz 2019) 325.

or appellate courts if necessary. In the past few decades, the French Supreme Court gradually began to exercise more control over interpretation of originality.[106]

To reiterate, it is generally accepted that originality must be manifested in the form.[107] In addition, originality must be manifested in certain aspects of the form, since originality 'does not lie in the style but in the manner in which it is materialised and expressed in a particular form'.[108] For instance, it has been established that originality of a musical work can be found in the melody, rhythm and harmony.[109] A novel can be original in its composition, including an outline or a construction, as well as its execution, including editing or style, etc.[110] This suggests that courts tend to engage with the final result rather than the process of creation.

Even though all works adhere to the same standard of originality,[111] originality manifests itself differently according to the respective genre of the work.[112] The burden of proof in relation to facts relevant to establish originality of a work is placed on the copyright owner,[113] but courts usually do not verify the existence of originality.[114] According to Lucas and Sirinelli, '[i]n practice, originality is rarely denied. It is, in fact, presumed, too'.[115]

Professor Vivant makes a similar observation that, in practice, the courts treat the traditional works of literature and fine arts as a priori eligible for protection and hence 'we are not far away from protecting a genre despite that being against the principles since it is each work in its singularity that must be examined by the judge'.[116] Caron concurs by questioning whether it is possible to use presumptions concerning originality. Sirinelli admits that judges rely on the statutory presumption of authorship and infer originality from it.[117]

This confirms the concerns expressed in this book. By way of illustration, courts tend to discuss originality more often in relation to the less traditional types of work such as computer programs or photographs. In such cases they showed more curiosity as to actual proof of originality. For instance, the first instance court in Paris held that the person seeking copyright in a database must demonstrate in which aspects it is original, including explaining originality in the choices made in the process of designing and making of the database.[118] In a different

[106] Carole Thomas-Raquin and Martin Le Guerer, 'Le controle de l'originalité d'une oeuvre par la Cour de cassation' [2017] *Comm Com Électr* 90.

[107] Pollaud-Dulian (n 69) [170].

[108] Pierre Sirinelli, 'Chronique de Jurisprudence' (2010) 226 *RIDA* 394. Translation by Margaret Platt-Hommel.

[109] Pollaud-Dulian (n 69) [209], [229]. Similarly Vivant and Brugière (n 105) 324.

[110] ibid.

[111] ibid [286].

[112] Laligant (n 68) 19.

[113] TGI de Paris, Decision of 6 October 2009 (2010) 226 *RIDA* 506.

[114] Lucas and Sirinelli (n 65) 260.

[115] ibid 255.

[116] '*on n'est pas loin d'une protection du genre, pourtant contraire aux principes puisque c'est chaque œuvre dans sa singularité qui doit être examinée par le juge*.' Michel Vivant and Jean-Michel Brugière, *Droit d'auteur et droits voisins* 4th edn (Dalloz 2019) 342–43.

[117] Sirinelli (n 108) 454.

[118] Pierre Sirinelli, 'Chronique de Jurisprudence' (2011) 230 *RIDA* 143, 172.

case, the author was successful in demonstrating originality of his photographs by explaining his own creative choices made in the course of creation of the examined photographs.[119] These cases show that once originality is in question, its presence must be demonstrated by explaining how the required effort or author's personality were translated into the final creation.

In sum, a work of the mind requires originality in the sense of a work amounting to a creation (in an appropriate form) (i) reflecting author's personality or (ii) personal effort of the author (in case of computer programs). However, as there is no legislative definition of originality, it still, to some degree, remains a 'notion of variable geometry'.[120] In practice, French courts appear to presume originality with respect to traditional works and search for originality in the process of creation with respect to less traditional types of work.

Application of the French Copyright Subsistence Criteria to AI Productions

From the present analysis of the case law, it follows that French courts have some chance to discover that an AI production has no author if they deal with certain subject matter such as photographs, applied art or conceptual art. It may be less clear how originality of a computer program would be assessed as there has been some development towards a test of personal intellectual contribution since *Pachot*. However, if *Pachot* is going to be followed, then courts will focus on distinctiveness rather than human origin. Any non-human origin of a computer program may thus remain undetected.

French legislation does not provide for the protection of computer-generated works. Bertrand refers in this connection to the conclusions of the Committee of governmental experts who stated that only those persons who furnished 'the element of creation without which the final work would not have been object of protection by author's rights'[121] are entitled to author's right.

There are cases discussing the protection of a computer-assisted subject matter which support this position. In 1997, the First Instance Court in Paris abstained from examining contributions allegedly made by a computer. In the process of creating a logo, different trials, studies and research of the graphic were realised on the digital material under instructions given by the claimant.[122] The court found that such contributions of the claimant were not of a sufficient specificity to give rise to author's right.[123] Similarly, in 2005, the Court of Appeal in Bordeaux found

[119] Sirinelli (n 108) 426.

[120] This idiom is attributed to the counsellor Jonquères according to Laligant (n 68) 19. Similarly, Lucas, Lucas-Schloetter and Bernault (n 104) [124].

[121] '*l'élément de création sans lequel l'œuvre finale n'aurait pu faire l'objet d'une protection par le droit d'auteur*.' André Bertrand, *Droit d'auteur* 3rd edn (Dalloz Action 2010) 107–08.

[122] TGI de Paris, Decision of 27 June 1997, *PIBD* 1997 III 661.

[123] ibid.

that a layout of a lorry storage that served to accommodate storing units designed with the aid of a computer was a work provided that it shows, at least minimally, originality which the person who conceived it wanted to contribute.[124] Again, the court preferred to look at the relevant contribution made by a human being and hinge any ensuing protection on it regardless of contributions made by a computer.

As for the scope of protection, in France, copyright in a work covers only its verbatim expression. Beyond the form of expression itself, the composition is protected to the extent that depends on, as put by Bertrand, '"capillarity" of its originality. The composition of a work is not original as a whole; it is [original] by multitude of elements that are interlocked into each other'.[125] Importantly, infringement can be claimed only in relation to the taken parts that are sufficiently recalling the personality of their true author.[126] Parts of work that are commonplace and do not translate author's personality do not attract protection.[127] As the scope of protection in France follows originality, ie the elements reflecting personality of author, the problem of unjustified scope of protection for AI productions with some minimal authorial contribution should not, in theory, arise.

Reflections of Authorship and the Epistemic Approaches in Germany

Protected Works

The German Author's Right Act provides a non-exhaustive list of protected works. Pursuant to § 2(1) of the Act, the following classes of work belong to the domain of literature, science and art: literary works (such as written works, speeches and computer programs), musical works, pantomimic works (including works of dance), artistic works (including works of architecture and of applied art), cinematographic works, photographic works, illustrations of a scientific or technical nature (such as drawings, plans, maps, sketches).

Pursuant to the next subsection, '[w]orks in the sense of this statute are only personal intellectual creations'.[128] This verbatim translation could be reformulated as follows: only those subject matter that are personal intellectual creations are works in the sense of this statute. As put by Professor Schulze, the two subsections

[124] Cour d'Appel de Bordeaux, Decision of 31 January 2005 as cited in André Kéréver, 'Chronique de Jurisprudence' (2005) 204 *RIDA* 298.

[125] '"*capillarité" de son originalité. La composition d'une œuvre n'est pas originale d'un bloc; elle l'est par une multitude d'éléments qui s'imbriquent les uns dans les autres*' Bertrand (n 121) 279.

[126] ibid 282.

[127] ibid 282–83.

[128] '*Werke im Sinne dieses Gesetzes sind nur persönliche geistige Schöpfungen*.' Urheberrechtsgesetz of 9 September 1965 (BGBl I S 1273), as amended by the statute of 28 November 2018 (BGBl I S 2014) (German Author's Right Act or Act) § 2(2).

supplement each other and the subsistence of author's right is conditioned on the works being personal intellectual creations.[129] This would correspond to the reading of 'presupposes' in the *Infopaq*[130] in its conditional meaning, ie that a subject matter is required to be an intellectual creation to constitute a protectable literary or artistic work (see Chapter 6).

According to Professor Schulze, 'it usually plays no role into which category a subject matter is put'[131] with the exception when special norms are to be applied with respect to certain kinds of work such as paintings or films.[132] The categorisation used to be meaningful for works of applied art for which there used to be a higher originality standard. However, this approach became outdated in the light of the CJEU's ruling in *Cofemel* with some uncertainty as to whether any other test, if at all, should replace it.[133]

In general, some subject matter such as a novel or a musical composition fall straightforwardly into a category and other are at the edge such as food recipes or contextual art.[134] As for the meaning of the categories literary works are understood as works of language that express 'ideas inhering in the content'[135] through letters or other signs. A musical work is a subject matter that consists of tones of any sort that must be created by a natural person; it can be improvised, but must be fixed.[136] Whether a subject matter is artistic (and hence falls into the category of artistic work) would be judged objectively and on the basis of how experts evaluate the work and on the basis of the overall impression the work makes on the audience.[137]

Personal Intellectual Creation

In Germany, the requirement corresponding to originality, ie personal intellectual creation, is enshrined in §2(2) of the German Author's Right Act.[138] German legal scholarship, which is traditionally highly regarded and followed by German

[129] Gernot Schulze, 'UrhG § 2 Geschützte Werke' in Thomas Dreier and Gernot Schulze (eds), *Urheberrechtsgesetz* 7th edn (CH Beck 2022) [2].

[130] Case C-5/08 *Infopaq International A/S v Danske Dagblades Forening* [2009] ECR I-6569, EU:C:2009:465, para 34.

[131] '*Meistens spielt es keine Rolle, in welche Kategorie das einzelne Werk eingeordnet wird.*' Gernot Schulze, 'UrhG § 2 Geschützte Werke' in Thomas Dreier and Gernot Schulze (eds), *Urheberrechtsgesetz* 7th edn (CH Beck 2022) [79].

[132] ibid.

[133] Case C-795/23, Request for a preliminary ruling, lodged 21 December 2023 by the German Federal Supreme Court.

[134] Matthias Leistner, 'UrhG § 2 Geschützte Werke' in Gerhard Schricker and Ulrich Loewenheim (eds), *Urheberrecht* 6th edn (CH Beck 2020) [133] and [173].

[135] Another plausible translation would be a work that 'contains thoughts', in original '*der Gedankeninhalt*' ibid [100].

[136] Schulze (n 131) [134], [135].

[137] ibid [62], [67].

[138] German Author's Right Act, § 2(2).

courts, further elaborates that there are, in essence, four originality sub-criteria within the §2(2) provision. In order to attract copyright, the work must (i) be a personal creation of its author, (ii) inhere an intellectual content, (iii) exist in a perceivable form and (iv) express individual character of its author.[139]

The sub-criterion of 'personal creation of its author' is understood as requiring the work to rest on human creative activity of the author.[140] The question is whether the creator of the underlying work was a natural person and any machine potentially involved was used as a mere tool over which the human creator had control.[141] Some argue that even an arrangement of found objects such as a stone or a tree branch that a natural person chooses to present as a piece of art would amount to a protected work.[142]

The second sub-criterion of an intellectual content requires a natural person being active in creating their work and in communicating the content that incorporates ideas or emotions originating from them.[143] Equally, within this sub-criterion, the work is supposed to have educating, entertaining or other, somehow stimulating effects on its human recipients.[144]

In one case, the Higher State Court in Düsseldorf found that the phrase 'We drive, drive on the highway' was deprived of any concrete intellectual content because the repetition of 'drive' lends itself to too many interpretations. For instance, it may evoke the flow of the journey, the distance to be driven, the speed of driving or the length of the journey, the joy from driving or the burden of driving.[145] In the words of the court, '[d]ue to the high number of and differences in the various plausible intellectual contents, this group of words does not carry, as it is, any certain thought'.[146] The court thus regarded the phrase to be a mere dependent building block to which something needs to be added in order to embody a protection-worthy intellectual content and for this reason it was declared, just by itself, ineligible for the protection.[147]

Similarly, the German Federal Supreme Court denied copyright protection for the manner in which individual works were arranged for publication on the

[139] Ulrich Loewenheim, *Handbuch des Urheberrechts* 2nd edn (CH Beck 2010) 55. Marcel Bisges, *Handbuch Urheberrecht* (Erich Schmidt Verlag 2016) 51–57. Or, alternatively, as put by Schulze, the protected work must amount to (i) a personal creation, (ii) an intellectual creation and (iii) a creation (in a sense of a result of employing creative forces, ie '*die Schöpfung*') (whereby the Loewenheim's fourth condition – individual character – is covered within the third criterion by Schulze) in Schulze (n 132) [8]–[18].

[140] Leistner (n 134) [38].

[141] Schulze (n 131) [8]. Loewenheim (n 139) 56.

[142] Schulze ibid [9].

[143] Loewenheim (n 139) 56.

[144] Schulze (n 131) [12].

[145] Decision of 1 December 1977, 20 U 46/77 [1978] *GRUR* 640, 641.

[146] '*Wegen der hohen Zahl und der Unterschiedlichkeit verschiedener denkbarer geistiger Inhalte der Wortgruppe ist diese nicht selbst Träger eines bestimmten Gedankens*.' ibid.

[147] ibid 641.

ground that the arrangement lacked concrete intellectual content. In the words of the German Federal Supreme Court, seeking protection for

> elements of the division and layout of the typographical arrangement of a specific genre of collected works [...] is not compatible with the leading principles of author's right, whereby only those specific [and] individual works that are characterised by an intellectual content are eligible for protection.[148]

The third sub-criterion of protection requires a work to be developed to such an extent that it is perceivable by human senses. This requirement also relates to fixation of the work. Even a temporary fixation is sufficient for copyright to subsist.[149] As this sub-criterion does not entail any human aspects of creation, it is not discussed here at any length.

The fourth sub-criterion means that the individualised character of work must be a result of author's individual intellectual creativity.[150] For instance, in case of a musical work, the German Federal Supreme Court held that 'creative individualisation lies in its own individualised aesthetical expressive power'.[151] Yet, the court continued, the standards for the individualised aesthetical content should not be set too high so that pop music can be covered as well.[152]

In relation to a brooch depicting a thistle, the German Federal Supreme Court found that if a subject matter imitates nature, it 'must not be a mere handicraft achievement but must also incorporate a certain individual and creative originality'.[153] The court emphasised the fact that the representation of thistle on the brooch differs from the natural thistle only in small details.[154] Professor Hofmann comments that it is uncertain whether the courts would follow the reasoning in the *Silver Thistle* judgment because, in the meantime, the German Federal Supreme Court had amended its approach to works of applied art so that no stricter rules should apply to them.[155]

In relation to a literary work, the German Federal Supreme Court affirmed the conclusion of lower courts that a novel inspired by a preceding, well-known novel and composed as its sequel while using its characters and their relationships and building on the preceding novel's scenes and plots, was found not to have its

[148] '*gewisse Merkmale der Einteilung und äußeren Anordnung des Schriftspiegels einer bestimmten Gattung von Sammelwerken anstrebt, ist mit dem leitenden Gedanken des Urheberrechts unvereinbar, wonach nur bestimmte einzelne, durch ihren Gedankeninhalt gekennzeichnete Werke urheberrechtsschutzfähig sind*.' Decision of 20 September 1955, I ZR 194/53BGHZ 18, 175/177 [1955] *NJW* 1753, 1754.

[149] Schulze (n 131) [13].

[150] Loewenheim (n 139) 57.

[151] '*Die schöpferische Eigentümlichkeit liegt bei Musikwerken in ihrer individuellen ästhetischen Ausdruckskraft*' Decision of 26 September 1980, I ZR 17/78 [1981] *GRUR* 267, 268.

[152] ibid. The same more recently in Decision of 16 April 2015, I ZR 225/12 [2015] *GRUR* 1189.

[153] Decision of 22 June 1995, I ZR 119/93 [1995] *IIC* 1997, 140, 142 (English translation by IIC).

[154] ibid.

[155] Franz Hofmann, Michael Grünberger and Adolf Dietz 'Germany' in Lionel Bently and Burton Ong (eds) *International Copyright Law and Practice*, vol 2 (annually updated, LexisNexis) §2[4][c].

own individualised character nor represent a sufficient departure from its source of inspiration and that the matter borrowed did not fade away and retreat in the new novel.[156] The lower courts' findings were supported by two expert reports in the field of literature which were commissioned by the parties.[157]

In the *Pippi Longstocking* case, the German Federal Supreme Court advanced a strict application of the individualised character sub-criterion in relation to literary or other characters. As put by the court, '[a]n individual character of a literary work […] can enjoy independent copyright protection on condition that the author gives this character a distinctive personality through the combination of pronounced character traits and particular physical features'.[158] The court added that describing external attributes or appearance of the character would not suffice to meet the requirement of individualised character.[159]

The Higher State Court in Berlin found that copyright subsisted in a 'Wrapped Reichstag' a work consisting of the Reichstag being wrapped in a thick woven polypropylene fabric with an aluminium surface.[160] The reason was mainly that the work was 'distinguished by its especially high level of originality and finds its only inspiration in the previous works of [the artists] such as wrapping of the Pont Neuf in Paris'.[161] The project was also found to have manifested 'a special level of inidividualised character'[162] through the constant change of shades of colours and movements of folding of the wrapping that were caused by the flow of wind and light.

These sub-criteria seem compatible with the EU requirements of author's own intellectual creation and liable to bring it to life. In particular, there appears to be an overlap of the sub-criteria of individualised character and author's personal creation with the EU requirement of the work reflecting author's personality. This comes through clearly in the *Wrapped Reichstag* case which may be interpreted as inferring the personal touch embodied in the work from artists' creative history of wrapping remarkable monuments and thereby creating aesthetic impressions that likely reflect their artistic personality. The requirement for an intellectual content appears to be the closest reflection of human authorship in German copyright law. For the time being, there seems to be no suggestion that AI-driven systems would be able to communicate any meaning through the expressive elements they determine. This criterion seems also somewhat additional to what is required at EU level.

[156] Decision of 29 April 1999, I ZR 65/96 [1999] *ZUM* 644, 648.

[157] ibid 646.

[158] *Pippi-Langstrumpf-Kostüm*, Decision of 17 July 2013, I ZR 52/12 [2014] *IIC* 467 (English translation by IIC).

[159] ibid.

[160] Decision of 30 January 1996, 5 U 7926/95 was affirmed by the German Federal Supreme Court, *Wrapped Reichstag – Christo*, Decision of 24 January 2002, I ZR 102/99 [2003] *IIC* 570 (English translation by IIC).

[161] '[…] *zeichnet sich durch ein besonders hohes Maß an Originalität aus und findet ein Vorbild nur in früheren eigenen Werken der Ast., so etwa in der Verhüllung des Pont Neuf in Paris*.' Decision of 30 January 1996, 5 U 7926/95, *GRUR* 1997, 128.

[162] '*zeigt das Werk* […] *ein hohes Maß an Individualität*' ibid.

Courts' Epistemic Approach to the Criteria

It follows directly from the German Author's Right Act that copyright subsistence is conditioned upon existence of a personal intellectual creation. German courts approach the 'protected work' as a normative, legal concept.[163] In the normal course of action, German courts rely on the manifestation of personal intellectual creation in the result rather than in the process of creation. The courts tend to rely on their own impressions and indications of originality as perceived from their intellectual engagement with the subject matter or audience opinion.[164] According to Bullinger, the German authorities are confident to pass such judgments because the questions of copyright subsistence fall within the remit of expert departments, expert chambers or expert senates at higher courts. As he continues, because of this work division and 'thanks to their constant practice the responsible judges are familiar with the matter also from the factual side'.[165]

For instance, in a case involving a simple metal chair with no hind legs, the German Federal Supreme Court did not interfere with the lower courts' factual finding and assessment as to 'the overall aesthetic impression'[166] of the constituting elements of the chair and their inherent characteristic aesthetic content.[167] The courts may also resort to external indications such as expert opinions, art exhibitions, reception of an award or appearance in a publication on art.[168]

This focus on the result may be due to the way in which the requirement of work is defined in the German Author's Right Act. Since it is defined as a work of certain qualities, the expressive subject matter becomes the centre of attention. Therefore, it is logical that courts would prefer to benchmark a result rather than a process against the statutory definition of a work. Understandably, it is more natural to compare an apple against an ideal apple.

A telling case study may be the copyright subsistence assessment in relation to computer programs. Pursuant to the German Federal Supreme Court in *Inkasso-Programm*, the individualised character of the work is to be ascertained based on a comparison of the disputed computer program with a plain and ordinary arrangement of elements or with previous works:

> This comparison does not entail [...] any novelty examination [...], but it just answers the question of whether the concrete design distinguishes itself from previously known designs through individual particularities.[169]

[163] Winfried Bullinger, 'UrhG § 2 Geschützte Werke' in Artur-Axel Wandtke and Winfried Bullinger (eds), *Praxiskommentar Urheberrecht* 6th edn (CH Beck 2022) [5].

[164] See also Schulze (n 131) [62], [67].

[165] '*Die urteilenden Richter sind deshalb mit der Materie auch von der tatsächlichen Seite her durch ihre ständige Praxis vertraut*' Bullinger (n 163) [7].

[166] '*den ästhetischen Gesamteindruck*' Decision of 27 May 1981, I ZR 102/79 [1981] *GRUR* 820.

[167] Decision of 27 May 1981, I ZR 102/79 [1981] *GRUR* 820, 822.

[168] Schulze (n 131) [62].

[169] '*Dieser Vergleich enthält keine [...] Neuheitsprüfung [...], sondern beantwortet die Frage, ob der konkreten Formgestaltung gegenüber den vorbekannten Gestaltungen individuelle Eigenheiten zukommen.*' *Inkasso-Programm*, Decision of 9 May 1985, I ZR 52/83 [1985] *GRUR* 1041, 1047.

Admittedly, in the above part, the case may be regarded outdated in the light of developments at EU level.[170] In general though, the case remains to be referred in the newest editions of commentaries.[171] In the meantime, German courts also devised other ways in which they assess the individualised character of a computer program. For instance, some courts require only statistical uniqueness.[172] Other rely on a judge-made factual presumption that any complex, specialised or 'lengthy' computer program does have a sufficient individualised character which makes it eligible for protection.[173]

Exceptionally, German courts would look at the process of creation. In *Inkasso-Programm*, the German Federal Supreme Court distinguished the process of solving a problem (the result being a literary description of the solution), the process of projecting the solution (the result being a graphic representation of the solution) and the process of coding itself.[174] Though these stages and their outcomes are recognised as important for copyright assessment, the copyright protection covers only 'the form and manner in which the materials are gathered, selected and arranged'.[175] For the purposes of identifying the intellectual creation, the room for making individual and creative choices as to the solution was found in all the three phases.[176] This exceptional attention paid to the process of creation does not, however, present any novel epistemic approach because, at the end of the day, the assessment is about comparing a computer program at hand with other computer programs known to date.

Application of German Copyright Subsistence Criteria to the AI Productions

The method that German courts employ to assess the presence of an intellectual content shows the most promise for the purposes of distinguishing authored works from AI productions with no human authors. As follows from the '*We drive, drive on the highway*' case, once an expression offers too many different interpretations as to the ideas inhering in the content (*der Gedankeninhalt*), it is doubtful that it will be found to constitute a personal intellectual creation. A variety of plausible interpretations of a AI production is likely to arise because of the lack of capability to fill the content with ideas and meaning.

[170] ibid.

[171] Schulze (n 131) [126], Michael Lehman and Gerald Spindler, '2. Abschnitt. Das geschützte Werk. §9 Werkarten' in Ulrich Loewenheim (ed) *Handbuch des Urheberrechts* 3rd edn (CH Beck 2021) [46].

[172] Malte Grützmacher, '§69a' in Ulrich Loewenheim (ed) *Handbuch des Urheberrechts* 3rd edn (CH Beck 2021) [36].

[173] Gerald Spindler, '§69a UrhG' in Gerhard Schricker and Ulrich Loewenheim (eds), *Urheberrecht* 6th edn, (CH Beck 2020) [22].

[174] *Inkasso-Programm* (n 169) 1046.

[175] ibid 1047.

[176] ibid.

The sub-criterion of author's personal creation should focus exactly on the issue of whether the expressive subject matter was authored by a human being. If there is an expressive subject matter with no human author and, as phrased by Dornis, the 'intellectual bond between the work and the creator' is missing, no author's right arises.[177] However, whether this will be checked by courts on their own motion seems rather unlikely. As Professors Loewenheim and Leistner write, even when the results of human work and computational creativity can hardly be distinguished from each other, the German Author's Right Act protects only human creative achievement and not results produced by a machine.[178] They argue that a case of a natural person who would create an essential basic plan for the work and make choices out of various versions of the work generated by a computer could be assessed differently.[179]

The other sub-criteria, eg individuality or perceivability, may not prove as helpful for the present purposes as they focus on external features of the expressive subject matter. Though the case of *Wrapped Reichstag* demonstrates that a track record of creating certain kinds of works, ie wrapping up monuments in a fabric, may lend itself to evidence an individualised character of an artistic work (as one in some sort of series).

As for the unjustified scope of protection for AI productions with some minimal authorial contribution, at least in theory, there are conceptual means to prevent it. The German Federal Supreme Court held that in general the scope of protection should correspond to the expressive elements brought about by the author:

> the aesthetic effect of the form can justify protection by author's right to the extent to which it is not owed to the utilitarian purpose [...]. Besides, it is to be noted that although it [the aesthetic effect] justifies protection by author's right, nonetheless a small level of creativity leads to a correspondingly narrow scope of protection of that work.[180]

Conclusion

This chapter showed that human aspects of creation are reflected in the UK, French and German copyright subsistence criteria, namely in the requirement for skill, labour, and judgment (the UK), reflection of personality (France) and personal intellectual creation (Germany). More specifically, in the UK, a subject matter must first fall into a statutory category and only after the bar of categorisation

[177] '*geistige Verbindung des "Werkes" zu einem "Schöpfer"*' Tim Dornis, 'Der Schutz künstlicher Kreativität im Immaterialgüterrecht' [2019] GRUR 1252, 1255. Simlarly Sven Hetmank and Anne Lauber-Rönsberg, 'Künstliche Intelligenz – Herausforderungen für das Immaterialgüterrecht' [2018] *GRUR* 574.

[178] Leistner (n 134) [39].

[179] ibid [41].

[180] *Geburtstagszug*, Decision of 13 November 2013, I ZR 143/12 [2014] *GRUR* 175.

is cleared it can be assessed as to its originality. The advantage of categories is that they predetermine the relevant creative activity for the originality assessment. When it comes to human authorship implicit in the copyright subsistence criteria, there is a requirement of person's own intellectual input that is of sufficient transformative character and poured into the activity of creating a particular type of work at the level of work's conception as well as its realisation.

In France, the concept of work depends on the conception of originality having more weight than the categories of work. The French 'work of the mind' requires originality in the sense of reflection of author's personality or author's personal effort. This clearly reflects the human aspects of the requirement. However, in practice, French courts seem to rely on a judge-made presumption of originality and are satisfied upon perceiving an expressive subject matter that belongs to literary or artistic domain.

In Germany, protected works are conditioned upon them being personal intellectual creations. In theory, the German understanding of personal intellectual creations as featuring personal creation of the author, intellectual content and expression of individuality of the author should lead to finding the origin since all these sub-criteria depend on human aspects of creation. However, in practice, the courts seem to rely on their own impression and aesthetical judgment and secondary indications of originality.

In general, the epistemic approaches usually applied by courts focus predominantly on the form of the expressive subject matter. If it is consistent with their previous experience of authored works, they tend to infer or presume that they have encountered another authored work. Therefore, the epistemic approaches regularly adopted by the UK, German and French courts are not robust enough to distinguish authored work from authorless expressive subject matter.

On a more positive note, there are also some promising signs of courts engaging with the process of creation as they ask for explanation of originality of choices (France) or identify ideas in the content of the work (Germany) or determine inputs of sufficient transformative character (the UK). The downside is that such examinations are likely to take place only in special contexts of less traditional works (France) or less intelligible works (Germany) or joint authorship (the UK).

9

Reforms and Ways Forward

Final Overview

We encounter AI-driven systems that have reached the stage at which they can determine expressive or non-obvious technical properties of their outputs without their human designers or operators intervening or understanding the properties before the outputs are completed. In addition, these outputs resemble traditional works and inventions so closely that they are often indistinguishable. Against these developments in AI and ensuing changes in the processes of creation and inventing, this book's main concern is as follows. When authorities encounter expressive subject matter with no human author or non-obvious technical advances with no human inventor, will they be able to distinguish them from authored works and human-made inventions?

The short answer is likely no. The authorities usually do not employ such epistemic approaches that would enable them to make the distinction. They focus almost exclusively on whether a subject matter has (convincingly) expressive or non-obvious technical properties without taking into consideration the underlying human activity required to render the subject matter eligible for protection.

More specifically, the invention test suffers from focusing solely on whether a subject matter falls within any of the technical fields and rarely examines whether it amounts to a human creation at all. The inventive step test takes the underlying necessary human intellectual activity for granted and is limited to the inventive quality of the invention. The inquiry whether a subject matter constitutes an authored work is reduced to engaging with its expressive elements. For instance, upon reading an arrangement of words which contains a rhyme and rhythm typical for a poem, the authorities infer that it is a poem which is traditionally regarded as a human intellectual creation. Admittedly, such inference is supported by the statutory catalogues of works and established assumptions about poems, music or paintings being created by human beings. The authorities practically infer the cause – the human author – from the effect – the poem.

As the present research shows, the statutory texts are not at fault. They appropriately conceive of works and inventions as human intellectual creations and formulate the copyright subsistence and patentability requirements accordingly. These requirements reflect the human aspects of creating and inventing sufficiently and with the aid of teleological interpretation even more clearly. The failings are due to the inadequacy of the established interpretation and application practices.

To illustrate the possible application scenarios, Chapter 8 shows how copyright subsistence requirements could be applied to AI productions in line with authorities' practices. This exercise revealed that even in cases of limited human authorial contributions, the UK authorities are at risk of warranting a scope of protection disproportionately larger than the contributions justify. In theory, this should not happen in Germany and France where the scope of protection follows the elements reflecting author's personality. Since the established epistemic approaches employed in patentability assessment provide almost no means to detect the lack of human inventorship, the application exercise was not conducted in the patent law part.

Authorship and inventorship were analysed to assess the adequacy of the interpretative approaches and application practices of authorities. This analysis also revealed some uncertainty regarding where the normative sense of authorship or inventorship ends and the examination of facts concerning the authorial or inventorial act begins. It is also unclear to what extent the conceptions of authorship and inventorship should be determined by policies, normative reasons and legal guidance produced by authorities as opposed to the facts of the case and practices in the industry. On the one hand, authorities currently treat authorship and inventorship mainly as questions of fact.[1] To recall, the act of creation and the act of invention are real factual acts. Hence, the semantic contents of the legal standards of authorship and inventorship are mainly informed by the current practices in the production of works and inventions. This is only reinvigorated by the legal presumptions of authorship and the designation of inventorship. In principle, a person who publicly presents themselves as the author or the inventor is deemed to be the author or the inventor.

On the other hand, as Biron and Bently point out, 'copyright law needs a conception of authorship that can be applied across a great diversity of cultural fields'[2] and hence be broad and abstract enough to encompass the real-life diversity. Therefore, and with a view to maintaining intellectual property reserved for human intellectual creations, this book argues that authorship and inventorship conceived of as factual creating and factual inventing may be good servants (to the established assumptions) but bad masters. At the end of the day, treating them as a matter of fact means merely giving a court stamp on the established social practices.

Biron and Bently also list the following downsides of social determination of the legal concept of authorship: the social norms and practices may not be stable enough, it may be impossible to align the concept with the sheer variety of creative

[1] Besides the national laws researched in Chapters 3 and 5, this is also supported at EU level. Recital 14 of the Term Directive states: 'The question of authorship of the whole or a part of a work is a question of fact which the national courts may have to decide.'

[2] Laura Biron and Lionel Bently, 'Discontinuities Between Legal Conceptions of Authorship and Social Practices. What if Anything, is to be Done?' in Mireille van Eechoud (ed), *The Work of Authorship* (Amsterdam University Press 2014) 260.

practices and, lastly, the concept could internalise the power relations already existing in the society.[3] By analogy, the same applies to the conception of inventorship in relation to its suitability to a diversity of technical fields. Applying this to the AI context, social determination of authorship or inventorship may lead to discrimination among the cultural and technical fields based on their implementation of AI-driven systems in their processes of creation. In some sub-fields, an AI-driven system may become regarded as genuine creator by way of custom, but not in all, or not as quickly. With this laid-back approach, the law would have to accept such developments despite the inconsistencies, fragmentation and feeding back to intellectual property policies that will come along. Therefore, this book calls for the law and regulation to gain the upper hand.

Additionally, the AI-generated challenges create a demand for conceptions of authorship and inventorship that are somewhat narrower and more selective so that the scope of protection is limited to those subject matter or to those of their properties that are genuine human intellectual creations. Such better management of the scope of protection (which currently extends to more abstract parts of authored works and technical equivalents of claimed inventions) seems necessary to sustain the essence of copyright as rights for authors-creators and patents as rights for inventors-creators and justify the limitations they place on the society.

Therefore, this book advances a normative approach. It advocates for treating authorship and inventorship (and thus the activities of creating a work and inventing an invention) as implicit legal requirements. As for the implementation, this book proposes that to distinguish human intellectual creations from other subject matter, the authorities should interpret the existing statutory copyright subsistence and patentability criteria in the light of the implicit human authorship and human inventorship requirements. More concretely, the aspects of authorial and inventorial contribution that play a crucial role in the context of entitlement, namely their specificity and their presence in a circumscribed process of creation, should be equally required and scrutinised in the context of application of the statutory copyright subsistence and patentability criteria.

Further, the authorities should amend their epistemic approaches to the application of copyright subsistence and patentability criteria so that they focus on the process of creation or inventing with the ultimate view to checking whether the expressive elements or non-obvious technical features respectively owe their existence to the relevant human intellectual creative activity.

To clarify, the proposed changes in interpretation and the shift of focus on the underlying processes of creation should not insert subjectivity or arbitrariness into the assessment. Rather, this book maintains that while human intellectual creative activity matters for patentability and copyright subsistence, whether activities corresponding to the legal standards in fact occurred and whether they were of required quality (expressive or inventive) should be assessed in an objective

[3] ibid 259–62.

manner and against objective standards. For instance, to achieve more flexibility and avoid detachment from real-life industrial practices, it would be desirable to adjust the obviousness test, eg so that it includes a person skilled in the art of designing AI-driven systems, and to assess the 'reflection of personality' against scientific knowledge in psychology and authorial traditions.

Refining the Conceptions of Human Inventorship and Authorship

Refining the conceptions of authorship and inventorship should procure reliable and abstract legal concepts of authorship and inventorship. To reiterate, the guiding logic is that these legal concepts would be applied to the facts of each individual case and, if a corresponding human activity has indeed occurred, the result is eligible for copyright or patent protection. If the required activity was not involved in the process, it means that the result falls outside the current patent and copyright systems. In other words, current patent and copyright laws are not applicable to subject matter whose creation did not involve the required human intellectual creative activity.

To make this proposal work, first the nexus between authors and their works and inventors and their inventions should be expressly appreciated. Second, the conceptions of human inventorship and authorship should become more nuanced. As Chapter 4 shows, the law already appreciates inventorship by recognising the right to the invention which warrants the right to file a patent application. This means that inventorship has legal effects preceding the grant of a patent. In addition, inventorship is protected even when a patent is not granted, eg the inventor was the second-to-file, by a right to continue use begun before priority date.[4] As Chapters 6 and 7 show, the legal significance of authorship for copyright subsistence is more widely recognised.

Building on research documented in Chapter 4, human inventorship should be conceived of as a relationship established by a human creative intervention[5] and human intellectual activity of inventive quality involved in a circumscribed process of creation. In more specific terms, the circumscribed process of creation means, in the UK, the process of coming up with an inventive concept; in Germany, the process of solving a concrete technical problem and disclosing a teaching; and in France, the process of conceiving an essence of invention.

To address the differences in national approaches individually – UK law seems to support the narrowest construction of the process of creation and the closest

[4] Patents Act 1977, s 64; Patentgesetz of 16 December 1980 (BGBl 1981 I S 1) (German Patent Act) § 12, Code de la propriété intellectuelle (Loi n° 92-597 du 1er juillet 1992 relative au code de la propriété intellectuelle, as amended) (French Intellectual Property Code) art L613-7.

[5] *Rote Taube*, Decision of 27 March 1969, X ZB 15/67 [1970] IIC 136, 138. *Tomatoes/State of Israel*, G 0001/08 of 9 December 2010, EP:BA:2010:G000108.20101209 [6.4.2.3].

link between the inventive heart of the invention and its origin in a human being's mind. French law puts the emphasis on the conception phase, which standard permits also more abstract inputs to count as inventorial. A good example is the case in which inventorship was recognised for suggesting to make a novel printable coated-like paper by layering known materials without making any specific technical contributions in the process of making such a paper.[6] German law understands the process of creation as including any 'human contribution that substantially influenced the overall success'.[7] However, before the *DABUS* case, German law perceived the process of creation and relevant activities more narrowly, eg in *Motorkettensäge*, coming up with a technical solution to a narrowly defined technical problem was required, coupled with its completion and disclosure.[8]

In principle, the process of inventing is predominantly understood narrowly and is limited to the intellectual activities expended on the immediate solving of the underlying technical problem. In other words, the relevance of certain activity is thus assessed in the light of the process of creation which is circumscribed through the underlying technical problem. Activities such as contributing technical features known in the prior art, entrepreneurial or managerial contributions, providing funding, labour, setting up tools, testing prototypes or fulfilling other assistant tasks do not give rise to inventorship because they do not immediately determine the non-obvious technical features. This should be elevated to a normative status and become part of the refined conception of human inventorship in those jurisdictions. Also considering the intrinsic and social values of human intellectual creations, human-centred justifications for patents and the purpose and objectives of patent law, inventorship in Europe should be interpreted as requiring origination of those technical elements of an invention that imply an inventive activity.

At European level, the EPC Contracting States should open a debate on inventorship. Historically, the states agreed that inventorship and derivation of title to a patent remained in the competence of national authorities and under governance of national laws. But this was roughly 50 years ago and since then their economies have become much more interdependent. In addition, the Board of Appeal of the EPO has recently found itself competent to decide on inventorship under the Article 60(1) of the EPC.[9] This may be another signal of necessity towards a common approach to inventorship for European patent purposes.

Further, unification appears desirable because national laws do not conceive of the activity that gives rise to inventorship in exactly the same way. For instance, whereas in Germany a complete solving of a specific, concrete technical problem and disclosure of the teaching are required, in France it is sufficient to formulate the idea which forms the essence of the invention without necessarily completing it.

[6] TGI de Paris, Decision of 16 October 2001 *PIBD* 2002 744 III 265.

[7] '*ein menschlicher Beitrag, der den Gesamterfolg wesentlich beeinflusst hat*' *DABUS*, Decision of 11 June 2024, X ZB 5/22 [38].

[8] *Motorkettensäge*, Decision of 20 June 1978, X ZR 49/75, [1978] *GRUR* 583.

[9] See Chapter 4.

Harmonisation of the concept of inventorship and delegation of the respective competence to the EPO would make sense also considering the European unitary patent system.[10] Pursuant to Regulation on enhanced cooperation, the unitary patent as an object of property will be governed by national laws of the state where the applicant had his residence or place of business on the date of filing of the application for the European patent.[11] In effect, if only one of the states accepts inventorship by a machine in their national law, the applicants with AI productions would just need to set up a place of business in that state and apply from there. (Though when dealing with the EPO, pro forma they would have to name a human being as the inventor.) If none of the applicants has a residence or place of business in any of the states (the Contracting Parties of the Agreement on a Unified Patent Court), the unitary patent as an object of property will be governed by German law, which adopted a generous inventorship standard in *DABUS*.[12]

The lack of a shared conception of human inventorship and the lack of an agreement on whether machines can be recognised as inventors under the national laws of the EPC Contracting States only add to the current inadequacy of the interpretation and application practices. This also potentially contributes to generating false positives by the European patent system.

In copyright law, formulating an EU conception of human authorship presents its own challenges due to incomplete harmonisation of EU copyright law. At EU level, it is argued that human authorship amounts to a relationship established through choosing, sequencing and combining the building blocks so that the result reflects the personality of those who made the decisions as to that choice, sequence and combination.

This book advances adoption of an EU-wide conception of human authorship which is conditioned on the following: (i) the interpretation of creative choices as choices that immediately lead to creation of the work; (ii) *Cofemel*'s emphasis on the reflection of personality as the only substantive condition defining the EU concept of work; and (iii) *Brompton Bicycle*'s directive to look for the personal creative choices in the process of creation.

In the UK, France and Germany, it is well established that the conception of human authorship entails providing intellectual and creative inputs of the right 'type and amount'[13] (creative choices in EU copyright law idiom) in relation to the subject matter at stake, ie authorial contributions. The current copyright law

[10] A system of enhanced cooperation established by the Agreement on a Unified Patent Court 16351/12 [2013] OJ C 175 (pending notification), Regulation EU 1257/2012 implementing enhanced cooperation in the area of the creation of unitary patent protection [2012] OJ L 361 and Regulation (EU) No 1260/2012 of 17 December 2012 implementing enhanced cooperation in the area of the creation of unitary patent protection with regard to the applicable translation arrangements [2012] OJ L 361.

[11] Regulation EU 1257/2012 implementing enhanced cooperation in the area of the creation of unitary patent protection [2012] OJ L 361, art 7(1).

[12] ibid, art 7(3); DABUS, Decision of 11 June 2024, XZB5/22.

[13] Lionel Bently and others, *Intellectual Property Law* 6th edn (OUP 2022) 136–37.

doctrine recognises that, as a matter of fact, abstract and general contributions made outside the process of creation do not count as authorial. Bringing this to a normative level, human intellectual creative activity giving rise to authorship should entail making personal choices that immediately lead to the creation of a work so that the work reflects the personality of its author. Such choices must be made in a circumscribed process of creation, ie they should occur already in the conception of a work and then flow through composition to the materialisation of the work. Conversely, choosing a motive, a particular technique, a piece of technology, setting up a piece of technology without determining the concrete expressive elements of the final outputs or any other preparatory activities preceding the circumscribed process of creation should not count towards authorship.

Amending the Epistemic Approaches

Besides adjusting the interpretation of copyright subsistence and patentability criteria, authorities should amend their epistemic approaches so that they examine the human aspects in the processes of creation. This signifies a paradigm shift: from the focus on the expressive subject matter to the focus on the underlying creative process. In exceptional circumstances, the authorities do look at the process by which a work came to existence, eg when they ask for explanation of originality of choices (France) or identify ideas in the content of the work (Germany) or determine inputs of sufficient transformative character (the UK). However, in general, authorities tend to come to quick conclusions when facing an expressive subject matter which falls within a well-established category (eg a musical composition, a poem) with unquestioned authorship. Such shortcuts are no longer appropriate or justified.

In copyright law, the relationship between an author and their work can legitimately be scrutinised under the concept of original work properly construed. The handling of *Martin v Kogan II* by the High Court presents a recent example of how this can be done. Putative joint authors gave accounts of individual characteristics of the process of creation, their respective contributions and their nature. The specific contributions were followed from the conception of the work, through its composition, to its materialisation. At the same time, this did not detract from the normative standard of joint authorship.

Hence, the bit of flexibility lost owing to adoption of the normative approach to authorship could be offset by the flexibilities inherent in the procedure modelled on *Martin v Kogan II*. A flexible procedure would allow the author (or copyright owner) to claim those authorial contributions in relation to which they have the best evidence. In the copyright infringement setting, the evidence would be limited to the origin of those expressive elements that are alleged to have been copied.

Although the approach that looks at the process of creation (adopted in *Martin v Kogan II* and *Brompton Bicycle*) appears theoretically sound and promising,[14] it is also prone to abuse. At the moment, there seems to be no in-built checks against fabricating the story of the process of creation and ex-post implanting personality where none has initially been present.

Some remedy may come in the form of a narrow and true-to-life conception of personality under the requirement of a reflection of personality. For instance, personality may be understood as a collection of qualities which makes a person a distinctive individual (in the present), while those qualities are enduring, inherited or acquired throughout the person's life (legacy of the past), and help the person to actualise their potentiality, capacity and potency when the person is wilfully and consciously projecting themselves into the world (for the future) when giving a form to their work. In this vein, the analysis of *Martin v Kogan II* (see Chapter 7) shows that attribution of musicality in the screenplay seems to have been guided by the musical personality or identity of Ms Kogan.

Since the question of who did what and when in the actual process of creation are questions of fact in the competence of first instance judges,[15] then the necessary checks will have to be implemented at the national level and will likely stem from general fact-finding practices and examination of evidence. It will primarily be the task of the party asserting copyright to supply enough of reliable (ie time-stamped) evidence for judges to conclude whether the contributions of putative authors were such that the result reflects the author's personality.

The proposed amendment to the epistemic approaches – the shift of focus onto the process of creation – would also make the statutory presumption of authorship redundant. However, there is little to regret because the presumption that human beings who publicly present works under their names are their de facto authors were designed to protect the true authors (and their successors in title; not those in possession of expressive subject matter). Nowadays, recording

[14] This approach was identified as relevant for copyright assessment by Professor Leistner: 'From the perspective of copyright, it is not decisive whether the ultimately resulting and to be disseminated result is comparable with human personal intellectual creations, but rather whether its form was given in the underlying creative process [that is] personal, free and creative in the copyright sense.' In the German original: '*Damit kommt es aus urheberrechtlicher Sicht nicht entscheidend darauf an, ob das letztlich resultierende und zu verbreitende Ergebnis mit den persönlich geistigen Schöpfungen von Menschen vergleichbar ist, sondern vielmehr auch darauf, ob der diesem zugrundeliegende Schöpfungsprozess im urheberrechtlichen Sinne persönlich frei und kreativ gestaltet ist*' in Matthias Leistner, 'KI-basierte Werke im Urheberrecht – eine Einordnung'/ 'AI-Based Works in Copyright Law – A Utilitarian Argument against Protection' 9 (*SSRN*, 6 April 2022). Available at: https://ssrn.com/abstract=3987928, last accessed 24 October 2022.

[15] Matthias Leistner, 'Einheitlicher europäischer Werkbegriff auch im Bereich der angewandten Kunst' [2019] GRUR 1114, 1120. To the same effect the CJEU: 'Consequently, the graphic user interface can, as a work, be protected by copyright if it is its author's own intellectual creation. It is for the national court to ascertain whether that is the case in the dispute before it. When making that assessment, the national court must take account, inter alia, of the specific arrangement or configuration of all the components which form part of the graphic user interface in order to determine which meet the criterion of originality.' Case C-393/09 *Bezpečnostní softwarová asociace v Ministerstvo kultury* [2010] ECR I-13971, EU:C:2010:816 paras 46–48.

technologies and devices are in our pockets. One may record creative processes and store the recordings at minimal cost. Thus the reason for having the presumption because it saves time and expense is now less compelling. It is questionable whether its other benefits such as increased certainty for third parties, outweigh the costs of protecting ineligible subject matter in some cases (as a result of the judicial presumptions of originality in France or lower standard of authorship in Germany as both these practices evolved from the presumption of authorship). In the nineteenth or twentieth centuries the presumption might have been validated by the factual assumption that every work has a human author. However, in the light of the advancements in AI and the ensuing necessity to question authorship, neither the assumption of human authorship nor (*a maiori ad minus*) presumption of individual authorship are legitimate.

If the paradigms are indeed shifted as proposed here, ie the legal presumption of authorship is abandoned and the process of creation becomes scrutinised, copyright owners would also have to prove their rights to enforce them. They would need to think ahead and introduce practices of collecting evidence about the process of creation, its stages and versions of the work for potential litigation. This does not necessarily open a controversial (and in some cases still technically impossible) task of explainability of AI-driven systems. Rather, the information of who did what and when would need to be supported by evidence. That some artists already monitor and record their creative practices and processes in real-time and in a reasonably cost-effective manner was demonstrated in the UK case *Sheeran v Chokri*.[16] The practice of recording one's own creative activity makes sense also for the purposes of proving independent creation in a potential infringement case (as it was the case in *Sheeran v Chokri*).

In the patent grant procedure, the authorities have limited powers to access and request information about the process of inventing. Therefore, this book proposes a reform that would enable a patentability assessment that takes into account the implicit human inventorship requirement. This would equip patent offices, courts and the public with information as to whether any AI-driven system was involved in the process of invention and, if so, its role in the process.[17]

Correspondingly, applicants' disclosure duties should be extended. They should disclose if, and to what extent, an AI-driven system was used. More specifically, applicants would be required to disclose the nature of the AI-driven system, a basic specification of the training dataset and functions of the algorithms, describe the system's basic workings and the role it played in the process of devising the invention, namely which steps in the process were undertaken by the system and their results.

[16] *Sheeran and others v Chokri and others* [2022] EWHC 827 (Ch) [2022] FSR 15 [54].

[17] An AI-driven system could be defined for this purpose as a system that can perform tasks such as decision-making, problem-solving, etc which normally require human intellectual activity. This proposal builds on definitions of AI offered in Stuart Russell and Peter Norvig, *Artificial Intelligence: A Modern Approach* 3rd global edn (Pearson 2016) 1–2.

The information provided under this more robust disclosure duty should be clear and sufficiently complete to assess, on a case-by-case basis, whether the non-obvious technical features were due to a human creative intervention and human intellectual activity. For instance, if the invention is found to be non-obvious, it should also be possible to ascertain whether the gap in the chain of obvious steps occurred in the process run on an AI-driven system (which may be superior to the state-of-the-art AI-driven systems which should become part of the PSA test for non-obviousness) or a human brain.

In the EPC system, such a disclosure could be part of the description of the technical problem and solution according to Rule 42 of the Implementing Regulations.[18] At the moment, Rule 42 specifies that the description in the patent application should contain, inter alia, such a description of the invention that 'the technical problem, even if not expressly stated as such, and its solution can be understood'.[19]

According to the EPO's Guidelines for Examination, the purpose of the Rule 42 (in concert with Article 83 of the EPC) is 'to enable a skilled person to put the invention as claimed into practice; and [...] to understand the contribution to the art which the invention as claimed has made'.[20] It seems logical that another, perhaps even more immediate, purpose of the current disclosure duty is to enable the EPO to understand the invention to examine its patentability. The proposed extended disclosure duty would add to the EPO's understanding of the invention, including whether the technical advance constitutes an invention at all and whether it involves an inventive step.

Whenever an applicant fails to declare and sufficiently explain the steps undertaken by an AI-driven system and their significance for the invention, the EPO would give them a chance to rectify the declaration. If it is not amended, then the EPO would eventually refuse the application under Article 90 of the EPC for not complying with the formal requirements of patentability. In cases where the patent applicant would provide a prima facie complete and coherent declaration, the ensuing question is how to verify its contents.

Some verification of the information by the EPO should take place although it will likely be constrained due to the lack of finances and competence. As Professor Lemley argues in his essay, it is unlikely that extending the examination time by a patent office would bring any significant fruits in terms of increased quality of patents.[21] Yet, some basic collection of information and inquiries into the process

[18] Implementing Regulations to the EPC. See also European Patent Office, *Guidelines for Examination* (EPO 2021) Part F, Chapter II [4].

[19] Implementing Regulations to the EPC, Rule 42(1)(c).

[20] European Patent Office (n 18) [4.1].

[21] Lemley argues that 'money spent improving the PTO examination practices will largely be wasted on examining the ninety-five percent of patents that will either never be used or will be used in circumstances that don't crucially rely on the determination of validity'. Mark Lemley, 'Rational Ignorance at the Patent Office' (2001) 95 *Northwestern University Law Review* 1495, 1511. It is curious, however, how he arrived at the exact number of 95% in his final argument when the preceding statements

of creation should be undertaken by the EPO as part of its ordinary duties. It remains true though that the EPO may not be able to verify the statements as to what happened behind the closed doors of applicants' laboratories and research departments since it does not have any investigative powers, eg to enter and search premises.

However, the limited EPO's competence and powers may be compensated by intensifying the incentives to disclose the truth on the side of those involved in drafting patent applications. At the end of the day, either the patent applicant, the designated inventor, or those who act on their behalf will be natural persons. Therefore, the EPO form 1001 Request for grant of a European patent and the form 1002 Designation of inventor should be amended so that they contain a safeguard against false statements and misrepresentation made by natural persons. A form required by the United States Patent and Trademark Office containing the following pledge may serve as an inspiration: 'I hereby acknowledge that any willful false statement made in this declaration is punishable […].'[22]

Curiously enough, the current EPO forms do not contain any similar pledges. At the same time, the disclosure of false information (when under a legal duty to disclose) or acting under false pretences with the intent to unjustifiably enrich oneself is a recognised criminal offence in Europe.[23] Therefore, any false or incomplete declarations should be prosecuted according to the laws of the EPC Contracting States and by national enforcement forces.

Some of the incentives to produce a truthful declaration could be allocated to legal representatives of patent applicants too. The legal representatives should be required to make a person willing to declare themselves as the inventor aware of the possible legal consequences of false declaration and to provide a *vidimus* attestation of that person's signature on the declaration. Nonetheless, the applicant's pledge and the ensuing risk of prosecution and punishment should be the main measure to disincentivise dishonesty.

Any potential fraudulent attribution of inventorship would likely be discovered only as a consequence of post-grant verification of the information disclosed. To ensure a wider scrutiny of involvement of human inventorship, competitors, downstream innovators and the public in general should be able to challenge the accuracy of the disclosure. This could be done either through opposition under Article 99 of the EPC whereby any person may give notice to the EPO of opposition or revocation under Article 138(1)(a) of the EPC before national authorities, both on the ground that the subject matter is not patentable. Invalidity for lack of

about the numbers of licensed and litigated patents (and the reasons why they were litigated or not litigated) which supposedly substantiate this final argument are acknowledged to be mere guesses and speculation.

[22] USPTO, 'Declaration (37 CFR 1.63) For Utility Or Design Application Using An Application Data Sheet (37 CFR 1.76)' (*uspto*, no date available). Available at: www.uspto.gov/patents/apply/forms, last accessed 14 November 2022.

[23] See the UK Fraud Act 2006, s 3; German criminal code *Strafgesetzbuch* of 13 November 1998 (BGBl. I S. 3322) as amended, § 263 *Betrug* and French criminal code *Code pénal*, Art 313-1.

patentability either for lack of invention or lack of inventive step can be argued as a defence in infringement lawsuits too.[24]

The challenge to patentability for lack of human inventorship (under lack of an inventive step as the explicit requirement) could be made by asserting that the disclosed AI-driven system was used in a way in which any person skilled in the art would have used such a system, ie the use of an AI-driven system corresponding to the description as well as the way in which it was used would have been obvious to a PSA. Alternatively, the challenge (for lack of an invention) could be made by asserting that the non-obvious technical features owed their existence to the steps undertaken by the AI-driven system and not to any human creative intervention. The burden of proof would inevitably have to be reversed or distributed between the parties.

The most precarious case would be to substantiate the challenge to patentability in case no use of an AI-driven system is admitted in the description. Then the challenging party could likely only rely on circumstantial evidence of the increased patentee's patenting activity (of the same type of invention) and the speed with which the patentee has been generating new inventions provided such performance could not be explained in any other way, eg years of research or acquisitions. Taking the example of the antibiotic *halicin* from Chapter 2, the AI-driven system used to discover *halicin* is likely to identify new antibiotics and thus likely to generate new medical uses for known compounds extremely quickly compared to human researchers. The involvement of an AI-driven system in the inventive process can therefore be discernible from the frequency of patent applications claiming alike inventions. If, on the balance of probabilities, the court finds that the disclosure duties were not dutifully met, the process of devising the invention would become subject of fact finding before the court with the burden of proof being placed on patentees.

In practical terms, the reform to epistemic approaches, including the disclosure duty, could be easily implemented. It would require an extension of the existing disclosure duty (in the description of the technical problem and solution under Rule 42) with a view to equipping examiners with more relevant information.[25] In addition, the amendment of the text of the relevant EPO forms would require the insertion of an inventor's pledge and a legal attestation of signatures. The reform would not be in conflict with the EPC Contracting States' commitments in the realm of patent law because it does not introduce any new patentability condition, nor does it impede the grant of patents procedurally.[26]

[24] Patents Act 1977, s 74, German Patent Act, § 81 (though there are specifics given the German bifurcated patent litigation system) and French Intellectual Property Code, Art L613-25.

[25] This is inspired by arguments made by Professor Sherman in relation to disclosure of biological resources and indigenous knowledge with a view to learning their role in scientific and technical developments. Brad Sherman, 'Regulating Access and Use of Genetic Resources: Intellectual Property Law and Biodiscovery' (2003) 25 *EIPR* 301, 307–08.

[26] By analogy, Nuno de Carvalho, 'Requiring Disclosure of the Origin of Genetic resources and Prior Informed Consent in Patent Applications Without Infringing the TRIPS Agreement: The Problem and the Solution' (2000) 2(1) *Wash U J L & Pol'y* 371, 372 and 382.

Naturally, these suggestions to address the knowledge gap problem have their limitations. The hope is that they could at least start a discussion about what is feasible and what could be effectively improved within the European patent system. As the pertinent questions around the involvement of AI-driven systems largely depend on a case-by-case technical analysis, it would be helpful to consult experts from various technical fields as to the questions which technical aspects may be the most telling, how to distribute the burden of proof, how to maintain some reasonable level-playing field and share responsibility for preserving patents for human intellectual creations.

Admittedly, the proposal to examine the process of creation goes against the intuitions of many patent lawyers. The objections raised may be along the lines that the process of inventing is irrelevant and should not be subject to scrutiny. These objections are usually supported by reference to historical sources. For instance, Terrell on the Law of Patents 1965 refers to *Liardet v Johnson* when stating that '[p]atents have been held valid for inventions that have been the result of the merest accident'.[27]

Contrary to what one may infer from Terrell on the Law of Patents 1965, the patent at stake in *Liardet v Johnson* did not involve an invention by accident and neither party claimed it did. Rather, Lord Mansfield used the word 'accident' when explaining the rationale for patent system to the jury. Lord Mansfield in *Liardet v Johnson* as reproduced in an article of 1902:

> So in the play of the Alchymist, when Sir Epicure Mammon was looking for the philosopher's stone he found out a cure for the itch. Thus, if they don't get what they are looking after, they find something else, and some of the greatest inventions we know of have been hit upon by accident.[28]

After reading the passage in its context, it becomes clear that Lord Mansfield only tries to shield inventors from being deprived of a patent if an accident occurred in the process.

A serendipitous event of finding a substance or observing a phenomenon does not amount to making an invention in the sense of the EPC and *Tomatoes/State of Israel*.[29] Making an invention in the sense of the EPC requires at least such understanding, perhaps following an accident, that it allows to teach others how to repeat the process or re-create the invention or (if already known) then how to use it to achieve the claimed novel and non-obvious technical effects. Hence, the disregard for the process of inventing is relevant only to the extent to which it protects inventors from being deprived of patents just because a lucky or serendipitous event occurred in the process of them making the invention. Deployment of an AI-driven system in the process of inventing is hardly analogous to a lucky or serendipitous event.

[27] Guy Aldous, Douglas Falconer and William Aldous, *Terrell on the Law of Patents* 11th edn (Sweet & Maxwell 1965) 120.

[28] Wyndham Hulme, 'On the History of Patent Law in the Seventeenth and Eighteenth Centuries' (1902) 18 *L Q Rev* 280, 285 reproducing *Liardet v Johnson* as reported in *Morning Post* of 23 February 1778 (No 16667, p 2, col 4).

[29] *Tomatoes/State of Israel* (n 5).

There is seemingly some basis for these objections under the US Patent Act which states that '[p]atentability shall not be negated by the manner in which the invention was made'.[30] However, even this provision states that the invention must be 'made'. As was held by the Supreme Court in *AMP v Myriad Genetics*, to be made under the US patent law means to amount to 'a product of human ingenuity'.[31] In the context of the US DABUS patent applications, a US District court affirmed that inventors are those individuals who conceive of the invention.[32] Therefore, the correct reading of § 103 is that as long as an invention has been made (in the sense of conceived) by a human being, it does not matter in which way it was made (conceived). A serendipitous event does not amount to making an invention under US patent law either, as recently clarified in the USPTO guidelines on inventorship.[33]

Finally, one may plausibly ask whether the extended disclosure duty would not create disproportionate costs or be otherwise too cumbersome to patent applicants. In effect, the additional costs associated with meeting the obligation should be, at least in case of employees' inventions, limited to the technical description of the AI-driven system. This is because many national legal regimes already provide for collection, storage and processing of the relevant information concerning the process of inventing.

Some countries, including the UK, Germany and France, legislate for the appropriation of employees' inventions in favour of their employers and for employees' compensatory schemes.[34] These compensation regulations are based on knowledge of the process by which an employee's invention was devised. More specifically, pursuant to the UK Patents Act 1977, to determine the amount of compensation for the employee, it must be considered, among other things,

> (b) the effort and skill which the employee has devoted to making the invention;
> (c) the effort and skill which any other person has devoted to making the invention jointly with the employee concerned, and the advice and other assistance contributed by any other employee who is not a joint inventor of the invention; and
> (d) the contribution made by the employer to the making, developing and working of the invention by the provision of advice, facilities and other assistance, by the provision of opportunities and by his managerial and commercial skill and activities.[35]

In the AI context, employees' contributions would range from providing advice, assistance (ie activities outside inventorship) to producing the inventive concept

[30] 35 US Code, § 103.

[31] *Association for Molecular Pathology (AMP) v Myriad Genetics Inc*, 133 S Ct 2107 (2013) 2116, 2217.

[32] US District Court for the Eastern District of Virginia Thaler v Hirschfeld 1:20-cv-903 (LMB/TCB) (ED Va Sep 2, 2021). The District Court referred to the Federal Circuit in Max-Planck 734 F3d at 1323 which held that 'it is axiomatic that inventors are the individuals who conceive of the invention'.

[33] USPTO, 'Inventorship Guidance for AI-Assisted Inventions' Docket No PTO-P-2023-0043.

[34] Jan Jonczyk, 'Employee Inventions' (1989) *IIC* 847. This is based on national reports received from 24 countries.

[35] Patents Act 1977, s 41(4). Similarly, ibid s 41(5) in respect of an invention which originally belonged to the employee.

(ie activity that gives rise to inventorship). Employers' contributions may be in the form of providing an AI-driven system which may support the inventive activity of employees or replace it. Given the focus of the Patents Act 1977 on individual contributions, it is in the best interest of employees-inventors in the UK to have already developed practices to gather the relevant information about the process of devising inventions, including who and when contributed to the inventive concept. UK employers, when acting as patent applicants in respect of their employees' inventions, would only need to collect the information from their employees.

German and French regulations specifically state that employees must report inventions to their employers, including details of the process of their devising and individual inventor's contributions. In France, an employee is obliged to report the subject matter of the invention, its anticipated applications and circumstances under which the invention was made.[36] In Germany, a notification must contain description of the technical problem, the solution and the inventive process, including the inventor's own contribution.[37] Therefore, German as well as French employers, when acting as patent applicants in relation to their employees' inventions, are already equipped with the necessary information to meet the proposed extended disclosure duty.

Employees, team leaders or even executive directors may be tempted to overstate their contributions. However, according to recent research by Professor Harhoff and Hoisl, this does not happen as often as it might have been expected. As they state, '[s]uperiors are mentioned as a co-inventor, not due to their inventive performance or participation in the inventive process, but due to their position within the firm. Given the notoriety that this phenomenon has received in the literature, our results suggest that its importance may have been overstated considerably'.[38] Additionally, the proposed amendment to the EPO forms and the requirement to pledge inventorship under the threat of prosecution should discourage such practices.

[36] French Intellectual Property Code, art L 611-7, 3 in conjunction with ibid arts R611-1 and R611-2, *partie réglementaire*.

[37] Gesetz über Arbeitnehmererfindungen of 25 July 1957 (BGBl I S 756) as amended. Matthias Reute, 'The German Employee-Invention Law: An Outline' in Jeremy Phillips (ed) *Employees' Inventions. A Comparative Study* (Fernsway Publications 1981) 189.

[38] Dietmar Harhoff and Karin Hoisl, 'Institutionalized Incentives for Ingenuity – Patent Value and the German Employees' Inventions Act' (2007) 36 *Research Policy* 1143, 1158.

10

Conclusion

Chapter 2 of this book argues that the advancements in AI challenge copyright and patent laws in novel ways. For the first time in human history, there may be no human beings involved in the processes of production of literature, art or technical advances who would be the immediate intellectual creators of those productions. This does not mean to suggest that AI-driven systems could initiate creative processes or were consciously engaged as creators. But what if an AI-driven system identifies a novel, efficacious drug and hence comes up with a non-obvious solution to a narrowly defined technical problem? Does this make the drug an inventive invention? What if an AI-driven system determines expressive elements of a painting through its inner, obscure processes outside the control of its human deployers or designers? Does copyright subsist in the painting? Should there be copyright and patents available for such productions? If these productions fall outside the scope of copyright and patent protection, how do we distinguish them from authored works or human-made inventions? Answers to these questions will have a significant impact on technological progress, the future of arts and culture and operation of markets with innovative and creative productions.

To answer the above questions, Chapter 3 shifts its attention away from AI and its accomplishments and focuses on what copyright and patent laws are really about: the protection of authors and inventors and their intellectual creations. Chapter 3 demonstrates that copyright and patents have traditionally been justified by theories relying on human authorship and human inventorship and they have been reserved for human intellectual creations. Chapter 3 argues for upholding the status quo. To this end, the chapter reasons and explains that any potential expansion of copyright or patent protection to subject matter other than human intellectual creations is not justified by the current human dignity, fairness, labour/desert-based theories and incentives to create. Incentives to produce and invest, market failure or fair competition reasons cannot, on their own, justify copyright or patents.

All then turns on the concept of human intellectual creations and their required properties. In this book, the term 'human intellectual creations' captures the essence of inventions and works, ie that they are productions of human mind. Authorship and inventorship are understood as relationships between an author-creator or an inventor-creator and their work or invention respectively. These relationships are regarded as having been established through human intellectual creative activity.

This book proves to be original by adopting the prism of human intellectual creative activity. Under this prism, it analyses entitlement disputes in the UK, France and Germany to find out what a natural person must do to become an inventor (Chapter 4) or an author (Chapter 7). Chapter 4 argues that human intellectual creative activity that establishes inventorship entails coming up with the inventive concept (UK), complete solving of a specific, concrete technical problem, including the disclosure of the teaching (Germany) and formulating the idea which forms the essence of the invention without necessarily completing the invention (France). It also argues that in European patent law, human inventorship matters for patentability. More specifically, the requirement for an invention requires a human creative intervention and the requirement for an inventive step requires human intellectual activity of inventive quality.

Chapters 6 and 7 argue that human intellectual creative activity that establishes authorship entails making personal choices that immediately determine the expressive elements of a subject matter so that they translate author's personality into the final subject matter. Only the natural person whose identity is channelled in an undisrupted fashion from the work's conception, via its composition to its materialisation, can claim authorship (*Cala Homes*, *Guino v Renoir* and *Buchhaltungsprogramm*).

Chapters 5 and 8 demonstrate that despite copyright (in authorial works) and patent laws being concerned only with human intellectual creations, neither the European Patent Office nor the authorities in the UK, France or Germany are equipped with such epistemic approaches that would adequately distinguish an authored work or a human-made invention from other subject matter.

Chapter 9 offers certain improvements to the interpretation of existing copyright subsistence and patentability criteria, amendments to the epistemic approaches and reforms to implement them. It argues that the conceptions of human authorship and human inventorship should be refined (through adding specificity, immediacy and occurrence in a circumscribed process of creation) and generally recognised as implicit normative standards (ie forming part of the copyright subsistence and patentability statutory criteria).

The authorities should also amend their epistemic approaches to application of copyright subsistence and patentability criteria so that they examine the processes of creation with the ultimate view to checking whether the expressive elements or non-obvious technical features respectively owe their existence to the relevant human intellectual creative activity. As for the implementation, Chapter 9 argues for abandoning the presumptions of authorship and assumptions about inventorship, placing the burden of proof of their rights and eligibility for protection to putative copyright owners, patent applicants and patentees and extending disclosure duties to close the knowledge gap.

This book admits that these are significant reforms that are unlikely to be popular because, essentially, they mean more work for bureaucrats, judges and those claiming copyright or patent protection. Yet, more transparency, and more information about the origin of information around us is going to be required in some form anyway. Such transparency requirements are mainly spearheaded by the EU. The Preamble to the AI Act states that given the advancements in AI, and

> the need for new methods and techniques to trace origin of information, it is appropriate to require providers of those [AI] systems to embed technical solutions that enable marking in a machine-readable format and detection that the output has been generated or manipulated by an AI system and not a human. Such techniques and methods should be sufficiently reliable, interoperable, effective and robust as far as this is technically feasible, taking into account available techniques or a combination of such techniques, such as watermarks, metadata identifications, cryptographic methods for proving provenance and authenticity of content, logging methods, fingerprints or other techniques, as may be appropriate.[1]

This is accompanied by a duty of those who deploy AI-driven systems to 'disclose that the content has been artificially generated or manipulated'.[2] In artistic and creative contexts, such disclosure is satisfied by disclosing 'the existence of such generated or manipulated content in an appropriate manner that does not hamper the display or enjoyment of the work'.[3] Chapter 9 proposes similarly spirited reforms which are, in many aspects, aligned with the EU's regulatory approach.

Second, some copyright owners and patent applicants may even endorse these reforms as they would wish to be honest and inform their audiences, users, trade partners or the public in general about the origin of their (AI-free) works and inventions and it may be easier for them to do so as part of an industry-wide practice. This applies even more in these times of uncertainty about how authorities will assess copyright subsistence in or patentability of AI productions. For instance, authors-creators may be willing to share the information that they did not use any AI-driven systems with their collecting society so that persons other than the real authors-creators or their successors in title are prevented from claiming a share from the common cake.

Third, as for the authorities, this book reveals that to improve their epistemic approaches, there are things they can do now and are obligated to do (regardless of the proposed reforms). For instance, they ought to be watchful of argumentation fallacies. For instance, some have misinterpreted the law by effectively claiming that since no one can come up with a better title for the production (of unknown or claimed AI origin) then the person who claims the protection is entitled to it.[4] The work with facts is the domain of first instance judges. They ought to engage in a genuine fact-finding when it comes to enforcement of property rights instead of relying on judge-made presumptions of originality (France) or presumptions of authorial or inventorial quality of contributions with respect to named authors

[1] Regulation (EU) 2024/1689 laying down harmonised rules on artificial intelligence (Artificial Intelligence Act) [2024] OJ L144/1, rec 133.

[2] ibid, art 50(4).

[3] ibid.

[4] Justice Birss fell for this in *Stephen Thaler v Comptroller General of Patents Trade Marks and Designs* [2021] EWCA Civ 1374, [2021] 9 WLUK 172 [85].

or inventors (Germany). Equally, the judges ought to follow the *Infopaq* granular approach and thus be cautious about granting protection over the whole subject matter if the human origin of the whole is not properly evidenced.

Coming back to the questions from the beginning: what if an AI-driven system identifies a novel, efficacious drug and comes up with a non-obvious solution to a narrowly defined technical problem? Does this event make the drug an inventive invention? The answer given by this book is no. The mere event of an AI-driven system identifying the drug does not give rise to inventorship and thus the ensuing technical teaching to use the drug for a specific medical use cannot constitute an inventive invention. If, however, coming up with the inventive concept (identifying the specific drug with the specific therapeutic effect) involved some inventive combination of the required properties of that drug that was made by a human being or any other specific human intellectual input determining the characteristics of the drug that make it liable to have the specific therapeutic effect and that would be regarded non-obvious then the drug could be claimed as an inventive invention. (This is because the human inventor determined the inventive technical features of the invention even though they did not find the drug having those features.)

Further, what if an AI-driven system determines expressive elements of a painting through its inner, obscure processes outside the control of its human deployers or designers? Does copyright subsist in the painting? Likely not, because such expressive elements are not the direct and immediate result of personal choices made by any human being in the process of the painting's conception and channelled through its composition to its materialisation. Hence, they do not reflect anyone's personality.

If these productions fall outside the scope of copyright and patent protection, how do we distinguish them from authored works or human-made inventions given they are prima facie indistinguishable? Chapter 9 proposes to distinguish them based on whether their process of creation involved the required human intellectual creative activity. This is to be achieved by amending the interpretative and epistemic approaches and extending disclosure duties of those who claim protection. These reforms would enable authorities to assess, on a case-by-case basis, whether the non-obvious technical features or expressive elements originated in the relevant human intellectual creative activity or not.

Finally, what if the conceptions of inventorship and authorship are not refined nor the epistemic approaches amended? What if the corresponding reforms are not made? In terms of consequences, this would mean that the authorities may end up granting proprietary rights in any productions resembling works or inventions, regardless of whether they fulfil the legal requirements for protection. Eventually, this would increase the risk of copyright and patent systems generating false positives and thus unjustifiably depriving the public of expressive subject matter and useful technical advances. This would also undermine the coherence and integrity of the modern copyright and patent law systems and compromise the systems' justifications.

This could also have an adverse impact on competition in the markets with works and inventions. Accomplished expressive subject matter imitating the style of existing author-creators would become substitutes for authors' own creations and thus interfere with authors' economic incentives to create new works. (Besides losing control over the supply, by creating new works, authors would produce new training data for AI-driven systems and thereby directly contribute to better outputs of their potential competitors.)

Nor is the current patent system geared for the speed and power with which AI-driven systems can generate non-obvious technical advances. To continue with drug discovery as an example, Demis Hassabis stated that Isomorphic Labs had adopted as its 'mission to reimagine the entire drug discovery process from first principles with an AI-first approach and, ultimately, to model and understand some of the fundamental mechanisms of life'.[5] This could lead to discovering and formulating new drug discovery principles and new meta-methods of drug discovery similar to what Isomorphic Labs' AlphaFold2 achieved with respect to protein folding[6] and AlphaFold3 managed with respect to 'all life's molecules'.[7]

Eventually, if this mission is successful, it could lead to gaining a monopoly over a large portion of the technical field (eg through patenting individual drugs for individual medical uses). Such a scope of protection could not have been envisaged by those designing the modern patent system. Even though the monopoly may be temporary, for a consolidated market 20 years may well be long enough to eliminate competition and stifle innovation.

This book is far from suggesting that the human intellectual efforts and investment in the AI or innovations brought by AI should not be appreciated, rewarded or incentivised. Or that Europe should sacrifice its competitiveness in AI to coherence of some outdated property(-like) systems. On the contrary, one could argue that AI is so promising and the recent accomplishments so ground-breaking that patents and copyright (despite their international acceptance) may just not be suitable and sufficiently flexible to protect them.

[5] Demis Hassabis, Founder and CEO of Isomorphic Labs (and DeepMind). Demis Hassabis, 'Introducing Isomorphic Labs' (*isomorphiclabs*, November 2021). Available at: www.isomorphiclabs.com/blog, last accessed 31 December 2021.

[6] John Jumper and others 'Highly Accurate Protein Structure Prediction with AlphaFold' (2024) 596 *Nature* 583.

[7] Isomorphic Labs and the Google Deepmind AlphaFold team, 'AlphaFold 3 predicts the structure and interactions of all life's molecules' (*isomorphiclabs*, 8 May 2024). Available at: www.isomorphiclabs.com/articles/alphafold-3-predicts-the-structure-and-interactions-of-all-of-lifes-molecules, last accessed 30 July 2024. Demis Hassabis and others, 'Accurate Structure Prediction of Biomolecular Interactions with AlphaFold 3' (2024) 630 *Nature* 493.

BIBLIOGRAPHY

Abbott R, 'Artificial intelligence, big data and intellectual property: Protecting computer generated works in the United Kingdom' in Tanya Aplin (ed), *Research Handbook on Intellectual Property and Digital Technologies* (Edward Elgar 2020).

—— 'I Think, Therefore I Invent: Creative Computers and the Future of Patent Law' (2016) 57 *BCL Rev* 1079.

Agé S, 'Introduction de la session' in IRPI (ed), *L'Activité inventive* (Acte de colloque 2019).

Aldous G, Falconer D and Aldous W, *Terrell on the Law of Patents* 11th edn (Sweet & Maxwell 1965).

Aldous W and others, *Terrell on the Law of Patents* 13th edn (Sweet & Maxwell 1982)

Ann C, '§ 19. Erfinderprinzip und Erfinderrecht' in Rudolf Kraßer and Christoph Ann (eds) *Patentrecht* 7th edn (CH Beck 2016).

—— 'Erfinderische Leistung' in Rudolf Kraßer and Christoph Ann (eds) *Patentrecht* 8th edn (CH Beck 2016).

—— '§ 21. Arbeitnehmererfindungen' in Christoph Ann (ed) *Patentrecht* 8th edn (CH Beck 2022).

Aplin T and Davis J, *Intellectual Property Law: Text, Cases, and Materials* 3rd edn (OUP 2017).

—— 'Creativity and the Law' in Lee Martin and Nick Wilson (eds), *The Palgrave Handbook of Creativity at Work* (Palgrave 2018).

Aplin T and Pasqualetto G, 'Artificial Intelligence and Copyright Protection' in Rosa Maria Ballardini, Petri Kuoppamäki and Olli Pitkänen (eds), *Regulating industrial internet through IPR, data protection and competition law* (Wolters Kluwer 2019).

Arnold R, 'Content Copyrights and Signal Copyrights: The Case for a Rational Scheme of Protection' (2011) 1 *Queen Mary J Intell Prop* 272.

—— 'Walter v Lane Revisited (Again)' (2021) 2 *IPQ* 67.

Asendorf C and Schmidt C and Tochtermann P, 'Erfindung auf Grund erfinderischer Tätigkeit' in Georg Benkard (ed), *Patentgesetz* 12th edn (CH Beck 2023).

Azéma J and Galloux JC, *Droit de la propriété industrielle* 7th edn (Dalloz 2012).

—— *Droit de la propriété industrielle* 8th edn (Dalloz 2017).

Bacher K, 'PatG § 1 [Voraussetzungen der Erteilung]' in Georg Benkard (ed), *Patentgesetz* 12th edn (CH Beck 2023).

Balganesh S, 'Causing Copyright' (2017) 117 *Colum L Rev* 1.

Barry B and Chan A, 'Intrusion Detection Systems' in Peter Stavroulakis and Mark Stamp (eds), *Handbook of Information and Communication Security* (Springer 2010).

Beier F-K, 'Zur historischen Entwicklung des Erfordernisses der Erfindungshöhe' [1985] GRUR 606.

Bently L, 'Copyright and the Death of the Author in Literature and Law' (1994) 57 *MLR* 973.

—— 'Patents and Trade Secrets in England: The Case of Newbery v. James (1817)' in Rochelle Dreyfuss and Jane Ginsburg (eds), *Intellectual Property at the Edge: The Contested Contours of IP* (Cambridge 2014).

Bently L and Lee YH, 'Computer Programs Directive, Art 2' in Bernt Hugenholtz and Thomas Dreier (eds), *Concise European Copyright Law* 2nd edn (Kluwer Law 2016).

Bently L and others, *Intellectual Property Law* 5th edn (OUP 2018).

—— *Intellectual Property Law* 6th edn (OUP 2022).

Bertrand A, *Droit d'auteur* 3rd edn (Dalloz Action 2010).

Biron L and Bently L, 'Discontinuities Between Legal Conceptions of Authorship and Social Practices. What If Anything, Is To Be Done?' in Mireille van Eechoud (ed), *The Work of Authorship* (Amsterdam University Press 2014).

Bisges M, *Handbuch Urheberrecht* (Erich Schmidt Verlag 2016).

Blanc E, *L'inventeur breveté, code des inventions et des perfectionnements* 3rd edn (Cosse 1852).
Blanco White T, *Patents for Inventions and the Registration of Industrial Designs* 3rd edn (Stevens & Sons 1962).
Blok P, 'The Inventor's New Tool: Artificial Intelligence – How Does It Fit in the European Patent System?' (2017) 39 *EIPR* 69.
Bodenhausen G, *WIPO Guide to the Application of the Paris Convention* (BIRPI 1968).
Bonadio E and Lucchi N, *Non-conventional Copyright: Do New and Atypical Works Deserve Protection?* (Edward Elgar Publishing 2018).
Boyden B, 'Emergent Works' (2016) 39 *Colum JL & Arts* 377.
Breyer S, 'The Uneasy Case for Copyright: A Study of Copyright in Books, Photocopies, and Computer Programs' (1970) 84 *Harvard L R* 281.
Bridy A, 'Coding Creativity: Copyright and the Artificially Intelligent Author' [2012] *Stan Tech L Rev* 5.
Bruguière JM, *Code de la propriété intellectuelle* 25th edn (LexisNexis 2024).
Buccafusco C, 'A Theory of Copyright Authorship' (2016) 5 *Virg L Rev* 1229.
Buckle S, *Natural Law and the Theory of Property: Grotius to Hume* (OUP 2002).
Bullinger W, 'UrhG § 2 Geschützte Werke' in Artur-Axel Wandtke and Winfried Bullinger, *Praxiskommentar Urheberrecht* 6th edn (CH Beck 2022).
—— 'UrhG § 24 Freie Benutzung' in Artur-Axel Wandtke and Winfried Bullinger, *Praxiskommentar Urheberrecht* 6th edn (CH Beck 2022).
Burrell R and Kelly C, 'Parliamentary Rewards and the Revolution of the Patent System' [2015] CLJ 423.
Burrows A, *Thinking About Statutes: Interpretation, Interaction, Improvement* (CUP 2018).
Caddick N, Harbottle G and Suthersanen U, *Copinger and Skone James on Copyright* 18th edn (Sweet & Maxwell 2020).
Campbell D and others, *Terrell on the Law of Patents* 20th edn (Sweet & Maxwell 2024).
Caron C, *Droit d'auteur et droits voisins* 5th edn (LexisNexis 2017).
—— *Droit d'auteur et droits voisins* 6th edn (LexisNexis 2020).
Chakroborty M, '§3 Ownership A. Inventor and Inventor Right' in Maximilian Haedicke and Henrik Timmann (eds), *Patent Law: A Handbook on European and German Patent Law* (CH Beck 2014).
Chio C and Freeman D, *Machine Learning and Security: Protecting Systems with Data and Algorithms* (O'Reilly 2018).
Clifford R, 'Intellectual Property in the Era of the Creative Computer Program: Will the True Creator Please Stand Up' (1997) 71 *Tull Rev* 1675.
Cooper E, *Art and Modern Copyright: The Contested Image* (CUP 2018).
Cornish W, 'Rights in Employees' Inventions: The United Kingdom Position' (1990) 21 *IIC* 298.
Correa C, *Trade Related Aspects of Intellectual Property Rights: A Commentary on the TRIPS Agreement* 2nd edn (OUP 2020).
Davies C, 'An Evolutionary Step in Intellectual Property Rights – Artificial Intelligence and Intellectual Property' (2011) 27 *Computer Law & Security Review* 601.
de Carvalho N, 'Requiring Disclosure of the Origin of Genetic Resources and Prior Informed Consent in Patent Applications Without Infringing the TRIPS Agreement: The Problem and the Solution' (2000) *Wash U J L & Pol'Y* 371.
Deazley R, 'Commentary on the *Statute of Anne* 1710' (2008) in Lionel Bently and Martin Kretschmer (eds), *Primary Sources on Copyright (1450–1900)* Available at: www.copyrighthistory.org, last accessed 20 April 2021.
Desbois H, *Le droit d'auteur en France* 3rd edn (Dalloz 1978).
Deltorn JM, 'Deep Creations: Intellectual Property and the Automata' (2017) 4 *Frontiers in Digital Humanities*. Available at: https://doi.org/10.3389/fdigh.2017.00003, last accessed 19 April 2021.
Deltorn JM and Macrez F, 'Authorship in the Age of Machine Learning and Artificial Intelligence' in Sean M O'Connor (ed), *The Oxford Handbook of Music Law and Policy* (OUP 2019).
Derclaye E, 'The Court of Justice Copyright Case Law: Quo vadis?' (2014) 11 *EIPR* 716.
Desbois H, *Le droit d'auteur en France* 3rd edn (Dalloz 1978).
Devant P and others, *Les brevets d'invention* 4th edn (Librairie Dalloz 1971).
Derclaye E, 'The Court of Justice Copyright Case Law: quo vadis?' (2014) 36 *EIPR* 717.

——, Opinion of the European Copyright Society in relation to the pending reference before the CJEU in *Brompton Bicycle v Chedech/Get2Get* (C-833/18) (2020) 42 EIPR 207.
Di W and others, *Deep Learning Essentials: Your Hands-on Guide to the Fundamentals of Deep Learning and Neural Network Modeling* (Packt Publishing 2018).
Dickenson J, Morgan A and Clark B, 'Creative Machines: Ownership of Copyright in Content Created by Artificial Intelligence Applications' (2017) 39 EIPR 457.
Dietz A, 'The Concept of Authorship Under the Berne Convention' (1993) 155 RIDA 26.
Dornis T, 'Der Schutz künstlicher Kreativität im Immaterialgüterrecht' [2019] GRUR 1252.
Dorotheou E, 'Reap the Benefits and Avoid the Legal Uncertainty: Who Owns the Creations of Artificial Intelligence?' (2015) 21 *CTLR* 85.
Drahos P, *A Philosophy of Intellectual Property* (ANU Press 1996).
Dreier T, 'Berne Convention, art 2' in Bernt Hugenholtz and Thomas Dreier (eds), *Concise European Copyright Law* 2nd edn (Kluwer Law 2016).
du Sautoy M, *The Creativity Code: How AI is Learning to Write, Paint and Think* (4th Estate 2019).
Duignan B, 'Inventors and Inventions of the Industrial Revolution' (*Britannica*, unknown date). Available at: www.britannica.com/list/inventors-and-inventions-of-the-industrial-revolution, last accessed 12 January 2021.
Duncan L, *The role of theoretical debate in the evolution of national and international patent protection: from the French Revolution to the Paris Convention of 1883* (Brill 2021).
Escarra J, 'Le projet de la loi français sur la propriété littéraire et artistique' (1954) *V RIDA* 3.
Fisher M, 'Classical Economics and Philosophy of the Patent System' (2005) *IPQ* 1.
Floridi L, 'The Method of Levels of Abstraction' (2008) 18 *Minds & Machines* 303.
—— 'Artificial Intelligence, Deepfakes and a Future of Ectypes' (2018) 31 *Philos & Technol* 317.
Fromm E, *To Have or to Be?* (Bloomsbury 2012).
—— *Strach ze svobody* (Portál 2014).
Frosio G, *Reconciling Copyright with Cumulative Creativity: The Third Paradigm* (Edward Elgar Publishing 2018).
Gajac R, 'Comparative Study of Substantive Law in Force in the Countries Represented on the Committee of Experts on Patents' *EXP/Brev* (53) 18.
Galloux JC, 'La progression du critère de l'activité inventive en droit français' in IRPI (ed), *L'Activité inventive* (Acte de colloque 2019).
Gautier P-Y, *Propriété littéraire et artistique* 11th edn (Presses Universitaires de France 2019).
Geiger C and others, 'Towards a Balanced Interpretation of the "Three Step Test" in Copyright Law' (2008) 30 *EIPR* 489.
Gervais D, 'The Machine as Author' (2020) 105 *Iowa L Rev* 2053.
—— 'Human Cause' (2021) Vanderbilt Law Research Paper No 21-39 (2021). Available at: https://papers.ssrn.com/sol3/papers.cfm?abstract_id=3857844#, last accessed 19 April 2021.
Ghidini G and Cavani G, 'The Relationship Between the Unfair Competition Regime and IP Law' in Niklas Bruun and others (eds.) *Transition and Coherence in Intellectual Property Law* (CUP 2021).
Gibbins D and Grant G, '"Inventive concept" – Is It A Good Idea?' (2005) 5 *EIPR* 170
Ginsburg J, 'Moral Rights in a Common Law System' (1990) 1 *Ent L R* 121.
—— 'A Tale of Two Copyrights: Literary Property in Revolutionary France and America' (1991) 147 *RIDA* 125.
—— 'The Concept of Authorship in Comparative Copyright Law' (2003) 52 *DePaul L Rev* 1063.
—— 'People Not Machines: Authorship and What It Means in the Berne Convention' (2018) 49 *IIC* 131.
Ginsburg J and Budiardjo L, 'Authors and Machines' (2019) 34 *Berk Tech LJ* 343.
Goodfellow I, Bengio Y and Courville A, *Deep Learning* (MIT Press 2016).
Goold P, 'Artificial Authors: Case Studies of Copyright in Works of Machine Learning' (2020) 67 *J Copyright Soc'y USA* 427.
—— 'The Curious Case Of Computer-generated works under the Copyright, Designs and Patents Act 1988' (2021) 2 *IPQ* 120.
Goudkamp J and Nolan D (eds), *Winfield & Jolowicz Tort* 20th edn (Sweet & Maxwell 2020).

Grimmelmann J, 'There's No Such Thing as a Computer-Authored Work – And It's a Good Thing, Too' (2016) 39 *Colum JL & Arts* 403.

Grünberger M and Dietz A, 'Germany' in Burton Ong (ed), *International Copyright Law and Practice*, vol 2 (annually updated, LexisNexis 2024).

Grützmacher M, '§69a' in Ulrich Loewenheim (ed) *Handbuch des Urheberrechts* (3rd edn, CH Beck 2021).

Guadamuz A, 'Do Androids Dream of Electric Copyright? Comparative Analysis of Originality in *artificial intelligence generated works*' (2017) 2 *IPQ* 169.

Haedicke M, '§3 Ownership A. Inventor and Inventor Right' in Maximilian Haedicke and Henrik Timmann (eds), *Patent Law: A Handbook on European and German Patent Law* (CH Beck 2014).

Haertl K, *Study on the Fundamental Problems of the Creation of a European Patent which Stands Next to the National Patents* (Bonn 1960).

Hardin G, 'The Tragedy of the Commons' (1968) 162 *Science* 1243.

Harhoff D and Hoisl K, 'Institutionalized Incentives for Ingenuity – Patent Value and the German Employees' Inventions Act' (2007) 36 *Research Policy* 1143.

Hassabis D and others, 'Highly Accurate Protein Structure Prediction with AlphaFold' 596 (2021) *Nature* 583.

Hassabis D and others, 'Accurate Structure Prediction of Biomolecular Interactions with AlphaFold 3' 630 (2024) *Nature* 493.

Hattenbach B and Glucoft J, 'Patents in an Era of Infinite Monkeys and Artificial Intelligence' (2015) 19 *Stan Tech L Rev* 32.

Hegel G, *Philosophy of Right* as translated in Thomas Knox, *Hegel's Philosophy of Right* (OUP 2015).

Heller M and Eisenberg R, 'Can Patents Deter Innovation? The Anticommons in Biomedical Research' (1998) 280 *Science* 698.

Hess P, 'EPC 2000, Art 62' in Richard Hacon and Jochen Pagenberg (eds), *Concise European Patent Law* (2nd edn, Kluwer Law International 2008).

Hess P, Tilman MS and Martin W, 'Are Patents Merely "Paper Tigers"?' (*Bardehle Pagenberg* November 2014). Available at: www.bardehle.com/en/ip-news-knowledge/publication/detail/are-patents-merely-paper-tigers, last accessed 3 December 2021.

Hetmank S and Lauber-Rönsberg A, 'Künstliche Intelligenz – Herausforderungen für das Immaterialgüterrecht' (2018) GRUR 574.

Hindmarch W, *A Treatise on the Law relating to Patent Privileges for the Sole Use of Inventions; and Practice of Obtaining Letters of Patents for Inventions* (V&R Stevens & GS Norton, and W Benning & Co 1846).

Huard A and Pelletier M, *Répertoire de législation et de jurisprudence en matière de brevets d'invention* (Librairie générale de jurisprudence 1885).

Hugenholtz B, 'Works of literature, science and art' in Bernt Hugenholtz and others (eds), *A Century of Dutch Copyright Law* (deLex 2012).

—— 'Neighbouring Rights are Obsolete' (2019) 50 *IIC* 1006.

Hugenholtz B and Quintais J, 'Copyright and Artificial Creation: Does EU Copyright Law Protect AI-Assisted Output?' (2021) 52 *IIC* 1190.

Hughes J, 'The Philosophy of Intellectual Property' (1988) 77 *Georgetown LJ* 287.

Hulme W, 'On the History of Patent Law in the Seventeenth and Eighteenth Centuries' (1902) 18 *L Q Rev* 280.

Johnson J and Johnson H, *An Epitome of the Law and Practice Connected with Patents for Inventions* (Longmans Green, & Co.= 1894).

Johnson P, 'EPC 2000, Art 56' in Richard J Hacon and Jochen Pagenberg (eds), *Concise European Patent Law* 2nd edn (Kluwer Law International 2008).

Johnson R and Cureton A, 'Kant's Moral Philosophy' in Edward Zalta (ed), *The Stanford Encyclopedia of Philosophy* (*plato.stanford*, spring 2021). Available at: https://plato.stanford.edu/archives/spr2021/entries/kant-moral/, last accessed 11 December 2021.

Jonczyk J, 'Employee Inventions' (1989) *IIC* 847.

Jumper J and others 'Highly Accurate Protein Structure Prediction with AlphaFold' (2024) 596 *Nature* 583.

Kamina P and others, 'France' in Burton Ong (ed) *International Copyright Law and Practice* (annually updated, LexisNexis 2024).
Kaminski M, 'Authorship, Disrupted: AI Authors in Copyright and First Amendment Law' (2017) 51 *UC Davis L Rev* 589.
Keukenschrijver A, 'Einleitung' in Alfred Keukenschrijver and Rudolf Busse (eds) *Patentgesetz* 8th edn (De Gruyter 2016).
—— '§ 4 Erfinderische Tätigkeit' in Rudolf Busse and Alfred Keukenschrijver (eds), *Patentgesetz* 8th edn (De Gruyter 2016).
—— '§ 6 Recht auf das Patent' in Rudolf Busse and Alfred Keukenschrijver (eds), *Patentgesetz* 8th edn (De Gruyter 2016).
Kim D, '"AI-Generated Inventions": Time to Get the Record Straight?' (2020) 69 *GRUR International* 443.
Kitch E, 'The Nature and Function of the Patent System' (1977) 20 *J Law Econ* 265.
Kohler J, *Deutsches Patentrecht* (Verlag von F Bensheimer 1878).
Kostylo J, 'Commentary on the Venetian Statute on Industrial Brevets (1474)' in Lionel Bently and Martin Kretschmer (eds), *Primary Sources on Copyright (1450–1900)* (2008). Available at: www.copyrighthistory.org, last accessed 20 April 2021.
Koukolík F, *Já. O mozku, vědomí a sebeuvědomování* (Karolinum 2024).
Koziol H, 'Natural and Legal Causation' in Luboš Tichý (ed), *Causation in Law* (Eva Rozkotová – IFEC 2008).
Kroher K, 'Art 56' in Dieter Stauder und Stefan Luginbühl (eds) *Europäisches Patentübereinkommen* 9th edn (Carl Heymanns Verlag 2023).
Kühnemann H, 'Report on Technological Progress and Creative Effort as Patentability Criteria' EXP/BRev (60). Available at: https://rm.coe.int/090000168072965b, last accessed 29 March 2021.
Kur A, 'Unité de l'art is here to stay – Cofemel and its consequences' (2020) 4 *JIPIL* 290.
Ladas S, *International Protection of Industrial Property* (Harvard University Press 1930).
—— *Patents, Trademarks and Related Rights. National and International Protection. Vol I* (Harvard University Press 1975).
Laddie H, 'Patents – What's Invention Got To Do With It?' in David Vaver and Lionel Bently (eds), *Intellectual Property in the New Millennium* (CUP 2010).
Laddie H, Prescott P and Vitoria M, *The Modern Law of Copyright and Designs*, vol I 4th edn (Lexis-Nexis 2011).
—— *The Modern Law of Copyright and Designs*, vol I 5th edn (LexisNexis 2018).
Laligant O, *La véritable condition d'application du droit d'auteur: Originalité ou création?* (Presses Universitaires d'Aix-Marseille 1999).
Landes W, Posner R, and Posner R, *The Economic Structure of Intellectual Property Law* (Harvard University Press 2003).
Lavik E, 'Romantic Authorship in Copyright Law and the Uses of Aesthetics' in Mireille van Eechoud (ed), *The Work of Authorship* (Amsterdam University Press 2014).
Lee Y H, 'United Kingdom Copyright Decisions and Legislative Developments 2023' [2024] *IIC* 422.
Le Stanc Ch, 'The New French Law on Employees' Inventions' in Jeremy Phillips (ed) *Employees' Inventions. A Comparative Study* (Fernsway Publications 1981).
Lehman M and Spindler G, '2. Abschnitt. Das geschützte Werk. §9 Werkarten' in Ulrich Loewenheim (ed) *Handbuch des Urheberrechts* 3rd edn (CH Beck 2021).
Leistner M, 'Einheitlicher europäischer Werkbegriff auch im Bereich der angewandten Kunst' (2009) GRUR 1114.
—— 'UrhG § 2 Geschützte Werke' in Gerhard Schricker and Ulrich Loewenheim (eds), *Urheberrecht* 6th edn (CH Beck 2020).
—— 'KI-basierte Werke im Urheberrecht – eine Einordnung'/ 'AI-Based Works in Copyright Law – A Utilitarian Argument against Protection' 9 (*ssrn*, 6 April 2022). Available at: https://ssrn.com/abstract=3987928, last accessed 24 October 2022.
Lemley M, 'Rational ignorance at the patent office' (2021) 95 *Northwestern University Law Review* 1495, 1511.
Levin M, The Cofemel Revolution – Originality, Equality and Neutrality' in Eleonora Rosati (ed), *The Routledge Handbook of EU Copyright Law* (Routledge 2023).

Lindenmaier, 'Die schöpferische Leistung als Voraussetzung der Patenterteilung' (1939) 3 GRUR 153.
Locke J, *Second Treatise of Government* (Alex Catalogue 1994).
Loewenheim U and Leistner M, '§ 6 Schutzvoraussetzungen' in Ulrich Loewenheim and Matthias Leistner (eds), *Handbuch des Urheberrechts* 3rd edn (CH Beck 2021).
Loewenheim U, *Handbuch des Urheberrechts* 2nd edn (CH Beck 2010).
—— '§ 10 Der Urheber A. Der Werkschöpfer' in Ulrich Loewenheim (ed), *Handbuch des Urheberrechts* 2nd edn (CH Beck 2010).
—— '§ 11 Miturheberschaft und Werkverbindungen' in Ulrich Loewenheim (ed), *Handbuch des Urheberrechts* 3rd edn (CH Beck 2021).
Long P, 'Invention, Authorship, "Intellectual Property" and the Origin of Patents: Notes toward a Conceptual History' (1991) 32 *Technology and Culture* 846.
Lucas A, *Propriété littéraire et artistique* 5th edn (Dalloz 2017).
Lucas A and Sirinelli P, 'L'originalité en droit d'auteur' (1993) 23 *JCP* 253.
Lucas A, Lucas-Schloetter A and Bernault C, *Traité de la propriété littéraire et artistique* 5th edn (LexisNexis 2017).
Lucas-Schloetter A, 'Folklore' in Silke von Lewinski (ed), *Indigenous Heritage and Intellectual Property* (Kluwer Law International 2004).
Machlup F, *An Economic Review of the Patent System* (Committee Print 1958).
MacLeod C, *Inventing the Industrial Revolution* (CUP 2009).
Mansfield E, *The Economics of Technological Change* (Longman 1969).
Margoni T, 'The Harmonisation of EU Copyright Law: The Originality Standard' in Mark Perry (ed), *Global Governance of Intellectual Property in the 21st Century: Reflecting Policy Through Change* (Springer 2016).
Mathély P, *Le nouveau droit français des brevets d'invention* (Librairie du journal des notaires et des avocats 1991).
McCutcheon J, 'Curing the Authorless Void: Protecting Computer-Generated Works Following IceTV and Phone Directories' (2013) 37 *Melb U L Rev* 46.
Mellulis KJ, 'Patentfähige Erfindungen' in Georg Benkard (ed), *Europäisches Patentübereinkommen* (CH Beck 2002).
—— 'PatG § 6 [Recht des Erfinders]' in Georg Benkard (ed), *Patentgesetz* 12th edn (CH Beck 2023).
Menell P, 'Intellectual Property: General Theories' in Boudewijn Bouckaert and Gerrit De Geest (eds), *Encyclopedia of Law & Economics. Vol II* (Edward Elgar 2000).
—— 'Einleitung' in Georg Benkard (ed), *Patentgesetz* 12th edn (CH Beck 2023).
Merges R, *Justifying Intellectual Property* (Harvard University Press 2011).
Metzger A, 'Interpretation of IP Treaties in Accordance with Articles 31-33 VCLT' in Henning Grosse Ruse-Khan and Axel Metzger (eds), *Intellectual Property Ordering beyond Borders* (CUP 2022).
Mollet-Viéville T, 'L'instauration du critère d'activité inventive en France' in IRPI (ed), *L'Activité inventive* (Acte de colloque 2019).
Mossoff A, 'Who Cares What Thomas Jefferson Thought about Patents – Reevaluating the Patent Privilege in Historical Context' (2007) 92 *Cornell L Rev* 953.
Moufang R, 'Art 52(2) u (3) EPÜ Ausgeschlossene Nicht-Erfindungen / excluded non-inventions' in Rainer Schulte (ed), *Patentgesetz mit Europäischem Übereinkommen* 10th edn (Carl Heymanns Verlag 2017).
—— 'Erfinderische Tätigkeit / inventive activity Art 56 EPÜ, § 4' in Rainer Schulte (ed), *Patentgesetz mit Europäischem Patentübereinkommen* (Carl Heymanns Verlag 2017).
—— 'Patentfähige Erfindungen / patentable inventions Art 52 EPÜ, § 1' in Rainer Schulte (ed), *Patentgesetz mit Europäischem Patentübereinkommen* (Carl Heymanns Verlag 2017).
Mousseron JM, *Le droit du breveté d'invention* (Librairie générale de droit et de jurisprudence 1961).
Murphy K, *Machine Learning: A Probabilistic Perspective* (MIT Press 2012).
Nack R, 'Inventions and their Amenability to Patent Protection' in Maximilian Haedicke and Henrik Timmann (eds), *Patent Law: A Handbook on European and German Patent Law* (CH Beck 2014).
Ng A, *Copyright Law and the Progress of Science and the Useful Arts* (Edward Elgar 2011).
Ohly A, 'Concluding Remarks: Postmodernism and Beyond' in Justine Pila and Ansgar Ohly (eds), *The Europeanization of Intellectual Property Law: Towards a European Legal Methodology* (OUP 2013).

Ong B, 'Originality from Copying: Fitting Recreative Works into the Copyright Universe' (2010) 2 *IPQ* 165.
Passa J, *Droit de la propriété industrielle* 2nd edn (LDGJ 2013).
Peifer K-N, 'UrhG § 11 Allgemeines' in Gerhard Schricker and Ulrich Loewenheim (eds) *Urheberrecht* 6th edn (CH Beck 2020).
Pelletier M and Vidal-Naquet E, *La Convention D'Union pour la Protection de la Propriété Industrielle* (Librarie Recueil Sirey 1902).
Phillips J, 'Employees' Inventions: An Analysis of the Nature of the Subject' in Jeremy Phillips (ed) *Employees' Inventions. A Comparative Study* (Fernsway Publications 1981).
—— 'Authorship, Ownership, Wikiship: Copyright in the 21st century' in Estelle Derclaye, *Research Handbook on the Future of EU Copyright* (Edward Elgar 2009).
Pila J, 'An Intentional View of the Copyright Work' (2008) 4 *MLR* 535.
—— 'Copyright and Its Categories of Original Works' (2010) 30 *OJLS* 229.
—— *The Requirement for an Invention in Patent Law* (OUP 2010).
—— *The Subject Matter of Intellectual Property* (OUP 2017).
—— 'The Authorial Works Protectable by Copyright' in Eleonora Rosati (ed), *The Routledge Handbook of EU Copyright Law* (Routledge 2021).
Pila J and Torremans P, *European Intellectual Property Law* 2nd edn (OUP 2019).
Piotraut JL and Dechristé PJ, *Jugements et arrêts fondamentaux de la propriété intellectuelle* (Technique & Doc 2002).
Plaisant M, *Traité de droit conventionnel international concernant la proprieté industrielle* (Librairie du Recueil Sirey 1949).
Pollaud-Dulian F, *La propriété industrielle* 2nd edn (Economica 2011).
—— *Le droit d'auteur* 2nd edn (Economica 2014).
Portron A, *Le fait de la création en droit d'auteur français* (LDGJ 2021).
Pottage A and Sherman B, *Figures of Invention: A History of Modern Patent Law* (OUP 2010).
Pratt D, 'Good Teaching: One Size Fits All?' (2002) 93 *New Directions for Adult and Continuing Education* 5.
Proudfoot D and Copeland J, *The Oxford Handbook of Philosophy of Cognitive Science* (OUP 2012).
Quaedvlieg A, 'Authorship and Ownership: Authors, Entrepreneurs and Rights' in Tatiana-Helenē Synodinou (ed), *Codification of European Copyright Law: Challenges and Perspectives* (Wolters Kluwer Law & Business 2012).
Radin MJ, *Reinterpreting Property* (University of Chicago Press 1994).
Ramalho A, 'Patentability of AI-generated Inventions: Is a Reform of the Patent System Needed?' (2018). Available at: https://papers.ssrn.com/sol3/papers.cfm?abstract_id=3168703, last accessed 1 April 2019.
—— 'Will Robots Rule The (Artistic) World? A Proposed Model for the Legal Status of Creations by Artificial Intelligence Systems' (2017) 21 *J Internet L* 1.
Reute M, 'The German Employee-Invention Law: An Outline' in Jeremy Phillips (ed) *Employees' Inventions. A Comparative Study* (Fernsway Publications 1981).
Ricketson S, *The Berne Convention for the Protection of Literary and Artistic Works: 1886–1986* (Kluwer 1987).
—— 'The 1992 Horace S Manges Lecture – People or Machines: The Berne Convention and the Changing Concept of Authorship' (1991) 16 *Colum-VLA JL & Arts* 1.
—— *The Paris Convention for the Protection of Industrial Property A Commentary* (OUP 2015).
Ricketson S and Ginsburg J, *International Copyright and Neighbouring Rights: The Berne Convention and Beyond*, Vol I, 2nd edn (OUP 2006).
Roberts A and Wooldridge M, *Artificial Intelligence* (Penguin Books 2018).
Robin A, 'Question de procedure: une présomption prétorienne' in Michel Vivant (ed), *Les grands arrêts de la propriété intellectuelle* 3rd edn (Dalloz 2020).
Robinson W, *Law of Patents for Useful Inventions* (Little, Brown 1890).
Rosati E, *Originality in EU Copyright: Full Harmonization Through Case Law* (Edward Elgar 2013).
—— 'CJEU Rules that Copyright Protection for Designs Only Requires Sufficient Originality' (2019) 12 JIPIL 931.

—— *Copyright and the Court of Justice of the European Union* (OUP 2024).
Rosenblatt F, *The Perceptron: A Theory of Statistical Separability in Cognitive Systems (Project Para)* (Cornell Aeronautical Laboratory 1958).
Roubier P, *Le droit de la propriété industrielle* vol 1 (Recueil Sirey 1952).
—— *Le droit de la propriété industrielle*, vol 2 (Recueil Sirey 1954).
Russell S and Norvig P, *Artificial Intelligence: A Modern Approach* 3rd global edn (Pearson 2016).
Samuelson P, 'Allocating Ownership Rights in Computer-Generated Works' (1986) 47 *U Pitt L Rev* 1185.
—— 'AI Authorship?' (2020) 63 *ACM* 20.
Samuelson P and others, 'A Manifesto Concerning the Legal Protection of Computer Programs' (1994) 94 *Colum L R* 2308, 2315–20.
Saxby S, 'Employees' Inventions and English Law' in Jeremy Phillips (ed) *Employees' Inventions. A Comparative Study* (Fernsway Publications 1981).
Schippel H, 'BGH 05.05.1966 Ia ZR 110/64 "Spanplatten"' (1966) *GRUR* 558.
Schulze G, 'UrhG § 2 Geschützte Werke' in Thomas Dreier and Gernot Schulze (eds), *Urheberrechtsgesetz* 7th edn (CH Beck 2022).
—— 'UrhG § 7 Urheber' in Thomas Dreier and Gernot Schulze (eds), *Urheberrechtsgesetz* 7th edn (CH Beck 2022).
—— 'UrhG § 8 Miturheber' in Thomas Dreier and Gernot Schulze (eds), *Urheberrechtsgesetz* 7th edn (CH CH Beck 2022).
Schumpeter J, 'The Creative Response in Economic History' (1947) 7 *Journal of Econ Hist* 149.
Senftleben M and Buijtelaar L, 'Robot Creativity: An Incentive-based Neighbouring Rights Approach' (2020) 42 *EIPR* 797.
Seymore S, 'Serendipity' (2009) 88 *NC L Rev* 185.
Shapiro C 'Navigating the Patent Thicket: Cross Licenses, Patent Pools, and Standard Setting' (2000) 1 *Innovation Pol'y & Econ* 119.
—— 'Competition and Innovation: Did Arrow Hit the Bull's Eye?' in Josh Lerner and Scott Stern (eds), *The Rate and Direction of Inventive Activity Revisited* (University of Chicago Press 2012).
Shapiro C and Varian H, *Information Rules* (Harvard Business School Press 1999).
Shemtov N, 'A Study on Inventorship in Inventions Involving AI Activity' (EPO February 2019). Available at: http://documents.epo.org/projects/babylon/eponet.nsf/0/3918F57B010A3540C125841900280653/$File/Concept_of_Inventorship_in_Inventions_involving_AI_Activity_en.pdf, last accessed 17 December 2021.
Sherman B, 'From the Non-original to the Ab-original: A History' in Brad Sherman and Alain Strowel (eds), *Of Authors and Origins: Essays on Copyright Law* (Clarendon Press 1994).
—— 'Regulating Access and Use of Genetic Resources: Intellectual Property Law and Biodiscovery' (2003) 25 *EIPR* 301.
—— 'What is a Copyright Work?' (2011) 12 *Theoretical Inq L* 99.
—— 'What Does It Mean to Invent Nature?' (2015) 5 *UC Irvine LR* 1193.
Sherman B and Bently L, *The Making of Modern Intellectual Property Law: The British Experience, 1760–1911* (CUP 1999).
Simone D, *Copyright and Collective Authorship* (CUP 2019).
Sirinelli P, 'Chronique de Jurisprudence' (2010) 226 *RIDA* 394.
—— *Code de la propriété intellectuelle* 19th edn (Dalloz 2019).
Sirinelli P and others, *Code de la propriété intellectuelle: annoté & commenté* 24th edn (Dalloz 2024).
Sirinelli P and Bensamoun A, 'Case Law Section' (2018) 255 *RIDA* 125.
Spence M, 'Justifying Copyright' in Daniel McClean and Karsten Schubert (eds), *Dear Images: Art, Copyright and Culture* (Ridighouse 2002).
Spindler G, '§69a UrhG' in Gerhard Schricker and Ulrich Loewenheim (eds), *Urheberrecht* 6th edn (CH Beck 2020).
Steel S, *Proof of Causation in Tort Law* (CUP 2015).
Sterckx S and Cockbain J, *Exclusions from Patentability: How Far Has the European Patent Office Eroded Boundaries* (CUP 2012).
Stokes J and others, 'A Deep Learning Approach to Antibiotic Discovery' (2020) *Cell* 688.
Straus J, 'Biotechnologische Erfindungen – ihr Schutz und seine Grenzen' (1992) *GRUR* 252.

—— 'Artificial Intelligence and Patenting: Some Lessons from "DABUS" Patent Applications' (2022) 44 *EIPR* 348.

Synodinou TH, 'Pluralism or Universalism in International Copyright Law' in Tatiana Eleni Synodinou (ed), *Authorship in International Copyright Law* (Wolters Kluwer 2019).

Taddy M, 'The Technological Elements of Artificial Intelligence' (NBER February 2018). Available at: www.nber.org/papers/w24301.pdf, last accessed 22 December 2021.

Tappin M and others, *Laddie, Prescott and Vitoria: The Modern Law of Copyright* 5th edn (Lexis 2018).

Tehranian J, 'Sex, Drones & Videotape: Rethinking Copyright's Authorship-Fixation Conflation in the Age of Performance' (2017) 68 *Hastings LJ* 1319.

Thomas-Raquin C and Le Guerer M, 'Le controle de l'originalité d'une oeuvre par la Cour de cassation' [2017] Comm Com Électr 90.

Thorley S and others, *Terrell on the Law of Patents* 15th edn (Sweet & Maxwell Ltd 2000).

Thum D, 'UrhG § 7 Urheber' in Artur-Axel Wandtke and Winfried Bullinger, *Praxiskommentar Urheberrecht* 6th edn (CH Beck 2022).

—— 'UrhG § 8 Miturheber' in Artur-Axel Wandtke and Winfried Bullinger, *Praxiskommentar Urheberrecht* 6th edn (CH CH Beck 2022).

Torremans P, 'Copyright (and Other Intellectual Property Rights) as a Human Right' in Paul Torremans (ed), *Intellectual Property Law and Human Rights* 3rd edn (Wolters Kluwer 2015).

—— 'The Role of the CJEU's Autonomous Concepts as a Harmonising Element of Copyright Law in the United Kingdom' (2019) 4 *IPQ* 265.

Turing A and others, 'Can Automatic Calculating Machines be Said to Think?' (1952) in Jack Copeland (ed), *The Essential Turing* (OUP 2004).

van Eechoud M, 'Voices Near and Far. Introduction' in Mireille van Eechoud (ed), *The Work of Authorship* (Amsterdam University Press 2014).

van Gompel S, 'Creativity, Autonomy and Personal Touch. A Critical Appraisal of the CJEU's Originality Test for Copyright' in Mireille van Eechoud (ed), *The Work of Authorship* (Amsterdam University Press 2014).

van Gompel S and Erlend Lavik, 'Quality, Merit, Aesthetics and Purpose: An Inquiry into EU Copyright Law's Eschewal of Other Criteria than Originality' (2013) 236 *RIDA* 101.

Vivant M and Brugière JM, *Droit d'auteur et droits voisins* 3rd edn (Dalloz 2016).

—— *Droit d'auteur et droits voisins* 4th edn (Dalloz 2019).

von Lewinski S, *International Copyright Law and Policy* (OUP 2008).

—— 'Database Directive' in Michel Walter and Silke von Lewinski (eds), *European Copyright Law. A Commentary* (OUP 2010).

—— 'Information Society Directive' in Michel Walter and Silke von Lewinski (eds) *European Copyright Law. A Commentary* (OUP 2010).

—— 'Principles of Interpretation' in Jörg Reinbothe and Silke von Lewinski (eds) *The WIPO Treaties on Copyright* 2nd edn (OUP 2015).

Vousden S, 'Infopaq and the Europeanisation of Copyright Law' (2010) 2 Wipo J 197.

Waldron J, 'The Rule of Law' in Edward Zalta (ed), *The Stanford Encyclopedia of Philosophy* (*plato. stanford*, summer 2020). Available at: https://plato.stanford.edu/archives/sum2020/entries/rule-of-law/. last accessed 31 December 2021.

Walter M, 'Term Directive' in Michel Walter and Silke von Lewinski (eds) *European Copyright Law. A Commentary* (OUP 2010).

Wooldridge M, *The Road to Conscious Machines. The Story of AI* (Penguin 2020).

Yanisky RS and Liu X, 'When Artificial Intelligence Systems Produce Inventions: An Alternative Model for Patent Law at the 3A Era' (2018) 39 *Cardozo L Rev* 2215.

Yu P, 'Reconceptualizing Intellectual Property Interests in a Human Rights Framework' (2007) 40 *UC Davis L Rev* 1039.

Zech H, 'Technizität im Patentrecht – Eine intra- und interdisziplinäre Analyse des Technikbegriffs' (2017). Available at: https://papers.ssrn.com/sol3/papers.cfm?abstract_id=3063183, last accessed 7 May 2020.

Zemer L, *The Idea of Authorship in Copyright* (Ashgate 2007).

Other Sources

Banks B, *The British Patent System* (Her Majesty's Stationery Office 1970) Cmnd 4407.

City of Munich, 'Kurt-Haertel-Passage' (*muenchen*, 2003). Available at: www.muenchen.de/rathaus/Stadtverwaltung/Kommunalreferat/geodatenservice/strassennamen/Strassenneubenennung-2003/kurthaertelpassage.html, last accessed 2 December 2021.

Czech Constitutional Court, 'Emeritní funkcionáři a soudci Prof. JUDr. Jiří Malenovský, CSc.' (*usoud* 2015). Available at: www.usoud.cz/emeritni-funkcionari-a-soudci?tx_odjudges%5Bdetail%5D=18&cHash=575a0e8402d2e6bbdd63027c0325b843, last accessed 25 October 2021.

Department of Trade and Industry, Intellectual property and innovation (White Paper, Cmnd 9712, 1986).

European Patent Office, *Guidelines for Examination* (EPO 2021).

European Patent Office, 'Press Communiqué on decisions J 8/20 and J 9/20 of the Legal Board of Appeal' (EPO 21 December 2021). Available at: www.epo.org/law-practice/case-law-appeals/communications/2021/20211221.html, last accessed 22 December 2021.

Etzioni O, 'No, the Experts Don't Think Superintelligent AI is a Threat to Humanity' (*MIT Technology Review*, 20 September 2016)). Available at: www.technologyreview.com/s/602410/no-the-experts-dont-think-superintelligent-ai-is-a-threat-to-humanity/?utm_campaign=internal&utm_medium=homepage&utm_source=top-stories_3&set=602438, last accessed 22 December 2021.

Fenzel B, 'Patent solution in a canning jar' (*Max-Planck-Gesellschaft*, 11 August 2014). Available at: www.mpg.de/8361429/flashback-ziegler, last accessed 31 December 2021.

Food container, European patent application EP3564144A1. Available at: www.worldwide.espacenet.com/patent/search/family/063915228/publication/EP3564144A1?q=pn%3DEP3564144, last accessed 13 December 2021.

Fraze D, 'Cyber Grand Challenge (CGC) (Archived)' (*US Department of Defense*, unknown date) www.darpa.mil/program/cyber-grand-challenge, last accessed 22 December 2021.

Gambardella A and others, 'The Value of European Patents – A Survey of European Inventors – Final Report of The PatVal EU Project' (*europa*, January 2005). Available at: https://ec.europa.eu/invest-in-research/pdf/download_en/patval_mainreportandannexes.pdf, last accessed 31 December 2021.

Hardesty L, 'Explained: Neural Networks' (*MIT News*, 14 April 2017). Available at: www.news.mit.edu/2017/explained-neural-networks-deep-learning-0414, last accessed 22 December 2021.

Hartmann C and others, 'Trends and Developments in Artificial Intelligence Challenges to the Intellectual Property Rights Framework' (*invir*, 2020). Available at: www.ivir.nl/ivir-study-for-european-commission-on-ai-and-ip/, last accessed 13 December 2021.

Hassabis D, 'Introducing Isomorphic Labs' (*isomorphiclabs*, November 2021). Available at: www.isomorphiclabs.com/blog, last accessed 31 December 2021.

Hawking S, Tegmark M and Russell S, 'Transcending Complacency on Superintelligent Machines' (*Huffpost*, 19 April 2014). Available at: www.huffingtonpost.com/stephen-hawking/artificial-intelligence_b_5174265.html?guccounter=1, last accessed 22 December 2021.

House of Commons, *Copyright and Designs Law* (Whitford Report) Cmnd 6732, 1977.

ING, 'Video on making the Next Rembrandt' (*Next Rembrandt*, undated). Available at: www.nextrembrandt.com/, last accessed 22 December 2021.

Institut national de la propriété industrielle, *La délivrance des brevets et des certificats d'utilité* (INPI 2016).

Intellectual Property Office, *Manual of Patent Practice* (UK IPO 2016).

Isomorphic Labs and the Google Deepmind AlphaFold team, 'AlphaFold 3 predicts the structure and interactions of all life's molecules' (*isomorphiclabs*, 8 May 2024). Available at: www.isomorphiclabs.com/articles/alphafold-3-predicts-the-structure-and-interactions-of-all-of-lifes-molecules, last accessed 30 July 2024.

Janečková E, 'AI as an Inventor: What We Can Learn from the Australian DABUS Case' (*Oxford Business Law Blog*, 30 September 2021). Available at: www.law.ox.ac.uk/business-law-blog/blog/2021/09/ai-inventor-what-we-can-learn-australian-dabus-case, last accessed 14 December 2021.

Japan Intellectual Property Strategy Headquarters, 'Intellectual Property Strategic Program 2016' (*kantei*, May 2016). Available at: www.kantei.go.jp/jp/singi/titeki2/kettei/chizaikeikaku20160509_e.pdf, last accessed 17 December 2021.

Karras T and others, 'Nvidia Original GAN StyleGAN' (*This person does not exist*, December 2018). Available at: www.thispersondoesnotexist.com/, last accessed 13 December 2021.

Knight W, 'The Dark Secret at the Heart of AI' (MIT Technology Review, 11 April 2017). Available at: www.technologyreview.com/s/604087/the-dark-secret-at-the-heart-of-ai/, last accessed 22 December 2021.

Lau JH and others, 'Deep-speare: A joint neural model of poetic language, meter and rhyme' Proceedings of the 56th Annual Meeting of the Association for Computational Linguistics (*arXiv*, 10 July 2018). Available at: www.arxiv.org/abs/1807.03491, last accessed 22 December 2021.

Levin S, 'Uber crash shows "catastrophic failure" of self-driving technology, experts say' (*Guardian*, 22 March 2018). Available at: www.theguardian.com/technology/2018/mar/22/self-driving-car-uber-death-woman-failure-fatal-crash-arizona, last accessed 22 December 2021.

Madison J, 'Federalist No. 43' (*Library of Congress*, undated) Available at: www.guides.loc.gov/federalist-papers/text-41-50#s-lg-box-wrapper-25493407, last accessed 21 March 2021.

Mathewson K and Mirowski P, 'Improvised Comedy as a Turing Test, 31st Conference on Neural Information Processing Systems' Workshop on Machine Learning for Creativity and Design (*arXiv*, 23 November 2017). Available at: https://arxiv.org/abs/1711.08819, last accessed 22 December 2021.

Mammen C and others, 'Creativity, Artificial Intelligence and the Requirement of Human Authors and Inventors in Copyright and Patent Law' (*Ssrn*, 17 July 2024). Available at: https://papers.ssrn.com/sol3/papers.cfm?abstract_id=4892973, last accessed 31 July 2024.

Maxmen A, 'South African scientists copy Moderna's COVID vaccine' (*Nature*, 3 February 2022). Available at: www.nature.com/articles/d41586-022-00293-2, last accessed 4 February 2022.

Moderna, 'Program Patents' (*moderna*, undated). Available at: www.modernatx.com/patents, last accessed 4 February 2022.

Neural network based prototyping system and method, US patent 5852815A expired. Available at: https://patents.google.com/patent/US5852815A/en, last accessed 22 December 2021.

Okorie C, 'Artificial Intelligence system as inventor in South African patent application: The case of DABUS' (*ipkitten*, 16 August 2021). Available at: https://ipkitten.blogspot.com/2021/08/artificial-intelligence-system-as.html, last accessed 15 December 2021.

Oxford English Dictionary Online (*EOD*, December 2020) www.oed.com/, last accessed 31 December 2021.

Proceedings of the 1st meeting of the Patents Working Party held at Brussels from 17 to 28 April 1961, Document IV/2767/61-E. Available at: www.epo.org/law-practice/legal-texts/epc/archive/epc-1973/traveaux.html, last accessed 29 March 2021.

Proposal for a Council Directive on Rental Right and Lending Right and on Certain Rights Related to Copyright in the Field of Intellectual Property of 30 April 1992, COM(92) 159 – SYN 319 final. Available at: https://eur-lex.europa.eu/legal-content/EN/TXT/PDF/?uri=CELEX:51992PC0159&from=EN, last accessed 31 December 2021.

Proposal for a Council Directive on the legal protection of computer programs COM(88) 816 final – SYN 183; 89/C 91/05.

Proposal for a European Parliament and Council Directive on the harmonization of certain aspects of copyright and related rights in the Information Society of 10 December 1997, COM(97) 628 final 97/0359 (COD).

Russell B, 'The Role of Individual' (BBC, 9 January 1949). Available at: www.bbc.co.uk/sounds/play/p00hgk48, last accessed 31 December 2021.

Russell S, 'BBC Reith Lectures 2021 – Living with Artificial Intelligence. Transcript of the Lecture' 5 (BBC, 1 December 2021). Available at: www.bbc.co.uk/programmes/m001216j, last accessed 12 December 2021.

Savage N, 'Tapping into the drug discovery potential of AI' (*Nature*; 27 May 2021). Available at: www.nature.com/articles/d43747-021-00045-7, last accessed 31 December 2021.

Seamless can, US patent US5803301A, Decision of the US PTO of 8 September 1998. Available at: https://worldwide.espacenet.com/patent/search/family/063915228/publication/EP3564144A1?q=pn%3DEP3564144, last accessed 13 December 2021.

Searle J and Floridi L at the conference 'Technology and the Human Future' (YouTube 25 October 2016). Available at: www.youtube.com/watch?v=b6o_7HeowY8, last accessed 6 September 2018.

Shead S, 'Britain, France and Germany fight it out to be Europe's AI leader' (*Forbes*, 26 April 2018) www.forbes.com/sites/samshead/2018/04/26/britain-france-and-germany-fight-it-out-to-be-europes-ai-leader/, last accessed 31 December 2021.

Special edition 4/2007 Revision of the European Patent Convention (EPC 2000) Synoptic presentation EPC 1973/2000 – Part I: The Articles Part II Chapter I Article 52 EPC.

Tashjian R, 'How a Schiaparelli Couture Look Gets Made' (*Harper's Bazaar*, 4 October 2022). Available at: www.harpersbazaar.com/fashion/designers/a41443815/schiaparelli-couture-process/, last accessed 23 October 2022.

Travaux préparatoires to the EPC 1973, Minutes of the Munich Diplomatic Conference for the Setting up of a European System for the Grant of Patents, M/PR/I. Available at: www.epo.org/law-practice/legal-texts/epc/archive/epc-1973/traveaux.html, last accessed 29 March 2021.

Travaux préparatoires to the EPC 1973, Texts Drawn Up by the Drafting Committee of Main Committee I at the Meeting on 12 September 1973, M/74/I/R 1. Available at: www.epo.org/law-practice/legal-texts/epc/archive/epc-1973/traveaux.html, last accessed 29 March 2021.

Travaux préparatoires to the EPC 1973, Volume 42 E, EPO, Munich 1999, M/PR/I.

UK IPO, 'Impact Assessment' (*gov*, 29 October 2021) Available at: https://assets.publishing.service.gov.uk/government/uploads/system/uploads/attachment_data/file/1029930/impact-assessment.pdf, last accessed 16 December 2021.

United States Patent and Trademark Office, 'Public Views on Artificial Intelligence and Intellectual Property Policy' (*uspto*, 6 October 2020). Available at: www.uspto.gov/about-us/news-updates/uspto-releases-report-artificial-intelligence-and-intellectual-property, last accessed 17 December 2021.

United States Patent and Trademark Office, 'Inventorship Guidance for AI-Assisted Inventions' Docket No PTO–P–2023–0043.

US Food & Drug Administration 'Step 1: Discovery and Development' (*fda*, 1 April 2018). Available at: www.fda.gov/patients/drug-development-process/step-1-discovery-and-development, last accessed 31 December 2021.

Utrecht University, 'Prof. mr. dr. Peter Blok' (*Universiteit Utrecht*, undated). Available at: www.uu.nl/medewerkers/PHBlok/, last accessed 14 December 2021.

Veitich M, 'The story behind Rembrandt's last, 3D-printed masterpiece' (*IDG Connect*, 8 June 2016). Available at: www.idgconnect.com/article/3579984/the-story-behind-rembrandt-s-last-3d-printed-masterpiece.html, last accessed 22 December 2021.

Williams G, 'Inside DeepMind's epic mission to solve science's trickiest problem' (*wired*, 06 August 2019). Available at: www.wired.co.uk/article/deepmind-protein-folding, last accessed 31 December 2021.

WIPO, 'Berne Convention for the Protection of Literary and Artistic Works' (*wipolex*, undated). Available at: https://wipolex.wipo.int/en/treaties/textdetails/12807, last accessed 19 November 2021.

—— 'Contracting States' (*wipo*, undated). Available at: www.wipo.int/treaties/en/ip/berne/, last accessed 19 November 2021.

—— 'Revised Issues Paper on Intellectual Property Policy and Artificial Intelligence' (*wipo*, May 2020). Available at: www.wipo.int/meetings/en/doc_details.jsp?doc_id=499504, last accessed 17 December 2021.

INDEX

Abbott, Ryan 14
accidental inventions 54, 71, 183–4
AI-driven systems 1–3, 12–19
AI Act, Preamble to 188
AI, definition of 8–12, 20–1
algorithms 10–11, 41, 114, 179
authorship
application practice 148, 153–5, 161–2, 166–8
EU 99, 118, 121–2, 124
collaborations 126–7
communication functions of works 38
competition, effect on 190
computer programs 167
copyright subsistence criteria 153–5, 188
creativity
damaging 44
processes of 154–5, 173, 186
criminal offences 181
declarations 180–1
devise inventions or create works, whether AI systems can 20–2, 24, 179, 182
disclosure, duties of 179–84, 188
drugs, discovery of 16, 19, 49, 182, 186, 189–90
employees' inventions 184–5
epistemic approaches 87, 94, 171
EU authorship 99, 118, 121–2, 124
European Patent Convention (EPC) 63, 65, 66–9, 176, 181–4
expressive or non-obvious technical elements 21–2, 24, 67–9, 171, 180
drugs, discovery of 186, 189–90
Germany 166
relevant for IP, aspects of AI which are 12–19
value 49–50
false attribution of inventorship 181–2
false statements and misrepresentations by natural persons, safeguards against 181
France 6–7, 93–4, 133, 148, 161–2
Germany 6–7, 59–60, 87, 126–7, 148, 166–8
human intellectual creations 41–2, 189
indistinguishably of outputs 13–15, 24
inventive step 94
investigative powers 181
joint authorship 126–7, 140–1
named as inventor, right to be 63, 65, 66
natural persons 63, 65, 66
originality 133, 144–5, 162
patentability 68–9, 179–80, 182, 188, 190
persons skilled in the art (PSAs) 93–4, 174, 180, 182
presumption of authorship 142
relevant activities, list of 144–5
serendipitous events and accidents 183–4
social determination of authorship or inventorship 173
social values 38, 44
training data 41, 179, 190
United Kingdom 148, 153–5, 184–5
algorithms 10–11, 41, 114, 179
application practice *see* **application practice, authorship in; application practice, inventorship in**
application practice, authorship in 177–85
AI-driven systems 148, 153–5, 161–2, 166–8
epistemic approaches 177–85
France 7, 148, 155–62, 170, 172, 177, 187
Germany 7, 148, 162–9, 170, 172, 177, 187–9
United Kingdom 7, 148–55, 169–70, 172, 177, 187
application practice, inventorship in 7, 79–98, 174
argumentation fallacies 188–9
Arnold, Richard 5
artificial intelligence *see* **AI-driven systems**
artistic works 5, 107–8, 149–50, 154, 159, 163
see also **literary, dramatic, musical or**
artistic (LDMA) works categories
Australia 49

authorship 1–3, 5, 174–7 *see also* **application practice, authorship in; epistemic approaches to copyright subsistence criteria; EU authorship; France, authorship in; Germany, authorship in; joint authorship; presumption of authorship; United Kingdom, authorship in**
author-creator principle 28, 117, 134, 141–4, 147, 186–7, 190
author, definition of 28–9, 116, 126–7
copyright subsistence criteria 3, 173, 187
entrepreneurial works and authorial works, difference between 5, 126
human intellectual creations 28–30, 186
originality as synonymous with authorship 142
personality, reflection of 174
romanticisation of authors 29
social determination of authorship or inventorship 173
user-manipulators, blurred lines between 29–30
authorship in United Kingdom, conceptions of 125–31, 187
academic and practitioners' commentaries 126
acts of creation, significance of 125
AI-driven systems 126–7
author, definition of 126–7
checks, lack of 178
collaboration 126–7
computer software, testing 128–9
Copyright, Designs and Patents Act 1988 125–7, 141
creative activity 126–31, 176–7, 178–9
expressive elements 131, 177
human intellectual creation 125–7, 176–7
Infopaq test 127–9, 131
joint authorship 126–31, 141, 147
labour and effort, investment of 127–9
musical works 126, 128–9, 131, 178
originality 127–9, 131
personality 128, 130, 147, 178, 187
positive law 125–31
post-creative activity 128–9, 131
presumption of authorship until challenged 125, 141, 178–9
purpose and objectives 125–6
skill, time and effort 128–9
writing, mere act of 129
autonomy 13, 15–20, 29, 64, 83, 120
Azéma, Jacques 83

Bacher, Klaus 85–6
Balganesh, Shyamkrishna 112–13
Banks Committee 1970 33, 52, 81
Beier, Friedrich-Karl 34
Bentham, Jeremy 40
Bently, Lionel 4–5, 27–30, 107, 144, 146, 172–3
Berne Convention 1886 26, 31, 38
EU authorship 102, 106–8, 120
human intellectual creations 28–9
interpretation 107–8
moral rights 28
originality 143–4, 146
United Kingdom 143–4, 146, 148
Bertrand, André 131, 133, 135, 161–2
biotechnological inventions 23–4, 35–6, 74
Biron, Laura 172–3
Blanc, Etienne 33
Blanco White, Thomas 33, 52
Blok, Peter 17
Breyer, Stephen 47
Brugière, Jean-Michel 131, 133
Brunelleschi, Filippo 32
Bullinger, Winfried 136

cameras 22 *see also* **photographs**
Caron, Christophe 132–4, 160
categorisation of works 148–50, 153, 159, 163, 169–70
causal links 72–3, 85, 112–13
Cavani, Giovanni 49
checks on entitlement *see also* **disclosure, duties of**
designation of inventors 65, 66, 67, 171
European Patent Convention (EPC) 65, 66, 67, 180–1
false attribution of inventorship 181–2
false statements and misrepresentations by natural persons, safeguards against 181
France, inventorship in 187
Germany, inventorship in 187
inquiries into creative effort 181
investigative powers 181
naming natural persons to circumvent rules 65, 66
United Kingdom 179, 187
collaborations 30–1, 126–7, 135, 139–40

collective works 6, 132, *see also* **joint authorship; multiple creators**
common law countries 28, 38–9, 43
Comparative Study of Substantive Law 72, 76
compensation *see* **remuneration/ compensation**
competition 41, 48, 50, 186, 190
compilations 105, 148, 151
computer-generated works (CGWs) 22–3, 161, 169 *see also* **computer programs; United Kingdom, computer-generated works (CGWs) in**
computer programs
authorship
EU 99–102, 108, 115–17, 122–3, 158
France 157–8, 160, 161
Germany 140, 167–8
United Kingdom 128–9
computer program, definition of 100–2
Computer Programs Directive 100–2
copyright subsistence criteria 99, 101, 122–3
distinctiveness 161
graphic user interfaces 100, 101
human intellectual creations 123, 161
lex specialis 100–2
open-source software 23
originality 100, 101, 108, 115, 116–17, 160
personality, reflection of 102, 157–8
purpose-based definition 101
consciousness 19, 39–40, 128, 133 *see also* **self-consciousness**
contributions
AI-driven systems 161–2
computer programs 140
France 156, 161–2
Germany 137–40
musical works 152, 154
United Kingdom 126–31, 152, 154
Copinger and Skone James on Copyright 126, 144
copyright *see* **authorship; copyright subsistence criteria**
copyright subsistence criteria
AI-driven systems 20–2, 24, 121–2, 153–5, 179, 182, 188
authorship 99–100, 103, 109, 111, 121–3, 173, 187
computer-generated works 144, 146
computer programs 99, 101, 122–3
databases 99, 103, 122–3
epistemic approaches 7, 173, 187
EU 99–100, 103, 109, 111, 121–3
France 7, 148, 155–62, 169, 172
Germany 7, 148, 162–9, 172
human intellectual creations 171, 173
multiple creators 23
neighbouring rights 6
United Kingdom 7, 144, 146, 148, 153–5, 169, 172
Council of Europe (CoE) 62–3
Covid-19 pandemic and the Moderna vaccine 46
creation, processes of
AI-driven systems 154–5, 173, 186
authorship 140, 154–5, 168, 173, 178–9, 186
Germany 140, 168, 179
human intellectual creations 27–8
originality 28, 153
social values 44
United Kingdom 127–9, 174–5, 177–9
creativity 4–5 *see also* **creation, processes of; human intellectual creations**
aesthetic considerations, exclusion of 111–14
AI-driven systems 118, 121
author-creator principle 28, 117, 134, 141–4, 147, 186–7, 190
choices
authorship 104, 108–15, 117, 118–19. 123, 176
aesthetic considerations, exclusion of 111–13
human intellectual creations 109–10, 111–15, 123
originality 109–10, 111–15, 118–19, 123, 161, 176–7
personal choices 118
epistemic approaches 80, 83–4, 86
European Patent Convention (EPC) 63, 69
expressive or non-obvious technical elements 114–15, 123, 147
France 83–4, 125, 132–5, 141
Germany 59–60, 86, 137–40, 179
human intellectual creations 109–10, 111–15, 123
incentives and rewards 63
InfoSoc Directive 104, 108
inquiries into creative effort 181
inventive step 76
inventor-creator principle 31–4, 46, 186–7

inventorship
epistemic approaches 80, 83–4, 86
patentability 69, 70–4, 76
originality 109–10, 111–15, 118–19, 123, 161, 176–7
patentability 69, 70–4, 76
post-creative activities 128–9, 131, 135
pre-creative activities 128–9, 131, 135
recording creative activity 178–9
technical character/technicity of subject matter 80
United Kingdom 126–31, 176–9
utilitarian/mechanical works 102, 111, 120, 129, 133–4, 150–1, 169
criminal offences 181
culture 30–1, 42, 43–4, 172–3

DARPA 2016 Cyber Grand Challenge 16
databases
copyright subsistence criteria 99, 103, 122–3
database, definition of 102
Database Directive 102–3
EU authorship 99–100, 102–3, 108–9, 116–17, 122–3
InfoSoc Directive 100
interpretation 102
lex specialis 100, 102–3
natural persons 116–17, 122
originality 103, 108, 116–17, 160–1
purpose and function 102, 108
systematic or methodological way, arrangement in a 102, 103
Deazley, Ronan 42
Deep Mind 17–18
Desbois, Henri 37, 122, 132, 159
designation of inventors 20, 31, 63–7, 171
Dietz, Adolf 28–9
disclosure, duties of
AI-driven systems 179–84, 188
burden of proof 182–3
burdens, adding 187–8
challenging accuracy of disclosure 181–2
costs, creation of disproportionate 184
employees' inventions 184–5
extended duties 179, 180, 184–5, 189
incentives and rewards 181
industry-wide practice 188
knowledge gap problem 183
steps in the process, of 179
sufficiency 45–6
technical character/technicity of subject matter 98
transparency 44, 187–8
discoveries 34, 73–4
accidents and serendipitous events 54, 71, 183–4
drugs 16, 19, 49, 54, 186, 189–90
epistemic approaches 81, 82–3
distinctiveness 126–7, 161
Dornis, Tim 169
Drahos, Peter 31
dramatic works 127, 149 *see also* **literary, dramatic, musical or artistic (LDMA) works**
categories
Dreier, Thomas 108
Droz, Numa 26
drug discoveries 16, 19, 49, 54, 186, 189–90
du Sautoy, Marcus 10

economic rights 37, 59, 117, 136–7
Eisenberg, Rebecca 45
employees' inventions 56–8
disclosure, duties of 184–5
remuneration/compensation 57–8, 184–5
reporting to employers 185
United Kingdom 184–5
entitlement, checks on *see* **checks on entitlement**
entrepreneurial works 5, 56, 126
EPC *see* **European Patent Convention (EPC), inventorship in**
epistemic approaches *see* **epistemic approaches to copyright subsistence criteria; epistemic approaches to the inventive step requirement; epistemic approaches to the invention requirement**
epistemic approaches to copyright subsistence criteria 3–4, 6–7, 177–85
argumentation fallacies 188–9
authorship in application practice 173, 177–85
France 7, 148, 156, 159–61, 170, 172, 177, 187
Germany 7, 148, 167–8, 170, 172, 177, 187
United Kingdom 7, 148, 152–5, 170, 172, 177, 187

inventive step 79–87, 97
inventorship 79–97
personality, reflection of 122
epistemic approaches to the inventive step requirement 81, 87–98
devisers of inventions 88, 90–2, 98
European Patent Convention (EPC) 87–8, 93, 95
novelty 93
objectivity 87, 93
obviousness 87, 88–93, 96–7
persons skilled in the art (PSA) 87, 88, 89–92, 93–4, 95–8
prior art 87–8, 89, 92–7
priority date 89, 93
problem-and-solution test 87, 93
state of the art 88–90
technical character/technicity of subject matter 87–8, 90–2, 95–8
epistemic approaches to the invention requirement 3–4, 6, 79–87
creative activity 80, 83–4, 86
discoveries 81, 82–3
European Patent Convention (EPC) 79–80, 81–4, 97
industrial applicability 81, 83–4
natural subject matter, use of 84–5
novelty requirement 81, 82–3
patentability 172–3 187
technical character/technicity of subject matter 80, 82, 83–7, 97
essence of inventions 36, 57–8, 70, 78–9, 174–5, 186–7
EU authorship 7, 99–124, 158, 188
AI Act, Preamble to 188
AI-driven systems 99, 118, 121–2, 124
Berne Convention 102, 106–8, 120
CJEU, case law of 99–124, 131–2, 163
computer programs 99–102, 108, 115–17, 122–3, 158
Copyright Duration Directive 120
copyright subsistence criteria 99–100, 103, 109, 111, 121–3
creativity 104, 108–15, 117, 118–19, 123, 176
databases 99–100, 102–3, 108–9, 116–17, 122–3
definitions 99–103, 108–9, 116
expressive or non-obvious technical elements 101, 109–10, 114–15, 121–4, 147, 187
films 103, 117–18, 123
free choices 109–11, 114–16, 118–19, 121
harmonisation 100, 104, 123, 176
human intellectual creation 103–4, 106–21, 123–4, 187
InfoSoc Directive 99–100, 103–9, 117, 120–1, 124
joint authorship 127
justifications for IP 119–20
lex specialis 100–3
originality 100, 101, 104, 108–22
personality, reflection of 102, 119–24, 176, 187
purpose and function 101, 102, 104, 108–9, 124
remuneration/compensation 117
Rental and Lending Rights Directive 117–18
Retained EU Law (Revocation and Reform) Act 2023 (UK) 100
technical character/technicity of subject matter 110–11
Term Directive 116–18
two tracks 99–109
work, definition of 106, 121, 123–4
European Copyright Society 104
EU inventorship
AI Act 17
Biotech Directive 74
EPO, overlap between members of EU and 62–3
free movement of goods, purpose of patents in context of 63
secondary patentability requirements 45
European Patent Convention (EPC), inventorship in 6, 62–9
accidental inventions 183–4
AI-driven systems 63, 65, 66–9, 176
disclosure duties 180–4
non-obvious technical elements 67–8
burden of proof 182
checks on entitlement, lack of 65, 66, 67, 180–1
Council of Europe (CoE) and EPO, overlap between members of 62–3
criminal offences 181
declarations 181
designation of inventors 63–7
disclosure, duties of 180–4
epistemic approaches 79–80, 81–4, 87–8, 93, 95, 97, 182

EPO 62–77, 79, 180–1
 epistemic approaches 79–80, 82–4, 87–8, 93, 95, 97
 establishment 62
 EU and CoE, overlap of membership with 62–3
essence of inventions 36
EU inventorship 62–3
false attribution of inventorship 181–2
false statements and misrepresentations by natural persons, safeguards against 181
form 1001 Request for a grant of a European patent, amendment of 181, 182, 185
form 1002 Designation of inventor, amendment of 181, 182, 185
Guidelines for Examination 77, 180
harmonisation of laws 62, 175–6
historical interpretation 62
Implementing Regulations 65, 180
inquiries into creative effort 181
interpretation 62–4, 69, 74
inventive step 69–70, 74–6, 78, 87–8, 93, 95, 180, 182
investigative powers 181
named as inventor, right to be 63–5
national authorities, competence of 175
national laws 64, 66–7, 175–6
natural persons 63–7, 181
object and purpose 62–4
patentability 67–77, 180, 182
persons skilled in the art (PSAs) 182
Preamble 62
revocation attacks 66–7
right to a patent 65–7, 69
Strasbourg Convention 1963 62
successors in title 64, 66–7
technical character/technicity of subject matter 80, 83, 87–8, 180
travaux préparatoires 76
unitary patent system 176
European Union *see* **EU authorship; EU inventorship**
exchange-for-secrets theory 45–6
exclusive rights 56, 100
experiments 40, 42, 54–5, 58, 60, 90
expressive or non-obvious technical elements 8, 15–19, 45–50
 AI-driven systems 15–19, 21–2, 24, 69, 121, 171, 180, 186, 189–90
 authorship 45–50, 131, 173
  EU 101, 109–10, 114–15, 121–4, 147, 187
  France 158–9, 175
  Germany 165–6, 169, 170, 175, 177
  United Kingdom 131, 146–7, 175, 177
 autonomy 16–19
 computer programs 101, 123
 epistemic approaches 173
 EU authorship 101, 109–10, 114–15, 121–4, 147, 187
 fallacies 48
 incentives and rewards 47
 initiative, use of 17
 intelligence, definition of 18–19
 intentionality 17
 inventive step 171
 justifications for IP 45, 47–50
 market failure argument 47–8, 50
 originality 110, 114–15
 personality, reflection of 40, 120–1, 124
 property/proprietary rights 40, 45–6
 social values 38, 44, 50
 technical character/technicity of subject matter 110
 value 45–50

fairness 36–7, 41, 48–9, 50, 117, 186
fallacies 48, 188–9
false attribution of inventorship 181–2
false statements and misrepresentations by natural persons, safeguards against 181
films 117–18, 149
 authorship 103, 117–18, 123
 definition 103, 123
 directors 117–18
 fair compensation 117
 Rental and Lending Rights Directive 103
folklore 23
formulation of the problem 1–3
France *see* **France, authorship in; France, inventorship in**
France, authorship in 155–62
 academic commentaries 131, 159
 AI-driven systems 6–7, 133, 148, 161–2
 application practice 7, 148, 155–62, 170, 172, 177, 187
 artistic works 132–3, 159
 authors, rights of 131–2
 categorisation and typology of works 159, 170

collective works 6, 132
computer-generated works 161
computer programs 157–8, 160, 161
conceptions 131–5, 187
concretisation of an idea 158–9
contributions 156, 161–2
copyright subsistence criteria 7, 148, 155–62, 169, 172
creativity 125, 132–5, 141
databases 160–1
epistemic approaches 7, 148, 156, 159–61, 170, 172, 177, 187
essence of inventions 79
expressive or non-obvious technical elements 45, 158–9, 175
human dignity 37
human intellectual creations 125, 133–4, 155–8, 161, 176–7, 187
instructions as to the execution of works 135, 147
Intellectual Property Code 155–6, 159
joint authorship 135, 147
juridical persons 6, 132, 141, 142
literary works 132–3, 159–60
mechanical works 133–5
moral rights 131, 141
musical works 159–60
natural rights 131
originality 133, 148, 155–62, 170, 177, 179, 188
personal works 156–7, 161, 172
personality, reflection of 37, 133–5, 147, 156, 157–8, 161–2, 169, 170, 187
post-creative activities 135
pre-creative activities 135
presumption of authorship 125, 141, 179, 188
property/proprietary rights 131
remuneration/compensation 132
restoration and renovation of works 135
work of the mind 155–9, 170
France, inventorship in 4, 6–7, 56–8
AI-driven systems 94
checks on entitlement 67
co-inventorship 57–8
conception phase 22, 57–8, 78, 174–5
creative activity 83–4
date on which invention is conceived 57–8
declaratory, grants of patents as 33, 56
devisers of inventions 57, 64, 67–8, 78
disclosure, duties of 185
employee-inventors 56–8, 184–5
entitlement disputes 187
epistemic approaches 82–4, 92–5
European Patent Convention (EPC) 79, 93, 95
exceptions to rights of inventors 56–7
essence of inventions 57–8, 174–5, 187
history 82–3
imported inventions 33
improvements, proposed abolition of patents for 33
industrial applicability 83–4
Intellectual Property Code 56, 92–3
intuitive character of inventive activity 93
inventive step 77, 92–5
learning and education motive 43
mother-idea and fundamental 93
named as an inventor, right to be 64
natural persons 67–8, 78, 187
novelty requirement 82–3, 93
Patent Statute of 1844 33, 56, 82
persons skilled in the art (PSAs) 92, 93–4
presumptive of inventorship 67–8, 95
prior art 92–5
problem-and-solution test 93
revocation attacks 66–7
state-of the-art 94
technical character/technicity of subject matter 83–4, 94–5
free riders 48
freedom to conduct business 3–4
Fromm, Erich 18, 44

Galloux, Jean-Christophe 83
Gautier, Pierre-Yves 131–2, 159
Germany *see* **Germany, authorship in; Germany, inventorship in**
Germany, authorship in 6–7, 78, 79, 162–9
academic and practitioners commentaries 136, 139, 168
AI-driven systems 148, 166–8
application practice 7, 148, 162–9, 170, 172, 177, 187–9
Author's Right Act 136–7, 162–4, 169
categories of work 163
collaborations 139–40
computer-generated works (CGWs) 169
computer programs 140, 167–8
conceptions 136–40, 187
contributions 137–40
copyright subsistence criteria 7, 148, 162–9, 172

creative activity 137–40, 168, 179
economic and moral rights, unity of 136–7
epistemic approaches 7, 148, 167–8, 170, 172, 177, 187
equitable remuneration 136
expressive or non-obvious technical elements 45, 165–6, 169, 170, 175, 177
fixation of the work 165
human intellectual creations 125, 137–9, 162–5, 168–9, 170, 176–7, 187
instructions as to the execution of works 138, 147
joint authorship 138–40, 147
juridical persons 136–7, 142
labour and effort, investment of 39
literary works 163, 165–6
named as an inventor, right to be 64
natural persons 163–4, 169
originality 148, 163–6, 170, 189
overall impression 163
perceivable form, existence in a 164
personal creations 163–6, 169, 172
personality 136, 147, 187
photographs 136
preparatory stages, contributions at the 140
presumption of authorship 97, 125, 139, 142, 179, 188–9
property/proprietary rights 39–40
protected works 162–3
quality of contributions 139, 188–9
utilitarian purpose 169

Germany, inventorship in 4, 6–7, 33–4, 58–61, 67–9
AI-driven systems 59–60, 87
aiding inventors 61
checks on entitlement 67, 187
completion of invention and disclosure, right to patent on 59, 60, 78
contributions, ideas or suggestions which solve technical problems 60–1, 174–5
co-inventor threshold 61
creativity 59–60, 86, 175
devisers of inventions 64, 67–8, 78, 86
disclosure, duties of 185
economic rights 59
employees' inventions 184–5
epistemic approaches 84–7, 95–7
European Patent Convention (EPC) 79, 95
inventive step 77, 95–7
inventor doctrine 59, 86–7
natural persons 59–60, 67–8, 78, 87, 187
natural subject matter, use of 72, 84–5
novelty 34, 58–9
obviousness 96
Patent Act 1936 34, 58–60, 95–6
patentability 72, 76–7
personal rights 59
persons skilled in the art (PSAs) 60–1, 95–7
preconditions for existence of invention 61
prior art 95–7
purpose of patent law 58–9
revocation attacks 66–7
teaching, disclosing a 72, 78, 174–5, 187
technical character/technicity of subject matter 84–7, 95–7, 174, 185, 187

Ghidini, Gustavo 49
Ginsburg, Jane 28–9, 38, 43, 107
good faith 52, 74
Goold, Patrick 111, 146
graphic user interfaces 100, 101

Haedicke, Maximilian 61, 68
Haertel, Kurt 76–7
***halicin*, discovery of antibiotic** 16, 19, 182
Hardin, Garrett 45
Harhoff, Dietmar 185
harmonisation of laws 6, 62, 100, 104, 123, 175–6
Hassabis, Demis 190
Hawking, Stephen 9
Hegel, Georg 39–40, 119
Heller, Michael 45
Hindmarch, William 32
history 32–3
epistemic approaches 82–3, 88–9, 92
European Patent Convention (EPC) 62
inventive step 76, 88–9, 92
status quo, historical justifications for upholding the 7, 26–50, 175, 186
Hofmann, Franz 165
Hoisl, Karin 185
Hugenholtz, Bernt 110–11, 142
Hughes, Justin 40
human dignity 36–8, 39, 50, 186
human intellectual creations *see also* **intrinsic values of human intellectual creations;**
social values of human intellectual creations
AI-driven systems 41, 189

authorship 7, 27–31, 35, 149–53, 162–5, 168–9, 170, 174–7, 186
author, definition of 28–9
EU 103–4, 106–21, 123–4, 187
France 125, 133–4, 137–9, 155–8, 161, 176–7, 187
Germany 162–5, 168–9, 170, 187
United Kingdom 125–7, 149–53, 170, 176–7, 187
computer programs 123, 161
copyright subsistence criteria 171, 173
culture 30–1, 172
databases 103
EU 103–4, 106–21, 123–4, 187
European Patent Convention (EPC) 70–1, 183
expressive or non-obvious technical elements 173, 189
France 155–8, 161, 187
Germany 125, 137–9, 162–5, 168–9, 170, 176–7, 187
InfoSoc Directive 104, 106–8
intelligence, definition of 18–19
inventorship 31–5, 174, 186
labour and effort, investment of 27–8
material form, realisation in 133–4
notion of human intellectual creations 7, 27–36
originality 109–10, 116
personal choices 110, 115–18
personality, reflection of 120–1
public, collaboration with the 30
social preconceptions 30–1
United Kingdom 32–3, 35, 125–7, 149–53, 170, 176–7, 187
human rights 37

ideas/expressions 110–11, 127, 129, 159
imported inventions 33–4
incentives and rewards
computer-generated works 145
creative effort 63
disclosure, duties of 181
economic incentives 190
expressive or non-obvious technical elements 47
justifications for IP 27
market failure argument 47
prospect theory 46
reputation 44–5
social values 43, 44–5, 50, 186
indistinguishably of outputs 13–15, 24
industrial applicability 45, 58–9, 81, 83–4
InfoSoc Directive
AI-driven systems 121
authorship 99–100, 103–9, 117, 120–1, 124
CJEU, case law of 105–9
intellectual creation 104, 106–8, 121
lex generalis 104–8
lex specialis 100
objectives and purpose 104, 124
originality 100, 104, 108–9
Preamble 104
short extracts 104
work, definition of 106, 121
instructions as to the execution of works 135, 138, 147
intellectual creations *see* **human intellectual creations**
intentionality 17, 153–4
International Covenant on Economic, Social and Cultural Rights (ICESCR) 37
interpretation
Berne Convention 107–8
creativity 128
Database Directive 102
European Patent Convention (EPC) 62–4, 69, 74
literal interpretation 4, 146
ordinary meaning 62, 74, 106, 149, 153
originality 4, 159–60
systematic interpretation 4, 73, 104, 146
teleological interpretation 4, 62–3, 171
textual interpretation 62
Vienna Convention on the Law of Treaties 1969 (VCLT) 62, 74
intrinsic values of human intellectual creations 25–6, 36–42
AI-driven systems 41–2
economic rights 37
fairness 36–7, 41, 50, 186
human dignity 36–8, 39, 50, 186
labour and effort, investment of 37–8, 39–41, 50, 186
moral rights 36–8
natural rights 38–40
personality-based reasons 36–7, 39–40
practice, mere reduction to 42
property/proprietary rights 39–40

inventive step 4, 7 *see also* **epistemic approaches to the inventive step requirement**
creativity 76
European Patent Convention (EPC) 69–70, 74–6, 78, 87–8, 93, 95, 180, 182
expressive or non-obvious technical elements 45, 171
inventive concept 54–5
natural persons 74–7, 78
objectivity 75–7
persons skilled in the art (PSAs) 75–7, 78
presumption of inventorship 75–7
state of the art 74, 76
subjectivity 77
United Kingdom 54–5, 77, 81
inventorship 1–4, 174–7 *see also* **European Patent Convention (EPC), inventorship in; France, inventorship in; Germany, inventorship in; patentability and human inventorship; presumption of inventorship; United Kingdom, inventorship in**
application practice, inventorship in 7, 79–98, 174
biotechnological inventions 23–4, 35–6, 74
checks on entitlement, lack of 65, 66, 67, 171
designation of inventors 20, 31, 63–7, 171
devisers of inventions 74, 76–7
European patent law, notion in 7, 51–78
expressive or non-obvious technical elements 175
human intellectual creations 31–5, 174, 186
imported inventions 32–3
invention, definition of 34, 70–4, 81–2
inventor-creator principle 31–4, 46, 186–7
inventor, definition of 49, 52–3
natural persons 67–8, 78
natural rights 26–7, 31
property/proprietary rights 25–7, 32
right to a patent 59, 64, 65–9
investigative powers 181
Isomorphic Labs' AlphaFold2 and AlphaFold3 190

joint authorship *see also* **contributions**
AI-driven systems 126–7, 141
collaborations 30–1, 126–7, 135, 139–40
France 135, 147
Germany 138–40, 147
musical works 128–9, 131, 155
presumption of authorship 139, 140–1
unitary concept, as 126, 155
United Kingdom 126–31, 141, 147, 152–5
juridical persons 6, 132, 136–7, 141, 142
justifications for IP rights *see also* **labour and effort, investment of**
coherence and integrity of system 189
deontic justificatory theories 25
EU authorship 119–20
expressive or non-obvious technical elements 45, 47–50
learning and education motive 43–4
market failure argument 47–8, 50
personality, reflection of 119–20
property/proprietary rights 25–7
status quo, historical and theoretical justifications for upholding the 7, 26–50, 175, 186
utilitarianism 25, 46–7, 146

Kant, Immanuel 18–19, 119–20
Keukenschrijver, Alfred 61
Kim, Daria 17
Kitch, Edmund 46
Koukolík, František 30
Koziol, Helmut 113
Kühnemann, Herbert 76

labour and effort, investment of 127–9, 144–6
computer-generated works 144–6
human intellectual creations 27–8
intrinsic values 37–8, 39–41, 50, 186
labour/ desert justification 38, 41–2, 50, 186
skill, labour and judgment 144, 150–2, 169
Ladas, Stephen 26–7, 38
Laddie, Hugh 91–2
Laligant, Olivier 156–7
Landes, William 47
Lavik, Erlend 112
learning and education motive 43–4
Leistner, Matthias 169
Lemley, Mark 180
Lindenmaier, judge 34

literary, dramatic, musical or artistic (LDMA) works categories 148–53 *see also* **artistic works; dramatic works; literary works; musical works**
computer-generated works 143–7
correct categories, importance of 148–9, 153
expressive or non-obvious technical elements 45, 47
filter, functioning as a 152–3
intentionality, importance of 153–4
originality 143–6, 148–53
United Kingdom 143–53
literary works *see also* **literary, dramatic, musical or artistic (LDMA) works categories**
Berne Convention 107–8
computer programs 149
definition 148–9, 154, 159
France 159–60
Germany 163, 165–6
United Kingdom 127, 129, 148–9, 154
Locke, John 39
Loewenheim, Ulrich 136, 137, 169
Lovelace test 10, 16, 19, 23
Lucas, André 156, 158, 160

Machiavelli, Niccolò 46
machine learning 10–11, 12, 13, 17, 24
Machlup, Fritz 43, 45
MacLeod, Christine 38
Madison, James 42–3
market failure argument 47–8, 50
Mathély, Paul 56, 83
mechanical/utilitarian functions, works with 102, 111, 120, 129, 133–4, 150–1, 169
Melullis, Klaus-Jürgen 59, 61, 66, 68, 73–4, 86
Merges, Robert 36, 39
Mill, John Stuart 40
monism 59, 136–7
monopolies 32, 43, 47, 52, 91, 154, 190
moral rights
Berne Convention 28
common law countries 38
economic rights, unity with 37, 136–7
France 131, 141
Germany 136–7
integrity of work, right to 36
intrinsic values 36–8
inventor-creators 31–2
name, right to be 63–4, 141
paternity eight 36
remuneration/compensation 36–7
United Kingdom 53
Mossoff, Adam 40–1
Moufang, Rainer 73
multiple creators *see also* **joint authorship**
compilations 105
copyright subsistence criteria 23
France, co-inventorship in 57–8
Germany, co-inventorship in 61
open-source software 23
musical works *see also* **literary, dramatic, musical or artistic (LDMA) works categories**
contributions 152, 154
creative activity 128–9, 131
definition 149, 154, 159
Germany 163
joint authorship 152, 154
originality 160
United Kingdom 126, 128–9, 131, 149, 152, 154, 178

Nack, Ralph 86
named as inventor, right to be 63–5
natural persons
AI-driven systems 63, 65, 66
author, definition of 28
computer programs 122
databases 116–17, 122
epistemic approaches 87
false statements and misrepresentations by natural persons, safeguards against 181
France 6, 67–8, 78, 187
Germany 59–60, 67–8, 78, 87, 163–4, 169, 187
inventive step 74–7, 78
inventorship 52–5, 67–8, 75–8, 187
named as an inventor, right to be 63–5
persons skilled in the art (PSAs) 75–7
presumption of authorship 141
United Kingdom 52–5, 67–8, 78, 141, 187
natural rights 26–7, 29, 31, 38–40, 131, 146
natural subject-matter, patentability of
biotechnological inventions 23–4, 35–6, 74
epistemic approaches 84–5
Germany 72, 84–5

neighbouring rights 5, 6
neural networks 12, 13, 14, 24
Next Rembrandt project 13, 15–16, 19
Ng, Alina 31
non-obvious technical elements *see* **expressive or non-obvious technical elements**
novelty requirement 34, 58–9
epistemic approaches 81, 82–3, 93
expressive or non-obvious technical elements 45
inventive step 93

objectivity 34, 75–7, 93, 156, 158–9
obviousness test 54, 88–92
epistemic approaches 87, 88–93, 96–7
human intellectual creations 28
inventive step 87, 88–93, 96–7
multi-factorial approach 89
persons skilled in the art (PSAs) 174
Windsurfing/Pozzoli test 89–91
originality
AI-driven systems 121, 133, 143–6, 162
artistic works 148–53
authorship
causal relationship 112–13
EU 100, 101, 104, 108–22
France 133, 148, 155–62, 170, 177, 179, 188
Germany 148, 163–6, 170, 189
United Kingdom 142
Berne Convention 143–4, 146
burden of proof 160
choices
creative choices 117, 118, 161, 177
free choices 109–11, 114–16, 118–19, 121
personal choices 110, 115–21
computer-generated works 142–7
computer programs 100, 101, 108, 160
creative choices 117, 118, 161, 177
databases 103, 108, 160–1
dramatic works 143–6, 148–53
EU authorship 100, 101, 104, 108–22
form, manifested in the 160
France 133, 148, 155–62, 170, 177, 179, 188
free choices 109–11, 114–16, 118–19, 121
Germany 148, 163–6, 170, 189
human intellectual creations 28, 35, 109–10, 111–16, 121
implied, as 156, 160
Infopaq test 127–9, 131, 149, 154, 163, 189
InfoSoc Directive 100, 104, 108–9
interpretation 4, 159–60
judge-made conception 159–60, 170, 179
law, as a question of 159–60, 170
literary works 143–6, 148–53, 160
musical works 143–6, 148–53, 160
objectivity 156, 158–9
personal choices 110, 115–21
personality, reflection of 119–21, 156, 161–2
Rental and Lending Rights Directive 117–18
slavish copying 150–2
subjectivity 156–7
technical character/technicity of subject matter 110–11, 127
Term Directive 117–18
two model conceptions 156
United Kingdom 127–9, 131, 142–53, 154, 177
overall impression 163

Paris Convention 1883 26, 38, 51–2, 67–8
Passa, Jerôme 83–4
patentability and human inventorship 3, 67–78, 175
AI-driven systems 68–9, 179–80, 188, 190
biotechnological inventions 23–4, 35–6
creative acts of inventors 69, 70–4, 76
disclosure, duties of 98, 179, 188
discoveries 73–4
epistemic approaches 172, 173, 187
European Patent Convention (EPC) 68–77, 180, 182
exclusions 80
expressive or non-obvious technical elements 173
human intellectual creations 171, 173
human intervention, requirement for 70–5
inventive step 69–70, 74–7, 78
national laws 75
natural persons 75–7
natural subject-matter 23–4
objectivity 75–6
persons skilled in the art (PSA) 75–7
process/method, subject matter claimed as a 72–3
product, subject matter claimed as a 72
repeatability requirement 72
requirement for an invention 70–4
patents *see* **inventorship; patentability and human inventorship**
Peifer, Karl-Nicholas 137

personal works
computer programs 158, 161
France 133–5, 147, 156–7, 161, 172, 187
Germany 59, 136, 147, 163–6, 169, 172, 187
right to a patent 66
personality, reflection of
AI-driven systems 174, 189
authorship 102, 119–24, 174, 176, 187
computer programs 102, 157–8
EU 102, 119–24, 176, 187
expressive or non-obvious technical elements 40, 120–1, 124
France 37, 156, 157–8, 161–2, 169, 170
identification of author's personality 122
intrinsic values 36–7, 39–40
originality 119–21, 156, 161–2
personality, definition of 119–21
scientific knowledge in psychology 174
United Kingdom 128, 130, 147, 178, 187
persons skilled in the art (PSAs) 60–1, 89–94
AI-driven systems 94, 174, 180, 182
epistemic approaches 87, 88, 89–92, 94–8
inventive step 75–7, 78
photographs 114–15, 120, 136, 151, 160–1
Pila, Justine 34, 68, 105–6, 142, 152–4
piracy 26
Plaisant, Marcel 27
plastics 47
Pollaud-Dulian, Fréderic 83
Portron, Alexandre 133, 135
positive law 51–61, 69, 125–31, 142
Posner, Richard 47
post-creative activities 41–2, 128–9, 131, 135
Pottage, Alain 34, 68
power relations 173
pre-creative activities 22, 41–2, 57–8, 78, 102, 135, 140, 151, 174–7
presumption of authorship
AI-driven systems 142
burden of proof 187
challenged, until 125, 141–2, 179
fact, as a question of 172
France 125, 141, 179, 188
Germany 97, 125, 139, 142, 179, 188–9
joint authorship 139, 140–1
juridical persons 141
natural persons 141
originality 160, 179
recording creative activity 178–9
statutory presumptions 140–2, 178
time and expense, saving 179
United Kingdom 125, 141, 178–9
presumption of inventorship
burden of proof 187
fact, as a question of 172
France 67–8, 95
Germany 67–8
indications 95
inventive step 75–7
presumptions *see* **presumption of authorship; presumption of inventorship**
prior art 14–15, 54, 87–8, 89, 92–7
priority date 89, 93, 174
private property *see* **property/proprietary rights**
probability theories 10–11
problem-and-solution test 87, 93, 180
property/proprietary rights 4, 25–6, 32, 188–9
collaborations with the public 30
expressive or non-obvious technical elements 45–6
France 131
Germany 39–40, 59
intrinsic values 39–40
justifications for IP 25–7
labour and effort, investment of 39
overlapping patent rights 45
patent thickets 45
self-consciousness 39–40
social contract theory 45–6
Vienna Patent Congress 1873 38
prospect theory 46
public interest 43, 52, 120
Pufendorf, Samuel 39

Quaedvlieg, Antoon 44, 116–18
Quintais, João 111

Radin, Margaret J 39
recipes for works, following 10, 18, 23
reforms 1, 171–85, 187–9
remuneration/compensation
employees' inventions 57–8, 184–5
equitable remuneration 136
fair compensation 36–7, 117
United Kingdom 184–5
Rental and Lending Rights Directive 103, 117–18
repeatability requirement 10, 16, 71–2, 183
reputation 44–5
research
methods and scope 4–7
significance 3–4

restoration and renovation of works 135
revocation attacks 66–7
rewards *see* **incentives and rewards**
Ricketson, Sam 28, 52, 107
right to a patent 59, 64, 65–9
Robinson, William 34
Rosati, Eleonora 116
Rosenblatt, Frank 12
Roubier, Paul 82, 93
Russell, Stuart 8–9

Schulze, Gernot 136, 162–3
Schumpeter, Joseph 46
sculptures 118, 134, 137–8, 149, 152
self-consciousness 39–40, 45
serendipitous events and accidents 54, 71, 183–4
Shapiro, Carl 45, 49
Shemtov, Noam 22
Sherman, Brad 4, 27–8, 34, 68, 107, 109
Siemens, Werner 34
Sirinelli, Pierre 156, 158, 160
skill 5, 30, 128–9 *see also* **persons skilled in the art (PSAs)**
- computer-generated works 144
- joint authorship 127
- skill, labour and judgment 144, 150–2, 169

slavish copying 150–2
Smith, Adam 40
social contract theory 45–6
social values of human intellectual creations 25–6, 42–5
- AI-driven systems 38, 44
- attribution 38
- culture 42, 43–4
- expressive or non-obvious technical elements 38, 44, 50
- incentives and rewards 43, 44–5, 50, 186
- learning and education motive 43–4
- power relations 173
- science, advancement of 43–4
- stability 172–3
- utilitarian justificatory theories 25

Spence, Michael 48
state of the art 69, 74, 76, 82, 88–90, 94
Statute of Anne 1709/10 (UK) 42
Statute of Monopolies 1623 (England) 32–3
Steel, Sandy 113
subjectivity 75, 77, 97, 156–7, 173
sweat of the brow test 150

technical character/technicity of subject matter
- disclosure, duties of 98
- EU authorship 110–11
- epistemic approaches 80, 82, 83–8, 90–2, 95–8
- European Patent Convention (EPC) 80, 83, 87–8, 180
- expressive or non-obvious technical elements 110
- France 83–4, 93–5
- Germany 84–7, 95–7, 174, 185, 187
- inventive step 87–8, 90–2, 95–8
- means, involvement of technical 80
- originality 127
- patentability 74–5
- United Kingdom 82, 90–2, 97–8

Tegmark, Max 9
Term Directive 116–18, 123
Terrell on the Law of Patents 81, 89, 183
theoretical and historical justifications for upholding the status quo 7, 26–50, 175, 186
trade marks 30, 38
trade secrets or unfair competition 41, 48
tragedy of the commons 45
transparency 44, 187–8
trial and error 54
Turing test 9–10, 15, 19, 23

unfair competition 41, 48–9
unitary patent system 176
United Kingdom, authorship in 148–55
- academic and practitioners' commentaries 126
- AI-driven systems 6–7, 126–7, 148, 153–5
- application practice 7, 148–55, 169–70, 172, 177, 187
- artistic works, definition of 149–50, 154
- author, definition of 126–7
- Berne Convention 148
- categories of works 148–50, 153, 169–70
- checks, lack of 178
- collaborations 126–31
- computer-generated works 146–7
- computer software, testing 128–9
- Copyright, Designs and Patents Act 1988 125–7, 141, 149
- copyright subsistence criteria 7, 148, 153–5, 169, 172
- creative activity 126–31, 176–9
- dramatic works 127, 149

epistemic approaches 7, 148, 152–5, 170, 172, 177, 187
expressive or non-obvious technical elements 45, 49, 131, 146–7, 152, 175, 177
human dignity 37–8
human intellectual creations 32–3, 35, 37–9, 125–7, 149–53, 170, 176–7, 187
ideas and expressions 127, 129
import of new technologies 32–3
Infopaq test 127–9, 131
joint authorship 126–31, 141, 147, 152–5
labour and effort, investment of 37–8, 40–1, 127–9
literary, dramatic, musical or artistic (LDMA) works categories 148–53
literary works 127, 129, 148–9, 154
mechanical functions 129, 151
musical works 126, 128–9, 131, 152, 154, 178
originality 127–9, 131, 142, 148–54, 177
personality 128, 130, 147, 178, 187
positive law 125–31
post-creative activity 128–9, 131
preparatory activities 177
presumption of authorship until challenged 125, 141, 178–9
purpose and objectives 125–6
skill, labour and judgment 150–2, 169
skill, time and effort 128–9
slavish copying 150–2
Statute of Anne 1709/10 42
Statute of Monopolies 1623 32–3
sweat of the brow test 150
writing, mere act of 129

United Kingdom, computer-generated works (CGWs) in 142–7
AI-driven systems 6–7, 144–5
authorship 142, 146–7
Berne Convention 143–4, 146
computer-generated works, definition of 143–4
computer programs 149
Copyright, Designs and Patents Act 1988 143–4
copyright subsistence criteria 144, 146
epistemic approaches 81–2
incentives and rewards 145
labour and effort, investment of 144–6
literary, dramatic, musical or artistic (LDMA) works 143–7
literary works 143–7, 149
named as an inventor, right to be 64
originality 142–7
skill, labour and judgment 144

United Kingdom, inventorship in 4, 52–6, 67–9
AI-driven systems 184–5
Banks Committee 33, 52, 81
checks on entitlement 67, 187
commercial considerations 91
creation, process of 174–5
devisers of inventions 33, 52–3, 55, 64–5, 67–8, 78, 79, 90–2, 98, 174, 184–5
discoveries, utilisation of 81
employees' inventions and compensation schemes 184–5
entrepreneurial or managerial contributions 56
epistemic approaches 81–2, 88–92, 97–8
European Patent Convention (EPC) 79
exclusions 82
history 88–9, 92
industrial applicability 81
invention, definition of 81–2
inventive concept, persons coming up with the 52–5, 78, 174, 187
inventive step 54–5, 77, 81–2, 88–92, 97–8
moral rights 53
natural persons 52–5, 67–8, 78, 187
non-enabling ideas 55
novelty 81
obviousness 54, 88–92, 97
Patents Act 1949 88–9
Patents Act 1977 52–3, 81–2, 89, 184–5
persons skilled in the art (PSAs) 89–92, 97–8
state of the art 82
technical character/technicity of subject matter 82

United States
AI-driven systems 20, 184
biotechnological inventions, patentability of 35–6
Congress, powers of 42–3
Constitution 42–3
false statements and misrepresentations 181
labour and effort, investment of 40–1
learning and education motive 43
originality 35

Patent Act 1836 41, 184
patentability 184
serendipitous events 184
US Patent and Trademark Office (PTO) 42, 181, 184
Universal Declaration on Human Rights 1948 (UDHR) 37
utilitarian/mechanical works 102, 111, 120, 129, 133–4, 150–1, 169
utilitarianism 25, 46–7, 146

values 25, 26–50 *see also* **intrinsic values of human intellectual creations; social values of human intellectual creations**
verification of entitlement *see* **checks on entitlement**
Vienna Convention on the Law of Treaties 1969 (VCLT) 62, 74
Vienna Patent Congress 1873 38
Vivant, Michel 131, 133, 160
Von Gompel, Stef 112
von Lewinski, Silke 102, 108
von Neumann-Morgenstern's utility theory 9

Whitford Committee 145
Wikipedia 23
Wooldridge, Michael 8–9, 17–19
work, definition of 106, 121, 123–4
work, right to 4

Ziegler, Karl 46–7
Zemer, Lior 30

www.ingramcontent.com/pod-product-compliance
Ingram Content Group UK Ltd.
Pitfield, Milton Keynes, MK11 3LW, UK
UKHW020809290926
15470UKWH00003B/1041

9 781509 976232